The Childhood Emotional Pattern in Marriage

Other Books by Leon J. Saul, M.D.

EMOTIONAL MATURITY

BASES OF HUMAN BEHAVIOR

TECHNIC AND PRACTICE OF PSYCHOANALYSIS

THE HOSTILE MIND

FIDELITY AND INFIDELITY

DEPENDENCE IN MAN (With H. Parens)

PSYCHODYNAMICALLY BASED PSYCHOTHERAPY

PSYCHODYNAMICS OF HOSTILITY

THE CHILDHOOD EMOTIONAL PATTERN: THE KEY TO PER-
SONALITY, ITS DISORDERS AND THERAPY

THE CHILDHOOD EMOTIONAL PATTERN AND COREY JONES

The Childhood Emotional Pattern in Marriage

Leon J. Saul, M.D.

Emeritus Professor of Psychiatry
Medical School of the University of Pennsylvania

Honorary Staff, Institute of the Pennsylvania Hospital

Emeritus Training Analyst
Philadelphia Psychoanalytic Institute

VNR VAN NOSTRAND REINHOLD COMPANY
NEW YORK   CINCINNATI   ATLANTA   DALLAS   SAN FRANCISCO
LONDON   TORONTO   MELBOURNE

Van Nostrand Reinhold Company Regional Offices:
New York   Cincinnati   Atlanta   Dallas   San Francisco

Van Nostrand Reinhold Company International Offices:
London   Toronto   Melbourne

Copyright © 1979 by Litton Educational Publishing, Inc.

Library of Congress Catalog Card Number: 78-17400
IODII. 0-442-27358-4 pbk.
          27358-4 pbk.

Manufactured in the United States of America

Published by Van Nostrand Reinhold Company
135 West 50th Street, New York, N.Y. 10020

Published simultaneously in Canada by Van Nostrand Reinhold Ltd.

15 14 13 12 11 10 9 8 7 6 5 4 3 2 1

Library of Congress Cataloging in Publication Data

Saul, Leon Joseph, 1901-
    The childhood emotional pattern in marriage.

    Includes index.
    1. Mentally ill—Family relationships. 2. Marriage.
3. Psychoanalysis. I. Title. [DNLM: 1. Childhood
behavior disorders—Complications. 2. Personality dis-
orders-Etiology. 3. Marriage. WM190 S256c]
RC455.4.F3S17   362.8'2   78-17400
ISBN 0-442-27359-2
ISBN 0-442-27358-4 pbk.

TO MY WIFE

Who, by providing a loving, stable home and raising happy, independent children has contributed as much as myself to everything I have written or done, and

TO MY SISTER

Who meant so much to my development and has been a faithful friend for life.

PREFACE

In my early years of struggle to understand the unconscious of every patient and for a decade afterward, I concentrated so hard during each therapeutic hour that I could not also write notes. Instead, I allowed 20 minutes between appointments, and during that time wrote notes reconstructing the associations while their sequence in the session was still fresh in my mind. This provided a review of each session immediately following it, which was invaluable for learning to "read" the unconscious, by following the "red thread," the common element, in the associations. It also provided material for some of the clinical research at the Chicago Institute for Psychoanalysis. Occasionally I used a conference microphone and dictating machine to record a session verbatim.

It is from these detailed notes on patients at the Chicago Institute that most of the examples for this book are drawn. In this book we study marriage not at the superficial level of influence of such things as changing customs, morality, movements such as "women's liberation" or evolving technological and political and socioeconomic conditions. Instead our focus is on marriage at the deepest levels of sexual attraction and feelings, and of interaction of the basic psychodynamics of personality. These fundamentals seem to be unchanged since the beginning of written history. When we read the writings of the Greeks, the Romans, the Bible, the ancient story of Buddha or the earliest cuneiform translations of the Sumerians, we can still identify with those universal emotions of sex, love, marriage, parenthood and personality. Thus in Kramer's *History Begins at Sumer* we can read the first recorded love song, "to be recited in the course of the most hallowed of ancient rites, the rite of sacred marriage.*

All names in this work are fictitious, and any similarities to present-day persons and marriages are purely coincidental.

*Kramer, S. (1959): *History Begins at Sumer.* New York: Doubleday Anchor, p. 215.

This book is not written by a statistician, sociologist or theoretician, but by a clinician engaged in the therapeutic practice of psychoanalysis and its psychodynamic modifications. Its basic observations are of human beings who come for help in understanding and relieving the causes of their emotional suffering. If one knows what to look for, their individual life histories, supplemented by earliest memories, dreams and associations, reveal the sources of their distress. Our few introductory formulations of fundamentals lead us into the personal stories that comprise a large portion of this book (I dislike referring to a person as a "case," convenient and brief though this term is). Using clinical presentations to make basic observations is a correct scientific procedure. Others may reach different interpretations as the techniques and knowledge of the dynamic unconscious increase in breadth, depth and accuracy. I can only present what these observations have taught me, with few qualms or doubts about their basic validity but with acute awareness of my inability to convey the sense of drama I have experienced in trying to help these mostly superior persons who have turned to me.

LEON J. SAUL, M.D.

ACKNOWLEDGMENTS

Special thanks to Dr. William Kephart, Department of Sociology, University of Pennsylvania, for Chapters 6 and 7 on the sociology and the ethology of marriage, and to Dr. William Davenport, Department of Anthropology, University of Pennsylvania, for Chapter 8 on the anthropology of marriage.

It is again a pleasure to thank publicly my super-secretary, editorial assistant and personal bosun, Susan (Mrs. Vernon) Bender, whose general saving of my time and energies and whose specific editorial help has made this book possible. It is also a pleasure to thank Anna Meigs Haiman, Howard Weir III and Ginny (Mrs. John) Briscoe for reading and helping with parts of the manuscript.

As always, my wife's understanding, patience and support were of indispensible help in this writing.

Portions of Chapter 31, "The Children," are modifications of previously published articles and used here with the kind permission of the publishers and authors: *Man and Wife,* edited by Emily Mudd, W. W. Norton & Company, Inc., 1957; *The Meaning of Love,* edited by Ashley Montagu, The Julian Press, 1953.

CONTENTS

The Childhood Emotional Pattern in Marriage

SECTION I:
DYNAMICS OF MARRIAGE

1
SEX IS NOT LOVE

Marriage is a thing of the soul and heart as well as of the body and you can't separate them out and have much left . . .

Patricia O'Brien,
Philadelphia Inquirer, 1977

It is believed in the village . . . that Henry loved me with a husband's love, But I proclaim from the dust That he slew me to gratify his hatred.

Edgar Lee Masters,
Spoon River Anthology

Physical sex, normal or perverted, is often referred to as "the act of love." Yet it often does not express "love."

Years ago, a letter came from a young woman married only a few months saying, "I am starved emotionally and physically." This is a common complaint heard in the author's practice; it may vary in form and intensity, but makes the distinction between love and sex. Then, one sometimes hears a wife complain of unhappiness because her husband wants sex so much that she has no peace! She cannot go to sleep early if she is tired or ill, for he will awaken her for sex in the middle of the night, nor can she sleep late in the morning for the same reason. It is too much of a good thing and may actually impair her health, causing her to lose her normal desire for sex even to the point of distaste.

One of my patients, a model by occupation, quite beautiful and a keen observer, discussed at just what point in the evening on a first date she must be prepared for the "sexual attack." In the past week, the daily press has reported that 25 members of a gang raped a teenage girl, after which one or more members hung her and dismembered her body. Here the sex was definitely not love. There is no need to belabor the point at a time when rape has so increased

3

as to be in the public eye. Most people know rape is not basically even sexual but a hostile attack. Yet there is still confusion between sex and love. Probably teenage girls are more sophisticated than they were a generation or two ago, but I have seen many who interpret a boy's "pass" as a signal of love, to their own later sorrow.

Why this confusion between two motivations that are so different? Is it because they have enough in common to blur the contrast? They share the characteristic of "closeness" and intimacy. Each person sees the world very much in terms of his or her own needs, reactions and desires: "Each person's ego is the yardstick by which he measures the world" (Saul, 1971, p. 78). The boy, driven by his sex urge, may be only trying to get the girl to permit or cooperate in sex, to satisfy his own sex drive and perhaps egotistically to boost his vanity by "scoring," by conquering the girl through overcoming her resistance. But that teenage girl may be lonely, craving a close friendship with the boy and hoping eventually for marriage. She may interpret his physical sex urge to intercourse as an interest in her personality, a potential form of love, i.e., of interest in her welfare, well-being, happiness. As people grow older, some learn a bit more about this, but it does not necessarily ensure that they will be more loving of anyone other than themselves. We have all seen men who try to stay married although they have left their wives or separated from them, men who walk out but prolong the divorce settlement to continue in their married state as long as possible. The goal for such men is often to live in an apartment where women can be brought for sex, but to continue married so as to prevent any personal involvement and responsibility for their transitory "amours."

It may be that the sexual and reproductive drives are more diffuse and pervasive in women; certainly they are less comprehensible to young and inexperienced girls, which makes girls more vulnerable. On a date with an attractive young man, a girl's hormones flow and give a certain glow and lift to the companionship. The boy may still want only intercourse and orgasm, but the girl may enjoy the companionship even more than he, because of the sexual aura, and she may want to keep on enjoying their closeness, doing things together, having fun together, while excluding overt sexuality and staving off intercourse until marriage or at least an engagement. The lift or glow one can experience from companionship with a normal attractive member of the opposite sex blurs the distinction between physical sex attraction and love.

We interpret sex as body contact, consisting of foreplay and intercourse, culminating in orgasm. Its complication is that sex is part of the reproductive process and culminates in babies, plus the interminable and infinitely difficult task of rearing those children to independent adulthood. The good times, surrounded by an erotic glow, are complicated by the fact of reproduction. For mating, love is needed; love involves not just physical closeness but psychological closeness, to the point of an identity with one's partner, an identity so full that both are as one, and giving and doing for one's partner is like giving and doing for oneself. One may forego a return for what is given and even sacrifice one's self-interest for the other and the children.

Now we begin to glimpse the instinctual and psychological tangle that underlies the relationship between the sexes, even those relationships that seem most naive, innocent and simple. We see why Freud, in his first explorations of the human mind, insisted on the fundamental importance of sex and used the term to mean more than sexual intercourse. He called it the "psychosexuality," including what was perceptible in the mind, and in disguised form in dreams, and he was willing to be pilloried rather than retract the observations he felt sure of, asking others only to look at what seemed to him so evident in the dreams, associations, conscious thought and behavior.

People have feelings for each other through two main processes: *identification* (empathy, sympathy) and *object interest* (viewing the other person as an object to be used, for dependence, for sex, to vent anger on, to enslave for service, and so on) What we call love, that strong attraction between two people of the opposite sex, contains elements of both the above processes. An exceptionally strong element is the mother's (and father's) feelings for the newborn child. We emphasize "newborn" because it is likely that at birth there is a flow of hormones which heightens the parent's feelings for the child. All such tender and protective close feelings, indicative of the love of every mother throughout the animal kingdom, love that causes the female to fight "like a tigress" even to her own death for her young—these feelings seem to be the purest kind of love as *object* interest. For the mother it is all giving with no immediate return from the helpless child. Such love never completely dies;

the child's response to it forms a kernel lasting the child's whole life, forming by identification a capacity to love that enters into love between the sexes. For example, a man may call his girlfriend "baby," and the girl might say if she breaks up with a boyfriend, "I feel as though I've lost my only child."

If an infant is not raised with parental love, it may never develop the capacity to give love to others, and woe to the woman who marries a man who did not grow up with such a warm, close, loving relationship to his mother or substitute. He will not have love to give his wife and their children. And if the wife did not get love, woe to her husband!

Sex, then, is a physiological process of the body but enters into the mind and emotions. It can be linked with other emotions such as anger and hostility, making sadism, rape and lust murders. Sex in marriage must be embedded in love, because marriage is mating, a process of increasing and *preserving* the species, not destroying it. Love involves both *identification* with one's partner and tender, protecting, disinterested, giving *object interest,* that is, interest for the other's own sake rather than one's own well-being and happiness. The nature of love is seen in this object interest and identification with one's child. What the child receives, it becomes able to give later to its own mate and children.

Identification and the consequent warm, affectionate, empathic "feeling with" and sympathy are conspicuously absent in such cases as those described in the chapter on divorce, where "I," "Me," and "Mine" predominate. We might even say that as long as husband and wife use "We," "Us," and "Ours," divorce is not imminent. If a husband says, "It is my money, I earned it and I will say how much to give you and how it is to be spent," then the wife usually feels seriously rejected and lonely, and accumulates resentment.

2
LOVE, SEX AND PSYCHODYNAMICS

MARRIAGE: The union of persons of opposite sex as husband and wife, forming new family, sanctioned by custom and religion. Marriage is generally initiated by rite combining words and symbolic acts, dramatizing and making public the new relationship. Where group is divided into clans, the individual usually must marry outside his clan, a practice known as exogamy. At same time, he must marry within his tribe, a practice known as endogamy; in small tribes this results in inbreeding. Monogamy is dominant form of marriage in all groups, even where polygamy is permitted. Of variant forms of marriage, polygyny, or marriage of one man to more than one wife, is more frequent than polyandry, the marriage of one woman to more than one husband. In polygynous unions, usually one chief wife ranks above the others . . . in Christian countries, the Church exercises close supervision over marriage, but civil marriage is now permitted in most countries. *

There are no laws or religious or social sanctions pressuring people to eat and breathe, but there are many pressures upon couples to remain married. This must be because people eat and breathe naturally, of their own accord, but many do not naturally stay together faithfully in marriage. Rather, many individuals have strong tendencies to escape from marriage, which must be held in check by powerful social, religious and legal sanctions. Does this mean human marriage is not a natural state? Or can it be that the almost universal neurotic difficulties that exist in human relations burgeon with special force in marriage?

General principles, however important, are not always interesting reading, but we gain time and understanding from them. So we will first summarize briefly some dynamics underlying marriage and some forces that make a marriage effective and happy. Then, following reviews of the sociology, ethology and anthropology of marriage, we will make our points by describing actual marriages with problems and the forces we can discern behind them.

* Definition from *The Columbia Viking Desk Encyclopedia*, 3rd Ed., 1953.

A great deal has been written, especially by Freud and later authors, on the interrelations of sex and personality, but it is not a settled question. Without a review of the extensive literature, the essentials, in somewhat oversimplified form, seem about as follows:

The young of animals, at least of the higher species, form attachments very soon after birth. Normally such attachment (which is roughly equivalent to what is technically called *imprinting*) is to the mother; but if she is not present, the attachment forms to a substitute. For example, a baby bird in a cage was fed by hand and became attached to the hand. When it reached adolescence, it mated sexually with the hand—not with other birds of its own kind. Konrad Lorenz, who introduced the term "imprinting," tells of a crow that was thus "in love" with a vacuum cleaner (1952). In a study of dogs, it was found that if newborn puppies were kept totally isolated from human beings for at least 14 weeks, they forever lost the capacity of forming the attachment to people that is so characteristic of our canine friends. Studies of many species show that sexual drives and social relations follow the path of the original imprinting—that is, the sexual and social attraction of the adult is toward the species, or even the inanimate object to which the initial attachment of the newborn was made. Hence, a monkey can become attached to a cloth "mother" and not to other monkeys, sexually or socially. This causes gross disorders toward other monkeys later in life. These disorders are to some degree correctable, in monkeys as in human beings (Harlow, 1952, 1950), if the fault in imprinting was not too severe and did not occur too early in the infant's life.

Although attachments, including imprinting, of the human young have only recently been studied systematically, it seems clear from clinical observation that attachment occurs in human babies and is of the greatest importance in their entire future emotional lives. In fact, since an outstanding feature of psychotic children is their inability to form emotional attachments to other humans, we may speculate that this inability is a result of failure to form such an attachment normally in the first hours, days, weeks and months because of the way they were treated; or that if they did imprint normally, later experiences were so traumatic as to disrupt the attachment. Therese Benedek studied the early "symbiosis" of infant and mother (1969; Anthony and Benedek, 1970), and

Margaret Mahler (1965) has studied this attachment and the growth process of "separation-individuation."

The first big step of the child in developing feelings for other persons is to achieve a healthy attachment at the proper time. The second step is the child's learning to react to the mother, or substitute, in order to *keep* this attachment. If the mother is loving and provides good care, the baby forms an image ("imago") of her as loving and providing, and reacts with pleasure to the relationship. But if the mother is depriving, loveless and harsh, the baby forms a threatening, frustrating image of her and is in conflict. Because he must have her care and love to survive, his need for love is unquenchable; but if her presence brings psychic or physical pain, he cowers and resents it (reacts with fight and flight impulses). Once formed, these images and patterns of reacting last for life, however well the rest of the child's personality develops.

The development of this process of reacting is a form of learning that is a kind of *conditioning*. To keep love and pleasure and to avoid rebuff and pain, the child unconsciously forms certain patterns of reacting that soon become permanent.

In normality and health, pregnancy is uneventful and desired, and the newborn baby is welcomed by loving parents into a loving home. The baby responds by attaching properly and is conditioned to enjoy the love of the parents and others who are close to him and responsible for him. Later his sexual desires follow this line of attachment and are directed toward a loving member of the opposite sex. From her or him, the postadolescent adult seeks the love he or she needed all through childhood and also sexual gratification. Sex is normally part of mating, and we may say that an individual's sexual urges and his whole mating mechanism follow the pattern of the original attachment and seek satisfaction with one of the opposite sex in a setting of love, such as he enjoyed all through childhood. With love and security the child identifies with his parents and matures normally in his adult capacities for giving love to others and for relative independence, responsibility, productivity and sense of reality. These processes are not free of problems; e.g., the baby boy's close attachment to his mother leads naturally to a woman for love and sex in maturity, but how does the baby girl's first attachment, also to her mother, lead to her adult attachment to a man? There are theories about the dynamics of this, but nothing is established with certainty.

In general, the younger the child, the more malleable he is. The complex of motivations and reactions at the core of the personality is mostly shaped by about the age of six or seven. After the initial imprinting and attachment are achieved, in the hours, days, weeks and months after birth, the first six years (0 to 6, for short) are critical. Love and security and respect for the baby's personality during that time provide a healthy base for whatever comes afterward. But lack of them or actively injurious treatment of the child fosters patterns of faulty feelings to others and to itself for life, however well the rest of the personality matures. Natural catastrophes excepted, disordered feelings toward oneself and others underlie all the problems and miseries of life, from headaches to murder—for life is almost entirely human relations.

Every personality involves such a complex interaction of passionate feelings that one hesitates to identify the essentials in simple terms. But these essentials are themselves relatively few, although they produce so many combinations that each personality is unique. So, too, are the designs of snowflakes, each different although each one is six-pointed; or the limitless number of chemical compounds, each made from some of only about 102 elements. Therefore we may hazard the observation that only a half dozen forces underlie or are prominent in almost all emotional problems. For a discussion in some detail of these individual emotional forces in the personality, e.g., dependence to independence, needs to get love versus ability to give love; inferiority, egoism, competitiveness and power-seeking; training, ideals and conscience, hostility and violence, sexuality, and grasp of reality, see: Saul, L. J., *Emotional Maturity,* 3rd Ed., Philadelphia: Lippincott, 1971.

All of these major emotional forces in the human mind are what the analyst deals with daily, but they are not all on the same level. They often overlap and are interrelated. For example, dependence and needs for love overlap one another. Both of these, by offending the adult pride and vanity, enter the inferiority-narcissism-competition conflict; through the need to please they also enter the domination-submission complex; and all frustrations provoke the fight-flight reaction. The very position of being small, weak and helpless means that every child must contend with all these forces, but in varying degree, depending upon how he is treated: with love or rejection, indulgence or deprivation, respect or domination, appreciation or depreciation, and so forth.

Loving others and being responsible for them is an attribute of maturity exemplified by the love and responsibility of parent to child. If all humans were thus mature, divorce, crime, cruelty, revolution and war might vanish. But there are other forces also, such as needs for self-esteem, so that the dependent-love needs of childhood cause shame and anger in the adult; when frustrated, they cause more anger, they cause exaggerated competition and much else.

Hostility is part of the fight-flight mechanism of adaptation (Saul, 1976). Any threat or frustration arouses impulses to eliminate the threat by fleeing from it or by destroying it. This is an invaluable reflex in the wild, but in society it threatens our existence, which depends upon a different mechanism of adaptation—social cooperation (Allee, 1951; Lorenz, 1966). Through social cooperation we defend ourselves against animals, forces of nature and even disease. It is the hair-trigger archaic fight-flight mechanism within us that now is our greatest enemy, for in this technological age our fight response can be made with atomic bombs instead of with rocks.

Hostility is not only readily aroused by threats and frustrations that are external, but also by those within our own makeup (such as shame, inferiority feelings, hurt pride and envy, stemming often from too strong dependent-love needs). Hostility generates guilt and fear of retaliation and often is turned against oneself, making a person "his own worst enemy" (a "loser"). Through all these complications one has a first very rough guide to any personality if he can see the two poles: dependent-love needs, and all that underlies them and results from them; and the terrible hostility, and what generates it and results from it.

These two poles of the personality—dependence and hostility—create a basic battle between the sexes which exists in addition to the many differences and conflicts in individual personalities that cause inner turmoil and marital discord. A male's first experience with a woman, namely with his mother when he is a baby and small child, is so overwhelming that it leaves effects that are never entirely outgrown or obliterated. They live on and shape his expectations in every subsequent relationship he may have with a woman.

The details vary with the hereditary potentials of each child and the personality and life setting of its mother, but the two basic features are never absent: the infantile dependence and the hostility from the fight-flight reaction.

Sooner or later a husband is almost certain to react toward his wife, as all men do to women they are close to for any protracted period, with much of the pattern he had toward his mother. Central in this pattern is always the original dependence on his mother. As it develops toward his wife, it leads to *hostility* along three routes: the most direct route is frustration of his emotional dependence, which often appears as demands on the wife.   He might insist she make decisions for him, sit with him while he watches TV, cook what and when he wants, permit him other women, and so on. These demands may be unreasonable or exaggerated, resembling his demands as an infant or small child upon his mother.   Even if the wife complies with these demands, the man usually feels inferior, although he is unaware that this feeling is the result of his childish or infantile dependence.   For this dependence wounds his masculine vanity, creating the second route to anger and hostility, often to the point of violence.   Of course, dependence is not a feeling limited to the husband.   An unusually perceptive divorced woman puts it poetically:

> For four days before Christmas a pitiful starving cat meowed outside my door and wouldn't go away.   Finally on Christmas, with its ears dripping wet with rain, it meowed at me so terribly pitifully I took it in. I am really very hardhearted about animals. It's a good cat.   I guess somehow I identified with that pitiful cat with the dripping wet ears . . . that's exactly how I felt . . . please somebody, I'll be a good cat.

Sex is a third route.   Dependence upon his mother transferred to his wife is apt to dampen a man's sexual interest in his wife because of the incest taboo toward his mother—usually the more a man is reminded by a woman, however unconsciously, of his childhood relation to his mother, the more inhibited the sex interest in her. In some men, however, because of the balance with other forces, the dependence actually heightens the sex, but the wife can often no longer enjoy it because she senses that her husband is not giving love and understanding, but making more demands upon her. Thus, by either decreasing or heightening the sex drive toward his wife, it results in frustration and more anger for the man. His wife feels more and more that the strong man she married in the normal expectation of getting male love and support is only another child whose demands she must meet along with the demands of her children. Even if the wife herself is relatively mature and free of disturbed childhood patterns, she finds herself in a "battle of the sexes," fighting to preserve her integrity as a person and even her health and life. It is all the more difficult for her if she does not perceive what is going on.

In examining what might be the causal factors in "the battle of the sexes," we approach a thicket of unresolved, vital and fundamental questions, including those of to what degree man's propensity for hostility and violence is intrinsic to his nature and to what extent it is due to conditioning by his early frustrations. When we consider why humans, inhabitants of earth for such a relatively short time, torment and kill one another and themselves, we must consider the problem in quantitative terms—how much is nature and how much is nurture? We know that a large part of hostility is the result of early conditioning, and is therefore susceptible of prevention and cure in theory, no matter how difficult it is practically to accomplish any large-scale improvement in childrearing (Saul, 1976).

Freud noted the hostility that springs from "narcissism with respect to minor differences" (1914), mentioning as examples the countries Spain and Portugal. Schools such as Harvard and Yale, and other similar groups or institutions with obvious similarities and rivalries, would also fall into this category. Perhaps such hostility is not necessarily the effect of similarity or minor differences, however, but part of a basic instinctual xenophobia seen in all animals when approached by a strange member of its own or another species, an innate suspiciousness, a caution until the stranger is identified as friend or foe. A dog's initial response is to race at every moving object in the field; he might continue the chase or attack if the object is a squirrel, groundhog, cat or bird, but he slows down to investigate if it is another dog. Konrad Lorenz (1966) described a turkey that attacked small creatures but was inhibited from attacking its own offspring. When a surgical procedure rendered the bird deaf, and it could no longer hear the cheeps of its young, it lost its inhibition and attacked and killed its babies.

In this case there was a biological instinctual force to hostile attack, and only an acoustical mechanism inhibited it toward its own young.

Most human hostile aggression and violence proneness seen in the analyst's office is the result of pathological childhood emotional patterns caused by mistreatment (by omission or commission) during the patient's early childhood. But this does not rule out the possible presence of an instinctive hostile drive to attack and kill.

This leads us to the possibility that in every individual there exists some hostility and violence proneness in the motivations, and they are controlled by certain psychological mechanisms that inhibit attack, just as the turkey was inhibited by physiological mechanisms. There is no positive proof of such physiological or biochemical causes, but we do know a psychodynamic mechanism exists. This is the narcissism Freud wrote about, taking the term from the myth of Narcissus who fell in love with his own image in a pool. Narcissism is probably part of the instinct of self-preservation, having to do with needs to be valued and esteemed by oneself and others. Although people do commit suicide, everyone normally has a powerful instinct toward self-preservation, toward health, well-being, esteem and self-interest. This protectiveness and normal love of self extends to others close to us with whom we identify. An obvious example is the young mother with her newborn child, which is indeed a part of her. We identify with our children and often would protect them with our own lives. Humans identify with their horses, dogs and other pets, and even with their homes, books and other inanimate possessions. So, too, ideally each spouse identifies with the other. Yet there is a slight and very basic difference between husband and wife, the sex difference.

In a locker room full of men there are often some who talk about "the women" as though they were different creatures, and who want to exclude women from men's sports altogether. Insofar as the narcissistic identification with another person is weakened, that individual loses the protection of the narcissistic love of self, and is more open to hostile attack. The more set apart a man feels his wife to be, because of the sex difference, the less protection she has against his hostility, protection she would have derived from his narcissistic identification, and the more free he feels to vent his hostility on her. The same situation can exist in the woman's feelings toward her husband. The source of this hostility might be either instinctive or from the childhood emotional pattern.

We can see clearly the operation of this principle in sociological terms; we are shocked if a person attacks "one of his own," with whom we expect him to *identify*, but we are less shocked if he attacks a stranger who is viewed as an enemy.

The sex differences that exist between husband and wife should bring only closeness, because of the sex attraction and love. Yet because of this difference, the narcissistic identification is weakened, and so also is the subsequent protection each has against the hostility of the other, whatever its basic source.

Marriage is a human relationship that consumes more than two-thirds of an average lifetime. The purpose of this book is to demonstrate what underlies typical problems of marriage in the hope that we may learn from these examples how better to prepare for family life and make it more gratifying. For family life shapes the child and provides the base for his personality and the rest of his existence, transmitting patterns to the children down through the generations, which in turn create the world in which we live.

References

Allee, W. (1951): *Cooperation Among Animals.* New York: Schuman.
Anthony, E. J. and Benedek, T., eds. (1970): *Parenthood: Its Psychology and Psychopathology.* Boston: Little-Brown.
Benedek, T. (1969): On frustration in infancy, *The Psychoanalytic Quarterly,* 38: 236–237.
Freud, S. (1914): On narcissism: an introduction, *S. E.* 14.
Harlow, H. F. (1950): Analysis of discrimination learning by monkeys, *J. of Experimental Psychol.,* 40: 26–39.
—— (1952) with R. Davis, P. Settlage and D. Mayer: Analysis of frontal and posterior association syndromes in brain-damaged monkeys, *J. of Comp. Physiol. Psychol.,* 45: 419–429.
Lorenz, K. (1952): *King Solomon's Ring.* New York: Crowell.
—— (1966): *On Agression.* New York: Harcourt, Brace and World.
Mahler, M. (1965): On the significance of normal separation-individuation phase, in: *Drives, Affects, Behavior,* Vol. 2, M. Schur. ed. New York: Intl. Universities Press.
Saul, L. J. (1976): *Psychodynamics of Hostility.* New York: Jason Aronson.

3
COMPONENTS OF MARRIAGE

The child we once were lives on in all of us.

Sigmund Freud

Good God, from your Heaven you see old children, and young children, and that is all, and your son proclaimed long ago in which of them you take the greater pleasure.

Goethe, *The Sufferings of Young Werther*

The interrelations of humans with each other are incredibly complex and sensitive. To live closely with another person, no matter what the age or sex, is extraordinarily difficult. Perhaps there are exceptions, but they must be rare. Even relatively loose, alterable relationships, such as those one might have at work, in social groups or among friends and acquaintances, are not noted for stability and harmony. What, then, of living with a person to whom one has bound oneself in closest intimacy for life? And what are the consequences of adding children to this union?

Why are emotional relations to others so trying? The answer seems to lie in the almost infinite differences within personalities. We are all in some ways so similar, but in others so different—for each of us is born into a different family and circumstances and each is subjected to different attitudes, feelings, nuances of behavior and treatment. The child's reactions to all these varying influences upon it from conception shape the core of his own personality for life, affecting how well and fully the forces of maturation operate. If all adults were adequately mature, then relationships would not be so frustrating, painful and hostile.

For each individual is motivated by a mostly unconscious childhood emotional pattern of impulses, feelings and reactions that was formed basically from conception to the age of about six by the interactions of his inherited potentials with the emotional and physical influences and pressures of the environment, most especially by the treatment received from parents and others close to and responsible for him.* This pattern, once formed, persists in its essentials for the rest of the child's life. Although often hidden from view, it is never entirely extinguished. The child grows up and moves away from home, his parents divorce or die, but the pattern remains.

This pattern is the key to the personality. The dynamic pattern of our 0–6 is our destiny. (By *dynamics* or *dynamic pattern* we refer to a certain equilibrium reached between the often conflicting impulses and reactions, i.e., the "emotional forces" in the mind.)

The dynamic pattern is the basis of maturity and nobility in some, and of all manner of psychopathology in others: psychosomatic disorders, neurosis, psychosis, perversions, addictions, criminality and "irrational hostile acting out," expressed as individual hostility or expressed collectively in violence which is frankly criminal, or rationalized as political action for some worthy cause.

The patterns of reaction to the *dramatis personae* of one's early childhood live on in us all; and no matter how appropriate in our early years, they are apt to be unworkable and even destructive when they emerge in adulthood toward others. It is these underlying forces that bring couples together in marriage and then may make them viciously hostile and drive them apart.

Thus, an emotionally deprived, lonely boy meets a girl who likewise is isolated and needful. Their common, underlying, lonely hunger for closeness and acceptance enables them to understand each other. They can relate closely to each other because they can *identify* with each other. But if they are intimate for long, if they marry, the boy's needs may make him turn to the girl as an object; he craves more love, care and attention than she can give. And she too changes from identification with him to an *object relation,* in which she yearns for more than he can gratify in adult life. The mutual need that brought them together now generates the frustrations that bring hostility and flight in varying forms and degrees.

---

* For smoothness and brevity, we will freely use "his," "he" or "him" as a general term for the individual, whether male or female. This in no way negates equal respect for both sexes, but is simply an attempt at stylistic simplicity.

True love means responsible disinterested caring for another for his own sake, and not for ulterior, selfish reasons. This love is seen throughout the animal kingdom, most clearly in the devotion of mothers to their young.

But marriage requires more than love. It is also composed of sex, which presumably should be an expression of love, but which often breaks loose from love and becomes a thing apart. It can be a channel for infantile dependent love needs, or even serve the most hostile, cruel impulses of which humans are capable, e.g., in lust murders—in a violence that far exceeds anything in the so-called lower animals.

With love and sex there must also be an enduring sense of romance. Marriage also requires responsibility for breadwinning and for care of one's home and family members. In fact, we might define maturity as the ability to accept responsibility. Mental health, Freud is reputed to have said, is the ability to work and to love and, we add, to play (Saul, 1977, p. 9).

In youth, the pressure of sex is usually so strong that its relation to reproduction and parenthood is often forgotten or seems incidental. But this, after all, is what sex is all about. With prostitutes or in seductions and certain affairs, reproduction plays no part; the chances of conception are a nuisance and a threat. The goal is to have sex, romance, companionship, money, or whatever each seeks, while eliminating reproduction. In our modern age of "the pill," this goal is readily attainable. In many marriages the goal is to have children, but when they arrive they may be found burdensome, interfering nuisances; and their parents' irritation with them may impair the children's good feelings toward their parents and thereby toward others for life.

Even if there are no problems with love, sex, children or daily responsibilities, there must be a "fit," a "meshing," of the childhood emotional patterns. Otherwise these patterns can generate tensions that may exceed what a person can stand. It is fortunate when domination-submission trends sometimes mesh rather than clash, as when the husband assumes the role of unquestioned boss in his business or profession, and the wife is unchallenged boss in the home.

Reasonable harmony in a marriage thus depends upon the adequacy in each partner of the following components:

1. *Love*—meaning a lasting desire to be with and close to the partner, identification with him or her and disinterested devotion to his or her welfare or with minimal ulterior, egocentric motives. Central to love is lasting loyalty.

2. *Sexual attractiveness, desire and healthy functioning and enjoyment,* a physical relation to the partner with relative freedom from exaggerations, perversions and impairments.

3. *Some sense of romance.* This is hard to define; perhaps it is in part whatever biological sense leads certain animals and birds to reject some suitors while mating, in some species, for life with an acceptable one. Perhaps it is the end result of many elements, culminating in what we call "being in love." It usually diminishes in quantity after marriage ("when the honeymoon is over"), but its quality often continues even into old age in "the love that has weathered the storms of life."

4. *Parenthood,* one of the deepest and most enduring satisfactions that life affords. But good childrearing is a long, trying, difficult job; what is best for the child often clashes with the parents' own comforts, desires and self-realizations and with the demands life places on them.

5. *Responsibility*—which comprises personal responsibility for spouse and children, including the children's direct emotional need of the parents, their dependence on and love needs for them and their requirements for the parents to be models of mature adults for them to pattern their own ideals and development on. Bread-winning has long been the primary nonpersonal responsibility of the husband with homemaking and childrearing the responsibility of the wife. But with the advent of the women's liberation movement, many wives have begun assuming part or all of this responsibility and gaining appreciation of the weight and pressure it entails. And husbands who take some responsibility for home, children, food, clothes and cleaning, experience the wife's isolation, dissatisfactions, frustrations and boredom. Perhaps this interchange and knowledge of one another's marital role will lead to increased understanding.

6. *Maturity,* which includes most of the foregoing points. The essence of maturity is seen in the contrast between, on the one hand, the baby and small child's utter dependence upon the mother and father for physical necessities and personal love, and, on the other hand, the parents' responsibility for and giving to the child.

The child is weak and helpless and therefore feels inferior, insecure and competitive, and is defenseless, afraid and hostile. A child is normally egocentric because his chief task is growing up, his own development. The parent, if his or her childhood attitudes are sufficiently outgrown, should be relatively independent, giving and capable, with minimal hostility and competitiveness, willing to live and let live as a responsible, productive, cooperative adult, spouse, parent, friend and citizen. Maturity includes a capacity for loyalty, identification, understanding, appreciation, encouragement and emotional support to one's mate; and, conversely, the strength for imperturbability in the face of hostility, negative criticism and wounds to one's self-esteem and pride from one's spouse. This *day-in, day-out* active affection and devotion is much more difficult than the relatively episodic giving during dating and courtship. Being in love is easy, but marriage is a long, hard haul. Its pleasures are quieter but deeper.

7. *Fit or mesh.* The more adequate the capacities listed above are, and the more adequate the outgrowing of childhood emotional patterns in favor of mature attitudes and feelings, the more easy, free and harmonious are the relationships in the family. But even if there is impairment and disturbance in any of these areas, a reasonably good home life is possible if the disorders in the couple *fit* each other sufficiently well. For example, a man who was deprived as a child developed emotional defenses against asking anything from anyone; he derived satisfaction from helping and giving to those dependent upon him. He married a girl who was herself deprived, which gave them a deep feeling in common. But the outcome in the wife was to remain dependent and needful, which just fitted her husband's emotional position of denying his own childish needs by playing the strong, giving, protective partner. The risk in such a situation lies in the possibility of a breakdown of the defenses and of the mature attitudes—if the husband should give out beyond his emotional means, or if the wife becomes less appreciative of him and demands more than he can comfortably give. Another risky situation is that of the man who was cruelly treated by his father as a child, identified with his loving mother and vows he will never treat his children as his father once treated him; he becomes a loving, excellent, understanding father and grandfather. This overcompensation often operates and holds for life, but must be at some risk. In the emotional life all is quantitative.

In a (typical) first interview a wife complains with bitterness of her husband's preoccupations with business or profession and other matters to the neglect and deprivation of herself, and she feels that she can no longer go on with the marriage in her state of frustration. She tells of disturbed relationships with her mother or father or both. This raises a vital diagnostic problem: This woman has had parental difficulties. Is the personality of her husband such as to frustrate any woman, no matter how good her relationships, and drive her to this desperation? If this is the case, then how did the wife come to marry such a man? Did she unconsciously select him to fit the disturbed relationships of her childhood, the kind of father or mother she grew up with and was accustomed to? Do these patterns continue her old feelings of deprivation even though the husband is basically a good partner and father, with warmth and consideration and not much internally generated hostility? If so, does the wife feel deprived or restricted mostly because of her ingrained childhood pattern, and unknowingly provoke her husband's feelings and behavior? Usually it is a matter of the interplay of all these components, in varying degrees—although one or another predominates.

This question is generally essential to understanding every individual: how much do one's feelings provide an appropriate response to the external situation, and how much do they express the constant, inner dynamics of the personality, i.e., how much is *reactive* to the externals, and how much *internal?* Some individuals unconsciously make for themselves, or involve themselves in, difficult and frustrating situations.

8. *Contrast.* This fit or mesh of the dynamics, although itself *internal,* is *reactive* to the childhood situation that shaped it and which continues in the mind. As such, it can be described as harmony through absence of too great *contrast.* This contrast is frequently heard by the analyst in complaints of one spouse about another.

A woman in her late fifties poured out a stream of complaints about her husband, always contrasting him with her father of childhood; she emphasized that her father, despite his faults, was constantly true to his wife and children, always interested in them, and understanding and supportive. The contrast of her inconsiderate husband with her most considerate father was more than she could bear. She responded to my taking a history of her 0–6 with: "I am amazed.   This is not my first experience with marriage after all, then! My first was with my own parents! That was so happy because of my loyal loving father and older brother. What a contrast now with my selfish egocentric, hostile husband."

Compare this with the purely *internal* dynamics of a wife whose father had died when she was only three years old. Her mother, after the father's death, was too busy working and seeking a new husband to give adequate care, attention and demonstrations of affection to the patient, who felt deeply rejected and neglected then and later. These feelings developed from *within* her toward her reasonably devoted, loving, conscientious husband, piling up irrational hostility to him because of her residue of inner feelings of rejection and neglect so ingrained in her growing up.

A husband who received much love as a baby and small child from his mother got much less demonstration of affection from his wife. He complained of the *contrast* that he was unconsciously feeling.

We can see how this works in the unconscious: A wife reported a dream (we will use only the relevant element of the manifest content) in which she entered a small, slightly dilapidated house and found herself in a cold bathroom lit by one hanging electric bulb. The house was irregularly heated. There was a party being held for the patient. One corner of the house seemed to be sinking. A man came in with a bright light to fix it [the analyst with insight].

What concerns us here is the association to the bathroom: "I was raised as a child in such a small, inadequate house. We had only one bathroom for my two parents and the three children. It was very warm and friendly. We were open with one another: one might have to wash while another was on the toilet. But each adapted to the others and waited or hurried up, doing what was needed to be helpful. When I was first married, we also had only one bathroom. My husband would sit on the toilet and read. I would have to wait—for as long as 40 minutes. Sometimes I could not stand it and even went next door to a neighbor's. Maybe I was too adaptable to my husband. I just thought 'It takes his body that long to eliminate.' The lightbulb reminds me of father. He was not just careful about turning out lights, he was a fanatic about it. But whatever his faults, he was a loving, devoted, understanding father, in sharp contrast to my husband, who is completely egocentric. I never realized this contrast until now, and how it has been tearing me apart, making me 'sink under' like the corner of the house in my dream, driving me to smoking three packs of cigarettes a day and drinking liquor to get to sleep at night. The house in childhood was like the one in my dream—simple, inadequate, slightly dilapitated and unevenly heated, but the family was all warm and loving in stark contrast to my present house and my cold, ungiving, egocentric husband. Yet I have always blamed myself for the strains in the marriage, and have done everything, even jeopardized my health, to make *him* happy."

9. *Intelligence, physical health, socioeconomic factors.* Although harmony and satisfaction in marriage are primarily the effects of emotional fit, there are other elements that affect this, such as health, money and intelligence. One partner with an intellect far superior to the other's may become bored or annoyed, and the partner with a lower I.Q. may feel inferior, unable to cope with his or her spouse. So, too, ill health can become tedious, as can poverty. These factors can aggravate emotional incompatibilities and play upon emotional sensitivities until the limits of tolerance are passed.

The success of a marriage and a family is largely a function of the total score on the above nine points. Some factors compensate for others. For example, the wife in one of the best marriages I have ever seen was relatively frigid sexually. Although she had never had an orgasm, she enjoyed sex, was faithful to her husband, bore five children and was a superior wife and mother. Her easygoing husband was well aware of the situation but entirely faithful to her, rejoicing in his good fortune in having a woman who was otherwise so excellent a wife and mother and companion.

Of course these nine points are not definitive but only a rough guide, and might be differently organized, but they do show why marriage is such a complex relationship.

A successful marriage means good relations, good feelings and happiness for all within its circle. It is from this soil that children grow up to be mature, responsible, internally satisfied spouses, parents and citizens.

Apart from the deeper motivations for marriage—the mating instinct and the psychological motivation to make a home, thereby satisfying the childhood pattern of growing up in a home—there are more immediate superficial motivations: for example, the simple convenience of having a home as a stable base and having a regular assured sexual partner without the squandered energy that goes into searching for a new one frequently.

The adult tends to repeat in his marital home with fateful precision the emotional patterns he developed in his parental home. This is the "interpersonal pattern" of childhood, revivified in an adult edition.

Every marriage is a drama—some are high drama. When a couple stand together at the wedding ceremony, their childhood emotional patterns come together, committing them to one another; in time, the traits of each are revealed to the other: the heroism and the cowardice, the bliss and the agony—making the tragedy and the comedy of our human scene.

This tendency to repeat a childhood pattern toward others in adult life occurs regardless of age or sex. Men thrown together, as in wartime, and women thrown together in close proximity repeat these patterns to one another. Marriage is only a special case of such repetition of childhood patterns toward another person.

An obviously complicating feature in the marital relationship is sexual intercourse. To have it at all, the man must have an erection, which is something beyond conscious control. The physiological sexual response is a phenomenon much affected by the emotional state. Paradoxically, the sex drive is both enormously powerful and also extremely sensitive emotionally.

Some degree of impotence in men and some amount of frigidity in women are said to occur in close to half of the adult population. This is not too surprising if one considers that the early training of children is generally inhibitory and conveys the idea that sex is "bad," wrong, sinful, except in marriage. Also, since sexual feelings follow the strongest emotional attachments, they are usually toward family members and therefore incestuous and subject to the usual taboos. One husband, a big strong attractive man, was only potent when in a certain internal state of mind, in which case, without warning, he would rush across the room and rape his wife. When in bed or in a tender relationship with her, he was impotent. Another husband had no problem with potency, but derived no satisfaction from coitus unless his wife had an orgasm, which she achieved only with difficulty, especially when she felt obligated by her husband's requirement.

Of course women have problems too; obviously girls as well as boys have been mistreated in their 0–6 and react to their parents in ways that later disturb their marital relationships. One couple was quite harmonious, but as time passed the wife lost sexual interest in her husband. She had no real complaints about him, but simply no longer desired him physically and even resented his sexual demands upon her. Yet she met another man, did not have intercourse with him out of fidelity to her husband, but found that even while fully dressed she spontaneously had an orgasm if this man merely put his arms around her.

A highly refined girl marries. Her husband at climax blurts out obscenities. This, for her, is an added thrill. To the beauty she finds in intercourse is added an earthy element that satisfies something in her animal nature. But another wife subjected to this only feels degraded and aesthetically revolted. One woman might like sudden, surprising initiations of sex by her husband in all sorts of circumstances; another requires the psychological preparation of long wooing, gradually leading up through dinner to soft lights and bed. Some relish the animalistic—but others are only satisfied if the act of intercourse is clearly, surely and deeply an extension of intensifying feelings of love. Some have mutual orgasms even though one or both may have to indulge in mad fantasies during the act or think of another partner or several. Manual help such as stimulating the clitoris may be resented or may be needed and agreeable. Thus the variations in physical sexual behavior are endless. And this colorful variety is an advantage to those men and women who have all sorts of mixtures of these desires. For them, in their fortunate marriages, the sexual act expresses endless variations of mood at different times. But usually some adaptation is required by each partner to the urges of the other.

Sex and love and their many interrelations and variations can cause further internal complications of feelings. In the romantic image they are one: love includes sex and sexual interest signifies love. But this is not necessarily true. A man may be "in love with" a woman, obsessed by her beauty and charm and desiring her sexually more than any other, his sexual feelings culminating in expressions of tenderness, affection and desires for closeness. In him, love and sex may fuse. But this same man, in a different time and mood, may feel less free sexually with this woman whom he loves and respects and be more aroused sexually by a purely animalistic situation or object, a female body with which he can do as he wishes with little regard or feeling for the woman's personality. Then love and tender feelings become interferences and even inhibiting forces to raw sex. So love and sex can either intensify or conflict with one another. Full fusion is an ideal, part of the desire to find *every* satisfaction in one single human being. Quite an expectation! Moreover, the choice of spouse on whom depends one's hopes for all marital satisfactions is normally made at an age when experience with human personalities and their motivations, and with one's own emotions including the sex drive, is slight.

In general, every person's reason is at the mercy and in the service of his emotions—the head is a servant and often a slave of the heart. What seems to be realistic reason is often mostly rationalization. As a young man once put it, "I cannot judge women because they have *beauty.*" A man's dynamics make him react to women with much more than the mating drive and sex alone: he reacts with emotional dependence, with submissiveness, with vanity and often with hostility—in fact, with all the attitudes and feelings of his childhood emotional pattern, especially toward his mother. Sometimes he may react because of extraneous motivational contaminants, such as money or social prestige. Small wonder his judgment is confused, and not only by the sex urge. Of course a girl's judgment is equally at the mercy of her own childhood patterns, plus perhaps a need for financial security and of course for a good father for her children.

Complicating that vital decision of choosing a mate is an equally crucial decision which arises about the same time: choice of career. Whatever your 0–6, whatever your basic dynamics, the mate and career you choose involve the lifelong influences of the childhood pattern, which are powerful forces working for your happiness or suffering, and form part of your development throughout life. The period of maximum vulnerability and conditionability for every individual is 0 to 6; probably the younger an individual is, the greater the vulnerability to trauma. Influences during later childhood and adult life leave their mark, but not so deeply. A child who was loved and respected during this early period usually has a healthy core of dynamics which can sustain him through difficulties later.

As we review the nine components of marriage in the light of the basic dynamics of the conjugal relation, it seems the husband has certain specific advantages and the wife has others. Marriage in the traditional sense will probably survive the currents of change because many men will want to live out their childhood patterns of pursuing their individual interests in a stable home environment, an environment that was maintained for them in childhood by their mothers. Also, many women will continue to prefer being supported financially, having the freedom they had as children, especially to raise their own young.

A husband who is a successful breadwinner, engaged in a job that yields both interest and enjoyment, has great advantages; his interests bring him into contact with other people, giving him both variety and emotional support and occupying his mind. He also has initial control of the family income, although in many of the best marriages he turns this over to his wife. If the marriage should develop serious difficulties, he can always turn his mind to his job and his coworkers. The dependent and relatively isolated position of the wife in such a situation is obvious: if she has not taken the precaution before marriage of preparing herself to earn a steady income, then her whole style and standard of living, even her very existence, is threatened by marital difficulties. In the case of a divorce, if her husband wants custody of their children, the wife may lose them if he as breadwinner can support them adequately and she cannot.

Does a wife have any specific advantages in the traditional marriage, with the accepted assignment of responsibilities? Superficially and mechanically, simply by running the home and providing sex, she gives her husband a high degree of freedom for his work. But, more deeply, she holds considerable power over him.* She is a woman he is attached to; he would not have been sufficiently attracted to her to initiate marriage if some elements within him had not responded to her as he once did toward his mother.

As Freud described the oedipus complex, the male is born of a female, and his first care is normally that given him by his mother

---

* "We must all be sorry for those who try to put a shape to dreams. We dream of lovers equal to the gaieties and the ardours of love—and all we get is a man in search of a mother .... I wish someone would tell me what flaw there is in men that makes them unworthy of straightforward gifts of which love should be the first." [Michael Arlen, "Legend of the Crooked Coronet"]

or a female substitute. It is a female he first imprints. It is a female who provides his first body care and closest body contact, a contact as intimate as the breast during feeding, and touching of the perineal region in changing diapers and bathing. It is now generally accepted that the male even in babyhood has sexual feelings. It is clearly observable in the erections from three months of age or earlier. Thus the male baby and small child is bound to his mother by powerful instincts, feelings and sensations before he is old enough to have sufficient "ego" to comprehend them. He is attached by his utter dependence. Without the mother's almost constant physical care in providing warmth, food, cleanliness, quiet for sleeping and watchful attention to his bodily health, he could not survive. His guarantee of this necessary care is his sense of being loved, expressed by his mother through physical and verbal demonstrations of affection. Mixed with these dependent-love needs are sexual feelings and responses that give the relationship a sexual tinge. All this psychological interaction of loving and being loved, combined with the physical elements suffused with erotic coloring, makes a mental and emotional state in the infant and child long before he has the maturity to apprehend it. Yet it is in this context that he, the tiny helpless child, experiences his first relationship with a woman who is to him all-powerful, and whose love and devotion constitute his entire emotional life and the only basis for his survival. Further, this relationship is in essence a "love relationship," no matter how rejecting, frustrating, punitive or unloving his mother makes it (which would engender hostility and hatred of women). Her treatment of him lays down a pattern for all future relations with women.

A man tends to repeat this early relationship with his mother toward every woman, sooner or later seeking a mother in her, and this gives women their power over men. It is this advantage that a wife possesses to counter the physical and financial strength of her husband.

Women, too, are born of women, and the pattern they establish toward their mothers is also fateful for their lives. A wife's pattern toward her mother persists for life and is apt to influence strongly her attitudes toward her husband, but less intensely if she established early, secure and good relations with her father.

Parents often ask how and when to introduce sex education to their children. Certainly the example of their own healthy, loving marriage is the first and best teacher. I sometimes wonder if "sex education" may not easily be overdone. Sex is an instinct deep enough to take care of itself. Is not part of the charm of young love finding out about sex for oneself? Is not some of this lost by anatomical and physiological lectures? Is not the real problem *psychological* rather than physical? Perhaps the best sex education is simply, as G. B. Shaw said, to answer your children's questions as soon as they are old enough to ask them.

References

Saul, L. J. (1977): *The Childhood Emotional Pattern: The Key to Personality, Its Disorders and Therapy.* New York: Van Nostrand Reinhold.

SOME ADDITIONAL REFERENCES:

Bowlby, J. (1953): *Child Care and the Growth of Love.* Baltimore: Penguin Books. (Based on *Maternal Care and Mental Health,* New York: Columbia Univ. Press, 1951. The subject is not marriage but a related topic, yet the thinking is dynamic and scientific.)

Eisenstein, V. (1956): *Neurotic Interaction in Marriage.* New York: Basic Books.

Flugel, J. (1929): *The Psycho-analytic Study of the Family.* London: Hogarth Press. (An early classic that is still valuable and contains the germinal concepts of many later developments; however, it deals hardly at all with marriage itself.)

Grotjahn, M. (1960): *Psychoanalysis and the Family Neurosis.* New York: W. W. Norton.

Masserman, J. (1958): *Science and Psychoanalysis II Individual and Familial Dynamics.* New York: Grune and Stratton.

Montagu, A. (1955): *The Meaning of Love.* New York: Julian Press.

Reiss, I. (1971): *The Family System in America.* New York: Holt, Rinehart and Winston.

Saul, L. J. (1972): *Bases of Human Behavior.* Westport, Conn.: Greenwood Press. (Originally published by J. B. Lippincott, Philadelphia, 1951.)

SECTION II:
A REVIEW OF THE SOCIOLOGY, ETHOLOGY AND ANTROPOLOGY OF MARRIAGE

4
LAWS OF NATURE AND MORAL LAW

Love is to the moral nature exactly what the sun is to the earth.

Balzac

Man that is born of woman is of few days, and full of trouble.

Job 14:1

The ancient interrelationship of natural and moral law, despite its theoretical and practical importance, is one that has never been fully clarified. Both natural and moral law not only operate nationally and internationally, but are vitally important to the smallest sociological unit—the human marriage.

Newton described certain laws in the area of terrestrial and astronomical mechanics. Einstein clarified some broader principles. Other physicists have made similar major contributions, e.g., quantum mechanics. Darwin discerned certain principles or laws in the behavior and evolution of biological organisms. Species that best adapted to the environment survived, while others did not. Since then ethologists, anthropologists, sociologists, psychologists, psychiatrists and others interested in the various aspects of behavior have provided certain guiding concepts.

One of these concepts is that each *individual* organism has a life cycle that it strives from within to live out, in its own way: birth, maturation, some form of mating, reproduction, provision for young, senescence, death. Another principle is that, just as the individual organism strives for its own survival, so it also participates in the survival of its species. Elephants do not destroy elephants, nor do mosquitoes live on mosquitoes. Fights between males for females are not to the death but only to establish dominance. Fights to establish territorial rights may be more serious, but members of a given species, say gorillas, use the threat of attacking to intimidate and bluff intruders to drive them off (Goodall,

1971), trying not to injure or kill and risk being injured and killed.

Almost all animals within their own species *cooperate* to some extent with each other. Man's cooperation with his kind to form societies is in accordance with natural law, using this term as a description of what is generally observable. Through cooperation we have developed our adaptation to nature. Cooperation makes possible science, engineering and processes that give us food, clothing, shelter and protection against the elements and even against many hostile microorganisms. If every man had to hunt or till the soil, we would have no scientists and no science or art. As long as men cooperate, they are reasonably secure on this planet. Ironically, their only major threat is from other humans. This destructiveness of man to man is contrary to the natural law of survival of the individual and the species. Destructive behavior toward one's own species is all but unknown elsewhere in the animal kingdom, with a few minor exceptions, and then usually only under special circumstances such as threat of starvation (as in the harvester ants). Organized crime and war seem to be uniquely human.

Superficially, morality varies from one age and station in life to another. For youth to have its fling is not the same as for a middle-aged clergyman to have his. But here we speak of a deeper morality—the *im*morality of man's hostility to his own kind, of cruelty, destructiveness and murder at any age, of what is *anti-human*, the worst of the corruption that we see everywhere—in government, management, labor and the home.

The destruction of one's own species and oneself on a massive scale is against natural as well as moral law, for the bomb or population explosion or pollution may eliminate man as an evolutionary failure. If war is a manifestation of fighting for property rights, as is seen throughout the animal kingdom, then in man it seems to be a pathological aberration of that instinct or its controls. I think killing, especially organized and on a wide scale, is at bottom a symptom of widespread emotional disorder, whatever other factors are involved. At least this element must be given due weight (Saul, 1976).

Moral and secular law against cruelty and killing expresses the natural process of maturation, reproduction and care of the young, and of social cooperation in all species. Its standard is love, which means it is *pro-life*. The breakdown of love, of moral law, is against life, a sign of warped emotional development, of failure to mature adequately. The mature human conforms to the natural law of his species: he is a responsible, loving spouse, parent and citizen in the community. In addition, he respects the natural law of other species. He may feel hostility and fight, but he does not destroy his species or himself.

Emotional warping, we now know, is chiefly the result of faulty childrearing in the earliest hours, days, weeks, months and years, causing the child's reaction of *egocentricity* and *hostility* and impairment of love toward its parents and siblings; this reaction is transferred or displaced to other human beings as a permanent pattern of *irrational, pathological, hostile acting out.* A child who is badly treated by its own mother and father may hate humans but love horses or dogs (who never mistreated him as his parents did) and continue to do so for life. Hence, a sadist may love animals.

The maturation of the individual, in accordance with *natural* law as seen in animals in the wild, into a responsible and loving spouse, parent and citizen is expressed in *moral* law. The need for moral law and secular law arises largely from the faulty childrearing that makes the child form patterns of behavior which are contrary to nature (Richette, 1970). Our laws proclaim the psychological pathology that makes them necessary.

Why are some humans brutal murderers and others loving people of good will? How can we prevent, control, check, sublimate, divert and weaken this destructiveness, most of which is obviously pathological, however rationalized? To raise emotionally healthy children is, of course, a monumental task, dealing as we do with so many warped, immature, hostile parents. It is a sad fact that most people are severely disturbed emotionally; the lives of many leave a legacy more of harm than of good.

The religious commandments and principles of both Old and New Testaments, moral law, social standards and secular laws all formulate the basic principles of natural law for the well-being of individuals and the species: the development of the young into good, responsible, loving mates, parents, citizens. In this respect they are more than intellectual rules. They express the biological instincts necessary for the existence of individuals and species and of human societies. They are deeply grounded in the biological nature of man and other species as well. It seems that those who go contrary to these laws are not simply being unconventional, but are manifesting disturbances in their psychological maturing to the status of mate, parent and citizen. It requires much maturity and mental and emotional health to handle the component drives that lead to the ability to make a happy home and thereby a stable society.

References

Goodall, J. (1971): *In The Shadow of Man.* Boston: Houghton Mifflin Co.
Richette, L. (1970): *The Throwaway Children.* New York: Dell Publishing Co.
Saul, L. J. (1976): *Psychodynamics of Hostility.* New York: Jason Aronson.

5
THE NATURE OF MAN

Man, biologically considered . . . is the most formidable of all the beasts of prey, and, indeed, the only one that preys systematically on its own species.

William James,
Memories and Studies

The author, by temperament an optimist, who still loves people despite all he has seen, has come to the following picture of man's nature, which, of course, cannot at present be finally proved or disproved.* Any hope for a basic biological standard for marriage from the study of animals in nature has not, at least yet, been fulfilled for humans. Nor has any such norm or ideal been provided by current knowledge of anthropology, history or sociology. There is no regular permanent mating known among animals except in a few species such as wolves and hawks. And the reviews of marriage among many different societies and cultures, primitive or far "developed" and at different stages in man's history, also yield no constant durable thread or standard. Why is this, why is monogamy, although practiced in every culture and the ideal of Western civilization, yet so unstable and unreliable?

I think one reason lies deep in the nature of man. Clinical experience with the deeper motivations, general observation, the news of the day and the study of all human history reveal what Freud phrased psychoanalytically as the conflict between Id and Superego (1930). This simply means humans are basically animals with certain conditioned, learned inner restraints; in Plato's famous words, "the good dream what the bad do." The animal nature is always

---

* "Thus, both [Harry Stack Sullivan and Erik Erikson] depart from the Freudian notion of man as the socialized savage. Both thinkers place tremendous emphasis on the interpersonal, and the meaning of what might be called 'the significant other.'" [Goethals, G. (1976): The evolution of sexual and genital intimacy: A comparison of the views of Erik H. Erikson and Harry Stack Sullivan, *J. Amer. Acad. Psychoanal.* 4(4): 529-544.]

present, whether acted out or kept in check; we can see this in the dreams if not the associations of even our most proper, most inhibited patients.   The greatest literature is tragedy; and fantasies of violence, of man against man, are used for entertainment in literature and on stage and screen.   Violent "murder mysteries" and "westerns" fill whole libraries.   At all stages in man's development violence has been acted out, as it is today all over our planet—in the Middle East, in Africa and as crime in U.S. cities or suburbs which makes it dangerous to walk the streets or countryside, or even to be in one's own home, flat, or high-rise apartment, where employees monitor visitors at a lobby desk, and in the elevators. *Homo hominis lupus*—man to man is a wolf.   Ironically, wolves are relatively good to one another, and "lions are good family men"; it is humans who are so often "brutes" to other humans.   Our chief fear of violence comes from other human beings.   Even disease is less dangerous statistically.   Few if any other species are as violent to their own kind as *homo sapiens.*

Men and women are basically animals, with especially hair-trigger and virulent *fight-flight* reactions, with propensities to *escape* into drugs and mental illness, as well as to *sadism* and *violence,* and this on a wider scale than is seen in any other species to its own kind. The human animal is *dependent* for so long on its parents that it must learn somehow to live within the family harmoniously.   This emotional pattern of behavior he transfers from his family members to other adults as he outgrows childhood and moves among them. Thus societies develop and provide powerful protection for the survival of the individuals that compose them against the forces of nature, including all sorts of disease.

But there is a price to be exacted: each human animal, to live in his society, must control his sexual drives and his fight-flight reaction.   If he takes flight into addictions and mental illness, he is a drain on the other animals in his society; and if he reacts with fight, his cruelty and violence will directly endanger his fellows. Therefore, for his own survival in society, he must learn to control these animal forces, i.e., he must develop a Superego to control his Id.   It is interesting to recall Freud's (1940) remark:

This general pattern of a psychical apparatus may be supposed to apply equally to the higher animals which resemble man mentally. A superego must be presumed to be present wherever, as is the case of man, there is a long period of dependence in childhood.

Normally the parents help the child to control his sex impulses and hostility by checking them during his formative years, from 0 to 6. If they do not help the child control these impulses with built-in restraints, he may spend his life in jail, or his flight into mental illness may lead to a mental hospital. Obviously the human animal cannot live as a wild animal does, by following his instincts in nature, but must adapt to a society, a culture, a civilization. To do so he builds up elaborate police and legal systems and develops religions that articulate basic standards of morality and ethics to inhibit internally the animal drives and reactions.

Dictatorships openly sacrifice individual freedom to achieve safety by direct police control. For that price you can walk safely in the streets of communist Prague, for example, but not in the streets of New York or small-town America, nor can you feel safe in your own home in the U.S. Humans have speech and have built up vast literatures of books and plays, all dramatizing for our amusement the struggles in the human animal of its primitive instincts against the necessary inhibitions of society, depicting the adventures that occur when these inhibitions are distorted, defied or broken. Domestication is often unsuccessful in humans, as testified by the mounting crime rate, overflowing jails and mental hospitals and the rising divorce rate. (Of course, there are current "reactive" factors also, as in socioeconomic pressures.) This parallels the behavior of other animals which have also been domesticated only to a certain degree; we have all seen unpredictable and dangerous dogs and horses, and even chickens that behave in a strange or crazy manner. We can sum up this behavior in a time-tested adage, "Never trust an animal" (some are more securely and reliably domesticated than others, and are more trustworthy, but their essential animal nature is no different), and we can add, "Every man has his price."

For most of my professional life I have recognized that my innate optimism, born of much love in earliest childhood and considerable inhibition of hostilities, has made me believe that Freud was too influenced by his own pessimism in his view of man. Therefore, my writings (1976) have expressed the view that hostility in human affairs is primarily a result of disturbed interpersonal relations in earliest childhood—and if we were only to raise our children with good relations of love, respect and understanding, we would indeed approach Utopia itself.

I was fascinated by the idea of one lone English girl walking into the heart of Africa to live with chimpanzees, and began reading the observations of Jane Goodall (1971, 1972) and other ethologists. Meanwhile, my clinical experience plus time to observe my patients and formulate these observations has increased with age.

We can now say that the problem of man's hostility to man is no longer so simple as whether man is "natively good" or "instinctually hostile." Rather, enough is known of psychodynamics to say that there is in the human mind a mixture of emotional forces, some innate and instinctual and others conditioned and learned, that interact to produce a variety of outcomes in behavior. Among those forces favoring violence, physical and psychological cruelty and killing are (1) the hair-trigger fight-flight reaction to flee or destroy a threat, frustration or irritation, either external or internal, and (2) egocentricity and arrogance, which block sympathy, empathy and understanding. Among those forces counteracting violence are (1) a basic tendency to cooperation, (2) capacity for humility, learning, identification, sympathy, empathy and formation of conscience, as well as the requirements of civilization and culture, and (3) the capacity for love.

As understanding of these forces increases, we certainly cannot predict but at least can be justified in hoping that man, "having arrived on this earth as the product of a biological accident [will not] depart through human arrogance" (Leakey and Lewin, 1977).

Rather than "a socialized savage," it seems more accurate to call man "an animal that must live in a society, culture, civilization"—in brief, "a partially socialized animal."

It is man's animal nature that makes such serious problems for him, living as he must in societies with their civilized rules and cultures. That is why I believe civilization does not mean the production of art but the treatment of one's own kind in a civilized way, with empathy and love, not with hostility, cruelty and violence.

One of the animalistic forces on the side of inhibition is *parental love*. It is sometimes reinforced by the sex drive, but not always, for sexual feelings do not always enhance love but rather do the opposite, intensifying cruelty and violence and leading to rape and lust murders. The importance of nonsexual love as a countervailing force to the violence of the fight-flight reaction has not been missed by the great religions, yet it has not prevented the long history of hate and violence in Jerusalem itself, nor in the Protestant Reformation, nor in the current bloodshed between Protestant and Catholic in North Ireland.

Man as an animal is not straightforward and honest like animals in the wild. He is an animal warped and distorted by the necessities of living in a society, a culture, a civilization. The essence of civilization, as I have said, is not the production of works of art but the capacity of the human animal to treat his own kind *civilly,* without victimizing his fellow man by his sex drives, his regressive demands or his cruelty and violence. Inhibiting these animal impulses leads to fantasies—frank fantasies of the ideal lover or mate, of revenge on enemies who threaten or injure and so on, and fantasies distorted and complicated by their internal inhibitions. Some individuals, because of certain characteristics of these partially repressed fantasies and certain talents, create works of art, while others add to the structure of science. Anthony Gilbert, at the end of *The Puzzled Heart,* tells how she once took her young grandson to Madame Tussaud's famous waxworks where, in the chamber of horrors, the child looked upon the images of a handsome young poisoner, the gentle Dr. Crippen who cut up his wife's body, and other famous murderers. But the little boy was disappointed; he thought they would look different, but "they looked just like everyone else".

If the childhood emotional pattern is not basically loving, it is like a time bomb that can explode at any age. It is a common clinical experience to see a young man of 35, after more than ten years of a stable marriage, one day announce to his wife that he has not been honest with her, that he really has not loved her for five years and has had sexual affairs with other women. Two weeks later another couple in their early fifties come to see me because the husband has suddenly announced that he is walking out of the marriage, after 30 years. And later, in that same period of only a few weeks, I see a similar couple of 60; the husband after many years of marriage announces his freedom and his sexual involvement with other women. It is not always the husband who abruptly deserts the marriage: an acquaintance of mine suddenly had a

heart attack while playing golf. The pain was intolerable. He recovered but only to regret it, for his wife became paranoid to him
and, like the Ancient Mariner, told everyone she could get to listen
stories designed to ruin her husband, about how crooked and untrustworthy he was, that he was a homosexual and a thief, and so
on—all this from a hitherto devoted wife, out of the suddenly exploded time bomb of her infantile hostilities. Less dramatic is a
case like that in Ibsen's *Doll's House,* a wife of 40 who left the
marriage to find herself a career. Her husband was not one to
embrace other women lightly and loosely; his whole life was devastated by the loss of his wife and his home, just as the lives of the
wives mentioned above were devastated when they suddenly lost
their husbands.

   When you marry, you cannot escape the risk—you can only use
your head as well as your heart and hope that in your mate the
animal impulses will be so directed and used as to bring you only
love. Your mate can only bring you this love if sufficient love
existed in the object relations and identifications of his or her
childhood, with those persons during 0 to 6 with whom he or she
formed the basic childhood emotional pattern.

   Marriage, vitally important relationship that it is in so many ways,
can be viewed in different frames of reference. We have discussed
it in connection with mankind's essential animal nature, the breaking-
through of certain unbridled animal impulses—egotistical, hostile,
promiscuous, sexual. Marriage can also be seen in the slightly different perspective of development to maturity.

   It takes a certain level of maturity to enter into the responsibilities
of marriage in the first place, and it takes a great deal more maturity
to maintain them. So it should not be too surprising that many
people do not have the maturity to marry at all, while many others
have enough maturity to enter marriage but not enough to sustain
it—somewhere along the line they break in some way, or walk out
of their marriages with visions, usually false, of freedom from responsibilities and opportunities for self-indulgence.

   In a third frame of reference, marriage is an opportunity to
gain consciously or unconsciously a certain control over one's
spouse in order to act out on him or her the hostilities developed
toward one's mother or father or siblings during childhood. This is
like the Marquis de Sade: gaining control of the spouse for one's

own sadism. This is sometimes overt, as with "battered babies" and "battered wives," the extremity and frequency of which problems are just becoming recognized. But in many marriages the sadism is more subtle, indirect and psychological, as in the case of those infantile egocentric husbands who treat their wives as servants, coming and going according to their own desires, expecting complete service and subservience from the wives as though they were their overindulgent mothers, and having other women and even bringing them into the home and into contact with the children.

In all three of these views or types of marriage, the childhood emotional pattern plays a central part. But whether the part it plays in generating human hostility is predominant or not, one fact is incontrovertible: the greatest danger to man is man himself.

References

Freud, S. (1930): Civilization and its discontents, Part V, *S. E.* 21, p. 108.
—— (1940): An outline of psychoanalysis, the psychical apparatus, *S. E.* 23, p. 144.
Goodall, J. (1971): *In The Shadow of Man.* Boston: Houghton Mifflin Co.
—— and Van Lawick, H. (1972): *Grub: The Bush Baby.* Boston: Houghton Mifflin Co.
Leakey, R. and Lewin, R. (1977): *Origins.* New York: E. P. Dutton.
Saul, L. J. (1976): *Psychodynamics of Hostility.* New York: Jason Aronson, Inc.

6
THE AMERICAN FAMILY:
PAST AND PRESENT

In both a structural and functional sense, the family of today is not the same as the family of yesteryear. It is stronger, probably, in some ways, and weaker—certainly in others. On the strong side, for example, would have to be listed such things as a more democratic orientation, a more companionable relation between husband and wife and a fuller awareness of the personality needs of all members, including children.

On the weak side, it is self-evident that today's marriages are—in a statistical sense—fragile. The marriage rate itself has been falling, even as the divorce rate climbs.* Sex outside marriage is becoming more and more commonplace. The birth rate is now below replacement. The tide of juvenile delinquency that has engulfed the nation in recent periods must also be listed as a weakness in family organization.

Whether, on balance, today's family is weaker or stronger than formerly can be debated. That it is substantially different is beyond debate. To understand the difference, it is necessary to take a capsule look at those historical forces that have shaped present-day marital patterns.

Historical Background

The roots of our present marital system can be found, to a surprising degree, in the Judeo-Christian, Greco-Roman period. While there were many differences among the ancient Hebrews, Greeks, Romans and Christians, certain of their marital and familial customs were remarkably similar, and many of these similarities have come down to us in the form of deep-seated traditions.

To begin with, the family of antiquity was heavily patriarchal in nature. The father was undisputed master of the household.

---

* Currently, the divorce rate is 48.2 percent (*Today*, Feb. 12, 1978).

Among the Greeks, it was commonly believed that women were virtually of a different species. Athenian wives remained uneducated and were not permitted to leave their homes without their husband's permission. Their social contacts were almost nil, and in fact their entire function in life was that of childbearing and homemaking. The young Greek girl was not even consulted when it came to marital arrangements.

Hebrew wives had a somewhat higher status than their Greek counterparts, but by modern standards it was pitifully low. Hebrew women were not permitted to inherit property or to participate in commercial activities. Their behavior was carefully circumscribed, even to the point of wearing veils in public. Although upon occasion a Hebrew woman such as Deborah the prophetess could attain some rank, such occurrences were unusual.

It might also be mentioned that among both Greeks and Hebrews divorce was considered to be a male prerogative. A husband could divorce his wife for almost any reason, whereas for the wife there was virtually no legal escape. About the only recourse for a woman was to try to persuade her husband to grant her a divorce.

Children were also under the complete jurisdiction of their father. In fact, no account of ancient family life would be complete without mention of the infamous Roman practice of *patria potestas*—uncontested power of the father over his children. As Johnston (1969) points out:

The *patria potestas* was carried to a greater length by the Romans than by any other people, a length that seems to us excessive and cruel. As they understood it, the *pater familias* had absolute power over his children and other descendants . . . . He punished what he regarded as misconduct with penalties as severe as banishment, slavery, and death. He alone could own and exchange property—all that his descendants earned or acquired in any way was his. According to the letter of the law, they were little better than chattels . . . .

In practice, things were not as bad as they sound. True, the patriarch had vast powers, but there is no evidence that he systematically abused his authority. Most men were fond of their wives and children, even as they are today. Furthermore, in the village life of the times, public opinion was a more potent factor than it is today. A man who mistreated his family was likely to feel the wrath of his peer group. For the fact was that a patriarch was deemed to have responsibilities as well as privileges: he was supposed to feed, clothe, and protect his family, and when he reneged on his obligations he had to be prepared to pay the price.

Were the marriages of antiquity happier than those of today? There is no way to answer this question; indeed, it is the wrong question. Marriages among the Hebrews, Greeks, early Romans and Christians were not undertaken for reasons of personal happiness. The term "romantic love" had not even been coined; nor had such expressions as "personality," "emotional needs," "women's liberation" and the like.

People married because they were supposed to, most betrothals being arranged by the parents. Young boys and girls were taught early in life that family names were important, and that marriage was part of the orderly way of life. To marry early and have a large family—based on patriarchal discipline—was as natural to the ancients as our own small, happiness-oriented family type is to us. Divorce, incidentally, (except in the later Roman period) was a rather rare occurrence. All things considered, therefore, it would seem that marriage was a stable and societally integrating force.

The subject of sex deserves special mention, since so many of our sexual codes originated in the Judeo-Christian period. Many of the early Christian leaders considered sex *per se* to be a major evil, and both Hebrews and Christians placed severe restrictions on most types of sexual activity.

Hebraic taboos included premarital coitus, adultery, homosexuality, masturbation and any "unnatural" carnal practices. The Christians added or stressed such prohibitions as "contraception, abortion, the reading of lascivious books, singing wanton songs, dancing 'suggestive' dances, bathing in mixed company, and wearing improper clothing" (Queen and Habenstein, 1974).

Not only was sex outside of marriage considered sinful, but virginity itself was eventually considered to be an exalted state. Furthermore, in the absence of strong self-control, there was a danger of *internal* sexual contamination. That is, it was not necessary for a man to *indulge* in order to sin; it was considered lecherous and sinful even to have sexual *desires* for a woman.

There is no doubt that the Judeo-Christian influence has had a lasting effect on our sexual behavior. The issue, from a secular view, is whether this influence has had the effect of improving man's lot or whether it has actually tended to create sexual problems.

Some writers feel that—despite recent changes—our present sexual codes are still too restrictive, and that the early Judeo-Christian influence continues to have adverse effects. Premarital and extramarital coitus, masturbation, homosexuality, nudity, use of sexual "vernacular," are all, to a degree, looked upon as "wrong." For some people, even marital intercourse gives rise to guilt feelings.

These writers feel that normal, healthy attitudes toward sex will not be attained until the sex mores, based as they are on ancient Judeo-Christian codes, are changed. Proponents of this position do not advocate unrestricted sexual license. But they do contend that substantial modifications are necessary if the individual is to achieve a reasonably happy sex life.

Other writers, however, believe that the early Judeo-Christian codes were effective not only in eliminating the more widespread abuses of the period, but also in fostering a sound societal perspective that has lasted down to the present. They acknowledge that the codes have sometimes given rise to guilt feelings, but contend that, to be effective, societal sanctions *must* include the specter of individual guilt.

Although the sexual codes remained generally strict during the Middle Ages, certain changes did take place in the institution of marriage. Spurred by the advent of chivalry (and the wandering troubadours), the status of women was raised somewhat. During the Renaissance, females—at the upper-class level, at least—were sometimes permitted a classical education. And with the coming of the Reformation, the sex codes were loosened, if only slightly. Luther, for example, while conceding that sex was indeed sinful, believed that it entailed no more sin than other worldly acts.

Nevertheless, there is no gainsaying the fact that throughout the Middle Ages, the traditional concept of the family prevailed. Marriage was heavily patriarchal. In England a wife's property, including personal effects such as her clothing and jewelry, belonged legally to her husband. Children, too, remained under the tight control of their father.

The American Colonial Period

It is hardly surprising, in view of the above, that the early American family retained much of its traditional orientation. Puritan New England, for example, was a man's world, and there were few who would dispute the fact. Education was almost entirely a male domain, as was business and commerce.

Morgan writes that:

In 17th-century New England, no respectable person questioned that woman's place was in the home . . . . The proper conduct of a wife was submission to her husband's instructions and commands. He was her superior, the head of the family, and she owed him an obedience founded on reverence . . . .
    She should therefore look upon him with reverence, a mixture of love and fear, not however "a slavish Fear . . . but a noble and generous Fear, which proceeds from Love. [Morgan, 1966]

Children were believed to be flawed by original sin, and thus "damned" unless they could be made to see the light. As Demos points out:

Puritan writings which deal in some direct way with child-rearing share one central theme: The child's inherent "will-fulness" must be curbed—indeed, it must be "broken" and "beaten down"—as soon as it begins to appear. All other aspects of character development are dependent on this pro-cedure. Here, for Puritans, lay the central task of parenthood; and, in a profound sense, they regarded it as involving a direct confrontation with "original sin." [Demos, 1971]

Little wonder that Puritan parents often used biblical admonitions to support their childrearing philosophy; e.g., "Honour thy father and thy mother, that thy days may be long upon the land" (Exodus 20:12).

Sex problems were present in the New world, even as they were in the Old. Whether they were more numerous—or more serious—is a moot point. But that they received a fantastic amount of attention can hardly be doubted. The era of the scarlet letter, for instance, may have been history's most sexually repressive period.

In Puritan New England, holding hands in public, open displays of affection and the like were prohibited. As a matter of fact, kissing in public was a criminal offense! (And records indicate that jail sentences were actually served by some perpetrators!)

More significant, perhaps, than the harsh penalties were the colonial *attitudes* toward sex. To put it simply, all sexual activity outside of marriage was forbidden—and even marital coitus was forbidden on Sunday! Adultery was considered a heinous offense, records indicating that several persons—both male and female—were accorded the death penalty upon being found guilty!

The Woman's Rights Movement

As time went on, Puritanism—predictably—ran its course, and by the 1800s only the backwash was left. Sex codes remained stringent, and wives remained subordinate to their husbands, but change was in the offing. And while there were a number of social forces that were to alter the nature of family life—urbanization, industrialization, improved transportation and communication—one is deserving of special mention: the Woman's Rights Movement.

The first convention was held in 1848 at Seneca Falls, New York, with the following stated objectives: (1) to free married women from the absolute control of their husbands and to establish the wife as a legal personality; (2) to open the doors of higher education to all women; and (3) to procure full political rights for women.

In spite of severe opposition (remnants of which still appear), the Movement forged ahead. In the economic sphere, women proved that they could not only support themselves but could compete effectively with men at both the professional and managerial levels. Politically, women achieved the right to vote and to hold public office, and today they can be found at all levels of government. And in the realm of education women made great strides. Close to half of today's college degrees are granted to women; in fact, figures indicate that women are more likely to graduate from high school than are males.

By the 1900s—as a concomitant of the Woman's Rights Movement, perhaps—sexual codes began to be loosened. Prior to the Movement, American women, ideally at least, were placed atop a moral pedestal. Sex was believed to be abhorrent to them, and many felt that even after marriage sexual response by the wife was somehow undignified. Wives were presumed to submit to their husband's sexual desires out of a sense of duty, and even today some divorce courts routinely use the term "wifely duty" in referring to marital intercourse.

Gradually, however—particularly after World War I—sexual activity came to be regarded as a phenomenon that was pleasurable for both spouses. Terms like "sexual adjustment" and "sexual maladjustment" were popularized, and impotency by the husband was added to the grounds for divorce available to the wife. Today, of course, *mutual* pleasure in the sexual realm is considered to be an integral part of marriage, and—should there be any doubts about how to attain it—"advice" is readily available in the form of marriage manuals and sex counseling.

The Present Scene

Now, in the so-called modern period, what is the sociological assessment of American marriage and family life? Although from the perspective of young people growing up our family system may seem right and natural, from a sociohistorical view it is anything but "natural." As a matter of fact, it is quite different from anything mankind has ever experienced.

To begin with, many of the traditional functions are no longer performed by the family. Under an agricultural-type economy the family served as a producing unit, building their own home, producing their own food, and so forth, whereas today the economic function has long been removed. Formerly, the family fulfilled the functions of education and religion, but today these functions have been taken over by schools, colleges and churches. At one time—with doctors and hospitals in short supply—the family even fulfilled the medical function, most homes containing a miniature apothecary shop. Today this function has been largely taken over by outside health services. Similarly, the home traditionally served the function of entertainment, a function that has increasingly been usurped by (paid) outside entertainment.

Today's families are, obviously, much smaller than those of yesteryear. With the advent of child labor laws and compulsory schooling, children are no longer economic assets. On the contrary, they are staggeringly expensive, with the cost per child estimated as high as $50,000! Little wonder that, aided by the pill, the U.S. birth rate has fallen to an all-time low.

Another major change is the fact that a large percentage of today's wives work outside the home, a trend that shows every sign of increasing. In the wake of women's liberation, it comes as no surprise to learn that there are already some 37 million women in the labor force. Of the remainder, the large majority are not seeking paid employment. As recently as 1900, women comprised but 18 percent of the labor force, whereas today the figure has grown to 40 percent (Bureau of Labor Statistics, 1975).

Another point worthy of mention is the fact that the institution of marriage is not on as high a plane as it formerly was. Although it was once deemed to be the only honorable state, more and more people, it would seem, are by-passing marriage. Some are simply staying single. Others are cohabiting (living together without matrimony). Still others are living in communes. Vital statistics merely affirm what everybody suspected: namely, that for the last several years the marriage rate has been falling.*

Finally, of course, mention must be made of the alarming increase in the divorce rate. For better or worse, there are now well over a million divorces granted annually, as the figures in the table indicate.**

United States Divorce Rate
for Selected Years

Year	No. of Divorces	Divorces per 1,000 Population
1867	9,937	0.3
1887	27,919	0.5
1900	55,751	0.7
1910	83,045	0.9
1920	170,505	1.6
1930	195,961	1.6
1940	264,000	2.0
1950	385,144	2.6
1960	393,000	2.2
1970	715,000	3.5
1976	1,077,000	5.0

* See, for example, the Monthly Vital Statistics Report, National Center for Health Statistics, March 8, 1977.
** See the regular reports issued by the National Center for Health Statistics, U.S. Department of Health, Education, and Welfare.

The rate continues to climb. The most recent figure (1976) of 5.0 divorces per 1,000 population is exactly twice that of a decade earlier (2.5 in 1966). Moreover, divorce represents the legal severance of the marital bond and is by no means the only index of matrimonial disruption. In certain areas desertions and separations probably exceed the number of divorces; and while there are no national figures, the number may well run into the millions. All in all, it is a rather disconcerting figure.

On the other hand, there are many bright spots. Our marital system is hardly falling apart. Most of our young people look forward to marriage, and over 90 percent of them do marry. Indeed, most of those who marry stay married. Even those who get divorced usually remarry.[*]

Today's family is certainly the most democratic in history. Gone (or going) are patriarchal dominance and wifely submissiveness. Family decisions often involve children as well as husband and wife.

As a matter of fact, none of the alternative life styles mentioned above have proved to be a real threat to marriage. Communes, after a widely heralded beginning, seem to have lost most of their appeal. As Murstein (1974) observes, the future of the commune "seems largely limited to serving as a developmental stage on the road from adolescence to adulthood."

The much publicized wife-swapping, "swinging" and various forms of plural marriage have also tended to disappear from the headlines. Apparently they were little more than fads, and—given the nature of the daily press—they received headlines that were simply not commensurate with their importance.

Actually, while it is true that many traditional family functions—economic, educational, medical, religious, and so on—have disappeared, many still remain. Thus the vital function of childrearing remains a family-centered activity. Sexual gratification remains basically a marital function. Companionship, the sharing of experiences, socializing, the exchange of ideas, satisfying each other's emotional needs—all of these have come to be important marital functions.

The point is not that the family has lost certain functions, but rather that it has exchanged them for new ones. These new functions,

* In 1973, marriages performed totaled 1,846,501. Of these, one-fourth or 487,843 were remarriages. *Vital Statistics of U.S.* Vol III, Table 1-43, 1973.

in turn, have arisen not only in response to institutional changes but as a result of the *new role accorded the wife in our society.* No longer considered a homemaking automaton, today's wife is likely to be a productive member of the work force, either part- or full-time. Intellectually, she is assumed to be every bit the equal of her husband. In brief, she is likely to enter marriage—for the first time in history—as a full-fledged partner, with all the rights and responsibilities thereof.

Because today's marriage is much more of an interactive relationship than ever before, interpersonal difficulties are bound to occur. Some of the commonest of these will be dealt with in later chapters.

References

Bureau of Labor Statistics (1975): *U.S. Working Women: A chartbook.* Washington, D.C.: Government Printing Office for the U.S. Department of Labor.

Demos, J. (1971): Developmental perspectives on the history of childhood, *J. of Interdisciplinary History,* Autumn issue, pp. 320–321.

Johnston, H. (1969): The Roman family, in: *Marriage and The Family,* J. Hadden and M. Borgatta, eds. Itasca, Ill.: Peacock Publishers, p. 77.

Morgan, E. (1966): *The Puritan Family.* New York: Harper and Row, pp. 42–45.

Murstein, B. (1974): *Love, Sex, and Marriage Through the Ages.* New York: Springer Publishing Co., pp. 537–540.

Queen, S. and Habenstein, R. (1974): *The Family in Various Cultures.* Philadelphia: Lippincott, pp. 198–199.

7
ANIMAL BEHAVIOR

If man has evolved from lower forms of life, to what extent is human behavior a function of the drives and other innate forces that characterize the lower animals? This is a question that has fascinated generations of scientists; for while it is easy to demonstrate the evolution of structure, evidence for the evolution of function is more elusive, especially as it relates to the human animal.

To take a logical starting point, the term *instinct* is generally thought of as goal-directing activity that is both inborn and genetically transmissible; the nest-building instinct, for example, which is characteristic of many animal species, is an activity that is actually "built into" the organism at birth. As thus defined, it is doubtful whether humans have any full-blown instincts. To carry the matter one step further, however, it should be pointed out that instincts are "triggered" in some manner. To illustrate: At certain times, depending on either internal or external cues, the sex glands (gonads) of many animals release hormones into the bloodstream. In some way not fully understood, these hormones set off the nest-building instinct, and preparations are then begun to house the future offspring.

Many—perhaps most—of the mating and parental activities of the lower animals are initiated by a similar or comparable internal mechanism. Although such a mechanism is lacking in humans, the pituitary and other glands are quite active, and a variety of hormones are continually being thrust into the bloodstream, the full results of which are not yet understood. The term *hormone*, by the way, is from the Greek, meaning "to arouse." And this is precisely what hormones do. Usually secreted by a gland, the hormone moves—via the bloodstream—until it reaches the "target" organ. The hormonal system is part of a complex interrelated chemical system. And if there is a relation between our current sexual and mating patterns and those of the lower animals, it is probably to be found in terms of hormonal interaction.

Male Aggressiveness

A noticeable contrast in the animal world is the aggressiveness of the male and the relative indifference of the female when it comes to sexual matters. There are some exceptions, to be sure, and they have been widely described in the literature, but clearly the dominant-submissive or active-passive role of the sexes is the general pattern.

It is also true, as a rule, that the male of the (mammalian) species produces more gametes and expels them more often than the female. The productive capacity of some male animals is enormous. There is nothing in the female mammalian realm, for example, to compare with the 12 billion sperm in the stallion's ejaculate, or with the 85 billion in that of the wild boar. The ovaries of the human female contain at birth all the egg cells she will ever have, one of which she will pass monthly for fertilization; the human male keeps generating new sperm, and about 300 million are contained in his ejaculation.

As the sexes mature, it is usually the male who is the larger, stronger animal, and it is he who tends to take the active role in courtship. And during actual coitus it is the male animal who indulges in vigorous pelvic movements, while the female stands motionless. That the male sex drive is more demanding than that of the female is also suggested by the fact that in the absence of the opposite sex, masturbatory and homosexual activity sometimes occurs among male mammals, while such activity is less common among females.

The sexual prowess of the male animal is related to his dominant physical capacity, both traits apparently being regulated by male sex hormones. Castration, for instance, has been known to lower both sexual and fighting ability. Actually, fighting ability or "dominance" is an exceedingly important factor, for in the wild state the male animal must often compete for the favor of the female. The competition takes a variety of forms, one of the most frequent being the establishment of a "territory," which the male defends against all comers. In some species, such as the musk ox and the seal, the male collects a harem, driving off all competitors until he himself is vanquished. In most species, actual combat is avoided, superiority being quickly established by a display of antlers, teeth, claws, fins or other weapons.

The ethological literature contains any number of descriptions of male animals defending territory and/or mates. One of the most bizarre is that of the hippopotamus. When two males are putting on a ritualistic display, they "stand head to head, open their huge mouths as wide as possible, and angrily belch evil-smelling gases in each other's face" (Droscher, 1965).

The female of the species, as a rule, does not exhibit a territorial defense pattern or a tendency toward competitive dominance. During her relatively short period of heat the female may mate with any male and is generally unconcerned with the behavior of other females or of competing males. Naturalists have often written about the indifference of the female during a mortal struggle between two male competitors. She makes no attempt to assist the vanquished in any way, but waits passively for the victor to approach her. Her refusal to interfere actually represents an assist in the natural perpetuation of the species; that is, by remaining neutral during the struggle, the female ensures that her offspring will be sired by the more powerful male rather than by a weakling, acceptance of whom would have a dysgenic effect upon the progeny.

At the human level, is there any trace of the male-female differential in sexuality and aggressiveness? It would certainly seem so. Human males seem more aggressive, with a higher sex drive than human females, but, it is argued, are not these differences culturally induced? Perhaps so, at least in part; but in recent years evidence has accumulated pointing in the direction of innate hormonal differences.

Studies indicate that it is the androgen level—in both males *and* females—which is an important determinant of sex drive. Androgen is produced by both sexes, but in much greater quantities in males than females; in fact, it is commonly referred to as the male sex hormone. However, in both sexes androgen levels have been shown to have a marked effect on libido.

Some women undergoing treatment for "frigidity" have shown improvement when they were given androgen. Reduction of androgen levels has been shown to depress sex drive in both males and females. Interestingly enough, estrogen may have the opposite effect; i.e., of reducing sex drive.

Research has also shown that androgen does not generally become operative until puberty. Udry reports that:

Preadolescents of both sexes have low levels of androgens, compared with adults. Although they are capable of most adult sexual practices, and engage in most adult sexual practices in some cultures, preadolescents do not give much evidence of sex drive. Puberty brings a small increase in androgens to females, and a general increase over a several-year period in males—to a level of androgen circulating in the blood which is about ten times that found in females. Studies of adolescent males show that the rise in sexual interest closely parallels the rise in androgen levels. [Udry, 1974]

Sexual Periodicity

Courtship and mating activity in the animal world is closely related to the female estrous cycle. Indeed, it has often been said that a major difference between man and the other animals is that man drinks without being thirsty and mates all the year round. And it is true that among mammals, mating is restricted to the period of estrum, variously defined as heat, rut or mating season. It is during estrum that the ovaries, stimulated by a hormonal secretion from the pituitary gland, produce ripened eggs. It is during this period also that external changes often become apparent in the genitalia of the female, including swelling and coloration. In general, female animals are sexually receptive only during the period of rut; in fact, unwary males who attempt coitus at any other time may be bitten or clawed.

In practice, these out-of-season attempts by male animals are not as common as might be believed, since males are quick to learn the proper mating procedure. In some species, such as the mouse, rabbit, mole, guinea pig and certain squirrels, the vaginal entrance is covered by a membrane when the female is not in sexual heat. Whatever the reason, though, male animals do not generally try to force their attention on nonreceptive females. Available evidence indicates that rape is characteristic only of the human male (supporting the interpretation of human rape as basically hostile rather than sexual).

In some species, the male animal has a sexual period comparable to that of the female rut. In the buck deer, for instance, the sexual period is marked by a full development of the antlers and an enlargement of the testicles. The neck swells to almost twice the normal size, and the animal is formidable to behold. In this state, a buck is ready to fight off all challengers in pursuit of the female. Generally speaking, however, the male period is of much longer duration than that of the female, and, of course, in most species—including domesticated animals—the male is sexually active at all times. It should also be mentioned that both the female estrum and, in those species where it exists, the male sexual period can be induced experimentally by the injection of sex hormones.

At the human level, the counterpart of the estrous cycle is the menstrual cycle, and some women report a discernible increase (or decrease) in sex desire during certain portions of the cycle. (Reports on which particular portions are involved vary from one female to the next, and it is at present unwise to attempt a generalization.) As a matter of biological fact, however, estrum and menstruation represent two contrasting phases of the female fertility cycle: estrum signals the time of *optimum* fertility, whereas menstruation is the period of *least likely* fertility in the human female, except that there is usually a rise in fertility a few days after menstruation ends.

Special mention should be made of the periodicity among the infrahuman primates (monkeys, apes), since there has been some misunderstanding on this point. So far as we can tell, female monkeys and apes (including the gorilla) follow a definite estrous cycle. When the female's external genitalia are marked by swelling and coloration, for example, the animal is in heat, and the egg is ready to be fertilized. In general, it is at this time that the male is received sexually; indeed, when a female monkey is in heat it is quite common for her to crouch in front of the male and exhibit her genitalia, a phenomenon that ethologists refer to as "presenting."

More significant is the fact that "presenting" is sometimes seen to occur when the female is not in heat! The activity is sporadic and may be used to distract the male, or to get the latter to relinquish a morsel of food. Ethologists sometimes refer to these actions as "prostitution behavior." Observers have also reported instances where female monkeys and apes have shown a preference for certain male partners, and during nonrutting periods one male may be accepted while another is rejected. Infrequent though nonestrous receptivity may be, and whatever the motivating factors are, the significant point is that such behavior occurs at all. For it may be the first mammalian occurrence of female sexual receptivity being determined by nonhormonal factors.

Courtship Behavior

Mammalian courtship behavior is often a surprisingly complicated affair. To begin with, an animal must first seek out and *identify* a proper partner. This identification process—something taken for granted among humans—may cause difficulty in certain animal species. For one thing, many species are nongregarious, and because they lead solitary lives must literally track down their mates. Also, in some species, males and females are fairly similar, in a few cases remarkably so. And finally, many mammals have poorly developed vision; in fact, it is questionable how many species could identify the opposite sex through sight alone.

In view of the above factors, it is not surprising that mammals tend to identify through smell, sound and touch. A number of species have scent glands which emit distinctive odors, especially during mating season. Others use calls or sounds of some kind when they are in quest of a sex partner.

Sometimes overlooked is the fact that the sense of touch is also part of the male courtship technique. In many mammalian species the male pursues the female and attempts to "seduce" her by displaying his physical charms and indulging in nuzzling, licking, pawing, examining her genitalia and otherwise rubbing the female's body with his own.

On her part, the female is at once indifferent, standoffish and enticing. She runs—but not very far—and when she stops, she may look behind to see whether the male is following. After what appears to be a measured amount of resistance-enticement, the female's evasions become more perfunctory, and the chase slows in tempo. Finally she stands still: the pursuit is ended and the male is rewarded for his ardent endeavors. In many species, subsequent coital activities are marked by a relative absence of courting preliminaries.

It cannot be emphasized too strongly, however, that mammalian courtships run the gamut from alpha to omega. Some are low-key; others are at fever pitch. Some are routine and mechanical; others appear to embody genuine affection. Let us look at examples from the two largest land mammals: the elephant and the rhinoceros.

First the elephant:

One of the loveliest sights in any zoo is that of a bull elephant courting his sweetheart.   He moons after her, offering her any tidbit that comes his way.   He squirts water over her in the bath and rubs his head against hers as she walks away from him with pretended indifference.   And when she condescends to flutter her enormous eyelashes at him, they entwine their trunks and even put their mouths together in a grotesque kiss. [Johns, 1970, p. 93]

By contrast, many zoos house the male and female rhinoceros in separate enclosures, permitting them to come together only during estrous, which lasts only for a day or two. Estrous is marked by an enlargement of the female's vulva "and the shrill whistling noises she makes, to which the male responds with deep sighs!"

It is a frightening moment when the door is raised and the 2,000-pound rhino, capable of charging at 35 miles-per-hour, rushes in to attack his lady love.   She is no less belligerent, and all available keepers stand ready to intervene with pressure hoses if the fight should get out of hand . . . .

After an hour or more of continuous battle, the couple will either become more savage, or the female will consider the male a worthy mate.   This is not to suggest that she becomes loving; she does, however, begin to parry his lunges and to behave as coquettishly as her grotesque body allows . . . .

He mounts her from the rear . . . . He ejaculates about once every ten minutes, and after an hour or more he has penetrated so deeply that all his four feet are off the ground and the female is staggering under his weight.   When he withdraws, both animals are exhausted. [Johns, 1970, pp. 52–53]

In most species it is the male who is the aggressor during courtship.   There are some exceptions, however, one of the most unique being the phalarope. To quote from Ardrey:

The phalarope is a water-bird, vaguely related to the sandpiper, and it frequents the Artic in summer. It is a freak. Some chance mutation once affected the phalarope's ancestral line, and in consequence certain sexual characteristics suffered reversal.

The male is dun-colored, the female brightly feathered. The female arrives first at the breeding grounds and conducts the territorial scramble. The male arrives later and incubates the eggs while she defends the home place. The system works and evolution shrugs. [Ardrey, 1961]

Animal Coitus

Among most mammals coital activity takes place at night, and since this is also true at the human level it is tempting to think of man's nocturnal sex activity as more or less natural, when, if anything, the reverse is true. It just happens that most mammals are nocturnal in their habits: they eat, drink, play and prowl at night. Their eyes are well attuned to darkness, and the same applies to their reproductive processes.

Man seems to be a diurnal animal: his body adjusts to the warmth of the sun, and his eyesight readily adapts to daylight. He is poorly equipped to venture into the night. Cultural innovations, however, change the picture. Civilized man works during the day, and with the aid of artificial illumination much of his social life takes place at night. The fact that sex is primarily a nocturnal activity is due to cultural rather than biological factors.

In most societies coital activities take place in privacy, but this practice also may be due largely to cultural restrictions. The majority of animals, curiously enough, seem to mate as readily in the presence of a group as they do when the pair are alone. Why this should be is somewhat mystifying, since during coitus the partners are vulnerable to attacks by predators. (Perhaps the group provides some potential protection.)

In subprimate species it is the male who generally initiates coitus, and in practically all cases the coital activity is dorsal; that is, the male mounts the female from the rear. Among monkeys and apes the dorsal position is also used, although ventral copulation has occasionally been observed, particularly among gorillas. The latter, oddly enough, seem to have a rather low sex drive. George Schaller (1963), who, as an observer, lived among wild gorillas for over a year, reported witnessing but two copulations, an observation which accords with those reported by zoo keepers.

Mammalian coitus generally involves vigorous plevic movements on the part of the male with the female passive and stationary, except for an occasional swaying motion. In fact, female animals have been seen to eat food during coitus, and in the laboratory they are more easily distracted by external stimuli. It is inferred that the male of the species also experiences orgasm. However, since the latter is a subjective sensation felt at the time of sexual release, it would be more precise to say that the male animal *behaves as if* orgasm has occurred. On the other hand, there is no systematic evidence to indicate that orgastic experience is characteristic of mammalian females.

Sex Drive and Mating Forms

Different species—and individual animals within a given species—evidence tremendous variation in sex drive. Gorillas, as previously mentioned, mate infrequently, and when they do, mating is of short duration. Mink, marten and sable, on the other hand, have protracted matings, which range up to several hours in elapsed time.*

Chimpanzees seem to be the most highly sexed of the apes:
When copulation is successful, the female chimpanzee seems not to experience anything like orgasm, nor is she tired by the event. In fact, some lusty females are insatiable and during the week or so of estrous will present themselves, with every appearance of enjoyment, and be mounted 20 or more times a day. Even very immature chimpanzees are interested in sex play; they watch with interest as their elders mate, and they try it themselves, mounting each other and giving pelvic thrusts. [Johns, 1970, p. 20]

It is also true that there is much mammalian variation in terms of *actual mating forms*. In some species "polygyny" is the rule; that is, the male will collect, mate with and guard several females. The opposite form, however, "polyandry," or the mating of one female with several males on a regular basis, is rare, if indeed it occurs at all.

In a number of species, "group mating" is known to occur. The aforementioned chimpanzees, for example, live in flexible groups

---

* Gagnon and Simon observe that sex is rather low-key throughout most of the human life-cycle. They contend that passionate sex is found only in young males, early marriage for both sexes and extramarital affairs. (John Gagnon, and William Simon, *Sexual Conduct: The Social Sources of Human Sexuality*, Chicago: Aldine Publishing Co., 1973, p. 104).

that constantly change; as some members leave, others join. Among baboons, most groups seem to be more or less permanent. In some species, interestingly enough, the sexes tend to live separately, coming together only during the female estrum.

Occasionally a mammalian species can be found which is truly monogamous, but that is clearly the exception. Burns states that such species "are exceedingly rare, constituting perhaps less than one percent. Stranger yet, these few comparatively faithful mammals are drawn from the group which the human usually thinks of as killers, namely, the wolf, the fox and the weasel" (Burns, 1953). Among the primates, the gibbon is also known to be monogamous.

Is it possible to generalize from other animal mating forms to that of humans? The answer probably would have to be more in the negative than the positive. If there is any applicability, it is certainly limited. Most mammalian species seem to be promiscuous, a generalization that would probably include the primates. Human societies, on the other hand, tend to have strict rules regarding who may mate with whom.

The practice of having plural mates exists among both other animals and humans, but clearly "polyandry" (plural males, one female) is a relatively rare occurrence. Is it a coincidence, for example, that any number of societies follow the practice of plural wives, whereas plural-husband cultures are few and far between? Or is it possible that male sexual jealousy is a mammalian trait, a vestige of which may remain at the human level?

At the moment these questions are unanswerable. It is interesting, nevertheless, to quote the late Ralph Linton (1936), a world-famous anthropologist and pronounced cultural determinist: "It seems probable that the widespread occurrence of polygyny derives more from the general primate tendency for males to collect females than from anything else. The other factors involved are only contributory causes."

The Maternal Instinct

Throughout the mammalian kingdom, one of the sharpest differences between the sexes is that relating to the care of the young. Generally speaking, the protection, feeding, care and training tend to devolve upon the mother animal. In most cases, the latter discharges her duties faithfully, often to the point of risking her own life. She may hide her young, or set out by herself in order to lure the enemy away from the nest; or—on occasion—she may turn and fight against great odds.

On the other hand, the male's behavior is often rather unchivalrous, judged by human standards. It is not so much a matter of his abandoning the offspring in time of danger; the fact is that he himself is often a source of danger. Among some carnivores and rodents, for example, males have been observed to devour their own offspring. And in many other species, the male is either a threat or simply plays no part in the care of the young. In some species of fox and wolf, on the other hand, the male will bring food back to the den and otherwise assist in the training of the young, even though primary responsibility for their care may still rest with the female.

It is tempting to think of the female's actions as a manifestation of mother-love, but it should be remembered that we are dealing with a locked-in pattern of behavior over which the animal has little control. The female mammal protects her young because of the *maternal instinct,* and the reason the male is unconcerned is because there is no corresponding instinct. Interestingly enough, Dimond (1970) reports that in most species, virgin females generally do not show a marked parental response to the young. On the contrary, some virgin females will kill the young "as though they were prey."

Physiologically, the maternal instinct is triggered by the pituitary gland, which, at a certain time in the female cycle, releases a hormone. Maternal behavior will continue until the effects of the hormone wear off, at which time the offspring will have matured to a point where they are able to fend for themselves. In a realistic sense, therefore, what is termed "mother-love" among mammals is simply a reaction that is chemically circumscribed; in fact, maternal behavior can be induced in the laboratory simply by hormonal injections—and it can be terminated in the same way.

Is there any discernible trace of the maternal instinct among human mothers? Several earlier studies showed some interesting results along these lines. In the original study by Levy, a questionnaire was given to women for the purpose of measuring the strength of their maternal feelings (questions concerning number of children desired, age respondent stopped playing with dolls, attitude toward breast feeding, etc.). Survey results were then correlated with length of menstrual cycle. Investigators found a "significant positive correlation between maternal behavior and duration of menstrual flow (Levy, 1942).

Benedek (1952) examined the relation between hormonal level, based on vaginal smear tests, and psychoanalytic material, as judged by independent analysts, and found that there were cyclic alterations not only in sexual receptivity but also in feelings of maternity or motherhood. Newton (1955), in a survey based on interviews with mothers of newborn babies, discovered a behavioral relationship among such phenomena as menstruation, pregnancy, childbirth, sexual feelings, breast feeding and care of the baby.

In contrast to the above findings, any number of anthropological surveys have shown that child-care behavior varies a great deal from one society to the next. Sociological studies have indicated that maternal behavior varies among different social strata within the *same* society. And, of course, psychologists and psychiatrists have demonstrated that individual mothers—within the same social stratum—may have markedly different feelings and attitudes with respect to offspring.

Perhaps a safe conclusion would be to say that whatever trace of maternal instinct there may be left at the human level, cultural factors —such as sex role differentiation—are almost certainly more decisive.

Conclusions

In view of the wealth of ethological surveys and observations made in recent years, what conclusions can be drawn relative to human marital, sexual and familial behavior? To begin with, it is rather obvious that throughout the animal kingdom the sexual impulse represents a persistent and potent force, and that—being an animal— man is subject to much the same sexual imperatives that other animals are.

It is also quite obvious that throughout the animal world there are sharp differences in the sexual behavior of males and females, with the male being cast in the role of aggressor. This is also true at the human level, though the press of cultural forces tends to cloud the issue.

Among the subprimates the female mammal will receive the male only during estrum, whereas the male either has an extended rutting period or, as in so many species, is sexually ready at all times. At the human level there is no doubt that the male is sexually responsive throughout the year, whereas the female may be more receptive at certain periods of the menstrual cycle than at others.

In both animal and human male, sexual arousal is more likely to hinge on sensory perception than is the case with the female. At both levels, animal and human, the male is prone to copulate until ejaculation is achieved. Female animals apparently are not capable of achieving orgastic response, and at the human level the incidence of orgasm is possibly lower among females than among males.

Among both animals and humans there is a great deal of individual variation in sex drive, and at both levels it is the female who tends to "control" the sexual situation; that is, it is the female who more often determines whether or not coitus occurs.

There is no denying the influence of cultural factors on all of the above phenomena. Still, as Burton puts it: "If man has devised all these things for himself independently of what has been going on in the rest of the living world for a thousand million years or more, then the coincidence is most remarkable" (Burton, 1953).

Among the lower animals it is the mother who is the guardian of the young, and among *Homo Sapiens* the term "mother-love" has more literal meaning than does "father-love." Clearly, however, in the latter case cultural factors have come to assume a most significant role. Not only do most fathers love their children, but, as has been mentioned, childrearing practices themselves show a good deal of variation among certain societies and certain groups. While it is probably unwise to overlook the role of biological forces in human sexual and familial practices, it is fallacious to assume that these forces comprise the dominant or even the major role in human family-life practices.

It should be kept in mind that "family life" in the animal world is largely instinctive in nature. Sex responses, mating cues, male competition, infant care and the like are determined in good part by a sequence of "built-in" developments. Sentiments and emotions and other ties that are involved in human family living can not be assumed in the animal world. And in the last analysis it is *culture* that influences and regulates the patterns of marriage, divorce, the derivation of family forms, the role of the sexes, the status of children, the responsibilities of parenthood and all the other institutional aspects of human marriage. Let us turn to some of the cultural variations in these spheres.

References

Ardrey, R. (1961): *African Genesis.* New York: Atheneum Publishers, p. 50.

Benedek, T. (1952): *Psychosexual Functions in Women.* New York: Ronald Press, p. 340.

Burns, E. (1953): *The Sex Life of Wild Animals.* New York: Holt, Rinehart and Winston, pp. 56-57.

Burton, M. (1953): *Animal Courtship.* London: Hutchinson and Co., Ltd., p. 15.

Dimond, S. (1970): *The Social Behavior of Animals.* New York and Evanston, Ill.: Harper Colophon Books, Harper and Row, pp. 42-49.

Droscher, V. (1965): *The Mysterious Senses of Animals.* New York: E. P. Dutton and Co., p. 61.

Johns, J. (1970): *The Mating Game: Sex, Love, and Courtship in the Zoo.* New York: St. Martin's Press.

Levy, D. (1942): Psychomatic studies of some aspects of maternal behavior, *Psychomatic Medicine,* April, p. 225.

Linton, R. (1936): *The Study of Man.* New York: Appleton-Century-Crofts, p. 184.

Newton, N. (1955): *Maternal Emotions.* New York: Harper-Hoeber, pp. 70-71.

Schaller, G. (1963): *The Mountain Gorilla: Ecology and Behavior.* Chicago: Univ. of Chicago Press, pp. 233-234, 286.

Udry, J. R. (1974): *The Social Context of Marriage.* Phila.: Lippincott, pp. 81-82. See Also: Starka, L., Sipova, I. and Hynie, J. (1975): Plasma testosterone in male transexuals and homosexuals, *J. of Sex Research,* May, pp. 134-138.

The Following References Are Also Useful:

Carrighar, S. (1965): *Wild Heritage.* Boston: Houghton Mifflin Co.

Lorenz, K. (1966): *On Aggression.* New York: Harcourt, Brace and World.

8
MARRIAGE IN CROSS-CULTURAL PERSPECTIVE

Marriage is one of the few social relationships that appear to be universally recognized in all human societies, whether ancient or modern, simple or complex, tribal or industrial. It might also be considered a very distinctive aspect of human culture when compared with nonhuman cultures or patterns of social behavior. However, this sweeping statement must be accompanied by certain qualifications. In a few narrow sec'.ors of a few societies there is no form of relatively stable adult heterosexual union. The Roman Catholic clergy is one such instance well-known to all of us, and there are other similar occurences in which a portion of a society does not recognize marriage as a normal form of relationship for most adults.

It is also fully recognized that permanent adult heterosexual pair bonds do occur in a few nonhuman societies, in birds, especially. However, the similarities between animal pair bonding and human marriage are found in the cohabitational aspects alone. In human marriage there are always many other aspects beyond cohabitation and breeding. Human marriage is always embedded in a matrix of social and cultural values, and as far as can be determined at present there is nothing "instinctual" or "genetically determined" about marriage.* Marriage, in whatever form it may take, is a culturally determined and regulated relationship, and this seems not to be the case in other animals.

Anthropological studies of marriage and related features of society and culture have undergone a number of changes in perspective. At the end of the last century, when anthropology was becoming recognized as a scholarly discipline, various doctrines of social evolution dominated comparative, cross-cultural studies. Reliable

---

* This is not true for psychoanalytic observation, in which "instinctual" elements are evident in thoughts and feelings, as seen in dreams and free associations, e.g., sexual, dependent, competitive, infantile fixations.

ethnographic data were few; consequently such early anthropological studies of marriage were offered as proofs of evolutionary dogma rather than attempts to discover what the range of human cultural variation might be. In most of those evolutionary studies, marriage was considered a social relationship that clearly separated human from nonhuman societies. At the same time, it was assumed that in very early periods of culture history, marriage did not exist in human societies. Some evolutionary theories assumed that the just-barely-cultured human lived in a situation of sexual and marital promiscuity in which neither stable heterosexual unions nor restrictions on in-breeding among close consanguineal relatives existed. From such bestial beginnings the incest taboo and increasingly more stable and exclusive forms of heterosexual unions evolved from group marriage to polygamous forms to monogamy. Faithful monogamy, as strongly advocated by Christianity, was considered to be the pinnacle of social evolution, while all other forms of marriage still to be found among exotic peoples were assumed to represent earlier, arrested or fossilized, phases in the grand scheme of social progress.

Even Sigmund Freud subscribed to such assumptions, although his views were more directly influenced by some of Charles Darwin's speculations that were much more conservative than those of the so-called social Darwinists. In his controversial book *Totem and Taboo* (1912–13) Freud attempted, among other things, to present a psychoanalytic, yet still evolutionary, theory of some aspects of marriage, to which few cultural and social anthropologists have been receptive.

Extreme evolutionary theories, for the most part, were rejected and replaced with so-called historical studies, which sought to reconstruct specific historical antecedents for each society and its cultural forms, but this anti-evolutionist trend also came to grief by being as speculative and arbitrary as the evolutionary doctrines that it meant to discredit.

At present, most comparative studies of marriage (or other patterns of culture) are cast in what is loosely called the "functional model," which notes that marriage in all societies is related to and interconnected with many other aspects of culture, and in each the configuration of these interconnections is unique. Moreover, in complex societies such as ours, there may be different forms of marriage and cultural interconnections in different socioeconomic classes, ethnic groups, religious groups and so forth. For this reason, marriage must be studied with equal emphasis on both the form and functional interrelations.

With this approach, and with our current richer ethnographic data, we have gained a much better understanding of the extraordinary variation in marriage patterns that are to be found from society to society and within the same society at different time periods. Yet better understanding has precipitated several serious dilemmas, most serious of which is that the marriage concept has no longer any precise and universal definition, good for all cultures in all societies. We can only say that there is one or more unique configurations of values, rules and behaviors in each culture that roughly correspond to what we may think of as "marriage." Another serious dilemma has come about by the failure of the comparative-functionalist approach to develop applicable "social laws." So far, no important or statistically significant correlation (much less a "law") about relations between forms and interconnections in marital relations can be shown. There are hunches and attractive hypotheses, but none can be tested.

Nevertheless, the functional or interrelational approach has enabled anthropologists and sociologists to understand a given pattern of marriage in its own cultural and social contexts far better than ever before. No longer is the observer content merely to describe what is readily apparent about marriage, for our own ethnocentric views about marriage may bias our observations. As a result, in the past few decades descriptive accounts, or ethnographies, of marriage have become increasingly rich in detail and sophisticated in insight.

We shall summarize here a few of the major aspects of marriage, as cultural and social anthropologists usually view them, emphasizing the degree of variation among cultures. Marriage is thought of as a cultural configuration of relatively stable adult heterosexual unions from which children may be naturally born (or adopted) and placed legitimately in the society. The marriage configuration is viewed as an integrated complex of values and behavior patterns, each aspect of which has a separate cultural context (or environment). A change in any relevant context will set in motion a force for change in that relevant aspect of marriage, and a change in one aspect of marriage will set in motion a force for change in another aspect of marriage.

Major Forms of Marriage

The standard anthropological classification of marriage and related kinds of unions is as follows:

Monogamy
Polygamy (plural or compound marriages)
Polygyny (more than one simultaneous wife)
Sororal (all wives either real or classificatory sisters)
General (all wives not sisters, real or classificatory)
Polyandry (more than one simultaneous husband)
Ancillary or alternative heterosexual unions
Concubinage
Mistress relationships

Monogamy, of course, needs no explanation for us in North America, for it is strongly embedded in the Euro-American cultural tradition. It is also the characteristic form of marriage in many so-called primitive, tribal and peasant societies. One survey of known cultures estimates that 20 percent of cultures favor monogamy as either the preferred or required form of marriage.

Where strong Christian morality prevails, monogamy is associated with the ideals of sexual faithfulness between spouses, and marriage, ideally, is for life. In some monogamous societies, legitimate sexual relations may not be confined to husband and wife. Although those societies are strictly monogamous regarding cohabitation of spouses, some extramarital sexual relations, usually with very specific types of kinsmen, neighbors or associates, are explicitly allowed. In other words, monogamy is not inevitably associated with exclusive sexual relations between husband and wife.

In some monogamous societies, marriage may be very brittle and short-lived, the adults making several marriages, in sequence, but never with more than one recognized marriage in force at one time. Such patterns are sometimes called "serial polygyny," "serial monogamy" or "sequential monogamy."

Two interrelations that also enter into the ideal form of the Euro-American marriage pattern are the emphasis upon the nuclear (biological or simple) family as the core of the household or domestic group and a concentration of relations between adjacent generations within the parent-child roles. The latter arrangement reinforces the sociological independence of the nuclear family. Contrast this with a situation in which, even though observing strict monogamy, each nuclear family unit is strongly linked with the nuclear families of either or both sons or daughters, so that each nuclear family is compounded with parental and offspring nuclear families. Such compounded nuclear families are called "extended" or joint families. They are usually fused either by linking the males (father to son to son's son, etc.) or by linking the females (mother to daughter to daughter's daughter, etc.), or occasionally by combinations of both. Now, when such extended families become corporate, nuturing some highly valued capital and considering the perpetuation of the extended family and its estate to be a major goal, the cultural significance of marriage is quite different from a situation such as ours, in which the nuclear family is highly *independent* of others and each domestic group is formed anew by marriage, growing with the birth of children, dispersing with the marriage of those children and finally being extinguished with the death of its founders and the division of property through individual inheritance.

Contrast, too, our marriage and family patterns with one in which each spouse, after marriage, maintains extremely strong obligations to his or her siblings' families, and a part of the marriage obligations is to support one's spouse in those responsibilities to sisters and brothers. Put another way, marital relations in some societies do not always take precedence over sibling relations and may in some instances be subordinate to them. At marriage one may be as strongly linked to the family of one's wife's or husband's siblings as to one's own family. This may be equally binding upon both husband and wife, or the wife alone, the husband alone, siblings of either sex, or siblings of one sex alone.

The two situations just described, in which nuclear families are linked either lineally across generations or laterally across the same generation, are not mutually exclusive. Both can and do occur together in such a way that large extended families are linked through marriage bonds into larger political or cooperative units. More will be said below about such *political* aspects of marriage.

Plural or polygamous marriages can give to a society a different basic structure. Simultaneous marriages of one husband to several wives, polygyny, is the common form of plural marriage, and it is estimated to be permitted or preferred in about 75 percent of known societies. Obviously the human sex ratio is never skewed so heavily in favor of females as to make polygyny a social response to demography. In societies called polygynous, only a minority of men are able to have plural marriages. Still it is the ideal, achieved or enjoyed by only a few, and then not always until advanced age.

When a few men succeed in marrying several women each, it would seem that some less fortunate men would have to go wifeless. To some extent this is true, but nearly all males in polygynous societies eventually get married, a situation achieved by postponing the age of marriage for men and by tolerating wide age discrepancies between husbands and wives. For instance, a young man might marry a considerably older widow first. Each additional wife is younger, the last possibly, being very much younger than himself. Such wide age discrepancies can have an effect upon fertility rates, but it is usually not a dramatic effect.

Polygyny is usually associated with distinctive economic, political or social class orientations. Most commonly the motivation for aspiring to more than one wife has to do with a particular kind of economics in which the division of labor by sex and the economics of production make the wife a major asset in the domestic economy, while men are in control of the investment of domestic profits. As profit is accumulated, it is invested in more productive capital, such as land or livestock, which the wife tends, and which in turn requires another wife (also an investment) to exploit or manage it. In this kind of situation a first wife might well be pleased to have co-wives so that her labors will be lessened. In such societies economic competition is high; a successful man inevitably has several wives, while the unsuccessful man may marry late and have an older woman as an only wife.

In some societies with well-defined social class systems, polygyny may be associated not so strongly with the productive side of the economy as with privilege and conspicuous consumption. Close to these societies are ones in which polygyny is more of a political than a socioeconomic matter. In such societies a chief, king or potentate has a large number of wives, most of whom have been selected from or given by constituent groups which acknowledge the authority of the ruler. Political marriages of this sort maintain political lines of power and authority within the networks and sentiments of marital relations. For example, marriage might be thought of in some aspects as authority of a husband over his wife. By extension then, authority over a constituent group might be expressed as analogous to marital authority.

The compound family groups that result from polygynous marriages in some societies are unitary and cohesive, even though they may be somewhat stratified by the fact that wives are ranked by seniority or even the common husband's personal preference. However, in some societies each household of wife and her children may have its own property and the independence to manage its own affairs without great consideration for other households of other co-wives. In parts of Africa it is expected that a husband will spend equal time with and give equal attention to each of his wives; for him not to do so is valid grounds for divorce for an aggrieved wife.

In most polygynous marriage systems a man takes his wives with little or no concern for kinship relationships among them. That form is called general polygyny. In sororal polygyny, however, the wives must be sisters. A sister in this usage, however, is not always a biological sibling, but is any female from the kinship class "sister," which, like the class "cousin" in English, includes several genealogical types. Sororal polygyny is really a kind of contractual relationship in which a man, and often his close kin, agree to take all wives from the same group of kin; hence all of those wives are "sisters."

A related practice with similar contractual relations is the "sororate," in which, should a wife die or be barren, she is replaced by a sister. Another rather common form of guaranteed remarriage is the "levirate," in which a man takes the widow of his deceased brother as a wife, which, of course, must be associated with polygyny.

Polyandry, or several simultaneous husbands for one wife, is the rarest form of plural marriage. It occurs in less than one percent of known societies, and as a fully recognized and preferred marital form mainly in the Himalayan region. Elsewhere, polyandry seems to be an alternate form of marriage associated with extreme but temporary demographic or economic factors. Polyandry has been subdivided into fraternal (or adelphic) and general forms, as polygyny is divided into general and sororal; however, there is now doubt as to whether it ever occurs as a preferred pattern in any form but fraternal. At least its most well-known occurrences, in Tibet in particular, are fraternal.

There have been a few known societies with extremely variable marriage forms, even with households changing from one type to another over short periods of time.   In pre-Christian Hawaii, for example, while the majority of marriages were monogamous, both polygyny and polyandry also occurred.   The same was true with some Eskimo groups, in which marriage and domestic arrangements changed according to demographic and ecological situations in one of the harshest of all environments occupied by man.   Clearly the important feature in such societies, as with the sequential monogamy mentioned above, is the brittleness of the marriage bond and the influence on it of extraneous social, economic and ecological forces.

In addition to marriage there are a number of ancillary forms of heterosexual unions, usually quite stable or permanent.   Concubinage is the best known union of this kind.   It differs from marriage because in the societies where it occurs there is a clear status difference between a wife and a concubine, even though both are socially legitimate.   In China before the socialist revolution, a man could have only one wife, but he would take concubines according to his ability to provide for them.   The concubine was never mistress of a household, and she was under the authority of the wife insofar as the domestic domain was concerned.   The Chinese concubine could not be the legal mother to her own children.   Under Islamic law, a man can have no more than four wives at one time, but usually he may have concubines in addition to the legal quota of spouses.   The harems of Islamic rulers were made up of women who, for lack of a better term, were political concubines, gifts from individuals or groups seeking favor with a sultan.

It is difficult always to make the distinction between wife and concubine because in some polygynous societies the first or senior wife may have many more rights and privileges than junior wives, and she may also exercise strong and direct powers over her less privileged junior co-wives.

It is also difficult—perhaps not even necessary—to make a firm distinction between concubinage and mistress keeping.   However, there does seem to be a difference in the degree of legitimacy.   The status of concubine is recognized as such, and though distinguished from wife, it is socially legitimate.   A mistress usually has no or very little legitimate status, but there seem to have been many exceptions to this in the ruling courts of Europe. The matter of legitimacy will be discussed further below.

Sexual Rights

The confinement of sexual relations to marriage together with strong social sanctions against infidelity, contrary to many popular conceptions, is not solely a feature of European societies and the Judeo-Christian tradition. Many pagan tribal societies place great value on sexual fidelity in marriage and also impose harsh sanctions on violators. For example, on Santa Cruz Island, a Melanesian society in the southwest Pacific, until recently women were expected to be chaste before marriage and faithful to their husbands during marriage. Penalties for extramarital sex offenses were extremely severe for the male offender, in fact only slightly less than for murder, but not so severe for the woman offender. Before pacification by a colonial government, sexual offenses frequently triggered bloody feuds.

On the other hand, in many tribal societies spouses cannot demand sexual fidelity of each other. The pre-Christian Polynesians of the central Pacific are a notorious example of societies where extramarital sexual relations are common, even expected. Those breaches that were classed as sexual offenses were regarded as minor or trivial matters. Usually, however, in societies where extramarital sexual relations are condoned, they are condoned only with specific types of persons—a husband's brother, a wife's sister, a neighbor with whom one cooperates economically. Certain Eskimo societies are famous for offering the sexual favors of a wife to a visiting male as part of the etiquette of being a good host. The same Eskimo groups are also very tolerant of extramarital sexual relations for both sexes; but once a couple has had an affair, it establishes a permanent conjugal-like relationship between the two. Furthermore, the descendants of both regard each other as being in a relationship something like step-siblingship.

Not a few tribal societies, while enforcing the wife's sexual fidelity, permit a husband to have sexual access to women of special statuses, who are prostitutes of a sort but not stigmatized or female slaves. Yet paradoxically such societies may severely punish adultery or fornication with an unmarried person not in those social categories.

The accepted "public" female sex partners are, as long as they occupy their special status, not to be considered as either a single woman or a wife. The so-called double standard can appear in many forms!

Reproduction and Legitimacy

While only a very few known societies (Australian Aborigine and Trobriand Islands in the southwest Pacific) formerly denied the necessity of coitus and semen as essential for conception and pregnancy, all known societies place great value on the reproductive capacities of women and clearly separate the assignment of rights of sexual access to women from the assignment of authority over the children a woman might bear. This is most clear in societies that are most liberal about rights of sexual access. A man and woman, not husband and wife, may legitimately engage in sexual intercourse, but it does not follow that they are fully regarded father and mother to a child born of their affair. Looked at in another way, authority over the reproductive capacities of a woman is a matter of determining to whom the child belongs and from whom the child derives his or her societal identity. Viewed in this way, a very significant component of marriage is the assignment or reassignment of reproductive rights. Marriage usually establishes the social legitimacy of children born of the marriage.

The English words "legitimacy" and "illegitimacy" carry meanings that at best only apply to our society. When they are extended to other cultures, confusion is apt to occur; but because there are no other more suitable terms, anthropologists extend their usage, in special ways, to other cultures. Today in the United States "legitimate" and "illegitimate" carry a somewhat archaic pejorative meaning that refers to whether or not a child's parents are or were legally married at the time of birth. In most of the United States a child who is "illegitimate" may or may not be "fatherless"; may or may not (usually may not) suffer from some social stigmata; may or may not (usually may not) be deprived in a legal sense. In our European background this was not always the case, but in recent times statutory laws have mitigated much of the possible jural deprivation that a child might suffer due to his or her being "illegitimate."

In other societies the notion of legitimacy works in different ways, chiefly in deciding to whom the child belongs, and from whom it receives its full social identity. Take Santa Cruz Island again for an example: if a child is born outside of a fully recognized marriage, the physiological father (who is thereby guilty of a serious crime) cannot be a true father to that child unless a legitimate marriage can be arranged. The child is not fatherless, however. The sociological father of the child is, if he accepts the responsibility, the father of the child's mother. The reason for this is clearly indicated: control of the reproductive capacities of an unmarried woman resides in her father, and not until marriage does he yield them to her husband and his kin. Before European law was imposed upon the Santa Cruz Island people, the maternal grandfather could accept his unmarried daughter's child as his own, give it away to another person or kill it—the same privileges that he had over children born to him and his wife. If the daughter's child was accepted, and it usually was with alacrity, the child became the legitimate offspring of its maternal grandparents. Unfortunately, this made the child a younger sibling to its biological mother, which was a confusing situation and one to be avoided. No social disability or stigma was ever suffered by such a child. Any stigma generated fell onto errant genetic parents.

In many patrilineal African societies, marriages are legitimized by more than one transaction, simultaneously for some, sequentially for some. Only after the final transaction is completed can the husband and his patrilineal kin lay claim to children of the marriage. That is, the final part of legitimization is the transfer of authority over a wife's reproductive capacities from her own kin to the kin of her husband. If the final part is never completed, this transfer is never made, and the children of the marriage become members of their mother's kin.

In some societies with rigorously enforced prohibitions against certain kinds of conjugal unions, such as intercaste unions in some parts of India, children born to prohibited sexual partners cannot be assigned social status; they become non-persons, outcasts, truly illegitimate beings.

So important is the factor of legitimacy in marriage in most societies, that some anthropologists have argued that the only possible way to define marriage universally is to equate it in a minimum sense with legitimation of children. The difficulty with such a minimum definition is that a few societies have so many legal fictions by means of which children can be legitimized, regardless of the jural relationship of their genetic parents, that the association of legitimacy and marriage becomes quite tenuous. In contemporary United States only a vestige of legitimacy is left in marriage, for the state has come close to guaranteeing, by law, some form of legitimacy for every individual.

Kinship and Marriage

In contemporary United States society, kinship is conceived of as an organizing principle of narrow and sometimes even inconsequential importance compared with the other kinds of social relations that govern our lives. For most Americans, kinship concerns relations with primary relatives, parents-children, siblings-siblings. The effective range of kinship is narrow, at best, embracing only some of our cousins, aunts and uncles. When we marry, it is usually outside the range of kinship altogether, and a marriage does not unite in any way the close kin of the husband with close kind of the wife. An "affinal" or in-law relationship is a weak one that does not require more than the maintenance of polite social distance.

In many nonindustrial and tribal societies kinship is not only quite different from the way it is in our society, but is is a factor that enters into almost all relationships and activities. To be a complete person in a social sense, or fully legitimate, is to have a full roster of kin in each of the several categories of kinship. Furthermore, in many tribal societies all persons are assumed to be related in some way, and the limits of society are bound by the reckoning of kinship. Nearly everyone with whom one has dealings is some sort of kinsman or kinswoman, and the category of the relationship determines the character of the interaction. In such societies one usually marries a kin of some kind; a distant kin, perhaps, but nevertheless a kin. Marriage, then, transforms one category of kinship into another.

In such societies where one relies upon or gives to different kinds of kin different kinds of support, the socialization of young people involves more kinds of kin than just parents. In adulthood, one does not just look to parents or siblings for support or inheritance; for different kinds of assistance are received and given in many different directions, the primary and secondary directions being different categories of kin.

Given the pervasiveness of kinship, it is not surprising to discover that in such societies marriage is of great concern to many persons other than the bride and groom. Marriages may be arranged by those who are thinking as much or more about the social consequences of the marriage as they are about the personal wishes of the couple. This places a heavy onus on the couple to adjust to one another and make the most of their marriage, which has been arranged for and controlled largely by others.

Time was, in our European backgrounds, that, except for individuals who had control over important capital resources, marriage was a sociolegal matter left to families and kin. Nowadays in most modern, complex industrial societies, marriage very rarely concerns many individuals other than parents. It does not forge new or reinforce old relations of great social import. This shrinkage of the network of relations that in other societies, and formerly in our own, enveloped marriage is one important aspect of the continuing trend of individualization that societies the world over are undergoing. Marriage has come increasingly under the control of the personal preferences of the partners. At the same time, society as a whole, in the form of the state, has established an interest in marriage. In the United States it is an agency of the state, not families and kin, that legitimizes marriage, and only an agency of the state can grant divorce.

In kinship-based societies, one way in which a controlling force is exerted on marriage is to consider certain classes of kin—kinds of cousins, for example—either highly desirable or necessary as spouses. The most common form of this is in cross-cousin marriage, in which the children of opposite-sex siblings (a brother and a sister) are either the preferred or prescribed marital partners. It is well to remember, however, that in such kinship systems a cross-cousin is not just a child of one's mother's brother or father's sister but also a child of any kinsman a mother classes with her brother or a father classes with his sister, and this may include a large number of people.

In the Arab world there is a marriage preference between the children of two brothers—parallel cousin marriage. A man is not required to marry his father's brother's daughter, but he has a prior right to claim her as a bride. Should it be desirable for her to marry someone else, her male parallel cousin must yield his right over her. In both the cross- and parallel-cousin types it can be said that part of the marriage relationship is rooted in the kinship system.

Another way in which kinship and marriage become enmeshed is to require an individual to marry in some way that was predetermined by a marriage one, two or even more generations previously. For example, a young man may be required to find a wife from the same set of kin or family line from which his mother, or his father's mother or his father's father's mother, came. There are many variations of this, and it can be looked at as a required marriage between certain classes of kin (as above in the cross- and parallel-cousin examples), but it is more often viewed as a perpetual marital alliance that exists between sets of lineal descendents, an alliance that should be renewed every generation, every third generation, and so on.

What these few examples demonstrate is that marital rights may be allocated as are other nonmarital rights, through the kinship system or held by familial lines or actual family groups in such ways as to perpetuate interfamilial ties. In some Australian Aborigine societies, marital rights over females are held by males and are regarded as capital assets that can be traded; but, more to the point, future marital rights over females who are not even conceived yet are also recognized and utilized to form strategic social alliances.

In European societies the closest thing to this sort of alliance by marriage is those political manipulations that were made between dynastic lines and by some of the great mercantile families of the Italian city states. However, the differences are enormous, because the scale of the political aspect of the European alliances by marriage was so much greater than that of the peasant and tribal societies where such alliances are most often found.

Selection of Spouses

In every society there are so-called sociological rules governing how potential spouses are selected. Some of these were touched upon in the brief discussion of kinship and marriage in the preceding section. Now let us look at some other aspects of spouse selection.

Anthropological literature is full of discussions about "exogamy" and "endogamy," which are descriptive terms for kinds of prohibitions against marriage and preferences for specific kinds of marriage. Unfortunately, the meanings of these terms (and even another, proposed as "agamy") are so hopelessly confused that they will not be used here. In their place we will simply refer to rules or prohibitions that *exclude* certain categories of individuals from consideration for marriage (exogamy) and rules, preferences and prescriptions that positively designate certain categories of persons for consideration for marriage (endogamy).

Every society has prohibitions against marriage between certain kin considered too closely related to be married—the incest taboo. However, the definition of just what constitutes consanguinity (blood relationship) that is too close for marriage is one of the most variable of cultural definitions. For instance, there are some societies in which marriage is absolutely forbidden between individuals with any known blood relationship, and in some of these societies, consanguinity is reckoned for many generations back. There are also societies with such prohibitions that reckon the blood relationship back only one or two generations. In all but three known societies, primary kin (parents, siblings and children) are included under the incest taboo.   Only in ancient Egypt, the Inca of pre-Spanish Peru and pre-Christian Hawaii were there forms of approved marriage or mating between siblings (and in Hawaii very occasionally between father and daughter), but these were confined to persons of special political and religious status. Sometimes such notable exceptions to the general rule are referred to as "dynastic" incest.

Societies vary considerably in approving first-cousin marriages; our own society has been somewhat ambivalent about it. As suggested in the previous section, some societies prefer or permit marriages with first cousins of the cross type, while at the same time first cousins of the parallel type are within the prohibited degree of relationship. Thus, closeness of consanguinity as a geneticist would define it is not always the determining factor in a marriage.

In many societies marriage is absolutely forbidden between persons who are affiliated with the same unilineal descent category (lineage, clan, sib, descent group) even though the blood relationship between persons of the same category cannot be demonstrated and is only assumed to exist. Unilineal descent is a form of consanguinity (not recognized in western European countries or the United States) in which a common progenitor is recognized, and relationship to him or her is traced either through males only (patrilineal descent) or through females only (matrilineal descent), and all persons so related to the common ancestor are considered to have a special but close blood relationship to each other, no matter how far distant the genealogical distance.   Such unilineal categories often observe some common form of food restrictions or have a mystic (totemic) relationship with an animal or plant species.   A marriage between persons of the same descent category may be thought of as incestuous, just as a marriage between siblings is incestuous.

Besides prohibitions based upon the avoidance of incest, every society has further restrictions that forbid or discourage marriages with certain kinsmen (in-laws for example) or on the basis of wide age discrepancies, social rank, social class, wealth, religion, ethnicity, race, political considerations and many others.   Thus the field of eligible spouses is always narrowed by a combination of excluding rules.

Conversely, all societies recognize values for selecting partners otherwise not ruled out.   All of those just mentioned as possible exclusions in some societies may be positive factors in other groups, and there are personal attributes, such as virtue, temperament, industry, appearance, intellect and a host of others, that may further narrow the field.   In all societies, then, spouses are selected by a combination of positive and negative criteria, and as with so much else that is cultural, each culture has a unique configuration.

In contemporary United States, where the positive factors are so involved with romantic love and freedom from many other social considerations, together with a high degree of geographic mobility, we may have developed the most individualized mode of choice of marital partners that has ever been known.   This is quite consistent with the extraordinary value that we also place on personal freedom.

Marriage Transactions

Special marking or celebration of marriage, although common, is not a cultural universal.   In some societies, such as that of the eastern Solomon Islands, when a couple receive tacit approval of their marriage they gradually begin to set up their own household. Behind the scenes, however, many adjustments have to be made: land or other vital resources must be allocated for the couple's use; housekeeping equipment must be assembled; a dwelling must be constructed or altered.   If the marriage is between pagans, no public or private ceremony is given to mark the change in status of bride and groom. Christians in these same communities, however, celebrate marriage with a wedding; but it is usually held quite a long time after the marriage is consummated because the first few months of co-residence are considered to be a sort of test period which might not work out. When a child is born and if the couple is still living together amicably, then the marriage is considered to be somewhat secure.

In our society, the necessary formalities of a wedding are not intricate when viewed in cross-cultural perspective. Health certification, application for a license, agreement to and proper validation of the contract constitute the only essential legal requirement for those who have achieved majority. The religious ritual and social celebrations are optional, depending upon religious affiliation and strength of belief, social standing and the strength of kinship networks and friendships. Again, these are options which point up the degree to which marriage has become separated from kinship, family and church, but at the same time has come under the direct jurisdiction of the state.

In most tribal and peasant societies, the transition from single to married status is marked by lengthy and involved rituals and celebrations. These rituals and celebrations usually symbolically portray the salient aspects of the social transition.

An uncommon ritual, but one made much of in anthropological writings, has the bride being abducted from her kin (who may put up a vigorous, even violent, defense—all this occurring after negotiations for the marriage have been completed). Early anthropologists called this "bride capture," arguing that it was a ritualized survival of an earlier stage of culture when men had to "capture" their wives by force in much the same way they captured and held territory or other valuable assests. Accepting the interpretation as given, bride capture was also offered as proof of the existence of a stage in human cultural evolution before there were accepted rules governing marriage. Today such bride-capture dramas, exaggerated social displays of grief at weddings or acts that seem to attempt to prevent the marriage from taking place are seen as rituals that express deep sentiment about the loss of a member to the group in a similar way that exaggerated expressions of emotion at funerals and mourning observances express the departure of a group member.

In a few societies, especially Indians of South America and Aborigines of Australia, the marriages of men are interlocked with the marriages of their sisters. A man marries a woman only on the condition that his sister will be married to his bride's brother. A precondition for marriage in some parts of Africa is that the groom must work for the bride's family for a specified period before the marriage can be legitimized. This is termed "bride service," and for those societies demanding it, it can be little more than a gesture, or can amount to a firm indenture of the groom's labor for several years. In both brother-sister exchange and bride service is the obvious recognition that marriage calls for some kind of compensation. Brother-sister exchange is an equivalent exchange; in bride service, the groom's labor is a token exchange for what he and his kin will receive from his bride.

Some anthropological theorists regard the exchange aspect of marriage as its most pervasive and elemental feature. Following this line of reasoning, one set of persons (or kin) gives women in order to receive wives. In simple kinship-oriented societies the exchange aspects are most clearly seen. In complex societies such as our own where economics and social class considerations are powerful forces, the exchange aspect of marriage is masked by other considerations.

By far the most noteworthy sequence of events in marriage ceremonies, found in many societies the world over, is the "brideprice" or bridewealth exchange. This consists of negotiations, collection, transfer and distribution of either tokens or great wealth from the kin of the groom to the kin of the bride. Bridewealth has been greatly misunderstood by missionaries and colonial officials, who have often seen (still see) such transactions as a purchase of the bride, as if she were chattel. Actually, in no known instance does the conveyance of bridewealth signify a purchase in the same sense that one purchases a commodity under conditions of the marketplace. The payment of bridewealth, however, is a sort of compensatory gesture for the loss of a female kin. It is also a form of exchange in which expectation of profit is not or should not be the motive, and often its payment or its receipt is linked to the full knowledge that wealth received for a woman will merely go out when the next man must be married.

In some societies, notably in Africa, bridewealth may be paid in two or more installments, each installment clearly signifying some change in status of the bride. Bridewealth payments may continue to be distributed over long periods of time, most often at special events during the marriage, or they may always be countered by presents from the bride's kin which are of less or equal value. In brief, bridewealth and related distributions of wealth that flow from the husband's kin and friends to the wife's kin and friends symbolize the scope of the marriage contract, which is different in every society. If the exchange is linked to one made in the previous generation and sets up a similar exchange in the next generation, then usually it represents a continuing alliance of some sort.

As mentioned above, in parts of Africa a form of bridewealth may be paid in two installments, the first when the bride comes to live with her husband, a second later on to finalize the marriage. The two payments are clearly seen as compensations for different aspects of marriage. The first is for marital rights having to do with her domestic and sexual life with her husband; the second has to do with the derivation of legitimacy for the wife's children. As long as the second payment is unpaid, the husband's kin have no legitimate claims to the children; after the second payment the husband's kin are the primary group with which children will be affiliated.

On Santa Cruz Island in the southwest Pacific, bridewealth of great value is payable in a special all-purpose currency made of fiber and red downy feathers. Every bridewealth must consist of ten units of geometrically graded value so that number ten is worth half of number nine, which is worth half of number eight, and so on. Each unit is contributed by one kinsman or friend (who may have asked others to help him) of the groom or of whoever has volunteered to organize payment. Lengthy and often tense negotiations go into making up a full set of ten units that is satisfactory to the bride's kin.

Following delivery to the father of the bride, the units are distributed to his kin and friends to whom he is indebted for helping with former transactions of this kind. Of prime importance among such outstanding debts are those incurred on his behalf when his bridewealth was assembled. The bridewealth of the first daughter to be married must go to repay her father's bridewealth debts. There are many other smaller gifts, recognitions and tokens which are returned to the givers of bridewealth, but usually some part of the bridewealth is donated by receivers back to the bride herself, to take into marriage as a nest egg for her and her husband to nourish and increase.

However, the matter does not end with the payment of bridewealth and the minor counterpayments. As each child born to the married couple matures, he or she is made the focus of a number of observances, each occasion marking some significant aspect of maturation, and giving the kin of the child's father an opportunity to express their gratitude to kin of the child's mother with valuable gifts (usually meat) that are a continuation of the bridewealth transaction.

Another important aspect of bridewealth on Santa Cruz Island is the special relationship that the payment establishes. The payees of bridewealth become the only in-laws of the bride; the recipients of bridewealth become the only in-laws of the groom. Thus an economic transaction is transformed into a kinship network. To payers of bridewealth accrue still other rewards. The first child of the marriage must be named after the payer of the most valuable unit of bridewealth, the second child after the payer of the second unit, and so on. If a child dies in infancy, the next one born is given its name so that the payer once honored with a namesake does not lose that honor. Having one's name perpetuated is not the end of the matter either. The payer of bridewealth and his wife have the privilege of adopting their namesake child as their own. If this privilege is exercised, they become fully legal parents; the biological parents are relegated to secondary parental status. Thus, if a husband's father is honored for his contribution to his son's bridewealth with a namesake, and the husband's father also adopts the child, sociologically that child becomes a sibling to his or her biological father.

As the Santa Cruz people see it, the payers of bridewealth make the marriage possible and therefore have a prior right to the fruit of the marriage—the children. In terms of marital rights the payers of bridewealth are entitled to a share of the procreative resources of the wife commensurate with the amount they contributed. Contributors or their heirs, it will be recalled, will also recover the wealth they paid later when the first daughter of the marriage toward which they contributed is married.

The ways in which marriage, bridewealth and associated customs are interwoven with the fabric of kinship and many other societal matters make Santa Cruz Island culturally unique. But it is not unique in the fact that marriage, rather than birth, establishes an individual for the rest of his or her life. It determines who will be the major kin through adult life; it sets up obligations that carry over into the next generation; it squares debts carried over from the previous generation. There are many other societies in which adults as well as juveniles are fully located in the social milieu only by marriage.

Economics and Marriage

In most summary discussions of marriage a great deal of attention is paid to the economic function of marriage. The most obvious aspects have to do with the management and disposition of communal and individually owned property, the division of labor between husband and wife and allocation of the fruits of their labors; but, more precisely, these matters have to do with the entire domestic group rather than with marriage alone. In rural, agrarian and non-industrialized economies the domestic unit, or household, is a far more important unit of production and consumption than in highly industrialized economies.

All societies seem to recognize personal property of husband and wife, but the extent to which separate control over capital is recognized varies. As a whole in primitive and peasant societies, there is an unmistakable trend for men to control the important capital, just as men the world over tend to dominate that field of activities we broadly call "political." In some societies one spouse may bring little or no valuable capital to the marriage because it is not possible to remove it from the natal group. This places the spouse without capital in a relatively powerless position. In other societies that exercise tight control over communal property, both husband and wife may each bring considerable capital, such as rights over land, to the marriage, but these rights are never merged to form a unitary estate for children to inherit. This is most frequent in societies where the important capital is all held by corporate kinship groups within which marriage is forbidden. Thus, at marriage each spouse brings only rights of use to corporate holdings, and with the termination of the marriage the rights of each spouse revert to their natal groups. In a very few of these instances, even the income or produce from the separate assets is partly owed to corporate groups that hold the assets. In the Trobriand Islands of the western Pacific, for example, a man owes a large share of produce from his garden land to his sister, because the land is held by a lineage group to which his sister, not his wife, belongs, and the principal heir to his rights over land is his sister's son, not his own son. The Trobriands is a matrilineal society, and in many other matrilineal societies a man may bring very little capital with him into the marriage. He works the capital of his wife and her brothers; he also works the capital that he and his sister share, and the products of these separate labors are kept divided. An economic situation that places first priority on keeping capital and income within the kinship group seems to put great strain on the marital and domestic group.

More often, a wife comes to the marriage with little or no control over valuable property or capital; or if she brings valuable property, she surrenders some control over it to her husband. Frequently, however, the wife's weak economic position with regard to her marriage is offset somewhat by the recognition in her natal group that she still retains rights over property held there. Simply put, societies vary greatly as to which spouse is the source of important domestic capital and the degree to which husband and wife retains claims on capital controlled by their respective natal families. The ethnographic literature is laced with examples of cultures where women have strong economic positions in marriage. Yet statistically speaking, there is no question that women generally occupy inferior, less powerful economic positions in marriage compared to their husbands.

A special practice that has to do with women and their valuable property in marriage is the dowry. It is often presented as the mirror image of bridewealth because it appears to be a flow of wealth from the woman's side toward the man's. This is incorrect. The dowry is a prepayment, so to speak, of part of a woman's share of her claim to the parents' estate, given her at the time of marriage rather than at the death of the parents. The few societies that recognize dowry vary with respect to how much control over that property is retained by the wife and how much is given over to her husband.

Regarding property, labor and marriage, our society, again, is at one end of a distribution curve with most other societies at the opposite end. In contemporary United States society there is a strong tendency for husband and wife to hold capital jointly and to funnel the products of labor and income into a common nuclear family pool. Various economic obligations extending from marriage along kinship networks of both husband and wife are weak; everything tends to focus on the next generation, while very little focuses back on the parental generations or across to kin of one's own generation. This, of course, is just another way of saying that after marriage our kinship networks, such as they are, seem to shrink, whereas in most peasant and tribal societies the kinship system seems not to come into full effect until marriage. Next to children, the most important economic obligation for contemporary American society is the society itself (e.g., taxes and charities). Nothing expresses this better than the personal income tax form, in which a gift to a needy kinsman is not a recognizable deduction, but a gift to a charitable organization is.

Of some historical interest are the formulations of Marx and Engels in their political conclusions regarding women, property and marriage. Based upon very poor ethnographic data (and also upon a great deal of speculative fiction about the evolution of the human family), Marx and Engels saw the subordinate position of wives to husbands (in a kind of "prostitution") as due to women's inferior position regarding capital property. Once private property was abolished, and once many of the maternal responsibilities were assumed by the socialist state, and once women were guaranteed rights over the products of their labors, they would become the equals of men. Marriage then would become a purely private matter, and for rather obscure and complicated reasons monogamy would flourish.

The Marx-Engels position, with amendments by Lenin and Stalin, became the foundation upon which marriage in some Israeli kibbutzim was formulated. In these small-scale socialist experiments there is no marital property, childrearing and formal education of children are the responsibility of the corporate community, and all basic needs are provided communally. Marriage in the kibbutz has been reduced, as far as possible, to the realm of personal relations between husband and wife. Certainly, this is one further step in the reduction of interrelationships between marriage and other cultural elements, going beyond what was evolved, without conscious planning, in modern capitalist industrial societies.

In recent years considerable attention has been paid to the marriage pattern termed "serial monogamy" and the resulting household form called the "matricentric family." It is most commonly found in economically depressed black communities in the United States, among Caribbean peasants and in parts of poverty-stricken Latin America. As mentioned, in this marriage pattern (which is not the only pattern recognized for these societies) men and women both have a sequence of monogamous conjugal or cohabitational arrangements. Children may be born to each union, and there is a statistical tendency for later unions to be more long-lasting than early unions. Early unions are not fully legitimized with all the formalities of marriage, and are, by anthropologists at least, distinguished from regular marriage by the name of "consensual unions." After several consensual unions a stable domestic arrangement often is achieved and fully legitimized.

The matricentric family is the result of unstable consensual unions in which husbands drift away leaving children in the care of women. Young mothers often drift away from a household to enter the labor market, leaving their children with another often older female kin, who for a number of reasons is more able to maintain a permanent household. Thus, the households are made up of women and children without husbands.

There are several competing hypotheses as to how these marital and household patterns emerge. One, pertaining to Caribbean societies, traces fragile and sequential marital unions to the practice of polygyny in Africa. However, the prevailing hypothesis is an economic one, as follows: On the whole, women in poverty situations can eke out a more stable living than men, because they are in demand for menial domestic work. Men, having fewer opportunities for work, must be mobile to get what work—usually seasonal—is available. Under these conditions where men have only a precarious position in the labor economy, stable marriage is difficult to achieve. Not until a man finds a secure niche in the economy—and that is usually later in life, if at all—is he able to enter into a permanent union.

Had Marx and Engels known about consensual unions and the matricentric family, they would have been delighted at the economic evidence that supports the explanation of marital instability. However, they might have had to reformulate their ideas about the relationship of female labor to the capitalistic economy; they saw it as more precarious than men's labor.

Stability of Marriage

A great deal of sociological and anthropological research has been devoted to finding social and cultural factors that seem to influence the stability of marriage. Results of the anthropological cross-cultural studies are not clear and are often contradictory. Many cultural variables affect stability, and since marriage in each society is a unique configuration, very few generalizations can be made. However, when viewed cross-culturally the problem breaks down into two elements: One has to do with cultural values about the permanence of marriage, for some societies just do not think of marriage as an irrevocable situation, while other groups do not even acknowledge the termination of a marriage except, perhaps, by death. The other element has to do with how close the statistical norms of behavior conform to the ideational norms—that is, the degree to which a culture's views about the permanence of marriage (values) conform to actual behavior (performance).

There are among non-Christian peoples some who make no provision for divorce. As with Roman Catholicism, marriage can be terminated only by death. These societies also have legal fictions that, under exceptional situations, permit spouses to separate and be substituted, and marriages to be annulled without calling it divorce. One of the most (to European eyes) unexpected legal fictions appears in some African societies in which it is imperative that some widows be remarried to spouses from specified groups, but in which there are no available men. The solution is to allow a woman to stand in for a man. Thus, two women become partners to a fictional marriage.

There are societies, too, in which marriage in a legal sense does not even terminate with the death of one of the spouses. The surviving spouse remains married to the deceased's ghost. Usually, this kind of fiction is buttressed at the social level by some kind of continual alliance between the two groups that were joined by marriage. The alliance continues, and is expressed by a cultural metaphor (marriage to a ghost) on the interpersonal level.

There is some evidence to suggest that in societies with strong corporate patrilineal kin groups marriage is always more stable than in societies with strong corporate matrilineal kin groups. This is explained as being due to the fact that marital rights over women are usually held by men, not by women and not vice versa. Therefore, when rights over a woman are transferred to her husband's kin group at marriage, it is easier to keep her there too. Conversely, in matrilineal societies the marital rights over men are never fully transferred to wives' kin groups; hence they can go back to their matrilineal groups when the marriage falters.

The same argument seems to apply in explaining the high frequency of societies in which polygyny is practiced. Men have the power (over women) to take other wives (with or without divorce) because few if any cultures have ever assigned irrevocable marital rights over men to women.

Another way of looking at this is from the point of view of incorporation of either wife or husband into the other's kinship or family groups. Men rarely, if ever, are fully incorporated into their wives' kinship groups (replacing, as it were, the women's brothers who have left), but women often are more fully detached from their birth groups and fully incorporated into their husbands' birth groups. The more fully the latter, the more difficult is divorce.

In an overwhelming majority of known cultures divorce is possible, and the grounds for divorce are clearly defined. Here, too, variation is the most apparent cross-cultural phenomenon. Unfortunately, in most of the ethnographic data numerical divorce rates that can be placed against the cultural norms are lacking. For example, some Eskimo groups of northern Canada reportedly have very fluid marital relations. Divorce, until recently, was determined solely upon personal decisions of the spouses. The same is reported for the commoner class in pre-Christian Hawaii. In both cases, marriage seems to have been bound tightly to domestic economics, which in turn was closely linked to ecological factors. That is, marriage and divorce were matters strongly influenced by the amount and quality of resources commanded by the married couple.

Cross-cultural perspectives on divorce seem to support this truism: when marriage is not enmeshed in other cultural (e.g., religious beliefs) and social (i.e., kinship, political organization, wide social networks) relationships, then divorce is easy and often acted upon. When marriage is thoroughly enmeshed in many different sorts of social and political relationships, then divorce is relatively difficult to obtain, and there are many social forces that act against it. We can postulate a concept of social disturbance and assume that divorce always creates some degree of social disturbance. If this is correct, then the more enmeshed marriage is, the greater the potential disturbance, and the more social pressures will be brought to prevent divorce. Such a formulation runs somewhat counter to the Marx-Engels position, which assumes that once freed of social relationships, faithful monogamy will stabilize and flourish.

Marriage and Sentiments

In our society marriage has become nearly synonymous with sentiments of sexual love. Without it, marriage is incomplete or in jeopardy. We are not unique in this. Some Polynesian societies, both traditional and contemporary, give to the sexual aspect of marriage as much or possibly more importance than we do. In our own culture history we know that the emergence of romantic love and sexual compatibility as a major (if not *the* major) affective component seems to have occurred as individual choices in all matters concerning marriage have increased. In contrast, there are societies in which love and sex, except minimally for procreative objectives, are conspicuously absent from marriage. Some contemporary tribal societies in New Guinea seem to denigrate love and sexual attraction in marriage nearly to the vanishing point. In Manus Island society of the southwest Pacific region women are reported to abhor sexual relations with their husbands. On Dobu Island, also in the southwest Pacific, marital relations are often strongly colored by mutual fear and suspicion; in some New Guinea societies men live in constant dread of becoming polluted by their wives; and in still other New Guinea societies the husband-wife relationship is tinged by feelings of hostility because the social groups from which spouses come are frequently opposed to one another as enemies. For similar reasons the marital relations of the Gusii of Kenya are often tinged by mutual aggressiveness that is manifested mainly in sexual behavior.

   Most cases where fearful, hostile or other negative sentiments are conspicuous components of marriage are clearly due to the fact that the same or similar sentiments dominate relations between the two sociological groupings from which the spouses come, and the society also demands a kind of primary loyalty, or social identification, with one's natal grouping. In other words, there is a strong sociological component to the structuring of marital sentiments.

Unfortunately, we do not have an abundance of rich and reliable data on the sentiments of marriage for most societies. Such data are difficult to obtain and to translate from one language to another because linguistic terms on sentiments and affective states are often not semantically equivalent. Moreover, the entire psychological classification of affect and emotions seems hopelessly governed by the manner in which European languages classify them. Take the concept of "love," for instance. In English the term covers an extraordinary range of affective states. In the language of Santa Cruz Island there are at least two terms that must be translated as "love," one with a sexual denotation, one without it. These two affective terms stand in semantic contrast with something we might translate as "lust." However, the term for nonsexual love also contains a semantic component of duty and obligatory action, and the term for sexual love (or attractiveness) has contained within it semantic components of familiar respect (in contrast to restrained respect).

Even though the sentiments that are considered to be appropriate for social relations including marriage are exceedingly difficult matters to research, it seems quite clear that marriage and kinship systems in all societies are just as much patternings of different sentiments and affective states as they are patternings of rights and duties, authority and subjugation. Moreover, in some societies the marital relationship is clearly one in which a conflict of sentiments is built in, so to speak, because the values of that society demand of husbands and wives two or more sets of sentiments which are inherently incompatible. The ideal of a personal, tender, loving and mutually respectful relationship as a characteristic of marriage seems to be an ethnocentric view.

Marriage and Social Change

It is a postulate of anthropology that cultures constantly change. Thus, marriage is just as subject to change as other cultural patterns are. Differential rates of change for different aspects of culture are not clearly understood, unless specific pressures for such change stand out clearly. In our own culture history, changes in marriage appear to be occurring more and more rapidly. It took centuries for the Christian church finally to classify marriage as a sacrament.

The concern and establishment of the authority of the state over marriage, particularly marriages of poor and obscure persons, was also slow to develop. The gradual withering away of the family as a fundamental economic unit of production and its effect on marriage came quicker, with the rapid growth of industrialism, urbanism and dependence upon wage labor. More recently, the development of easy and efficient methods of birth control has quickly altered values concerning marriage and childbirth. It is clear, too, that in our society as the divorce rate continues to go up, there is increased questioning of traditional values about marriage. In the United States people seriously discuss whether or not traditional faithful monogamy is compatible with modern life, and a few are experimenting with alternative conjugal forms. In sum, in contemporary United States society there is a heightened consciousness of marriage along with less tendency to regard the values of marriage as bound by tamper-proof tradition.

But planned alterations to the marriage pattern are not exactly new to the United States. On the basis of religious reinterpretation, the Mormons once attempted to establish Old Testament polygyny in their communities. Another religiously based experiment was undertaken by the Perfectionist Community, more commonly known as the Oneida Community. To the Oneida faithful, monogamy appeared contrary to man's nature; hence it propelled him toward evil. In the place of monogamy the Oneida banned permanent heterosexual attachments, instituting a form of group marriage wherein all adult men were married to all adult women. Marriage became a holy bond of the community; sexual intercourse was a form of sacrament.

Then there was the United Society of Believers in Christ's Second Appearing, better known as the Shakers, who renounced all sexual behavior and redefined marriage as a completely chaste domestic arrangement between a man and a woman.

Today's experiments with alternative forms of marriage resemble those just briefly mentioned in their attempts to bring marriage into a more compatible relationship with the other requirements of living. In the eighteenth and nineteenth centuries, experimenters saw religion as the guiding force of life, and reinterpretation of the scriptures provided the bases for redefining marriage. Today's experimenters search in many directions to make their alternative marital forms more compatible. The communes seek freedom from the inhumaness of industrialism and are searching for relatively isolated self-sufficiency in which sexual love and gratification give cohesiveness to their familistic small groups. Others seek more individual freedom, especially from the legal restrictions imposed by law. The so-called consensual union is no longer confined to poor black sectors of our society. It has been adopted by some elderly poor, in order to combat loneliness and isolation and to make ends meet; and by young and relatively affluent white adults who for a variety of reasons do not wish to commit themselves to a legal contract that is both difficult and expensive to break. If the trend of the past two decades continues, alternative conjugal forms will become as much a social fact of American society as they are of, say, Caribbean societies.

In nonindustrial parts of the world, traditional patterns of marriage are being subjected to even more intense pressures for change. The most apparent of these demands come from Christian missionaries, usually the first heralds of change to arrive from the industrialized world. Their teachings and preachings are, on the whole, very successful. It is difficult to find a society now in which Christian missionaries are not at work, and in which some aspects of marriage have not been altered by their influence. The other force of change appears as formerly isolated and purely agrarian peoples are drawn into the industrial labor market. Traditional forms, even when changed by Christianity, often do not fit well with the demands of industrial labor, which may require geographic mobility and long-term separation of husband and wife.

Again, there is nothing really new about these kinds of changes, but what is unparalleled is the rapidity with which the are occurring. The kinds of changes in marriage that took centuries in our own histories may now come about in one generation. Another difference is the fact that urbanized industrial society is a unitary model toward which all societies are trending.

Many anthropologists see all culture change as a great adaptive process. In this light changing marriage patterns are no different from other cultural patterns. Sometimes in historical perspective it is possible to gain insight into what forces caused certain changes to occur. However, to project culture change forward is no more a possibility at present than the forecasting of long-range biological genetic changes.

The only aspect of social change that may be different in the contemporary world from what it was a century or more ago seems to be the *consciousness* and awareness of change. Every society today is aware of change; ours even accepts it as a permanent feature of culture, but not necessarily one that applies to all aspects of our culture. Some people think of marriage as perpetually undergoing change; but others see change in marriage not as continual adaptation, but as social disorganization and pathological. Even the social sciences are not at all in agreement as to what constitutes adaptive change and what is disorganization. The more than change is recognized, the more societies and governments will consider the possibilities of *planned changes*. Already the possibilities of comprehensive social engineering are being envisaged, although the pure theory to base such engineering upon is lacking. Limited social engineering is already a fact in some parts of our industrial and financial organizations. Good planning is considered to be good management, and professional specialists are already available. With recent rapid advances in medical technology we now support advisory agencies for planned parenthood. Can a fully and well-planned marital life be far behind?*

Author's Comment (LJS): A recent TV report indicated that California, which has "do-it-yourself divorce," has now adopted "instant marriage." Apparently a couple must only agree they are married, with no legal or religious ceremonies or requirements whatever. This, the report said, frees marriage from government interference, which is proper, since marriage is an entirely personal relationship between two persons. My reaction was this: an institution that has existed among humans from the beginning of recorded history, in the most primitive, isolated tribes and in the greatest civilizations, must have some important roots and should not be so lightly discarded. I believe that two of these roots are the mating instinct and the responsibility for the children. One of the most heinous crimes of which the human animal is guilty is bringing children into the world without providing a stable, loving adequate home that allows them to mature properly and adequately. A home without such a loving atmosphere dooms these babies to future lifelong neurosis, psychosis and criminality. As they become teenagers and then adults, our whole society is doomed in turn. It seems to me that marriage involves our deepest feelings and weightiest responsibilities to both partner and children, and these involve society. If our present forms of handling such feelings and responsibilities are not suitable, we must not jettison what we have but *improve* it.

References

Note: References 1–4 are different anthropological approaches to the material covered in this chapter. References 6–8 are good ethnographic descriptions of marriage in tribal societies. References 9–12 deal principally with marriage in our society. Reference 5 is a special cross-cultural approach to divorce. All contain excellent bibliographies.

1. Leach, E. (1972): Marriage, primitive, in: *Encyclopedia Britannica,* Vol. 14. Chicago: Encyclopedia Britannica, Inc., pp. 938–947.
2. Marshall, G. (1968): Marriage, comparative analysis, in: *International Encyclopedia of the Social Sciences,* Vol. 10. New York: Macmillan Co. and The Free Press, pp. 8–18.
3. Stephens, W. N. (1963): *The Family in Cross Cultural Perspective.* New York: Holt, Rinehart & Winston.
4. Fox, R. (1974): *Kinship and Marriage, an Anthropological Perspective.* Harmondsworth, Misslesex, England: Penguin Books A884.
5. Barnes, J. (1967): The frequency of divorce, in: *The Craft of Anthropology,* A. L. Epstein, Ed. London, New York: Travistock.
6. Schapera, I. (1941): *Married Life in an African Tribe.* New York: Sheridan House.
7. Malinowski, B. (1929): *The Sexual Life of Savages in North-Western Melanesia.* New York: Halcyon House.
8. Goodall, J. (1971): *Tiwi Wives: A Study of the Women of Melville Island, North Australia.* Seattle: Univ. of Washington Press.
9. Winch, R. and Spanier, G. (1974): *Selected Studies in Marriage and the Family,* 4th Ed. New York: Holt, Rinehart and Winston.
10. Winch, R. (1971): *The Modern Family,* 3rd Ed. New York: Holt, Rinehart & Winston.
11. Smith, J. and Lynn, G. (1974): *Beyond Monogamy.* Baltimore: The Johns Hopkins Press.
12. Neuback, G. (1969): *Extramarital Relations.* Englewood Cliffs, N.J.: Prentice Hall.

SECTION III:
PROBLEMS WITHIN
MARRIAGE

9
A PARADIGM OF MARRIAGE

Dynamics of childhood pattern in choice of mate, effects of discord and divorce, and transmission through the generations.

Therefore shall a man leave his father and his mother and shall cleave unto his wife: and they shall be one flesh.

Genesis 2:24

It was long thought that if any condition "ran in families" it must be hereditary, and each generation of that family had a predisposition to it. Gregor Mendel's pioneering studies confirmed this supposition in such matters as color of eyes, for example. It was extended to diseases like "consumption" and "syphilis." But then the "tubercle bacillus" was discovered, and also the "treponema pallidum" of syphilis, which proved that these terrible diseases were not inherited at all but were infections *transmitted* from one generation to the next.

Today an inherited tendency to the extremes of schizophrenic and manic-depressive *psychoses* is not entirely ruled out. A young person would prefer not marrying into a family in which many members suffered from these extremes of psychosis. But the accumulated clinical evidence shows byond all doubt that ordinary emotional problems which are termed neurotic are *transmitted* from parents to children, not only to the third and fourth generation but forever, unless interrupted by chance or conscious intervention.

Occasionally in private practice one meets a patient whom one senses would become a good friend if the meeting had been social instead of professional. This raises a special countertransference problem. Professionally, the analyst always risks being of less than maximum therapeutic help if he allows his personal feelings of any kind whatever to intrude in the slightest. Contrariwise, liking a patient as a person can be therapeutic in itself and stimulate the analyst to be of maximum help. I once met a mother and daughter who impressed me as being of the highest caliber. Many if not most human beings, we must sadly admit, are not impressive. Their childhood patterns contain such hostility that the effects of their lives are more destructive than constructive. Those who come for analytic help are usually of the best, for they have the emotional honesty to face their problems and to seek insight and help in their struggle for maturity. Jane D. and her mother, Enid, I soon reacted to as old, trusted friends. I determined that if human help were possible I would see that they got it, and that they would achieve as good, happy, satisfying lives as this world affords. This may have broken a psychoanalytic rule, but because I sought nothing but their welfare I believe it worked for the best.

My first reaction to Jane D. was, "What a superb girl!" I en countered her at the University of Chicago in a meeting of seniors who served as dormitory proctors, but of the nine girls she was outstanding in a quiet way—chestnut hair combined with light brown eyes that were warm and intelligent, a perfect complexion and a trim, graceful, athletic figure. It was a surprise when she asked me for an appointment. When she arrived, she was easy and unself-conscious. I learned later that she was doing what she believed was right for her, and therefore cared little about what others might think.

Jane told me her problem simply and frankly: "I lack confidence sexually and with boys." If ever a girl had no external reason for this it was Jane, but internal reasons are just as "real"; so I waited for her to begin.

"There are five of us in the family," she said. "Father, Mother, an older brother and my younger sister. We were all loved children, but there has been some discord between my parents for years, since before I was 10; yet I don't doubt that they each loved me. I guess I resented Sister as a baby. When I was small I had thoughts of hurting babies and I guess they came from jealousy of Sister. I looked up to Brother."

As our interview continued, it became evident that Jane was popular and had many friends, but no close ones and no close feelings with any boy or boys. There was nothing of alienation about her, however—she was very much a part of life. She moved with confidence, held part-time jobs, traveled and gravitated toward rather than away from challenges and dangers. Yet she moved through life with a certain distance, with a certain reserve.

She told of her social setting, and it gave a clue to her pattern. "My parents live in an elite area of Chicago. My father is in one of those giant corporations that move their young men to a new city every few years. Now my parents are settled but have a peculiar attitude. My mother wants social acceptance but fears she will never fully have it. This is not realistic and I'm glad to say that her anxiety about it is getting less. Father wants acceptance too, but is sure that he will not get it, and so he says that he has no use for people in our area and all they stand for—all their fine homes and cars and swimming pools and boats. This attitude of Mother and Father doesn't make much sense because they are white Anglo-Saxon Protestants with money and status. They are just not 'old' residents. But I seem to have been influenced by both of them, and now I have a distaste for it all, including a distaste for the young men of that set. Right now I am seeing a boy who is rather Bohemian, something of a beatnik. He is not too clean and is not considerate; in fact, he's a rat. He wants me to sleep with him, and that is why I came to see you. I don't have close friends and I'm afraid that if I don't sleep with him he will drop me entirely."

I looked at Jane and said, "What irony! Here you are a superior, highly intelligent, beautiful girl; yet you feel that you must have sex with a 'rat' in order to have his companionship. You are not the kind that, in my day at least, a fellow of any substance would seduce just for kicks. What do you think of yourself?"

Jane said, "I know that I am attractive and lots of boys are interested, and people like me. I see there's a real problem here, and that is why I came to see you."

At our next interview a week later I pursued the matter further and asked for details of her childhood:

"We were all loved, as I told you. We used to roll around on the floor together. Mother and Father would do little things for us, and they were affectionate and tender. I never made good friends in school because we moved so often. I would just get settled and then another move."

"It sounds," I said, "as though the moving prevented you to some extent from detaching some of your dependence and love needs from your parents and attaching them more to friends your own age and identifying with your peers." This led Jane to remark that, "There really is magic in words . . . I knew there was something not quite right about my attachment to my parents and you gave it a name when you called it my 'dependent love needs.' Since our last talk a lot in my understanding has crystallized and fallen into place. I realize that I do not shy away from tall, slim, clean-cut blue-eyed boys just because Mother and Father turned me against that set . . . there is something more, and much stronger. All during childhood people said how adorable I was, the nice little blonde with curls. I couldn't stand it; I hated it. Now I think I know why; it is because it meant I was Mother and Father's little angel, too dependent, too needing of their love, a baby attached to their apron strings, never at ease out in the world, never independent like other children. I was so dependent on my parents that I felt anxious at school and everywhere except at home.

"In school I had to be the teacher's pet. I was afraid of speaking in class for fear I would say something the teacher would not like. In fact, as I see now, I tried to be everybody's pet. I hated myself for being that way without realizing what it was I couldn't stand. Traveling so much now is certainly part of my effort to break this childish dependence on my home . . . . I take jobs, I face dangers, I act independently, all to get away from being my parents' darling little immature child. And now I can see that is a means to escape from what you call my too-strong 'dependent love needs.' I guess it follows that full independence will come only when I change these attitudes, and lessen my dependence and my need to be the adored child in everybody's eyes."

We talked about how this affected Jane's feelings toward boys, and she said "It influences how I get along with boys in two ways: the first is that the clean-cut WASPs represent my remaining a good little girl. Marrying one would mean giving in to my dependence on my parents and being swallowed up by them and their set. I guess in wanting to escape my dependence on my parents I want to escape from all the boys who represent what they expect of me.

"The other way this dependence thing works is that I am so afraid of getting involved with a boy that I stay away entirely. I never knew what I feared in an involvement, but now I can see that it is the dependent love needs. I fear being so dependent on a boy and wanting his love and attention so much that I will be held in bondage. I am not afraid of sex itself, but I fear that if I had sex then I would become so dependent on the boy I would be secondary to him forever, and no longer able to work but swallowed up in the relationship."

At our next meeting Jane volunteered some dreams. She had written them down over the past few months, and they were all variations on a similar theme. In one she was camping with some beatniks, and the group was attacked by hoodlums; she feared rape. In another, there was an attractive man, but he was replaced by a repulsive dangerous one. In yet another dream she shot a man and then was caught. I pointed out that consciously she longed for a good, strong, loving man to marry, but that her dreams were full of violence. I asked if she were conscious of being afraid of men or hostile to them, and how long she had had such dreams.

With some agitation Jane told the following: "I first recall being anxious when I was nine or ten. That was because some tension developed between Mother and Father. I was afraid they might get a divorce; I managed to shut my mind to it though. In fact, only now in this hour with you and your asking about my dreams have I remembered my anxiety. I have never faced it directly before. I was always popular and a straight-A student, but then I felt that I could not do the work and could not get along with the teachers or the students. Now I see that I was really frightened about my parents' getting a divorce, but it was too terrible to face. So I thought it was school I feared."

This seemed to suggest that her insecurity in the home made insecurity with others, including boys. I asked Jane if there were some connection between this and her dream of shooting the man, and she said with considerable emotion: "You are asking me about something which I have sensed since you first mentioned the importance of dependent love needs, shame on the one hand and hostility and guilt on the other. I know Father loves me and always has, and I love him, and that is why this is so hard to tell. The trouble between my parents really began as early as I can remember. I only began to see it consciously at age nine or ten and then I shut it out. And it is the same with my feelings about Father . . . I began to see that he was mean. Oh, I feel awful telling you about this because he never punished us; he was always pleasant to us children, but not always nice to Mother. But he did things such as not slowing down in the car, taking close chances that left us nervous wrecks. He teased in frightening ways, like letting us go in deep water before we could swim. It was a holier-than-thou, Spartan, bossy, dictating attitude. He has had an easy enough life and a successful one, but his tone is, 'I've worked so hard to give you everything, now what will you give me?' He loves us and my early memories of him are tender; yet in his *feelings* he does not pour love out. He is so self-righteous. He can justify himself in everything and has no insight into how he is rationalizing.

"Right now, pouring this out to you, is the first time I've let myself see how angry I am at Father. Yet I feel guilty, I guess, because he really does love us and we love him. But I feel he let us down. As you have told me, insecure children are apt to cling all the more to their parents. I am sure that describes me . . . when I was so terrified of Mother and Father divorcing I clung all the closer, was afraid of school and became more dependent on them. But when I felt this mean streak in Father, this coldness underneath, and felt he had let us down, then I partly turned to my brother and became dependent on him. I pushed off my little sister, who tried to cling to me.

"This brings another terrifying thought: my dependent love needs toward men are so strong that I fear closeness, fear I will lose my own autonomous life, my own identity, and this must come from my feelings toward my parents and my brother. Is it possible that my hostility toward Father could appear as hostility to boys? Am I really hostile to men underneath?"

In later interviews with Jane it seemed that her question was true, to some degree. This undercurrent of hostility to men was another cause of her confusion in relations with men. It made her gravitate toward weak, depreciated men who aroused this hostility and stirred her sadism. This intensified her sexual feelings, but the men also aroused her identification with them in their unsatisfied needs for dependence and love and aroused her maternal instincts. Also, her hostility to her father impelled her to revenge herself upon him by selecting a man of the opposite type—not handsome, clean-cut, masculine, successful like her father. And there was danger in this motivation because it was also fed by her guilt. She loved her father and felt loved by him; hence she felt profoundly guilty for her hostility, and this made her feel she should be punished or should punish herself. Her defenses against her feelings toward her father were rapidly crumbling. More and more honestly she could look at these feelings, disentangle them and clarify the main forces.

"I was always in a bind with Father," she said. I had to be the good submissive little girl in order to keep his love, which I felt I could not live without. If I were not, he would punish me—not physically, but by restrictions, by threatening to cut off my allowance. He was the lord and master; that was man's proper role. Women should be subservient. It just occurs to me that this is why I feel so guilty about refusing a man anything. If a boy wants to kiss me, for example, and it is no one I want to be involved with, it seems only good sense to refuse; yet I feel terribly guilty for not doing as the boy wishes. This would make me a pushover for any man at all. No wonder Mother resists Father and does not let him make her into a servant, a slave.

"I hope this picture of marriage that I have grown up with has not influenced my image of marriage or men too much . . . but I am just beginning to recognize how much anger I have had toward Father all these years. Could this unconscious picture of marriage keep me from making a good one myself? I do sense that this temptation to have sex with ineligible men is somehow a revenge on Father. It is a rejection of him because I pick men who are completely unlike him. There is some danger I think of getting myself into trouble and doing something I'd reproach myself for, such as cutting myself off from a good marriage by having an affair with someone I would never marry. I can see this, and I am now aware that this danger comes from the hostility toward Father.

"I have had another thought: Could I be attracted to these weaker men because it puts *me* in the stronger position? Am I attracted to men with whom I also can feel stronger, as well as threatened, submissive, inferior? Could I be trying to escape the submissiveness Father wants in me by getting a man who will not be controlling, but who will be submissive to me? Then *I* would be the controlling one. This would be a tendency to identify with Father . . . . I think all my dynamics come down to my need for love and dependence on the one hand, and the hostility and guilt on the other. If I felt only loving and true to Father, I would not be tempted to start a dead-end affair. I would want and find a husband like the Father I wholeheartedly loved and admired, instead of being tempted by the opposite."

There is much to be learned here: how conflict between parents, even if they both love the child deeply and wisely, can threaten the child's relations with his peers and jeopardize his love life by driving him or her to mishandle the sexual urges and make a marriage of misery.

A later interview with Jane brought certain of her dynamics into sharper focus:

"I see what you mean by conditioning," she said. "I want Father's love. But I can get it only by being subservient and submitting to his childish dictatorial ways. So I feel the love of any man as handsome and successful as Father will be the same way . . . I don't dare attract the love of such a man because I can't stand that subservient attitude in me   I flee from it. But since I am young and sexual I guess I compromise by trying to get love from a man who is as unlike Father as possible, and such a man is usually not husband material.

"And I see what you mean about my dreams being ones of violence, never happy or romantic ones. I had another dream in which I was dying of cancer, and was so sad about leaving the rest of my life behind; to this I associate my emotional involvement with the beatnik boy, who is all wrong for me, and this would mean leaving my normal true life. The cancer that is threatening my life is my anger at Father . . . some day I have to tell him what I think. I am so mad at him! I see that now; you are right, I can't think of revenge on him except in a masochistic way that hurts myself, such as throwing his money in his face, quitting school, having an affair, marrying a bum."

Her dream shows one of the most fateful mechanisms of the human mind: how a person's hostility can be turned against himself. His own hostility can be projected outward and experienced in dreams as being attacked, or projected inward and felt as attack by disease from within. In real life these dynamics are felt as symptoms such as anxiety, danger from people or from disease. This is the nucleus of paranoid and hypochondriacal thinking. On a larger social scale, it explains why economic, political and social changes often involve bloodshed—the hostility comes out directly toward others and masochistically toward oneself.

A subsequent interview with Jane went as follows:

PATIENT: Father is so hard on Mother. He's worn her down, and she is weakened by it. Mother loves Father, wants his affection, but is not getting it.

Mother has much love to give and could have had a wonderful marriage. But she is insecure and is tired out by Father and is hiding this at home. At times I have felt pessimistic and that they should divorce so Mother would have a chance for a better life. But should they now? Mother has no strength left.

ANALYST: Can you give me some examples?

P: A woman friend of Mother's is having a breakdown, and Mother thought they should go over to be with the woman, who wants them to come. Mother couldn't go early in the evening because of Grandmother, and Mother finally went about 9 P.M. Father was angry and said, "You should have thought ahead, etc.," as though it was Mother's fault.

Another example: When dinner is not ready at seven, Father is so angry as though Mother did it deliberately; it is the same if Mother forgets to heat the plates. Father has an image of Mother as what she is not, as though Mother is deliberately doing those things which will hurt him, but to me and Sister, Father is all love and affection.

A: Why do you suppose he does this?

P: He has an image of women and what he expected from his mother, and he wants his wife to fill that image instead of taking her as she is. He is constantly resisting any other image, and little squabbles or the chance to express his resistance are symptomatic.

A: What do you think are the underlying causes?

P: I'm not sure, but I think it is his hostility to women. Father has many fears and hostilities. Father does not have the love for people that Mother does.

They went to a concert at Mother's school, and Mother wanted to stay and socialize, but Father refused. That is awful. He should have stayed in the spirit of fun, but he made it clear he only did it because Mother was foolish enough to want to go. So I think Father initiates those squabbles, and Mother's hostility is in reaction. Yet if Father only showed a little love, Mother would forgive instantly. I guess I do think the trouble lies with my father. Mother supports Father in ways he needs, but Father does not support her.

For example, if Father does anything at work, Mother enters in and gets enthusiastic for and with him. But Father never enters into anything with Mother's work at the hospital. Mother is now weakened and self-centered and gushes on, about the hospital and her problems: but Father is strengthened—he is less shy and insecure with people. After a party we had, Mother was crying because she lost all her assurance and felt that all she said wasn't worth saying and that people picked on her.

A: Why do you think she feels this way?

P: If she had a happy marriage and really if she were supported by Father . . . but Father is not supportive at all. He only undermines her. Mother supports Father.

A: Have you spoken with Mother about this?

P: Oh, yes. She needs support and is not getting it from Father and talks to me, but now I've become bored with it. But Father speaks with me very little about it. Yet Mother does not want to talk with me about their problems and feels guilty doing so. I hear their problems so much that I have gotten self-righteous and will not talk with them about mine. Father asked what I thought of their problems and I told him.

I think Father wants Mother to be like his mother. Like a little boy who wants his mother to serve him, have his plates hot, give him this toy and that toy. As when Father made a list of petty demands, childish things. Mother makes almost no demands on Father; but he will insist on such things as one or two parties a week. Yet with me, Father is so loving, just unbelievable, couldn't be nicer. Yet it doesn't have the right quality of concern . . . it is sentimental and overdone. He makes no demands on Sister and on me.

A: Can you tell me something about your situation at school?

P: This year I am a senior and my friends have left. The whole bunch has shipped out. I have become shy with people—I can't speak up in class; but none of this is serious. Part of the time I think I am great and a senior, but wonder what to do with my life. My chief problem is my timidity. I cannot speak up in class, cannot speak up with boys, but actually I guess I *do*. But I act old-fashioned and not bold until I know them well. I think I give an image of being sweet and incompetent. I feel competition with girls; they'll do more with their lives than I will. I always hated those girls' schools. Mother feared that I had hostility to men, but I don't think so. I like boys, and they like me. I have been too much of a crusader in my family. Being

put upon. Can I help with Sister or with Brother, with other people's problems? My feeling now is that I can give support and love and let them solve their own problems.
A: That is very good. We can only help people to help themselves. Do you have any other problems or any other reactions to the home situation?
P: Not much, although I have thought it would be nice to have a stable home to bring people to. My brother and sister and I always stuck together. Brother was close and a great support to me. I don't think we have suffered much in the shuffle. I feel all my problems are in control if I work on them, and I am not timid toward situations (i.e., I hitchhike) or toward people I don't know. Only to contemporaries.

I hate to see Father and Mother struggling along like this; it's a waste of life. Mother is losing strength for a divorce and to begin afresh. What if psychoanalysis does not work? Father is so closed, not like Mother. When he asked what was wrong in his treatment of Mother, I told him but felt it only touched the surface, that I did not really reach him. And yet he tried for a day or two.

Father's mother is tall, imposing, rigid, *authoritarian,* she whipped her sons with belts, and is so negative to my sister and insecure. She has a fear of people. [No wonder, I thought, if she treats them so badly!]

Four months later a subsequent interview with Jane revealed the following:

P: I am working on a small newspaper and have applied to a school of journalism. Sexually I am insecure, relaxed with boys I like, but some of them tell me that I am afraid of sex and I have dreams about fear of sex. Sometimes this scares me. I had a dream in which a friend, a boy, took me to a beautiful stadium and there lived a group of his friends who were having a beautiful, free life with a beautiful view of the city; then Negroes and Puerto Rican hoodlums came up until there were six or seven and I thought it was the worst situation of my life, but at least I'd only be raped and not killed. Then the friends fought them.
[With no associations to this dream, we can only guess that there is a yearning for "a beautiful free life," which contains

some elements of escape from the rebellion against her parents and their conflicts, and that the hoodlums are projections of her own repressed hostilities, and that sex is a way of expressing rebellion and escape but also a pathway by which the hostility is turned—by guilt?—against Jane, making the rape fantasy.]

A: What about your home situation?

P: Mother gets on my nerves.

A: What more can you tell me about the period from 0 to 6?

P: I was happy: I loved Father and Mother and felt loved. I was happy with Brother and Sister. I remember Father picking ticks off us after a picnic and being very tender. One of my first memories was when Sister was born. Mother said for me to go tell Father that she had decided to call the baby "B___." and I thought something was wrong that Mother did not talk it over with Father. Brother used to put me down and say, "Oh, she can't tell time!" I wanted to hit babies, and wanted to see them cry. In kindergarten, a boy was angry and hit me, and I thought he would get sticks for Christmas because he was so bad. I was pretty and cute and Queen of the May.

Our family was very close. I was proud of my family, I thought we were the best, but later I found out we had problems too. In all our moves I felt I did not fit into the world but did fit into the family. Outside I was too thin or fat or did not fit in well. My family meant more to me than others' to them. Do all kids feel the same? I was not mature till later, and I was shy. But that is now behind me; now I can operate. Sunday mornings we all went into Father and Mother's bed together. That was pretty idyllic. I remember Mother coming home with Sister from the hospital and my having no feeling for Sister or about the whole thing. [And note above impulses to hit babies.] I once had a friend and wondered why Mother didn't like her. Something special was happening; Mother was making a dress for me. We were under the table pretending we were buttercups. Brother and I were punished by Mother for not acting better to our cousins. Father was cool and authoritarian, and we would do what he said, but we were closer to Mother. We could talk back to her.

Once I had a terrible problem of homesickness. When I was four years old, once overnight, I felt awful and attacked by a feeling of melancholy—a lonesome feeling; nor would I have gone away to boarding school.

I always thought of myself as the girl who fell out of the second-story window, although I have no memory of that happening. [There was no evidence to support this, but the thought flashed through my mind that it might mean Jane thought of herself as one who survived a danger, and it might signify confidence that she would overcome whatever difficulties she now faced, which indeed she did.]

Actually my first memory was about age four, when Sister came home from the hospital and Mother said something about her name. Maybe I thought of Mother as snobbish. I really liked Mother, but did she drive us to some extent, as with friends whom she thought were not appropriate?

In third grade I had a crush on a girl in sixth grade. I remember Father was in uniform, looked so wonderful. He must have served for a few years in the Army.

I remember a childhood dream. A man threw something around me and I couldn't scream, and was to be kidnapped. [Again the theme of leaving home, without responsibility for doing so, because it is forced upon her by the hostility of a man. Is this her own anger and guilt toward her father?] Once I screamed because I thought I saw a man and a dog, and Father rushed in. [Again anxiety—is it because there is more anger as a result of these problems than Jane realizes?] I liked Father very much. I thought of myself as lonely because I felt I was different and romantic. I usually had one very close friend.

When Brother married I couldn't stand it, could not stand the girl. I had been very close to Brother. As I grew older, I grew disillusioned with Father and Mother, especially Father, and perhaps turned to Brother as a substitute. We were so close, and I expected that we would be together all our lives. I was always pretty and was told I was, and thought Brother was not so good looking, although it was not important.

Brother was taking flowers to an old lady once on his tricycle. I remember little of Brother because he was off with the boys and he kept me at a distance. Do we like each other very much? I thought of him as a little boy with his business, like a big train project, and no time for me. Father teased Brother for having a girlfriend, and I feared to have a boyfriend. Brother once ran away from home and returned the same night. I used to go next door at night to visit, and Brother ambushed me, and I hated it.

A boy chased me once; and maybe because of Brother I thought that if that boy liked me, I would be hostile to him and feared how I would ever get rid of him. I fear boys will like me excessively. I had sex only once; I was dared into it by a boy when I was traveling. [Despite her early homesickness and fear of the world, in college Jane came to love traveling—possibly as part of the trend toward leaving home and her unconscious reaction against her dependence on her parents.] In childhood I feared new situations and new schools.

A: Do these fears become related only as to the family, that is, excessive closeness, or to outsiders, to whom you are *not* close because you moved so often?

P: Yes, I fear a boy will like me excessively and wonder how I can keep him away. When I left him, the boy I had sex with threatened suicide. It was a terrifying experience.

Later Jane said she heard her mother's voice and repeated that she had excessive dependent-love needs [an obvious theme of her dreams and first memories], and feared rejection. "I isolate myself as a defense. I still have hostility toward babies. I have identification with hostile boys and am attracted to them." [Which might indicate in part that Jane unconsciously felt it was safer to identify with Father than with Mother, who suffered under Father's hostility.]

Jane repeated her conclusion that she had excessive dependent-love needs as the result of being overly loved as a child, and because the many moves of the family during her youth prevented close, sustained attachments outside of the home to peers. She was never able to keep friends in one school for more than a year or two before having to move on. In addition, she felt insecurity, torn by the tensions between Mother and Father. Father seemed selfish and hostile. Her dreams were frequently of sex, but never satisfied and always with hostile boys and am attracted to them." [Which might indicate college graduation, when she was living alone, a man forced himself into her room when she opened the door and tried to rape her, but she fought him off so viciously that he fled.] Were the dreams of hostile unhappy sex due to the usual ubiquitous repressive upbringing, especially of girls, or to her excessive dependent-love needs, or to hostility toward her Father? Jane felt her main trauma was the fights between Father and Mother, her fear of their being divorced, from about the age of six on, and her anger at her father for his treatment of her mother, and guilt for this anger because she also loved him and felt he loved her. These feelings toward her father could well produce the dreams of threatened rape and the problems in getting along with men.

A short telephone interview with her father went as follows:

FATHER: I've been a hard worker for 30 years. I give to my family, and I want entertaining once a week. This is necessary to me, and if I do not get it, I want a divorce. I also want arrangements for a social life while my wife is away on vacations because Jane can't have people in or go out alone. [I am still amazed at the outright selfishness of so many husbands, which probably repeats their childish demands upon their mothers, and is so devoid of recognition of their wives' needs as adults. (See Chapter 33, "Divorce.") Of course, small girls are often poorly reared too, and wives can be as selfish as husbands.]

ANALYST: Why not go slow with the divorce and win over your wife?

[Jane commented, "Father is really very mean to Mother, and without any insight." This opinion was fully confirmed by my personal interviews with her father.]

In my next meeting with Jane, I initiated the hour:

A: I will start this hour for a change and ask you to tell or remind me of your chief complaints, why you came to see me and why you are still coming.

P: I am a little anxious, and Mother thinks I am a little depressed.

A: How is everything in your life? Do you have any problems in your schoolwork or with people?

P: Yes, in fact I guess the main problem is that I'm not married and do not seem able to find a boy I care that much for who is interested in me. I don't seem able to attract boys, or rather, one I want to marry. I'm rarely attracted to boys who are not attracted to me.

Here I thought again of the ironies of life and the paradoxes of personality. This girl was as attractive as any I had ever met, not only in beauty of face and form but in intelligence, kindliness and understanding, one of the few persons one meets in a lifetime in whom the inner light shines through. Jane seemed so wholesome and healthy. I would have guessed that she was irresistible to boys. And I thought of the unattractive girls whom I had met, who always had dates or a boyfriend and who married young. What was there about Jane? This was our main problem. Evidently it stemmed, as just mentioned, from the relationship to her father and that between her Father and Mother.]

A: How long have you had any of these problems?

P: When I was about nine years old, I very suddenly lost my confidence in school, in studies and in making friends.

A: What was going on emotionally in that time?

P: Nothing any different

A: Any different from what?

P: From the tensions between Mother and Father. Except for one thing: I overheard them mention divorce. On hearing this, an abyss opened. I could not see how I could live if they divorced. All I saw was a dark void, and all my security vanished. But now I see, looking back, that I simply could not face the idea as a reality that my parents might actually divorce. It just became a dark abyss that I must avoid to survive. Abruptly I lost all confidence in myself, in my ability to do my school work and to make friends. I became afraid of school.

A: This sounds a little as though you repressed some of your anxiety about the possible divorce and transferred it to the school. I do not know this at all, but think it worth mentioning.

P: We once mentioned the probability that I feared the school as a defense against or avoidance of living with my real fear, that Mother and Father would divorce and destroy the family, which with all the moves we made from place to place and school to school was my only haven and security. I guess that does seem possible. Now as we discuss these things, I realize that there is a type of boy whom I resent and would never marry, and that is the button-down-collar, clean-cut, Ivy League, successful suburban type.

A: Do you know why you have this antipathy?

P: Well, that is the type Father is, and the type both he and Mother try to steer me toward. I guess I have resented Father's treatment of Mother for so long that I resent him and his type, and also fear him and his type. Eager as I am to marry, I certainly do not want to have a marriage like Mother's. I guess it is awful to think this way, but I have built up a lot of hostility to Father because of all this.

A: Why do you say it is awful?

P: Guilt, I guess. Father has always been nice to me and I feel terribly guilty about being hostile to him, even though I can't help it.

A: This is just the kind of emotional situation that makes masochism, a tendency to defeat or in some way injure oneself as a way of expressing hostility to parents. Let us watch for any such tendency. We have seen it in your dreams.

P: Yes, I have already noticed it and think that this guilt has had a lot to do with my not attracting a good husband. I almost consciously feel that I do not deserve one. This is in addition to my fear and resentment of these attractive, successful men who are Father's type.

Two days later:

P: I do not have anything particular that I want to start with today.

A: I do not like to start any session, but it may save us time in the long run if we take stock, either now or in a later hour, and review what we know. So if you have something, please tell it.

P: No, I don't. I would rather take stock.

A: Most of your feelings, as you talk freely, seem to express a mixture of reactions toward your parents, especially sympathy and identification with your Mother and resentment against your Father, plus some resentment against being pressured to marry a boy of the clean-cut, Ivy League type, and subsequent guilt for this resentment of your father. This interplay of feelings, the dynamics as we call it, seems to enter into your attitudes toward boys and marriage, your security and independence.

P: I have tried to be very independent.

A: True, but is this in reaction to a still unresolved wish to be dependent?

P: Yes, it could be.

A: But are there other dynamics, too?

P: Yes, I have some guilt, in fact quite a bit, toward my younger sister. I was envious and jealous of her all through childhood.

She was so sweet and got such adoration from both Father and Mother, and my brother also got it because he was the oldest and a boy, and of course ahead of me in everything. I guess I shy away from boys who are too much like my brother, for I am too envious and competitive toward them to be comfortable and relaxed. Also I do not trust them because I became very attached to my brother, and then he got married and went off and left me alone with the tensions between Mother and Father.

A: What types of boys exist that are not like your father or brother?

P: I don't know. Maybe ones that very much need me, who are dependent on me so I don't fear what will happen if I am too dependent on them and trust myself to them.

Jane had two dreams several months after starting treatment that revealed gratifying progress. In the first, she saw a man who attracted her in real life. In the dream he was nice but obviously rather tough, which he was not at all in actuality. In the second dream, some rough teenagers burned down their school. In both these dreams she was not personally threatened as she had been in earlier dreams; the danger was all externalized. Her associations to these dreams were about her own resentment of her father, her feelings of being submissive toward him, her rebellion against being the obedient good little girl, her wishes to be defiant and tough and able to stand up to him. "Burning down the school," she said, "is hostility to authority, and I guess I feel that way toward all authority because of Father. I recognize now that I've always had a secret sympathy for the underdogs. That must be part of my interest in foreigners and minority groups."

Jane dreamed of hoodlums in her earlier dreams because they were hostile and could be overtly what she denied to herself. She felt rebellious and hostile to authority but dared not show it. They were a projection of a repressed part of her own feelings. The young man in her later dream who was nice in reality, she made tough in her dream; by changing him into someone who could be tough under authority, she gave him the ability to act that she wished for herself.

When questioned about it, Jane admitted to a latent rebellion against me (the transference of her pattern to her father), a resentment against coming to see me, an anger at having to be so careful, so she thought, to please me in every detail. It was a vicious circle:

needing to please enraged her, but in order to hide the anger she had to be ultracareful to please:

The dynamics of masochism are not easy to grasp, but they are as vital to understanding individual lives as to understanding mass behavior. Repressed hostility, often far from conscious awareness, can produce self-injury in many ways. In Jane it caused a fascination for hostile, dangerous underdogs. This might have even propelled her into marriage with one. Jane felt guilt toward the father with whom she was angry but whom she still loved, and from this guilt came tendencies to punish herself. The repressed hostility toward her father was turned against herself. This is the key to so much behavior in which an individual repeatedly defeats himself despite his best efforts to succeed—and it is why groups and nations so often do the same.

Follow up. This was not the end of the therapy, but should convey the main dynamics that need to be worked through. What happened to Jane was this:

She fell in love with a mature young man who was good to her, but for extraneous reasons marriage was not advisable. She had the willpower to see this and to go against her masochism and break off the relationship. A year or two later she married a man who was devoted to her and proceeded to make what seems to be an entirely harmonious marriage with two fine children. This man was just what her dynamics predicted and wanted: in part like her father and brother (in being handsome, clean-cut and having a superior intelligence) and in part not like them. Unlike Jane's father, he had a good, very close relationship with his mother that gave him the model to be a good husband and father.

Then Jane's parents did actually divorce. Soon both were remarried. I do not know about her father's second marriage except that it held; but Jane's mother, Enid, had been so criticized and put down for so many years by her husband that at first in her new marriage she felt unworthy and insecure. We met occasionally throughout all this, and then one day she phoned me and said, "I have never been so happy. Now at last I am beginning to think that I really *can* be a good wife." Enid's new husband was a superior man, I later discovered, who had had a fine marriage until his first wife died.

While there is much to be said for the analytic guideline of not having contact with members of a patient's family, this is only a guideline and must be balanced in individual instances against what are sometimes enormous advantages, such as seeing at first hand the principals in the patient's dynamics, and getting from them certain life views of the patient to balance the analyst's narrow office view.

After due deliberation and also after discussion with Jane and with her full knowledge, I did have talks with her Mother, Enid, and also Jane's father, Edwin.   Both confirmed the descriptions Jane had given me. Her mother was warm, outgoing, highly intelligent, sincere, eagerly seeking support and help.   She had been the baby of her family and much attended by her older brothers. Her dynamics were not entirely clear at first, but my impression was that Enid sought this brotherly devotion, interest and support from her husband and did not receive it. Also, she had been close to her mother, more so than to her father. Jane's father, Edwin, was also all I had been told: handsome, straightforward, with a keen mind, yet not psychological because he was defended strongly against seeing any hostility in himself or in his treatment of his wife and others, such as in his fast and dangerous driving deliberately to "tease" his wife and children when they were in the car with him. Asked about his background, he answered that the outstanding person was his mother. I subsequently met her and talked with her. She was all I had heard: tall, large-boned, with an overpowering personality. Her husband had been away a good deal, and she had raised the children alone, at times using strict discipline, with corporal punishment, until she could send the boys away to boarding school. Jane's father, Edwin, told me that he was terribly lonely at school, where he felt he had to fight to survive. He still had this psychology. He felt that after all he did and having worked so hard, yet he got little from his wife and children in return. He felt deprived; he wanted much, and resented giving. He showed a strong current of anger and resentment for all this, of which he was unaware. He also identified with his strong, dominating mother, and thereby showed a strength which no doubt was attractive to women and originally was part of what prompted his wife to marry him.

Thus the causes of Jane's problems could be traced back two generations, to her emotional interrelations with her parents, who affected each other and Jane in certain ways because of *their own* childhood patterns.   It was easy to see how Jane's mother, the warmly adored baby girl with doting older brothers, was attracted to the tall, strong, masterful young man and became his wife without seeing the deprived little boy underneath and the cruelty, hostility and resentment of giving within . . . resentment arising because of treatment by his mother in early life.   It was easy to follow the thread of how frustrations developed between them, out of each one's dynamics, and to see how these affected Jane in the ways mentioned above.

It is one thing to have adequate facts to trace back *causes*, but much more detailed and precise information is required to describe *determinants*   We can trace Jane's problems back through her parents to her grandparents, but I do not think that we can demonstrate from the grandparents why her parents would have such specific difficulties as to predetermine Jane's particular strengths and problems.   Our knowledge is not accurate enough quantitatively. Will it be a curse or a blessing when it becomes so?   If I had the skills of a novelist, I would start with Jane's paternal grandmother and with the mother and brothers of Jane's mother, tracing the emotional forces through these generations to Enid and Edwin and their outcomes in Jane's problems and great strengths.   Perhaps the literature of the future will be expected to do this more than it has been done in the past.

In trying to understand a person's dynamics in terms of his major emotional relationships as a small child to those closest to him and responsible for him (usually the members of his family or substitutes), we try to understand his feelings in terms of identifications and object relationships as previously mentioned; this seems to be a good general principle.   Children are generally disturbed and often form pathological patterns of reacting because of tensions between parents, and this is closely tied in with a child's identifications and object relations.   The child may be torn by his unconscious tendencies to identify with both parents equally; in some cases the child is threatened in his dependence on one parent, perhaps the mother, because of tensions with her husband.   We have seen that Jane identified mostly with her mother in the tensions between her parents.

With these thoughts in mind we now return to Enid, Jane's mother. She was an attractive, superior person in her mid-forties.   In the first interview, Enid complained vaguely that something was "not right." More than 90 percent of these first interviews yield insight into an area in which pathological dynamics lie. They are usually golden opportunities to gain a clarity of perspective that is often lost when treatment is begun (Saul, 1972, p. 136). With Enid, however, I could not see clearly the central dynamics in the first interview. I suspected that this vague sense of something being wrong had to do with her sense of guilt. She had very good relationships with both her parents, especially with her mother, but also an easy, loving relationship with her father. There was some tension between her parents, which Enid did not understand, and we could not yet connect it with her dynamics.

The deeper motivations, reactions and feelings, the unconscious forces, are revealed through the history and present pattern of the person's life, and through the first memories, dreams and associations and what they tell of the emotional pattern of childhood. Enid's current life situation was tension with her husband. As we have seen, she had a grown son and two daughters, all three of whom had some minor emotional problems. Her spontaneous material dealt with her resentment against her husband. How much of Enid's resentment against her husband was *reactive* to his bad treatment of her, arising from his childhood pattern, and how much was *internal*, with Enid blaming him and being hostile to him because of frustrations within herself that stemmed from her own childhood pattern?

Of course, the analyst must always see both marital partners, for each alone may tell a very convincing story that conflicts with the other's account.

Now it became clear in interviews with Enid's husband, Edwin, and with his mother that Edwin had indeed been dominated by a strong, controlling mother and had also been deprived by her. It seemed evident that he had great resentment toward his mother that was repressed, but which he was taking out on Enid after the pattern toward his mother. One certainly does not like to see a divorce, especially between good people in their mid-forties who have lived together this long, raised children and gone through the vicissitudes of adjustment. Neither of them likes the idea of making a "fresh start." The husband usually has his work to occupy him; so he has both financial independence and outside interests, but the wife usually finds herself all alone without means of support or proper skills and experience to make her own way. Usually her whole life and profession has been her husband and children. Now she faces a lonely life, with serious financial insecurity. The man usually has less difficulty supporting himself and finding another wife. This is especially true for those wives who grew up before the days of women's liberation.

I asked Edwin for details of the marital friction, and he related incidents in which his hostilities to Enid arose over what seemed to me to be trifles. For example, he became enraged if, after a breakfast that Enid had arisen early to prepare, she did not stand up to kiss him good-bye. Apparently it never occurred to him that he was the husband and maybe he should bend down to kiss *her*, thanking her for the breakfast. He would tease Enid in cruel ways, as by driving the car dangerously, knowing it frightened her, by splashing her with water, rocking a boat or canoe while on vacation. He often teased the children, annoying and frightening them and of course thereby upsetting Enid. Underneath it all were his domination and his demands for attention and service, exaggerated by emotional deprivation in childhood.

Enid felt she simply could not go on with her marriage. I stayed out of the decision, keeping to the role of merely helping as best I could to clarify the dynamics of each and their emotional interplay, and helping Enid to see what the future might be like if a divorce eventuated. In order to understand more fully, I asked Enid's husband to have his mother come in and tell me her view of the situation.

When she strode into my office, I immediately felt she was indeed the key. Our interview, as already mentioned, confirmed this impression of an overwhelming personality. Yet I found myself liking her. She too was the product of her own childhood; she was straightforward and doing her best. She did have love and had done a good job of raising Edwin; in most ways he was a fine man, in fact, in all ways except as a husband. But my first impression of her was correct and relevant: she had dominated her son using corporal punishment and rejecting him by sending him off to boarding school as soon as she could. Thus dominated and deprived, Edwin reacted with strong but unconscious hostility to his mother and later in life never let himself be in a submissive, emotionally dependent relationship, especially to a women. Partly as a defense, he identified with his mother, trying to dominate other persons without warmth or sympathetic understanding in order to avoid being dominated or deprived by them, yet still always *feeling* that he was. He unconsciously made his frustrated demands of childhood on his loving, intelligent wife, and took out on her his hostilities to his mother, and also treated Enid as his mother had treated him. Edwin could be kind to the children because they were small and helpless, and more remote from being mother figures who would dominate him and deprive him. Edwin's mother entirely repressed her negative feelings toward him during childhood, rationalizing it all as the best possible childrearing to develop a strong, self-disciplined, independent man (which worked insofar as there was love and gentleness for the son to identify with the strengths of his mother) Edwin in turn was totally oblivious to his own hostilities He came to see me about a dozen times; once he seemed to catch a glimpse of his childhood pattern with its demands and hostilities and what he was doing to his wife, and it seemed barely possible that he might work on these and soften them, freeing himself to develop enough love to be a tolerable husband.

But Edwin's insight soon vanished under his rigid repressions. It seemed to me that divorce was inevitable if, as Jane said, Enid's health was to be saved before he unconsciously beat her down further. (For example, he once invited her on a camping trip and Enid was delighted—but then Edwin plagued her unmercifully with practical jokes.) The central goal was now to save Enid. I had to let the relationship take its course.

Yet in a way the story ended happily, as happiness goes in this life. Edwin remained completely unconscious of his own hostility and had no interest in seeing me or any other psychiatrist to explore his own feelings. He came to see me only a few more times after Enid seriously threatened divorce.

Once she obtained her freedom, Enid felt tremendous relief. And then she met an outstanding man, George, whose wife had recently died. Thus fate or chance, or whatever one calls it, so often plays a crucial part in therapy, as in life. Many women were pursuing George because he was so attractive as a man and had been so good a husband. Enid came to see me again because she had a vague sense of guilt that she feared might get in the way of her relationship to George. I thought I could do little more than give her support, mostly through the classic method of trying to understand what was going on emotionally in each interview. I feared I was taking both my time and her time and money to no avail. But later, Enid told me that she never could have gotten through the divorce or the months of being alone, or have married George, without my help. This shows how very hard it often is for the therapist to know the therapeutic process until much later.

Her marriage with George was a resounding success, one of the happiest I had ever seen—not just for Enid but also for George. His relationship with his first wife had been excellent, but his marraige with Enid was more so. Enid kept in touch with me by occasional telephone calls and sporadic visits. Several years later she again came to see me, not because of acute problems she said, but "just to check up on things." Often as a person changes, his or her capacity for new insights also changes. Enid was now happy and free at last from Edwin's hostilities. In this interview I made a fresh approach to her basic dynamics. She still had a feeling of a lack of self-confidence, and this time, with little effort on my part or hers, the reasons emerged quite clearly:

Although her parents loved each other and loved her, Enid felt that her father was of lower caliber than the other men she met once she began to date. It was hard for her to define "caliber." I sympathized with her because it is indeed difficult to know what we mean when we use that word for a human being. It usually means the size of the bore of a tube, mostly applied to guns. We determined that for her it meant "moral level," merit, excellence of capability and character, and certainly included a capacity for love, generosity, identification and understanding. As a result of this feeling, Enid had been ill at ease out in the world with other men of "high caliber" whom she met and dated. She felt uneasily that she was not superior herself. This was an identification with her father, but a conflictful one. She was at ease with somebody of her father's caliber, but not with those whom she considered "above" him. This was all in her own mind. The vague uneasiness she initially complained about to me she herself considered to be guilt, but it turned out to be mostly shame connected with these inferiority feelings. Enid had no sense of harming anyone and deserving punishment, which is the essence of guilt; she only felt inferior to and therefore unworthy of others, which is more related to shame.

Some of this feeling persisted in her excellent marriage to George. It was improving, of course, under this blessing that life had afforded her, in addition to her fine children. Her new insight helped enormously. She could see her very real, superior traits with a realization that had developed and sustained her during the ordeal of her divorce and afterward. Now she could see that the inferiority feelings were not realistic in terms of her actual personality and behavior; she was in all ways superior and possessed none of the traits she felt uneasy about in her father. In fact, Enid was without question of the "highest caliber," mentally, physically and emotionally.

We might say that her problem had been shame for her father, but it did not surface until she was grown, out in the world, meeting other men. We did not continue therapy long enough to uncover the source of this low regard for her father. But with it went the feeling that she could love and be loved by a man like her father, but *not* by the highest caliber of man, which is what she wanted in a husband. This idea, connected with "narcissism," now seemed a form of masochism and perhaps was a reason she had married a man as hostile to his mother and wife as Edwin. This conflict now appeared resolved. She could see that fate was kind to her in giving her George, and kind to George in giving her to him. As George said, she was "true blue."

Enid's dynamics were a little different from the simple disordered relationship of a child to his parent or to a sibling, or to particular tensions within a family. I was glad that I had remained open-minded and told Enid those few years later, when she returned for the interview, that I had never understood her dynamics. Then, when we went through them again, she quickly illuminated the missing link in her childhood emotional pattern, which caused her feelings of uneasiness, lack of self-confidence, inferiority and insecurity, socially and even in her second marriage. I felt that Enid really got the essence of what I had to contribute by seeing this clearly at last and being well on the way out of it. Happily, her already excellent second marriage continued to improve. George adored her and could not believe his good fortune in finding her. Jane was by then happily married with two fine children of her own, and although we never again met professionally, we continued as friends. [As previously noted, only very rarely do I allow a professional analytic relationship to become at all social and friendly because no one is ever fully analyzed nor is the transference ever resolved completely, and there is no certainty that the person will not need you again professionally.]

Jane and Enid were two of my favorite people, "true blue" and of the "highest caliber." It was partly through analyzing their childhood emotional patterns that our goal had been reached: each was settled with a husband who was also of highest caliber. We could relax with confidence in the emotional health of their next generation, Jane's children.

The years flew by. Jane lived at a distance and was in town visiting her mother one early fall. It was an opportunity to take them to lunch; so I played "hooky" and the lunch was both leisurely and jolly. Little did we think then, after all we had achieved, with Enid happy in an excellent marriage, that nine months later she would be dead of cancer. But she lived on in Jane, who had identified with her and taken into herself her mother's strength and beauty of personality.

References

Saul, L. J. (1972): *Psychodynamically Based Psychotherapy.* New York: Science House.

10
DOUBLE BIND

Sex in humans can break loose as an almost impersonal mechanism, draining all sorts of nonsexual tensions; it can be used to serve every purpose other than love, mating and parenthood. A man goes to a prostitute for sex without love; she in turn gives herself to him for money, not for love. Certain men and women react to any buildup of tension—from studies, business, home, from any source whatever—by an intensification of sexual feelings that they feel compelled to relieve in some way, whether with a partner or by masturbation. We have noted that some people experience sex in so detached a fashion that for them love *inhibits* gratification. They can only feel sexually free with a partner who represents simply a body and not a personality. When the personality of the partner enters the picture, their sexual drive is not enriched but is dampened or even extinguished.

Emotional disturbances disrupt mating in many other ways. Here is a husband, Art, in whom the sex drive, partially separated from the human relation, was strong enough to begin a marriage until other feelings within him turned the relationship into an intolerable battle.

His wife, Amy, sat in my office, blonde and buxom, intelligent and tense. She seemed shy, but glowed with the freshness of her 24 years despite the strain she was under. This is what she told me:

"I am confused. I am deeply in love with my husband, and I am sure he is with me. He courted me for a year and a half. He swept me off my feet. He wined and dined me and tried in every way to seduce me. He could not live without me. I began to give in. Since we were to be married soon, I did give in. [These sexual aspects she tells with difficulty.] Sex was intense and he was insatiable. Maybe I became so too. But then he began to have doubts about getting married. I did nothing to hold him. I did not want him if he did not want me, even though we were so intimate. Finally I broke it off.   But no sooner was this done than the phone began ringing.   He couldn't stand it without me.   So it was on again.   But then he began to feel trapped.

"It was not easy.   I was so in love with him.   But then I just wanted peace, to be left alone, to have my own life back again.   But it was no use.   He phoned.   He came.   He could not stand it without me. At last I thought it was off for good and left for a vacation from it all.   But within the week he had found me and insisted on marriage— marriage immediately, and promises of everything.   I knew he could and would keep his promises.   He is enormously energetic and smart and generous.

"This time it stayed on, and three weeks later we were married and took off for our honeymoon in New Orleans.

"Even on the train he was not himself.   He was subdued.   The first morning in New Orleans the weather was perfect.   I was eager to go sight-seeing, to explore.   But Art had no interest in anything. He wouldn't leave the room.   He complained of a stomachache and a terrible headache.   He was depressed.   He began worrying about money.   It was terrible.   Have you any idea of what it's like to live with a depressed person?   Well, perhaps you do.   It is unbearable. After four days of this we returned to Chicago.   That was about a year ago.

"Art got back to work and came out of that depression.   But for the past few months he has been insisting on a divorce.   I am confused because, although he wants a divorce, he talks and acts as though he cannot live without me.   He makes love night and morning.   A few days ago he said he could not stand the marriage any more and definitely wanted a divorce.   Of course, I was upset. I'm still in love with him.   Last night I was listening to the radio to take my mind off all this, and he came in and insisted I come to bed with him, because he could not sleep without me.   And today he suggested we go up to Wisconsin for a skiing weekend together. Will you see him if I can get him to come?"

I looked at this young woman.   Some women are physically attractive but psychologically impossible.   Once at a dance I cut in on a gorgeous blonde, but there was something so wrong there that by the end of the dance, even though we had hardly spoken, my interest in her had vanished.   Young as I was, it flashed through my mind that something in her makeup must repel other men also and might be tragic for her. But I had no such sense about this girl. She seemed in all ways desirable.

It is difficult enough to evaluate one person, and five times harder to discern the interactions of two in a marriage. I could not but look forward with interest to an interview with this vigorous, smart, able, successful, generous, highly sexed husband who could awaken in a hotel room in a fascinating city with this charmer in his bed and thereupon get pains in his head and stomach and plunge into a depression. There was a disturbing possibility that this young wife's confusion might stem from her failure to discriminate between sex and love. Perhaps in herself sex and love and romance and responsibility were normally fused, and hence she could not perceive or perhaps even imagine their being split into separate components in her husband.

Her husband came for an interview, not reluctantly but eagerly. His eagerness sprang in part from a genuine belief that something was wrong in him which he wanted to change. But in part, as soon became apparent, he was also trying to use me to help him get a divorce immediately. This conspiratorial element I totally rejected, but said I would like to hear how it all seemed to him.

He was a rather small, wiry, intense muscular young man, with a shock of unruly red hair. He was 29 but exuded an air of authority that one might expect in an older man. If his barely controlled inner tension found expression in sex, one could easily see how he attracted girls and why his sexual activity was above average. The interview went as follows:

PATIENT: I've been so depressed, so exhausted, that I can hardly work. I have the weight of the world on me.

ANALYST: What do you mean by "depressed"? You seem energetic enough now.

P: That's only since yesterday. Until then I couldn't even think.

A: Was this improvement after you agreed to come to see me?

P: Yes—I see—yes. Maybe it's connected. The train trip for the honeymoon was rather delightful, but when we hit New Orleans I couldn't function. I was depressed, wanted an annulment. I almost stood the girl up and didn't marry her. I almost broke the engagement, but I had her on my brain. When I can go to bed with her, that's it. Do you think sex every morning and night for an hour or two is normal, or is it a strain? Why does she attract me so? Is it just her body? I think it is all sex, only sex. We are from different worlds. She reads her way through life. She likes ballet. She goes for doilies, place arrangements at parties, travel, books, interesting guests. I can't stand these things. What I like is food, drink, horses, skiing, the sports page, the comics, comfort, having my feet up. I was born behind the stockyards. I've come up the hard way, had to defend myself in fights with some rough characters, some of the lowest and toughest. I'm lucky enough to be real smart in business. I have a trucking business, and it's doing pretty well in spite of the Depression. [The business depression of the 1930s.] But I don't go for culture. I like a woman who doesn't care about musicales, and, if a policeman stops her car, she tells him to go to hell. I've slept with women all the time, all kinds.

A: What kinds?

P: Never prostitutes, if that's what you mean. I just go for a girl and she goes for me. We go someplace—her place, my place, a hotel. Sometimes it's great; sometimes I can't even get an erection. I've had all these women since I was 15, but I've never paid a girl.

A: When did you first have a depression?

P: I've had some all my life, but not so bad until three or four years ago. Oh, you think it's connected with all these women? It could be, because after being with a woman, many times I'd feel depressed.

A: Tell a little about the emotional relations in your family during your very earliest childhood.

P: My mother was in charge of the house. My two older brothers and father were subservient to her. I have a sister eight years younger, but I never had much to do with her. My mother threatened me with Father, told me if I was bad he would beat me. But he never did. She was always criticizing him and blaming him. He always acted guilty, as though he had to make up for something to her. He was only work, work, work. He works in the stockyards—for Armour. He is goodhearted but could never relate to me. We did nothing together. He never brought me anything. He never taught me anything, like playing ball. When I was older and went to a game or a movie or on a date, he never asked if I had a good time, but only why I came home so late. He never stood up to my mother. Neither did my brothers. In fact, my brothers beat on me just the way my mother did, and she let them. My mother babied me. She made special lunches, wouldn't let me eat what the other boys ate or dress the way they did. I guess she wanted me to be something better than they were. I was dependent on her but embarrassed by my dependence. The other boys didn't play with me much; so I kept returning to Mother all the time. She was the boss. I felt a lot of love and a lot of hate toward her. She rode my father too much. My brothers and I were never close. They tried to rule me too. Mother and Father said they could; so they tried, but I resented it. My father couldn't assert himself. Everybody rode him.

A: What are the very first memories in your whole life?

P: The first is that the kids would not play with me, and Mother was trying to be reassuring. Another memory was that Father forgot to do something for Mother, and she wouldn't talk to him, and he felt awful. Father was always subservient. He never was like other fathers. He never said, "Come on out and let's hit a ball," or "Come on to a ball game," or come and do anything together.

   [Mother seems to be the central theme in these earliest memories. Relationships with other children fail, and Mother is the consolation. Father demonstrates that one must please Mother or feel awful. But this implies resentment of Mother for having to do so. Mother is the central figure, as in his life women are. The love and hate for mother seem to be the key.]

A: Did you dream last night?

P: Yes, I dreamed my wife and I were in a train wreck. I tried to save her, get her out, but couldn't. Then a man got me out.

   [This dream seems like a frank expression of a wish for his wife to be lost. The man who saves him probably represents his wish toward me, the way he sees me and analytic help.]

P: You asked when I was first depressed. I was depressed when I was about 17. It was before the stock market crash. All the other kids found jobs, but I couldn't. Mother said I would be president of a giant corporation, and Father said he would get me started. But I went from one job to another. The reason was because I had to direct whatever it was. I had to run the business. I've always had great drive. When I got my own business—trucking—I did well, and it's not an easy business. I've handled every kind of person, some pretty tough ones. I've always had a lot of sex drive too. My mother joked about it. She knew about the girls from an early age, and later I used to tell her, and she'd make jokes and think it was cute.

A: We are running out of time, and I think I should tell you my impression. The way I understand what we call your dynamics is roughly something like this—and you tell me freely where I am wrong: The main pattern of early childhood seems to be toward your mother and to consist of spoiling, overprotection and especially domination by her. The brothers reinforced the domination, and your father gave no model for standing up to it. This involvement with your mother rather cut you off in your childhood from friendships with other boys and girls. Because friends rejected you, you fell back on your mother. But why did they reject you? Was it *because* of the close involvement with your mother? Correct me if this impression that you have never had any close friends is wrong.

P: No, I've never had a real close friend.

A: Your choice of attitudes to people is limited pretty much by the ones you had toward your mother. If others are strong, you are threatened with being subservient, as you were with your mother. The escape from that is to *be* the dominating one yourself—you dominate others, become the boss, run the business, handle every kind of person. It is as though, in order not to be the submissive child or father, you must be the directing mother—with everyone. *Identification with the aggressor,* it has been called. At the same time, cut off from playmates, with little relation to your father or brothers, you were thrown back on and close to one single person, your mother—all the love and all the hate you mentioned. Perhaps that is why, without close friends, you seek everything in human relations with a woman. With a woman you look for all the love, but also you feel all the resentment, the rebellion and the need to dominate.

P: You mean they are all Mother?

A: And the opposite. You cannot stand being subservient, as you were to your mother. These women are probably both the wish for Mother and the attempt to escape from her.

P: Then is that why I can't resist my wife sexually? She is absolutely passive sexually. I can do anything I want with her. Other women react much more, are much better in bed—but maybe this is why she excites me. I am completely in charge—can do anything. And is that why I sometimes don't even get an erection with another woman I like better?

A. Meaning?

P: Well, I've noticed that I may have a lot more in common with a girl who is more my type, but she doesn't excite me much sexually. With my wife the only thing we have in common is sex. There is nothing else. When that goes there will be nothing. Another girl likes what I like, but I can't care that much about sex with her. That's why I didn't marry earlier and why I couldn't make up my mind about marrying Amy.

A: And the resentment of Mother may make an undercurrent of hostility to all women.

P: I'm not hostile to my wife. I just can't stand her except for the sex.

[I thought of the dream of his wife's being killed in the train wreck. He could have dreamed that he was divorced, that the marriage was annulled, that he was single and had never been married. It is harder to consider dreaming of his wife's being killed in a wreck as not hostile, but the time was up, and we would wait and see. At least he did not dream of killing her or of a man doing so. If he had, I would have been concerned.]

Further dynamics were suggested more or less strongly by the material. The mechanism of *identification with the aggressor* has already been mentioned. Subservience to the mother and brothers was contrary to the child's natural growth toward independence; submissiveness in his father made the mother and brother look down upon him. Probably for other reasons as well, the patient feared and disliked the tendencies in himself to give in to maternal control. It seems that he defended himself against his mother's domination by identifying with her in this; as she was the boss in the home, so he had to be boss with women and in business. Thus he could not hold an ordinary job because he felt compelled to be the director of whatever operation or business he was employed in. He could only function as the boss, not as a subordinate. And, apparently, he was only fully potent with women so utterly yielding that he felt he could do anything with or to them.

The childhood pattern continued in his having no close friends but in seeking complete emotional satisfaction from women. He lived out toward them the pattern toward his mother: the closeness to his mother, the emotional dependence on her, the being thrown back upon her because of rejection by friends, the hostility to her (which came through to the sorrow of every woman with whom he became close); the guilt for the hostility that got him into situations with women, which he found intolerable and from which he sought escape; the impotence with women like himself, i.e., like his mother. As with his mother, he could not live with a given woman or without her. His success in business, when he became the master of his own firm, stood in contrast to his intense but tolerable involvement with women.

This very brief interview alone reveals the depth and power of the motivations that enter into all close human relations, especially so intimate a relationship as marriage. Not always do these motivations appear quickly. Sometimes signs of them are evident in the first hours of the honeymoon; sometimes, as in this case, after a day or two. But often the deeper patterns of reactions only emerge after months or years.

This interview illustrates an aspect of the technique by which the dynamics operating in a personality are discerned. There is a fit between certain factors:

1. *The present emotional pattern* of a person's life (in this case, toward his business, which he directs well, and toward his wife, with whom intense feelings clash, as they do also in himself).

2. *The childhood emotional pattern,* which, as here, is continued into adult life.

3. *The life history,* which reveals this same pattern (perhaps different facets of it at different ages).

4. *The first memories.*

5. *The current dreams.* These memories and dreams may reveal not the entire pattern, but rather one or two essential aspects of it. (In this case, the common pattern of being rejected by friends and thrown back into the relation to Mother appears in the earliest memory, but the hostility does not. This hostility, however, is

quite undisguised in the current dream, in which, years later, the pattern toward his mother, and the defense by identification with the aggressor, have appeared toward his wife.)

Consistency in these five kinds of data is the most potent clinical tool as yet available for insight into the dynamics, the interplay of emotional forces, derived as we have seen from the childhood emotional pattern.

A case such as this cannot fail to impress us with what terrible chaos and cruelty there are sexually and personally in human reactions as compared with the equally powerful, yet clear, calm and well-ordered, so much more considerate and loving reactions between the sexes in most animals. Of course, this is true not only of relations between human males and females but of all human relations—in which hostility, in the form of cruelty, crime and war, is intrinsic to the human scene, to human history, to human dreams. And the source is the same as here: in childhood, in the first hours, days, weeks and months of life, from conception through the earliest years. There and then, by the way a child is treated, is determined the adult personality.

In the case of Art and Amy, Art's conflict tossed him back and forth. No sooner had he finally won his wife, married her and gone on his honeymoon than he panicked. He felt trapped into the relation to his mother and that he might lose his sanity if he did not get a divorce without delay. Since he had so recently expressed to his wife his undying love and devotion in words, sex and marriage, she naturally was reluctant to grant a sudden and ostensibly senseless divorce. Finally realizing Art's feelings, she agreed. But then again be panicked and felt he was falling apart. He could not stand the idea of being all alone or of moving into an apartment and eating in restaurants. Amy was becoming upset by all this fluctuating emotion and insisted on going ahead with their separation. His fears of loneliness and lack of a woman (mother-figure) upon whom he could be dependent proved justified. No sooner was he living alone and eating out than his anxiety and depression became intolerable. He had managed before marriage by having many affairs. But now he was no freedom-loving bachelor. It looked as though his childhood mixture of feelings toward his mother was now fully aroused and attached to his wife. Feeling desolate, isolated and unable to exist without a home, he began to consider suicide. If only his wife could relent and take him back, he was sure that the pain of this present banishment would burn forever and force him to accept the adjustment to marriage. So he wooed and pressured her—and eventually wore down her resistance until she wavered. He saw that she was about to let him return, and this was enough to fill him again with panic. He could see that his return after the separation was irrevocable—that he could not go back to his wife and then again leave her without incurring her total and irrevocable antagonism and rejection. It was literally true that he could not live with her and could not live without her.

He had no pattern in childhood of playmates, friends or relationships other than the overclose domination-rebellion, love-hate conflict with a mother whom he could not stand and could not leave. Now the conflict centered exclusively upon his wife, Amy. He could find no surcease in friends, sports or social relations. His stability at work was endangered. Panicked by being married to her and panicked by being separated from her, he began to fear that he would break down mentally or be driven to suicide.

In the end his wife sensed the threat to him that lay in returning to her and felt that she had been through too much to risk reunion. As it turned out, it was she who insisted on the divorce that he had at first in terror sought and then in terror fought.

This was a few months before Pearl Harbor. When America entered the war, Art joined the Marine Corps and, once in the Service, became much more stable, stayed out of trouble and served well. Art was not the only man that the armed services rescued from an emotional blind alley in private life.

I heard from Art some years after the war and found his later story of great interest. Almost immediately after returning to civilian life he became engaged and also began analytic treatment. It was violently stormy. He could not return to his old free, promiscuous bachelor existence. His new love, Janice, was quite like Amy, but a little more earthy and doggedly, almost masochistically, attached to Art. Again he oscillated, leaving her and returning. They married. He left again and took up with a woman, Phyllis, for whom he had no respect whatever. His new wife, Janice, had a child. He hated himself for being with his mistress when he had a wife and child, but lost all feeling for his wife and had none for his small son, although he boasted of his love for children. He could not tear himself away from Phyllis, the mistress. It was a rough analysis. But surprisingly enough, virtue was rewarded. After two and a half years he suddenly returned to his wife and son. He arranged to set up his business in Los Angeles and took off, saying he would bring Janice and the baby as soon as he was settled and had a place for them. Janice did not know whether she would ever see Art again, but eventually he did send for her, and they stayed together. He located a good analyst in Los Angeles. Then his wife wrote me that Art had been killed in an auto accident. His first wife, Amy, remarried and settled down and had two children; her second marriage was a relatively good one, nothing like the first one with Art.

Art's case typifies how conflict causes indecision and oscillation, compulsions and compulsive doubt, that are seen commonly in many forms. Some men cannot live with or without a girl before marriage; then in matrimony some settle down but others continue the oscillation. Still others find that they cannot tolerate either matrimony or promiscuity and reach a balance in long affairs with women who, because of their own problems, are willing to live with them unfettered by the marriage state. Some escape by alcoholic binges; some only withdraw emotionally; some run to other women, either with sexual desires alone or even with some feeling, only to seek the wife again as the one true love. Of course, women also show disturbed behavior because they, too, are vulnerable to trauma during childhood. Many a husband or wife is so unhappy in a marriage as to think seriously of divorce, but hesitates at the prospect of the separation being worse than the union. These frequent doubts and fears, and what may be behind them—how much is realistic and rational, and how much from childhood patterns—can usually be seen more clearly when exaggerated, as in the example we have given. The extreme is like seeing the moderate through a magnifying lens. Hence we have presented not a mild, usual bind, but a desperate double bind.

The accustomed behavior of each of us, that is, our usual personality, is the result of a balance of many and strong forces; therefore, it can be tipped in new and surprising directions. Even in a man with such extreme and apparently fixed but kaleidoscopic patterns as Art, I have seen sudden and surprising changes. One such man, in a year of analytic treatment, gained much insight but had not resolved his conflict. His wife then divorced him. He suffered. But only for a month or two. Then he met another woman.

She was young and attractive and most loving and considerate. She seemed to fit his needs exactly. He became equally loving, considerate and giving toward her. His conflict vanished. He could love and be loved and could again work freely, effectively and successfully. Whether the analytic help had prepared him to react thus well to what life brought, or whether the fit with the personality of this girl operated alone, the fortunate result was more freedom from conflict than he had ever known.

How this marriage held up I do not know, but it does recall those men and women of about 30 who come for treatment with the belief that something must be wrong with them, since they have not yet married, although they are burning to do so. The majority of them are correct; many have internal inhibitions or conflicts that keep them from a final commitment to anyone, even though they can love and be loved and are healthy, attractive and successful, and nothing is wrong with their sexuality. Some have no problems. They simply have not met the right woman or man. One mature young man of 30 said, "Now I have been happily married for a year to a girl I deeply love. I would have waited until I was 40 rather than marry just for the sake of marrying. I was waiting for a girl I could truly love, no matter how long it took to meet her."

One young woman was 29, and her friends were beginning to think she was just not the marrying kind. On a rare trip, a conversation started with the man in the seat next to hers. She told her parents, whom she was going to see, about it and added, "I think this is the man I will marry." They were shocked. But she did, and the marriage has been most satisfactory.

Of course it does not always work out so well—but neither do many other marriages, even though they are off to the most promising starts. We will give examples later of fine girls who soon discover that their choices are very poor husbands, and excellent men who find their wives to be hostile, demanding children. Some of these good people realize that they have "goofed," as one girl put it, lose no time in getting a divorce and are soon remarried to the right person. It is certainly wise, for the sake of the children, to give a marriage two years to settle down before having babies. Other couples do not divorce but muddle through. Some of these couples drive each other to the breakdown, or near it, of mind or body or both, and doom their children to serious emotional disorders. But some reach a reasonable adjustment, which may develop in a few years, or which may not develop for most of a lifetime. One philanderer settled down when his children were grown and he was 50— "I'm not much of a threat any more," he told me—and he and his wife had 20 fairly good years together.

There are as many childhood emotional patterns as there are people in the world. As the sex drive brings couples together, the childhood pattern of the one meshes or clashes with that of the other, producing every conceivable interrelationship and the whole range of marital problems, and their effects on the children of these parents.

11
HOSTILITY AND MASOCHISM IN MARRIAGE

Misery seeks not man, but man misery.

Frances Burney

I hate one of whom you know; and somehow that hatred of him keeps me from loving any human being.

Charles Kingsley, Westward Ho!

Sex is a physiological and psychological mechanism in its own right, but it often serves as a channel, path or drain for all sorts of impulses and feelings. Rapes and lust-murders express sex cut off from love, mating and parental feelings and used as an outlet for hate, violence and destructiveness. This sexual pleasure in cruelty gets its name, sadism, from its depiction in the writings of the Marquis de Sade. Its converse, sexual arousal through suffering, is termed masochism, from Count Leopold Sacher-Masoch's novel *Venus in Fur,* in which a man finds sexual satisfaction through being whipped by a woman wearing a fur piece. Originally the word was used narrowly for sexual pleasure in being hurt. It has gradually come to denote any trend toward being one's own enemy. One way among many to assure self-suffering is to marry a person who plays upon this unconscious tendency. One may unconsciously choose a spouse who is overtly or unconsciously cruel; or one may choose a kind and devoted partner but suffer anyway because of inner frustration, hostility and guilt.

Brenda, a petite, blue-eyed blonde of 31, told the following:
PATIENT: I can't stand my husband—and I don't know why. We went together for two years and now we've only been married two years, yet I can't stand him. But if I'm real nasty to him, then I want to make up. I feel guilty, and I'm afraid of his leaving me. I'm hostile to my mother and father too. Since I was a kid, my

father has mostly been angry at my mother. When he was angry, which was often, he would lash out at everybody. But the worst part of my childhood was that I had no freedom. Both my parents would say, "Later"—you can do this or that "later." But later never came.

Father was a martinet, and I was always subjected to his tyranny. He was very strict—a real Prussian. He did give me some affection, though—when I was very young—although he was always a tyrant. My brother was nine years older and hardly ever home. He went away to school pretty young. He didn't play much part in my life. Mother never gave me any real affection, or at least I felt she didn't. She was very negative. I know later on I'll feel guilty for talking this way about my father. He worked hard and was fairly successful.

ANALYST: How do you sleep?

P: Pretty well, and I have dreams every night but I can't remember them.

A: Any recent ones at all?

P: I dreamt that a man I went with died. I'm always afraid of dreaming of someone who died. And I often dream about a girl I know who criticized me when I was only 15 years old, and I am always trying to please her. Why was I so impressed?

A: What is your very first memory—way back before continuous memory?

P: Father used to like to play with me in bed. I used to jump up and down on the bed. Once he kissed me on the mouth, and I said something about it and he got mad and told me never to say it again. Also I remember finding a Kotex of my mother's and asking her what it was. She said it was for some trouble she had that made her bleed. I must have been over five years old but those are the earliest I remember.

A: What about other people in your life, besides your husband?

P: I have one girl friend and we get along very well. Except for her I'm not very close with anyone.

Some patients talk freely about their present lives but not about the past. This young woman comes with a marital problem and talks freely about her past. This gives us a good initial insight into her pathodynamics, and arouses our interest in how this combination of forces has shaped her life and the inner emotional atmosphere of her mind. What she has told so far fits together about as follows:

The picture in childhood (the 0 to 6 and later) is of difficulties in the only two close relationships of her life. The brief allusion to her brother gives the impression that he escaped from the home as much as possible and played no significant part in her life. Her mother is described as negative and not affectionate; so there is no sign of a warm, easy relationship there, but no overt struggle either. The pattern toward her father is the most vivid. Her relation to him was as to a tyrant; yet also he was apparently her source of affection. This dual relationship appears in her earliest memory, which is highly illuminating. Here her father is a source of play and affection, but the affection has an unmistakable, openly sexual coloring and takes a forbidden form. Her father prohibits her from ever mentioning it. If borne out by further information, it means that she seeks her affection in the form of sex, but that sex is forbidden. Here is one conflict. Further, she only can expect the affection if she is obedient to the father's tyranny. Here is another conflict because she complains about it and probably represses much hostility toward him because of it. This hostility does not come out toward him overtly, presumably because of her fear of him, and because her need for his love and affection was exaggerated by getting so little satisfaction of her dependent-love needs from her mother.

Her hostility is probably much repressed, for it does not appear in the earliest memories, but its existence is made clear by the current dreams of men dying. The early memory of her mother suggests that her mother may have been more important to her than she at present consciously realizes, if only because of her dependent-love needs, which her father did not adequately satisfy. In this memory her mother is deceiving her or trying to, and the scene is again of a sexual nature. This means that there is some sort of problem about sex, probably of sexual acting out.

The only close relationship in childhood was with her father, and the only close relationship recently has been with a girl her own age. It is likely that this girl friend is in part a mother-substitute and in part provides another person like herself to identify with. The repetitive dream of distress at being criticized by the girl and of trying so hard to please her sounds like trying to please Father—and Mother—and now in adult life, herself. If she were not dissatisfied with herself, she would not be here talking to me.

What then of her chief complaint, her not being able to stand her husband? This is not intelligible, at least at a first guess from this meager but consistent information. With the pattern toward her father, she expects tyranny. She hides her hostility because of her fear, but in her dreams she wishes he were dead. She also expects love and affection from her husband as from her father in childhood, but mostly in the form of sex; yet she cannot freely accept love in this form, for by her father's training sex is forbidden. Hence she probably *feels* she is not really getting love and sexual satisfaction, no matter how giving her husband may be. With the pattern toward her brother, she can only expect her husband to go away and leave her; and by her identification with her brother, she would feel impelled to do as he did—escape from her parents in childhood, and from her husband in adult life. We can also suspect, pending further revelations, that if she is hostile and rebellious, openly or covertly, consciously or unconsciously, the defiance and retaliation might take the form of sexual acting out (which means using sex to express other feelings, such as rebellion against parents).

As we have already remarked, we each relate to other persons as objects (for dependence, sexual urges, hostility, love and the like) and by identification, that is, feeling outselves to be like another person. The child is thus dependent upon its parents as objects, but also in large part identifies with them, taking over into himself much of their feelings, attitudes and behavior. This identification is often less evident than is the feeling toward a person as an object, but is no less powerful. Others often recognize how much the offspring are like their parents.

If Brenda identifies with the figures of her childhood, feels like them, takes over their attitudes and behavior, how will this affect her feelings toward her husband? Being like her mother will make her distant and unaffectionate; being like her father will make her in part affectionate in a sexual way but in part tyrannical. Also her father's anger at her mother was one of the most disturbing features of her childhood. If she is like her father, she will be angry at her mate; and if she is like her mother, she will expect anger and tyranny from her husband and either accept it masochistically or else fight against it, *feeling* that is exists even if it does not.

She has told very little of good personal relationships so far. Unless she does, the therapeutic problem will be difficult because lack of a pattern of good feelings in the past means lack of a base for the development of good feelings toward her husband in the present. *A*

fateful fact about marriage is that each person tends to feel and be-
have in his marital home much the way he did in his parental home.

Wondering how her dynamics had, as has been said, lived her life for
her thus far, I began the second interview by asking her to tell the
highlights of her past from childhood on:

P: I guess the worst part of my childhood was my father's anger at
my mother. I couldn't stand it. I didn't know whose side to
take. Maybe this has something to do with my being so confused
and so indecisive. The other thing I couldn't stand was Father's
strictness. He was a tyrant, as I told you last time. I felt shackled
and not free—and that is how I feel now in this marriage.

A: Before telling about the marriage, please tell more about your
past. How did you behave in your home?

P: Well, like my brother, I got away from it as much as I could.
In fact, I used to run away from home—I began doing that as far
back as I can remember. When I got a little older I would go to
the girl friend I told you about. She was the only person I felt
at home with. We were close for years. I still see her sometimes.
When I got near to teen age I had other friends among girls but
no one else really close. Of course Father never allowed me to
date, but I was used to slipping away, and so I began to sneak off
with older boys. One of them fell in love with me, and we had
sex. He wanted to marry me, but Father forbade it. He was very
poor, and Father thought he had no prospects, and that I would
be stuck with him for life. He married another girl and has remained terribly poor. So Father was right. But at the time I
resented his control. I wanted to be free to live my own life. I
went with another boy, and after a while he seemed to be in love
with me, and we began an affair. I've always enjoyed sex, and
that wasn't the last affair.

A: Was this partly in defiance of your father's overly strict control?

P: I guess it was. And it seemed that only with sex was I close to
anyone. I guess you'd say my life then was escaping from home,
defying my parents, and finding love or sex or both with an older
boy or man. As I got out of my teens I continued this. It was
really a series of love affairs. I was satisfied just with the relationship. One day a woman I knew told me I was foolish to
make such a point of never accepting anything from a man. If a

man cared about me, and we had sex together, he would want to take care of me and give me expensive presents. So I tried it, and it was like a series of marriages. Not so many. Sort of a different one every year or so. I saved a good bit of money. All the men were extremely nice to me. They treated me better than any husband I know treats his wife. We always had a lot of respect for each other.

When I met the man I married, Ben, I was really impressed. He was handsome and wealthy, and crazy about me, both sexually and as a person. We went together for a year and a half, and then he said he wanted to marry me. He had had plenty of affairs with women, but for him this was love. I was what he wanted. He did seem like a prince in a fairy tale. He had everything—looks, friends, money, success (he is a lawyer) and devotion to me. He said he would give me anything and everything I wanted, and I knew he could do it. This seemed to be the real thing. We began living together, but when it came to actually getting married, I felt nervous about it. I couldn't figure out why. But I should have followed my instincts about it and not let myself be pressured into it. Since we've been married, he has not changed a bit, but I just haven't been able to stand him. I feel shackled again. And all the sex that was so great has become nothing. He's lost a lot of his drive, and I don't care much about sex myself any more.

A: What is it you can't stand about your husband?

P: He is cruel to me.

A: Cruel? I got the impression from what you just said that he was very kind, considerate and generous.

P: He is. He is too perfect. He is cruel because he makes me feel guilty. I think he does it on purpose. I lose my temper at him; I'm awful to him, but he is all patience, only wants to please me. If I don't like the cook, he'll get another one. If I don't like the apartment, he'll get another. If I told him I wanted to have an outside affair, he'd probably say yes even to that. He torments me with this. And part of it is that he can never make up his mind—all he wants is what I want. He never puts his foot down, never makes me do what he wants, never makes a decision except to please me.

All this fits the childhood pattern. It sounds as though her husband is in reality a paragon, and that she cannot tolerate a relationship so foreign to what she was accustomed to as a child. Unlike the hostile, tyrannical father and the distant mother, her husband is all devotion and giving, wanting to please her instead of to dominate her. Surreptitious, prohibited sex outside the parental home had the lure of defiance and closeness. Now in marriage it is forbidden, as it was in the parental home. The husband's attitude of only wanting to please his wife tempts her to be the tyrannical one herself ("identification with the aggressor," her father, similar to Art's identification with his mother in the previous chapter). As long as Ben was the forbidden lover, she could enjoy the relationship. But when he became the legitimate husband in a home, then her childhood patterns toward her mother and particularly toward her father were duplicated toward her husband.

Of course, I reserved opinion until interviewing the husband. It is hard enough to evaluate the dynamics of one individual; in a marital problem one must discern not only the dynamics of each of the partners but also how these mesh with or grind against each other. If this young woman's description of her husband is correct, it would fit with her inability to tolerate the marriage, but it is safer to get this view of what is going on between them. In many cases I discuss all these dynamics without delay, but this can only be done if they can be put in a way that clarifies what is going on without upsetting the patient. Here I thought it better to wait until I had seen the husband, and meanwhile we needed more information about the patient's feelings toward herself.

A: Can you tell me how you feel about yourself—apart from this problem with your husband? Have you other problems?

P: I have no confidence in myself. I'm still hostile to my mother. She tries to control and dominate me now more than my father does—to such an extent that I have no confidence in myself. And I'm hostile too. If I buy something and it's not right, I'm afraid to say anything about it. When we got married and moved into a beautiful apartment, I just remarked to Ben that I didn't care for the color of the walls in one of the rooms. So he said, "Okay, we'll change it." That's how nice he is, and that's how he makes me feel guilty, and the guilt makes me even angrier at him. I don't like housework, but I do it. Of course when I complain he offers to get help, but I'm afraid I wouldn't know how to deal with whomever it would be. And I'm afraid of social obligations. I talk too much and say all the wrong things.

A: If you don't see people and don't like housework, do you have any interests?

P: My father is in the building business, and for a while I was interested in houses and even in architecture, but not anymore. I want to be interested in the home, but I can't. I want to get away from it, but I'm afraid to. You'll probably say that I hated being home during my childhood, which I did, and still just don't like it in a home. I feel tied down, hemmed in.

A: You are right. I would raise the question of whether this traced back to your home in childhood. Have you and your husband any interests in common?

P· I wish I had interests. I wish I could get out of the apartment and do something—job, volunteer work, anything. I try to make myself, but I just can't. I rarely see people any more, even my girl friend. I've just got to get out of this marriage.

A: Into what?

P: Just to live alone, to be free again. Marriage just isn't for me. I just want to have a small place of my own and be free.

A: What about the interests in common with your husband?

P: As I said, I guess I don't have any, with him or without him.

A: And your husband?

P: Oh, he likes everything. He likes to be on the go. He likes going to political meetings, lectures, movies, all that. And he likes concerts, books and what he calls interesting people. And he likes parties. And of course he's absorbed in his law practice, and he's always buried in the *Wall Street Journal,* which he carries around with him.

Arrangements were made for her husband, Ben, to come see me. Very often in marital problems each partner reveals little of self but gives a picture of the other, frequently clear and accurate as far as it goes, but showing the other to be the source of all the difficulty. The wife may complain that the husband is totally absorbed in other interests and has no time or attention for her, while the husband tells of all he does for his wife, who is dissatisfied because she wants too much. But in this case, the husband's story and my impression of him fitted exactly what the wife had told me. He was a big fellow of 39, with thinning blond hair and blue eyes, who could have passed as her big brother. He was all she had said—handsome and charming and, as far as I could perceive, entirely devoted to his wife. He had been around and had had plenty of affairs. Now he wanted to settle down, but very specifically with this girl and no other. If it were impossible for her to stay with him, he would survive, he said; he would provide for her as best he could, and in time he would no doubt find another wife. But it was Brenda he wanted. What made this lusty young bear settle on this girl with such constancy after a life of such freedom could only be known from his own dynamics.

It is often said about marital difficulties that "It takes two to tango." I have not found this to be true in all cases. In many marriages the trouble arises entirely from one of the partners. The only generality, it seems to me, is that either husband or wife may contribute anywhere from nothing on up to 100 percent of the trouble. I do not know if the 20–80's or the 50–50's or the 0–100's are the most frequent. It would be an interesting statistic. A successful, that is, a reasonably harmonious, marriage depends not on the absence of neurosis (i.e., of disordered childhood patterns) so much as on how the childhood patterns of the pair *fit* each other. But probably the more mature the two are and the less disturbed their childhood patterns of human relations, the easier is their adjustment in marriage to each other and to the children and other responsibilities involved.

From these two interviews with the wife and one with the husband, it seemed that the problem lay with the wife.

We introduced Brenda to illustrate one way in which masochism works. How many women want to live alone instead of with a handsome, charming, sexy, wealthy, colorful, worldly, devoted husband? Having everything, she is miserable. She feels caged. Her childhood pattern toward her parents repeats itself toward her husband. Down underneath she feels toward him as she felt during all those previous years toward her parents. The old feeling of being trapped and tyrannized over, leading to rage and guilt, continues in the new home. This pattern of feelings, formed in childhood, lives its own life, with little regard for present reality.

To clarify the distinction between the child's outmoded feelings for her parents and the present realities of the wife's feelings toward her husband is the first big goal of treatment. Brenda's feelings toward her parents were a natural, normal, inevitable reaction to the treatment she received during her earliest, most formative, years.

But she is no longer a child, and her husband is a contemporary, not a parent. She has failed to outgrow her childhood feelings toward her parents so as to mature and develop the feelings of a wife for a husband. The conspicuous lack of any mention of children in my two interviews with Brenda is a manifestation of this failure, as are the repeated references to the specific parental warning against tying herself down for life. If her masochism wins out, Brenda will leave love and marriage to be isolated from people, devoid of interests and facing a bleak, financially insecure, lonely middle age. This is the challenge to the analyst: he cannot allow himself to influence her in the slightest by what might seem reasonable to him. He can only point out what seems to be going on in her feelings and motivations. Because Brenda feels trapped and dominated, the analyst must stay completely out of any decisions she might make; he can only warn her against any irreversible or consequential decisions while she is in the middle of an analysis.

The extent of this challenge becomes more apparent if we review the box score for each partner on the nine components of marriage. Enough has been said about Brenda and Ben to allow the reader to evaluate them on these points:

1. Love—defined as closeness, identification and selfless interest in the spouse.

2. Sexual attractiveness, desire and healthy functioning with the partner.

3. Sense of romance.

4. Parental drive and functioning.

5. Responsibility, personal and other, such as for home and in breadwinning, and loyalty to one's spouse.

6. Maturity.

7. Fit of the two personalities.

8. Harmony through absence of *contrast.*

9. Intelligence, health, socioeconomic factors.

When Brenda came to see me, she was headed for an emotional breakdown. This was not only avoided but, with considerable security, prevented for the future, chiefly by working through her hostility and guilt and their sources. The second threat was that her masochism would cause her to abandon the love of a devoted husband and superior person. If she were to scuttle her security by withdrawing from him and her few other human contacts, she would be left lonely with no adequate way to support herself as she entered middle age. Brenda's sexual activities, which she revealed soon after beginning treatment, largely had the meaning of secretly defying her father; this piled up guilt and increased her tendency to punish herself.

Immediately after the interview with her husband, Brenda's major dynamics as described above were discussed with her. Her insight was keen and realistic, but it alone could not remake childhood patterns of reaction to her parents, which began so early in life and which were in no way diluted by other relationships. There was no sibling, aunt, grandparent or near neighbor with whom she could have a free, easy, good friendship, feeling that that person understood her and was on her side. She did not escape to some other family from the stresses in her own, as so many children do. She ran away, but to nothing—later to loose relations with pre-teenagers, and to one girl friend. It was a struggle for her to try to free her adult attitudes and feelings, as a wife to her husband, from her all-encompassing patterns of reaction as a child to her parents. While slowly improving, she acted out many of these patterns, including the running away from home, and even the gestures toward surreptitious love affairs, which never materialized or were consummated, but remained gestures.

There were two impressive features: One was Brenda's perseverance in treatment despite her almost irresistible impulses of anger toward and escape from her husband. The other was the steadfast patience and fidelity of her husband, compounded no doubt of both mature and infantile patterns, in the face of his wife's hostile, provocative feelings and behavior. He knew that she had a problem but was getting analytic help, and he waited it out.

Hostility has a place in the emotional life similar to that of heat in the physical world. Just as all physical processes produce heat, so all psychic friction generates hostility. Any threat, frustration or irritation makes us angry. This is, I think, because a fundamental mechanism of adaptation is, as we have already mentioned, to meet every danger by destroying it or by escaping from it—by fight or by flight. When what distresses us arises from within, from inner conflicts, from an internal sense of inferiority, from self-made frustration, then we cannot destroy it or escape from it. Often in such circumstances we "project" our hostility onto others, attribute our troubles to them, blame someone or something outside ourselves.

Hostility threatens family and society; no one enjoys being the object of another person's hostility, and sometimes the condition becomes intolerable. Indeed sometimes one's *own* anger is intolerable. Hence children generally, and properly, are trained to control their hostilities. But hostility, checked by the parents, may be directed against the self ("I could kick myself") and cause the superego (conscience) to react with guilt and shame. Unfortunately, it may not cause enough guilt or shame in many people to prevent *irrational, pathological acting out,* as in much crime. Aggressive war is usually only a larger form of crime. We have to fight the aggressors to survive, just as we have to have a police force to combat crime. But in good, decent people hostilities cause guilt and are often self-directed, and hence people very often behave unconsciously in self-injurious, masochistic ways and are their own worst enemies. As Churchill said, it is very hard to know one's own best interest.

With analytic help, Brenda did not break down. She did get a divorce, however. In his generous way (which so many husbands promise but forget when it comes to a legal settlement), Ben recognized her helplessness and gave her a settlement that insured her security indefinitely. Brenda never remarried but achieved considerable satisfaction working in a hospital and traveling. As a volunteer she could feel free and not trapped in job or home. Her life might look lonely to others, but she took it as freedom and did not complain.

Marriage, we have noted, provides an ideal arena for the acting out of hostility to others and, masochistically, to oneself. In any close relationship the old emotional patterns of child to parents tend to emerge. Sometimes they come out almost as soon as the marriage ceremony is over; sometimes they take years, even decades, to reveal themselves openly. (SEE Chapters 15–18 and 33.)

Masochism or self-injury arises from guilt and self-directed hostility, whatever the source. In some cases self-injury in any of a thousand forms is no more than a threat. In other cases the threat is realized because the self-injury is to some extent acted out.

Examples are probably at hand in everyone's experience. I will describe another couple very briefly without going into detail. The wife was a most attractive girl, married to an equally attractive man, and was the mother of two boys. We might call this couple Cliff and Candy.

Candy had a deprived background; her parents and older brother and sister were in the home but showed very little interest in her. She had a childhood with no really good relationships within her family. Therefore, there was no emotional pattern for good feelings within a family in adult life. As we have stressed, people tend to behave in their marital homes as they did as children in their parental homes, however different the realities of the marital home may be, and tend to treat their own children as their parents treated them, i.e., identify with one or both of their parents. Cliff had a certain amount of deprivation from his parents also, and this drew him and Candy together. This was the deeper emotional element they had in common, that made them understand each other, that made them *simpático*. But Cliff had developed more effective defenses than Candy against his sense of deprivation and rejection. He also had the advantage of being a man, and having work he could lose himself in. Work itself can be a great escape, defense and compensation. Through work many men and some women can drive for the recognition, appreciation, rewards and love that they lacked in childhood from their parents and of which they continue to feel deprived, or for the love they had and strive in their work to hold. That is why there is a compulsive element in the unremitting drive of some people to work.

Candy felt, with some justification, that her husband was too devoted to his work (accounting) and not enough so to her. She complained, and he responded with a real effort to be home earlier, have cocktails before dinner, take her out to dinner and to the theater and in general to do all he could to satisfy her needs. But her needs were too neurotic, that is, too much an expression of the deprivations of childhood rather than of the realities of a mature, adult married life. Her complaints continued despite his every effort. It got so that he lived in the stream of her hostility and criticism. Nothing he did was right. She acted out her parents' rejection of her in childhood by rejecting her husband now in marriage. Of course, the children suffered. She saw an analyst but made little progress in changing the situation. In her mind all her frustration was caused by her husband, not herself. She failed to discriminate between the real frustrations of childhood and her hypersensitivity to even minimal frustration by her husband, which impinged on this emotional vulnerability.

Then it happened. Cliff met a girl who sincerely felt that he was the greatest thing that walked the earth. His wife continued to feel that he was totally inadequate. At last Cliff was offered what his soul craved, and he and the girl fell madly in love. He became determined to have a divorce. Now Candy woke up—but too late. She had pushed him beyond the point of no return and masochistically precipitated herself into a divorce. Freud called it the "repetition compulsion"; she had acted out the childhood pattern of deprivation, hostility, guilt and self-punishment and had recreated for herself in marriage the rejection by her husband that she had suffered as a child from her parents. The divorce went through, with great anguish for all involved. Cliff's new marriage was of course not idyllic but was an improvement. Everything was bitter for poor Candy, who was, in her ego, the innocent victim of her own unconscious, undone through her pattern of rejection by her parents asserting itself in her marriage. Lacking a childhood pattern of good relations with parents, she failed to make good relations with other men after the divorce. Too late she realized what she had lost—a husband to whom other men she met did not measure up and whom another woman appreciated. She became depressed and, when I last heard, was again seeing a psychiatrist, this time not to save a marriage but to prevent serious depression and potential suicide.

It seems terrifying that what parents do or omit doing during those early formative days, weeks, months and years of their child's life can so fatefully influence that child's destiny. Terrifying and grossly unfair. But the world of adults is only the world of these children a few quick years later. The destiny of humanity is determined by how its young are reared. If we do not face this reality squarely, we will continue, by unenlightened childrearing, to bring up generation after generation of hostile, suffering adults, who will bring about destruction and agonies compared with which the unhappinesses of divorce, bad health and poverty seem only minor inconveniences. Not only in their marriages and private lives do individuals act out their frustrations through hostility and masochism, but, acting with others similarly affected, they account for the hostility and self-destructiveness of whole groups and nations.

12
GIVE—GET IN MARRIAGE

No one has ever loved anyone the way everyone wants to be loved.

Mignon McLaughlin

Those who want much are always much in need.

Horace

The hand that gives, gathers.

Ray

There is a kind of marital problem so common that, if my practice has provided a representative sample, it can properly be rated a sociological phenomenon, at least among certain strata of our society. This might be called a simple "give–get" conflict, and it would be helpful if everyone contemplating matrimony were well acquainted with it. But then it seems self-evident that the fundamentals of the human emotional life—that is, our attitudes, feelings and behavior toward ourselves and toward others, their origins and development—should be taught in school from the lower grades on up through college. Marriage is only a special case of human relations, and the essentials of marriage should be taught as soon as young people are concerned with it in its earliest form, dating.

It would be more proper to say that the essentials of marriage should be taught as soon as these instincts and feelings begin to exert their power in adolescents and pre-adolescents. Actually, a background of knowledge of the human emotional life should be laid in advance, long before this period. Certainly such instruction should be made available not later than high school, for these forces are so powerful that every adolescent is to some extent confused by them, and needs all the clarification, insight and help available. These forces can make a person's greatest happiness or his most extreme misery.

John and Jane are an average middle-income American family with three children, all now in school, the youngest in kindergarten.

The husband was a loved child. His father was too occupied with his business to have been much in evidence. His mother was pretty well adapted to her husband's absence and to getting her chief satisfaction from home and children. She pinned great hopes upon John, and perhaps he was somewhat favored by her over his sister, perhaps not. Probably his mother felt that he would be a greater source of pride to her than her husband was. At any rate, she gave John the best of care and possibly a little too much devotion. Certainly she was always there during his grade school years; she served him breakfast, saw him off to school and was waiting there with milk and cookies when he returned. She was a good, orderly housekeeper, and she was pretty much the boss of the home. As John grew up, his picture of marriage, formed from that of his parents, was of a good, kindly father coming in from his affairs to a well-run home in which his mother was at the helm. His father acceded to her wishes and did so gladly, for it saved him the trouble of making decisions and it kept the peace. He worked and earned, and Mother was satisfied with home and children. John was a miniature of his father. He went to school instead of work. He earned high marks instead of money. He behaved well in the home, and his mother was delighted with him. He went on to college and then to business school.

The sex urge drove him, and he had some adventures and affairs. The mating instinct asserted itself and he married. Jane was very attractive and very bright. Their three children came in fairly rapid succession, and by the time the third child was two or three years old, John and Jane had been married nearly ten years. John was just passing his middle thirties. Sex with his wife was no longer the novelty and thrill and irresistible passion that it had been. As John's interest in his wife diminished, his absorption in his business increased.

The old pattern was emerging. As his father went out as breadwinner, now so does he. Now he must make top grades in his particular occupational field as he used to in school. Then his wife will, like his mother, be proud of him, his income and his other successes, and like his mother will have a well-run home and well-behaved children always awaiting him for dinner with open arms. He is satisfied with himself as a sincere, conscientious husband and father who is doing good work in his chosen occupation. His mother and father were pleased with him because of his behavior in childhood, and now he takes over their acceptance of him into his own self-image, his picture of himself. And it is confirmed by his friends and co-workers.

How could his wife see him any other way? Astonishingly though, at least to him, she does see him very differently. This is less surprising if one learns that despite their having chosen each other, her early emotional background was rather different from John's. In childhood Jane lacked warm, understanding, giving love. And this meant that she lived in a different emotional climate in her own mind and had other outlooks and attitudes toward herself and toward life.

John called me and made an appointment. He was a slender, fair, outgoing man, on his way up in a large company. He told the following:

PATIENT: Over the last few years, our marriage, now ten years old, has been getting worse. At this rate it will soon reach a crisis. Jane and I are getting to be at swords' points. Sex has become infrequent. Is it possible that these things could be my fault, that I am doing something wrong or not doing something I should without realizing it? Can our marriage be salvaged? I still want to save it, but it is meaning less and less to me. Marriage no longer means much, but the children do—they and their future. Jane is not stable and is a poor housekeeper. If we got a divorce, she would not raise the children well. I think the trouble is really all hers, but I hope there is something in me that can be changed to help matters. Jane is impractical, a poor organizer, can't run the house. Dinner is not cooked or is not on time. A water pipe leaks and she doesn't call the plumber. The furniture is not well arranged. The refrigerator is not stocked. The house seems empty, dark, depressing. Jane has no interest in my work and never asks about it. She is never satisfied sexually and complains so much about not enough love-making that I've given up trying to satisfy her. But Jane says that the only way to improve the marriage, or maybe even save it, is for me to get analyzed for my sexual inadequacy and for my lack of affection. She blames me for the whole trouble, because she says I never give enough affection and never want to have sex. She seems to be threatening me, telling me I'd better see a psychiatrist and be a good lover, or she will leave. Even when I try to be demonstrative,

she still accuses me, and the more she accuses me and attacks me
and neglects the house, the more I withdraw.

ANALYST: Please tell me a little about your home life when you
were young.

P: My parents did not have a very good marriage. They were
not terribly fond of each other, but they were good-hearted.
Mother was especially so. She was always very good and very
warm, and she babied me and catered to me. The only children were me and my sister, three years younger. Father was
almost always working, and I didn't see much of him. He tried
to do what was right, but there was no closeness between us
and we never talked about things that mattered.

A: Has your sister problems?

P: She seems to have an all right marriage and to be reasonably
happy.

A: What is the very first thing you remember, way back before
continuous memory?

P: Let's see. The first thing I can remember is Mother taking me
to kindergarten.

The very earliest memories are astonishingly revealing of central
major trends in the personality. The major trends seem to cause
one to select for remembrance just those little scenes which best
express them. Here we see the prominence of the mother and care
by her and the outside interest, the school.

This is as far as we got in the first interview. In the second he
went on:

P: This problem with Jane is the only thing really wrong in my
life. I've gradually been gaining confidence in myself. I have
gradually made good friends. I like my job and am doing well
in it. I get on well with the children. My relation to Jane is
practically the only bad one I have in life. She has blotted out
her childhood. She makes friends but often loses them. She
can be good with the children but then fails to make arrangements for something, say a party, and disappoints them.

The mutual respect, admiration, affection and interest Jane
and I had when we were first married have been lost. Jane likes
to discuss artistic and intellectual things, but I don't feel like
it when the house is in such a mess. When I come home, I

can't find anything, dinner often isn't ready, or she'll tell me to take her and the children out to dinner, although I have work to do that evening. If I want a snack, there is nothing in the refrigerator. I've given up expecting breakfast at home.

A: What do your complaints come down to?

P: Well, I guess you could call it domestic inefficiency that I object to—things misplaced, beds unmade, servicemen not called, all that. And social inefficiency as well—she's careless about letters of congratulation, gifts, entertaining.

A: What else bothers you?

P: I want my wife's interest. But no, maybe I don't. Maybe I rebuff her. I don't want her suggestions about what I should do.

A: Do you think a vicious circle is building up between the two of you? And if so, what does it reduce itself to?

P: As we have been talking, things have become clearer in my mind. My chief complaint is *inadequate house management;* her chief complaint is *inadequate love life.* And this is what makes the vicious circle you spoke of. If I phone to say I'm delayed at the office, Jane's tone makes it clear that she thinks I arranged it on purpose.

A: You mean she is very easily frustrated?

P: Exactly. When I come home at night I must be on guard because if she has had any problem or disappointment, she will be annoyed and hostile. What I want is for her to be *more responsible* and *less hostile.*

As usual the one spouse tells more of the pathology and dynamics of the other one than of his own. In this case John has shown Jane to be a deprived person underneath, which makes her constantly frustrated, demanding and hostile. He has depicted her ego (the conscious, official part of her personality, with all her higher powers) as childish and irresponsible. Often the description of one spouse by the other is correct or partially so, but I have learned that one cannot count on this. The other partner must be seen.

To emphasize this point it is worth a brief digression to mention another case. Tom, a handsome and apparently healthy and wholesome man, complained that his wife, Toni, was infantile, that she was extremely neglectful of the house and of their young children, that her person and house were filthy and that she was so hostile that she attacked him.   The picture was of a rapidly deteriorating schizophrenic.   But I got no clear idea of his own dynamics.   When I saw the wife, she presented a very different picture.   The husband, she said, from his own background held a belief in male supremacy and was so extreme and hostile in this that she simply could not tolerate it and was on a full scale sit-down strike.   We tested this by a brief separation in which she and the children visited her parents.   Overnight she became her old self.   This couple moved away because the husband was transferred, but I heard later that the wife had obtained a divorce despite the husband's resistance, has re-married, and was her former happy self.

There are two morals to the tale.   The first is the necessity of hearing both the husband and wife.   The second is the powerful effect people have on each other, especially when bound together in the intimacy of married life.   With this husband, Toni was behaving indeed like a schizophrenic.   What would this have led to if the marriage had continued?   I once saw a mature, stable man who was so depressed that he could barely function.   This turned out to be a reaction, unrecognized by himself, to his wife's internally generated hostility.   It was possible to get her into treatment, which was, happily, successful.   Remarkably, her hostility to her husband lessened in a few months and his depression disappeared.

I had to meet Jane and see the picture through her eyes.   I hoped that all was not so dark as it looked and that the drift to divorce might somehow be reversed, especially because of the children.

Speaking with Jane for only a few minutes quickly and sharply brought out the contrast between her personality and John's.   Both came through strongly, both were highly intelligent, but John, although outgoing, was deliberate and steady, while Jane, with bright blue eyes and a ready smile, would attract attention in any group by her quick mind and varied interests, as well as by her femininity.   If the two complemented each other, they would, other things being equal, have a good and interesting marriage.   In a way each provided qualities the other needed.   How Jane saw the problem will appear from the following abbreviated notes:

PATIENT: The problem is whether it is possible to make a go of the marriage.
ANALYST: What is the central difficulty?

P: It is John's lack of interest in me, generally and sexually. He apparently can go indefinitely without wanting me or even hardly touching me. I am the opposite. I respond strongly to people and to everything—art, literature, music—and there is always an erotic coloring to the enjoyment for me. John doesn't understand this at all, and his not understanding it makes me so angry. I feel so frustrated and blocked and angry that I cannot do anything—not even get a divorce or take a lover.

A: Tell a little about the emotional relations in your earliest childhood.

P: My father was mostly busy, and I saw very little of him. He traveled a lot, but when he was home he was always preoccupied with business. Mother meant well but we were never very close. My sister, three years younger, wasn't close to her or to me, either. Mother was always active in the community, always had something to keep her out of the house a lot.

A: Did you resent this?

P: Yes. I got used to it, but I think I always missed her and was very angry at her underneath for it.

A: What are your very earliest memories?

P: The first is of my father saying that I was spoiled. The second is having fun at a neighbor's whom I used to visit. I liked it better at my neighbor's house than in my own home. Then I remember, when I first went to school, being told that I was no good at the little paintings we did, and how devastated I was by this.

   [We note the criticism by father—overspoiling—the fun at the neighbor's in preference to her own home and again the criticism at school for her performance, which may appear today in criticism from her husband.]

   But the question is, how can I live with nothing from my husband and with no sex? I didn't want to come to see you because John thinks everything is my fault, and if I spoke to you, he would take it as proof that I was neurotic. He tells me all the things he wants done and I do them. He lacks any human feeling; he had it once but hasn't shown it for years.

A: You said you do all the things your husband wants done, but you know he complains of the opposite—that you don't run the house very well or handle entertaining well, or anything really.

P: That's only because I'm in such a rage at him. He gives me nothing and doesn't seem to have the slightest idea of my needs. I don't know if it's because of his talking with you, but he seems to be waking up a little to what is going on in his own home now and to be concerned about the children. Anyway, it's nothing at all for me to run a home efficiently, take care of the children and their activities, and do plenty of entertaining. I haven't done any of these things because of simple revenge. I told you I felt blocked. Divorce would harm the children. Somehow I haven't felt right about taking a lover. I've just taken revenge by letting the house go.

[Here is a most encouraging sign. If her neglect is the result of conscious hostility, it is of course much more easily reversible than if it were an unconscious internal sit down strike.]

A: Do you think that your revenge may have the opposite effect from what you want—that it may be causing a vicious circle by making John react with more anger to you and therefore with even more rejection and neglect of you? Sometimes in adult life we defeat ourselves if we demand too directly. Sometimes we get only by giving.

This comment began a discussion that launched "treatment," although the goals and the form were not yet evident. Jane quickly made clear that she wanted her husband to see me regularly for his part in their difficulties, but that she would not even consider going to a psychiatrist in a systematic way herself.

Since we were still in an exploratory, diagnostic stage, this was not unsatisfactory. A pattern of deprivation and hostility formed in her childhood seemed a central key to *her* side of the tussle with John. I discussed this pattern with her almost immediately, in as unthreatening a way as possible, without attributing to her any blame or neuroticism (neurosis being disturbed childhood patterns that cause difficulties in later life). At the same time it is important that only the truth be told. I said that, as she well knew, the extent, form and nature of one's wants and the way in which one handles his frustrations are largely conditioned by one's experiences during childhood. Therefore she and her husband had differences in their needs, in what and how much they expected from life and from others and in their reactions to frustration. But no matter what one's early childhood, every marriage involves *getting* somewhat less and *giving* somewhat more than each of us dreams of and anticipates. If she did the efficient job her husband desired, maybe the vicious circle of their marriage would be interrupted.

When John came in again, what he said confirmed my impression of his dynamics and I was able to discuss these impressions with him very openly. The essence of his dynamics was his continuing toward his wife the pattern toward his mother, taking her for granted and not fully appreciating her needs, which might, I agreed, be intensified by his wife's early deprivation. But every wife has some limitations; no wife is the ideal mother of our childhood wishes. For him, as for her, it was a matter of getting a little less and giving a little more in a real-life marriage than he had dreamed of since childhood.

The idea of giving and getting was the main theme of the therapy for both of them. The immediate goal was the clarification of how their present attitudes, formed in childhood, impaired their achievement of harmony. The object was to make the most of the present reality, since each had so much to offer, instead of pining hopelessly and angrily for some dreamed-of potentiality.

It was not clear at this point how much trouble would come from Jane's underlying residue of deprivation from childhood. She would certainly have to come to terms with her past. All the same, the trend in John's personality that contributed to the tug-of-war between them, although quieter and less obvious, was no less a contributing factor to their difficulties. As we have previously remarked, sometimes the difficulties come almost entirely from the husband or the wife. Not infrequently the problem stems almost entirely from the wife's persisting pattern of childhood deprivation, which makes her excessively demanding and chronically hostile. But in this case the husband's naivete and insensitivity about his wife's normal needs certainly increased Jane's sense of frustration. This was all to the good therapeutically because it increased the chances that insight alone without a long analysis would help John change appreciably, just as it promised to enable Jane to relinquish her tactic of revenge by passive hostility through her sit-down strike.

When I brought up with John his wife's feminine needs, he said, "At eleven o'clock I'm tired and want to go to sleep and not have intercourse first." I replied, "Sex is not just the physiology of intercourse. Your wife needs all the kinds of attention a man can give to a woman. If there is to be intercourse, the woman wants to be wooed and gotten into the mood. Her needs for physical sex are only part of what she wants more broadly: masculine attention, appreciation, affection and love. She wants to be told that she looks pretty, that she made a fine dinner, that she handled a difficult problem well, that she did a good job with the children, that she was attractive when you were out together and that she handled the entertaining at home well. She wants your interest in things that interest her. She will be less demanding of physical sex, which you rather resent, if you better satisfy her broader feminine needs, and she will be much more apt to handle her responsibilities well, which is what you want, if she gets plenty of appreciation for doing so."

Does it seem strange that it could be necessary to discuss these elementary matters with a man of middle age who is successful in life and who has a wife and three children? We traced back his attitudes toward his wife to their sources, in his relation to his mother. We also spoke to his wife's needs and reactions in relation to *her* childhood pattern.

The interactions of both and the sources in their childhood patterns were then discussed with Jane. Each one saw what was central to the struggle between them and what each must do to build reasonable harmony and happiness in its place. The positive attributes of each were also defined—all Jane's excellent qualities and all that John actually provided for her. For Jane to get a divorce and face life seeking a better mate, with or without her three children, seemed a poor risk compared with trying to make her relationship to John work. And how could John know whether a second wife would not have hidden troubles worse than Jane's?

The first goal of this therapy was to clarify the conflict and bring it into perspective. It was to show what each was feeling and doing, and why, and to visualize the alternatives. This was accomplished through insight and discussion. Its purpose was to achieve a reorientation of attitudes that would make both of them realize what they would lose by breaking up, and gain by true reconciliation. This was not full personal analysis, designed to change by therapy the childhood pattern of each. Instead it was what may be called "ego reorientation" to help them see what they would do to themselves and to each other and to their children if they did not change and build a good relationship between them. The hope was that the threat on the one hand and the promise on the other would be pressure enough. Working in this way through insight, I hoped for steady improvement in their feelings and behavior toward each other. The desire to find pleasure and avoid pain works with the drive to maturity; and nature's powers of healing are what help us to change, to free ourselves from the entrapments of the childhood patterns. "If you do not have a virtue, assume it."

This began working almost immediately. John showed more appreciation and attention; Jane easily ran everything efficiently, as she said she could. This improvement led to the resumption of sexual relations, although John's drive did not match Jane's need. The children became happy again.

With such a good start, I thought it best to continue as we were doing and not to bring in another psychiatrist for John or Jane. This does not mean that there were not ups and downs and backslidings, nor that I ignored the potential for trouble from the pathodynamic childhood patterns of each. But the trend, although saw-toothed, was toward improvement, and the difficulties were manageable as they arose. For example, John would feel at times that Jane was backsliding in her responsibilities, and he would flare up in anger in spite of his efforts. This I agreed was bound to happen, and, I reminded him, making a satisfying marriage was never quick or easy for *anyone.* It always takes many years. Jane objected that, although John's treatment of her had improved greatly, his behavior had an artificial quality. "Naturally," I said, "everything we learn is artificial and self-conscious in its first stages. This is a good sign, not a bad sign; it means that he is trying, and that he is moving toward change." Or Jane would at periods of anger become bitter about what she had missed over the last years and invoke her "rights as a woman." The important thing, I reminded her, was to keep this a winning game—the relationship was better, and the job was to keep it improving—not to pine over the past. As to rights, this term had only an abstract meaning. The only substance was the reality of what we knew of her and of John and how to get the most satisfaction out of what each could offer. And this was the point: marriage, like the rest of life, offers less and demands more than *any* of us wants. *Make the most of the reality; don't frustrate yourself over the potentiality.*

Of course the differences between John and Jane were clear. Different people use different physiological systems in varied proportions to gain satisfaction. Some especially enjoy eating, using the gastro-intestinal system; others get great pleasure from athletics, using the muscular system. John got his satisfaction chiefly through intellectual and man-to-man activity in his business. Sex was not the chief system for his gratification. Sex can be a great drain for any kind of feeling (hostility, dependence, love, togetherness, and so on), and for most people it is a great diversion, consolation and refreshment. Sex was all of these things to Jane; it was the chief channel for almost all of her feelings. This important incompatibility was apparently so deep-seated in their makeups that the chances of analysis changing either one appreciably in these outlets, intellectual and sexual, were slight, if indeed such an attempt were advisable.

Of course there were the deep-seated childhood patterns under lying the marital conflict. Could ego orientation and insight help? Would intensive analytic treatment for one or both be indicated later? Were there strong hostile and masochistic trends that would cause one or both to injure the other and himself? Or was the balance of forces in each personality and between them such that this ego re-orientation had halted the vicious circle and started them on a permanent path to ever increasing mutual satisfaction? The un-conscious is complex and powerful, its effects not always predictable. Meanwhile we were playing a winning game, and, since both John and Jane had so much to lose by breaking up, so much to gain by getting on better, we continued on this basis.

The outcome was fortunate. Improvement continued slowly over the years. Typically, it was easier for John than for Jane. There were two reasons for this: John had had more security and love from his mother than Jane had had, and he had the pattern of taking the home for granted while he made a success in school. So now, with a well-run home and success in the company, his pattern was pretty well satisfied. But Jane, with her inner dependent-love needs strengthened and sensitized by early frustration, was, as a woman responsible for home and children, largely cut off from outside contacts and gratifications. As she saw and worked through all this, she made steady progress in managing her needs and frustrations, and her husband was won over to accepting and even approving outside interests for his wife, although this ran contrary to his mother's narrow, undiverted concentration on the home. Jane, always interested in politics and community problems, became active, well known and popular. This helped to satisfy her needs as she worked analytically on them and on her inner sense of frustration.

Five years later they were doing well. They had come or were coming through the next shoals and rapids of marriage—the matrimonial passage in which the husband is at the peak of his career. It is a time when the husband is even more absorbed in his job and his increasing power in the business. He is more self-sufficient. He has gained recognition from his associates, and his success compensates for his passing youth in attracting certain kinds of women. He is more easily tempted into infidelity because, now in his mid-forties, he sees the shadow of age five or ten years ahead.

Jane had reconciled herself to the futility of expecting and demanding from John what it was not in his makeup to give; and she had learned how much of her frustration derived from her own inner pattern. So she ran the home and pursued her own outside interests, was exposed to her own temptations and made a life for herself as best she could, restraining her envy, feeling of deprivation and resentment toward John. In striving for an equilibrium they had grown further and further apart, and here lay the danger. The children were grown and one after another leaving for college. The maturity in John and Jane showed them in retrospect the life they had shared and the deep satisfaction, despite the battles, in marriage, home and children. They saw that the only choice was to make the most of what they had together and that nothing—neither success nor pride nor interests nor romantic adventures—was worth the sacrifice of the good that they provided each other. (But maturity does not always prevail, as the next chapter will show.)

John and Jane's situation illustrates another point: in order to understand a person one must usually maintain two opposing attitudes. We must be entirely open-minded and free of preconceptions, always ready for the unexpected, but at the same time we must be ready to draw on all our previous experience and knowledge.

Almost always, in my experience, there is some deep-seated emotional similarity in childhood patterns that draws two people together into marriage. In John and Jane's case the similarity was not clear. Perhaps it lay in their attachments to their mothers. John tried to gain his wife's love in the same way he had successfully gained love from his mother. But, unlike John, Jane had no established pattern to assure her of her husband's approving love.

In some cases the wife or husband has an intensified longing for maternal love because of being overindulged as a child; in others (and this is more common) there was deprivation. Perhaps the father, like most, was so preoccupied with the competitive struggle for existence, security and status that he was not much in evidence. If the family was in a low income bracket, the mother may have been fatigued emotionally and physically with the labors of home and children and not have had enough to offer in feelings, patience, time and understanding. If the family was in a relatively high income bracket, the mother may have been too busy pursuing her club and community activities. In either case the child feels insufficiently loved. And this feeling, a true, inevitable, realistic reaction during the earliest, formative years—continues for life. This created an inner emotional atmosphere that leads to several consequences.

It creates an *internal* sense of being deprived, unsatisfied and insufficiently loved. This comprises two feelings: an increased need to *be* loved over *giving* love, and a sense that one is not loved enough, a built-in feeling of frustration. These two feelings may in the days of courtship enhance a girl's attractiveness. Many such girls are especially alluring. They are so girlishly eager to be loved, and this eagerness shows through so clearly that most men find it an irresistible appeal to their masculinity. Perhaps this is particularly true for a man who has been in the position of the child craving his mother's love—for now he finds *himself* in the stronger, adult position, as the one to whom the girl appeals for *his* love. Thus he is "out from under" the childhood position to his mother. He may also be attracted, by identification, to someone who craves even more strongly than he what he himself yearns for, that is, maternal love. (And one who was deprived may be attracted to one who was gratified in childhood.) The girl, on her part, usually seeks maternal love through the channel of sex and romance; she turns her dependent-love needs from mother to men or to one single man. The most direct path for her to express her need is through sex in a setting of love, which becomes especially prominent in her relationship with a man.

In the case we are discussing, Jane, deprived in childhood, especially craves love and has particularly strong sexual needs and sex appeal. Since she is so attractive, we can see why John married her. However, wanting the reassurance and demonstration of love through urgent demands for attention and sex may well lead after the honeymoon to a vicious circle. With this couple the requirements of home and children took more and more energy out of Jane and thereby increased her already strong inner needs for replenishment. Meanwhile John's powers were being directed more and more toward his job. If Jane were strong and were firmly identified with her husband's orientation, she would tolerate the frustrations of being a wife with a hard working husband, who is wrapped up in his work but who is well-meaning and at heart devoted to hearth and home. Thus when I asked one wife how she liked having a husband with two jobs, she unthinkingly replied, "Great!" and then the conversation made clear that she was referring to her husband's enjoyment and enthusiasm for the two jobs he was then carrying. Another wife, somewhat younger and who had three small children, found it difficult to have her husband in a job that required many nights out; but she knew how important it was for them all, and was so proud of her husband and what he was accomplishing that she did her best to accept the deprivation.

Jane was much younger but not that strong. Strength is largely a matter of how much one can give and how little one requires. Jane felt increasingly deprived and became more insistent on what seemed to her to be her "rights"; and, of course, with the frustration came resentment. Not all wives identify with their husbands' successes. Jane felt that John was getting recognition and esteem at work while she got nothing and only did what a housekeeper and nurse could do. She was a little envious of what John got out of work, a little competitive with him. John sensed Jane's increasing need of him, her sense of deprivation, her resentment. He never liked his mother to be displeased with him, and he did not like his wife to be. He tried to give her more attention, time and affection, but he disliked her demands for them. Though he tried, he became somewhat cooler and more distant. Sex had lost its irresistible urgency. He was happier following his interests at work than doing what was becoming a chore in his home—the job of being husband and father. Jane felt this and noted an artificial quality in his feelings toward her. She felt more deprived, more demanding, more resentful. But John wanted a home like the home of his childhood, so that he could be free for his success, then at school, now at work. His reactions to Jane's mounting frustration increased further. The vicious circle between them was in full spin, spiraling downward.

The children, of course, are also affected by these increasing tensions. If they are involved long enough, strongly enough, from early enough in life, there will be effects upon them that will last all their lives. Today many parents know this or at least suspect it. Sometimes it is because of the children that they come for help— which is all the more reason for the efforts of the dynamic psychiatrist to arrest and reverse the downward spiral where possible.

13
PASSIVITY AND REGRESSION: THE PERENNIAL CHILD

The baby and small child are completely dependent on the mother (and father or substitutes) for satisfaction of their needs, that is, for their survival. The feeling that goes with this dependence is love. Being loved brings the assurance of the food, shelter and care that are necessary to survival. Thus we can conveniently speak of the dependent-love needs. Conversely the parent, originally the mother, who carries, bears and nutures the child from her own body, is responsible for meeting the child's needs; and the feeling that assures this is love for the child. The child must *be* loved and have responsibility taken for it by the adult—the parent *gives* the love and all that the responsibility entails. This is the "instinctual response system" between child receiving and parent giving.

On the long road from the helpless, love-needing dependence of infancy and childhood to the relative independence and responsibility of the adult, certain feelings and attitudes may, if the child is not properly treated, be left behind, may fail to mature. Some parts of the emotional development proceed; others are inhibited or warped and persist with little change in the adult. It is like the children once raised by traveling circus troupes in big vases of varying shapes, which let parts of their bodies grow normally but molded other parts grotesquely; or, a less grisly analogy, like a young tree growing in a dense forest, striving to mature fully and in perfect balance, aiming to catch the sunlight but becoming bent, stunted or twisted by darkness, crowding and climbing vines. Thus, because of the early influence upon them, many children mature well in certain parts of their personalities, while failing to do so in other parts; certain of the childish needs for love and dependence may persist and not be outgrown in favor of giving and responsibility. These may be in relation to wife, children, career, breadwinning or in any other area. A person may be quite mature in some areas and painfully infantile in others, depending on his early experiences.

A simple example came to my attention when a young mother of three came to see me about her husband. We will call them Eleanor and Ed. Eleanor said that Ed was a fine husband and father, devoted to her and the children, a good lover, and of a uniformly good humor. He had only one failing, and it was about this that she wished to consult me. His devotion was confined to his home; he had none for his work. A college graduate, he had had a series of rather poorly paying jobs—low level work in business, door-to-door selling and other employment suitable for college students during the summer but of no interest in itself, and not adequate for supporting a family of five, or for potential for the future. Her parents would finance treatment for him if I felt it held promise. I explained to her that my schedule was filled at the time but that I saved time each week for consultations and referrals of people to other analysts. Although some disagree, my own experience has demonstrated beyond doubt that the selection of the analyst is of the greatest importance: his personality as well as his interests and abilities should fit as well as possible the particular needs of the individual patient.

Ed came for an interview. What Eleanor said was completely confirmed by him. There had been very little model for responsibility in his mother, and his father had been away most of the time. His own efforts at any responsibility, such as helping to clear the table or running errands, were rebuffed and discouraged, apparently rejected as nuisances. He was most loved when he was inactive, passive. Then his mother was devoted. She was also overanxious about his playing and associating with other boys. His childhood pattern, his 0 to 6, was a loving family life as an only child, as long as he stayed home and was "good" (meaning quiet). His passivity was rewarded, his initiative blocked. Thus he became a homebody, at home in the bosom of his family but not at ease and effective out in the world. His wings were clipped.

The outlook for therapy for Ed was poor because no nucleus of independence and responsibility was discernible in his whole life to build on. Yet normal maturation includes a drive to use one's powers. He accepted referral to an excellent analyst for this problem. But as anticipated, treatment did not go well. A drive can be unblocked, but it is often impossible to develop what is missing.

Passivity, whether for breadwinning, as in this case, or in any other area, usually has four main sources: a fixation to the childish enjoyment of irresponsibility, hostility, inhibition of normal drives and regression.   Each of these sources may be present in a given individual in different strengths and proportions.

The simple enjoyment of inactivity is similar to the baby's and very small child's enjoyment of lying back and being taken care of, his every want fulfilled by others.   However, even in infants this passivity is only a small part of otherwise ceaseless activity.   Of course, rest from responsibility is normal and healthy.   We all withdraw into complete passivity for sleep, and only a balanced life is wholesome—a balancing off of responsible giving and effort by rest and replenishment.   But passivity can also be a continuation of childish needs to such an extent as to be pathological, a neurotic problem, as in the man just mentioned.   This kind of passivity is a fixation to a childish (really "babyish") attitude.

But this man also revealed another source for his deficiency as a provider for his family.   His mother's restriction of his natural exuberant activity, her gentle molding of him into the good little home boy, was a warping of his emotional maturation.   We all are impelled biologically to live out our lives, to fulfill our life cycles, to mature and then to grow old and die.   Impairment of the process of maturation is frustrating and threatening.   Failure to mature makes us inadequately equipped to cope with the world, inferior to others and insecure.   We react with the fight-flight response: attack and destroy the danger, or flee from it.   But if the danger is internal, it cannot be grappled with, destroyed or escaped; instead it generates an impotent rage.   Ed managed to hide his rage at his mother from her and even from himself.   She would not have tolerated it; he would not have been loved if he had showed it.

Married, Ed repeats toward his wife the old pattern toward his mother.   He is the good devoted boy in the home.   But besides being unaccustomed to making his way in the world and not wishing to, he uses this passive withdrawal as a weapon of hostility: "All right, Mother, you hold me back from growing up in the world, then I'll do what you say—but to such an extent that we'll just see how you like it!"   This passivity used to express hostility is the so-called passive aggression.   It is the sit-down strike that Jane, described previously in "Give–Get in Marriage," used consciously in neglecting the house as revenge on her husband.

Interestingly, treatment is more promising if the passivity expresses hostility than if it is a simple fixation, simple childish pleasure

pleasure in inaction. For hostility is mostly uncomfortable, and for this and other reasons is reducible.* But simple passivity gives satisfaction, and what gives pleasure is relinquished only with great difficulty. If a drive to responsible activity is there but is blocked by hostility, the task is only to unblock it; but if the passivity has never been outgrown in favor of this drive to responsible activity, then a long process is required for growth out of something that is clung to as pleasurable. Hence alcoholism, sexual perversions and misbehavior and generally all symptoms that give pleasure are difficult to change. It is almost like working with something that is not there. People only change if they feel strongly that the change will relieve suffering and increase pleasure.

If the passivity is the result of normal drives to activity and responsibility being blocked while they still exist strongly in the person, then therapeutically the most favorable situation exists. It is the third source: passivity as blocked (inhibited) mature drive. For example, a father insists too much that his son be a great success. The son has drive and wants to succeed but is on a sit-down strike against the excessive parental pressure. Another son is always criticized for what he does; his activity becomes blocked for fear of criticism. Another is so intensely competitive that success means to him defeating or killing off every rival. Striving is therefore so fraught with effort and anxiety as to become inhibited.

Sometimes the child is in such conflict with his parents or others, or as an adult is so burdened by internal pressures or by situations in life that exceed his capacities, that he gives up, breaks down, collapses and is unable to continue his responsibilities. This is passivity as regression from adult life, back to the dependence and helplessness of childhood. Such regression may affect only certain parts of the personality, or it may be comprehensive enough to necessitate hospitalization. Such passivity as regression from external situations beyond a person's tolerance are of course clearly seen in the neuroses of war (Saul, 1971). It is a matter of external pressures impinging too strongly on a person's "specific emotional vulnerability." Thus one man would break as soon as he was drafted. Another would

---

*As Coleridge wrote in "Christabel":
     And to be wroth with one we love
     Doth work like madness in the brain.

tolerate combat better than the next, but then would break when he heard that his wife had been unfaithful to him. Others would tolerate just about everything except the authoritarian discipline—and so on. The strongest men break and regress if the pressure hits them in their most vulnerable emotional spots.

Ed's problem turned out to be passivity as fixation. Of course these four categories (fixation, hostility, blocked normal drive and psychological escape into regression) are not hard and fast, are not mutually exclusive; all are usually present, but in varying proportions. In some persons one reaction predominates strongly over the others, as hostility did in Jane and as fixation did in Ed.

All this sounds, I fear, rather didactic, but it is of the greatest practical importance. Each person should understand the nature and strength of the passivity versus the responsible drives in himself—and in his prospective mate.

It is tragic when a good man finds himself wedded to a woman who turns out to be infantile in her lack of interest or capacity for responsibilities for home, husband and children. And what of the woman who, aglow with love, entrusts her security and that of her children to the breadwinning capacity of her husband? Certainly she should know that a man's relation to his work is no set, stable thing. It is subject, like everything else in the personality, to a whole range of variation. It is influenced by intelligence and energy and, of course, by the emotional relationships left from the man's childhood.

The capacity of responsibility is, as we have seen, an attribute of maturity, and conversely responsibility builds maturity. A man's capacity for interest and accomplishment in his work is a vital part of his personality for himself and for his family. He may be so compulsive in his application to his work that his wife bitterly objects, somewhat as Jane did. But before a wife objects, however legitimately, to her husband's excessive application to his occupation, let her consider the other extreme: the men like Ed, who, however charming in every other respect, are emotionally infantile and inadequate as providers.

It is difficult for most men to find a happy medium. Even if a man's own emotional balance and maturity make his desire a happy medium, external pressures of the world, in our society, bear down heavily upon him. When a man is young, he must make his way to a certain level of income and security, and this is no easy task. When older, he has responsibilities that he is usually unable to shed. He is caught in a more or less all-or-nothing position. Usually it is not possible, in certain strata at least, to do half a job or three-quarters of a job. The competition is strong. At any age and stage he may wish to let up and have more time for his family and for leisure, but life rarely lets him achieve this well-balanced situation.

Thus the balance between interests (work, family, society) and the balance between responsible effort and reaction are both difficult to attain because of the external demands of life and the internal balance of forces within the personality. Perhaps this is part of the reason why it is said that it is the very rich and the very poor who take the worst beatings from life.

Perhaps too it is because of the unremitting daily demands of life that so many people long for surcease from work—for passivity—and are apt to forget that the exercise of one's mature adult powers, if not excessive, is one of the greatest of all blessings. "Blessed is he who has found his work." Put conversely, one of the worst punishments for a man—and for a woman too—is to force him to be idle, to prevent him from using his abilities. For in this the personality is like the body. If vision is not used, it dims, as animals long in caves lose their sight. Muscles, even if in peak condition, weaken in a few weeks if they are not used. So too do the reflexes for sports and arts, from golf or skiing to piano playing or singing. The proper use of one's body, mind and feelings for mature, responsible, giving, constructive purposes is indispensable to the maintenance of health and strength. To let one's natural endowments atrophy bespeaks an emotional problem.

Looked at another way, the progressive thrust of maturation is opposed by a counterforce of fixation and regression back to the childhood patterns. These patterns affect different motivations. Some persons carry the weightiest responsibilities without flinching—Winston Churchill, for example (but he said he would not want to live through it all again). Others carry on, but the inner protest, the regression that is not given in to, contributes to ulcers, high blood pressure, or to other symptoms. Others under their first adult responsibilities do regress, even to the point of breaking down. And still others never get started at all.

Ed started, but barely. His wife suspected nothing while they were students together. Not until six years and three children later did she realize that he had a problem, and even then she did not perceive its severity. He accepted treatment, which was to be financed by his mother and his mother-in-law. The analyst knew that this arrangement played into the problem, but reasoned that if a start were made and any progress at all achieved, Ed might then gradually become willing as well as able to contribute financially. It was the only way an attempt could be made.

It was evident in a few weeks that the attempt would fail. There was no sign in his history, dreams, memories or present behavior of any motivation toward this or any other financial responsibility. His unconscious motto was: Anything is better than work. There was no therapeutic urge and hence no progress. The analyst cannot hypnotize or anesthetize the patient and actively *do* something, as the surgeon can; of course such methods have long been tried—hypnosis, Pentothal, shock and the like. Improvement on a sound, permanent basis is the result of alterations in the balance of basic forces in the personality.

In Ed's case, the progressive forces toward work were overwhelmed by the childhood fixation. It seemed clear that there was not enough for the analyst to work with, but he tried valiantly and far reduced his fee to bring it to something that Ed could afford himself. But Ed was more inclined to enjoy treatment at the expense of his mother than to use it for any real change in his attitudes and functioning. Despite all the analyst's resources, the treatment never took hold. Some persons from their first contact with analytic therapy feel that it was developed just for them. Some begin with a powerful resistance, usually from things within them that they fear to face or reveal or experience; but it is usually favorable for improvement to have this defensiveness appear early so that it can be dealt with immediately. The balance of forces in others is such that analytic intervention cannot influence them appreciably and start them toward health and maturity. Ed was a legitimate failure (in contrast to the illegitimate ones resulting from faults in treatment).

His analyst arranged to maintain contact with Ed by occasional visits and phone calls. This kept the relationship going and enabled the analyst to watch for anything that he might be able to do by way of prevention or help.

Ed dragged along earning less than his family could subsist on. He would keep an inadequately paying job for a time because he enjoyed it. One that required much work he soon relinquished. The parental families contributed in order to keep the family going, but their financial resources were limited and they could not or would not continue this support indefinitely. Their attitude gradually shifted from wanting to help Ed get up the first rungs of the ladder to impatience and dismay at the character deficiency they were being forced to acknowledge.

Faced with the withdrawal of their help, Eleanor, the wife, felt that she had no choice but to find remunerative work herself, in addition to the already weighty job of caring for home, husband and three children on a subsistence income. She found work that enabled her to pay for help in the home and still come out ahead financially. Fortunately she was sturdy physically, but the strain soon told. The chief effect was to make her irritable. She tolerated this irritability in herself toward her husband because it was his fecklessness that overburdened her. Even so, she was not entirely easy about her shortening temper with him because he was a warm, interested husband and father, and what with his shortcomings, could not but appeal to the maternal in her. She inevitably responded to this appeal, which derived so directly from his childhood pattern toward his mother. But her blowing up at the children filled her with guilt and self-reproach, and she became somewhat anxious and depressed.

Sex, as we have said, is the great diversion and consolation; it channels and drains every kind of tension and feeling. As Eleanor felt more and more deprived and increasingly resentful toward Ed, her give–get balance was tilted far over by little get and excessive give, and she began to think of a love affair. This might provide masculine consolation, a needed outlet, diversion and change from the home, and drain some of her hostile wish for revenge against her husband. She was not conscious of all this. All she was aware of fully was the buildup of this urge and these fantasies. Her background and training were such that her reaction to this impulse was guilt—and, when inevitably she met a man who might make such an adventure a reality, she panicked. She feared that yielding to such desires might carry her byond a point of no return and involve her in feelings and situations destructive to herself as well as to her family.

To save herself, she called her husband's analyst. That is how, in the position of consultant, I heard the story, told to me at her own request. His analyst, after discussion with me, referred her to another, not wanting to jeopardize any possibility, however slight, of helping Ed by seeing his wife also.

She was right to be afraid of such entanglement. It would mean too much to her. It had too hostile a meaning, which, intended for her husband, might cause suffering to the children; and she was already so filled with guilt that she could not trust herself to use such an affair for release and happiness without too large a component of self-punishment. But the temptation was so strong that she sought help in fighting it and allaying it.

The impulse to indulge in extramarital sex is very commonly stimulated by anger at the spouse. But some personalities are such that they do not react with infidelity no matter how angry they are—they respond, but by other mechanisms and in other ways.

While his wife was thus struggling with the pressures from her external circumstances and from her own emotional responses to them, Ed increasingly felt the strain. He was reproached, sometimes openly, sometimes silently, by his wife and their parents. Inevitably the children began to show signs of upset. He felt shame, which is a reaction to weakness and makes one feel undeserving of love; and he felt guilt, which is caused by injuring another and makes one feel he deserves punishment. He too found his outer and inner worlds less and less happy, more and more burdensome. His fixated passivity kept him from the one simple solution: earning a reasonable income by doing a proper job somewhere near the level of his abilities. His makeup, as we have seen, was deficient in fighting spirit and preseverance, so important in life and for analytic treatment.

I wondered what his unconscious would decide. His solution was just as pat as one might have anticipated. He could not relieve his wife's burdens and make his home happy; so be began to think of a change. He began to talk of divorce. Eleanor was now even harder pressed. She wished she could feel "good riddance," but now Ed's virtues were a handicap; apart from poor providing, he was, as she had always known, a good husband and father. And she loved him. Difficult as life was with him, what would it be without him—no husband for her, no father for the children and even less income from him or none? And if she stood the rejection emotionally and could in her heart accept another husband, what were the chances of finding one when all her energies were going into working to support herself and the children, while still running the home?

As for Ed, it gradually became apparent that his pattern from 0 to 6 was turning his wishes toward another home more nearly like his parental one; he was thinking of divorce and then a second marriage, this time to a wife who would be rich enough to be a good provider for him. And since his pattern was of warmth and charm toward women, especially older ones, he felt that this would work out.

Eleanor first endured the disillusionment of her husband's neurotic improvidence; then she sustained the burden of working in addition to running the home; now came the psychic pain of rejection and the prospect of a bleak future. Her strength was exceeded. The potential deterioration that began with the temptations to infidelity now progressed like a malignant disease. Her irritability increased. Instead of smoking a cigarette or two after lunch and dinner, she now reached for one at every minor demand, frustration or tension. She became an addict. Of course, I know the argument that smoking is a habit and not an addiction, but the distinction is, in my opinion, a sophistry. For smoking, instead of merely being a pleasure, comes to meet an emotional need and becomes more and more compulsive— the person is forced by inner compulsion to smoke, just as he may be addicted to overeating or to alcohol or to women or to drugs. Eleanor's smoking increased to half a pack a day, then a pack a day, and soon she was chain-smoking at least three packs a day. She tried to cut down and could not; tried to stop completely and could not; and finally gave in.

This giving in was the first real crack in her ego, her defenses, her character. Not able to resist smoking, she began drinking martinis before dinner every evening. She began to have trouble sleeping and tried to help this by drinking vodka at bedtime. She overate and began losing her figure. Life was too much for her. She fought, but a losing fight, always giving more ground.

The marital vicious circle was in full whirl. And the children, as always, were caught with the parents in the downward vortex. They became irritable, had nightmares, behaved badly, did poorly at school, and more and more became problem children. So the home was transformed more and more into a place into which Ed's pattern fitted less and less. It is said that divorce brings out the worst in people. No doubt it is often the best solution and the only solution. Couples who are destroying each other sometimes do divorce and make good second marriages. And in many an instance it is clear that no marriage is far better than a bad marriage; for a bad marriage can breed hatred and can destroy both body and soul. But the process of separation is apt to be nasty. At any rate, for better or worse for him and his wife and children, Ed finally insisted and won out. The divorce became a reality.

Eleanor and the children moved in with her parents, forced by the divorce to return to all the tensions she had had with them as a child. I have used as a slogan: G.D.M., meaning "generations don't mix." Eleanor and her parents were no exception. Through all this Eleanor had the indispensable help of a psychiatrist in a clinic and, for part of the time, of a social worker in an agency.

Needless to say, there can never possibly be enough therapists to help the millions who need them. The only practicable solution is prevention. This has many aspects. The basic one is of course the proper rearing of children so that they mature adequately and do not have pathological childhood patterns that disrupt their own lives as well as the lives of those to whom they are important.

Before our eyes the neurotics, dropouts and juvenile delinquents of the rising generation are manufactured where all of them are made—*in the home*. The only sound basis for control of children comes not from cold discipline, but from a good relationship with the parents, from loving and being loved, and from good parental examples of mature behavior. But, in this world, how many parents are themselves mature?

When I last heard, Ed was remarried, to a woman with a small but assured private income. Perhaps it was because of this support and freedom from the responsibilities of parenthood that he was now able to carry satisfactorily a simple clerking job, and he was interested enough to take some courses in a business school. Eleanor reached a frustrated stability, living near her parents, being helped by them and working half-time while the children were in school.

She was a superior person in energy and good will. But her position was vulnerable. When I heard from her recently, it seems her parents had lost what money they had, and she was fighting for survival against inflation and burdened by the emotional problems of her children—but she *was* struggling and was still afloat. She had developed enormously as a person, but at what a price. Possibly the world at large would benefit, for she had become a fine, strong and prolific writer.

Here is a similar case: Jack was attractive, strong, energetic and the son of financially comfortable parents. He seemed a fine catch for any girl. When Josie married him, their friends rejoiced for them both. It took a few years for Josie to realize that Jack was not capable of sustained work; he was like Ed. This marriage, however, did not run as tragic a course as Eleanor and Ed's. Josie managed a job as well as home and children, without breakdown or deterioration. Very few women in my experience have been capable of doing so. Jack's parents helped out to some extent, and the marriage survived. Jack's problem, and the tensions with Josie that it created, could not but have ill effects on their sons; but Josie was superior in her handling of the difficulties, and Jack, however childish in the workaday world, was a loving father; so the children had a reasonably good life. But it is still sad to think of so superior and talented a girl as Josie dissipating so much of her warmth and happiness in the internal heat and friction of a marriage to a husband with such pathology in his makeup.

It is quite different when such pathology (pathological dynamics or pathodynamics) shows up earlier. It would be a boon if these passive trends, and other disorders as well, could be spotted while the young men and women were still students. Sometimes they show up in the senior year of high school or college as anxiety or other symptoms. In interviews they are often found to result from the fear of graduating from the protection of school, which is all the student has ever known, into the unknown milling and mixing of life, with its responsible tasks, inexorable demands and many problems in understanding and dealing with people.

Book knowledge is essential for techniques, as in science, engineering, medicine or law; but for living it only supplements "street knowledge," which is what counts. Yet this truth is almost totally ignored and neglected by our educational system.

For example, a young woman, an excellent student, was courted in college by an ardent young man. In the beginning of their senior year they made plans to marry about six months after graduation. Let us call them Kay and Ken. As the year progressed, it was evident that Ken was not doing well in his studies. Actually, he had never

been an outstanding student.   It was not clear whether he had un-
realized capacities, but it seemed to be generally accepted that he was
extremely able but not working up to his potential.   It is interesting
how often one encounters this estimate of a student without any solid
factual basis for it.   In this case, it seemed to be deduced from Ken's
many talents.   He sang, he built hi-fi sets, he could draw, and he was a
superior dancer.   He was very good at tennis and other sports.   The deduction was that if he applied himself to his work, he would easily be
successful in whatever field he chose.   This assumption reflected his
opinion of himself and his parents' opinion.   He did poorly in his senior
year but graduated.   He obtained a position, but then worked only mar-
ginally.   This caused second thoughts in Kay, and a closer look.   She
came to talk with me about it.   Perhaps in the not too distant future,
when psychodynamics is more advanced scientifically and psychiatrists
are more skilled in its application, young couples contemplating marriage will profit in many ways from psychiatric interviews.   Kay was
highly perceptive as well as intelligent.   She had done what all girls and
all young men should do before letting themselves become seriously
involved.   She had pieced together from Ken and his parents enough
about his 0 to 6, his early childhood, and his later life as well to have a
pretty reliable picture of his underlying pattern.   It was this:

Ken was an only child.   He was a loved child.   This gave him the
warmth to which Kay responded.   But he was loved too well and not
wisely enough.   He was too much doted on.   Everything he did filled
his parents with pride, and they thought no child was ever so cute,
so bright or so accomplished in every activity he tried.   Ken quite
naturally took over his parents' extravagant opinion of himself.   He
grew up with this self-image.   Never was there a child who could do
so many things so well.   But as he became older, vague, disturbing
fears crept in.   On closer examination his performances in science,
music, sports and the social graces were those of a dilettante.   His
whole orientation was toward winning the praises of his fond parents;
but he was accustomed to winning praise by showing off skills and
not by solid, responsible accomplishment.   When he did not do well,
even in school, his parents had excuses: he had great potential but
had not yet found himself.   Thus he was warm and affectionate but
striving for praise, rather than geared to sustained responsible work,
even in studying and getting good grades.   All that he did was more a
subdued showing-off than an expression of any genuine interest.

This became very evident toward Kay herself. When she suggested postponing the marriage, Ken replied that this was not his idea of love—if she really loved him she would love him for himself alone and not be concerned whether he did well in his work or not.

This of course was the key. This revealed his immaturity. All his life he had been loved unconditionally by his father and mother. Now he wanted to marry but failed to see the difference between the love of a child by doting parents and the mature love between husband and wife. He failed totally to see the responsibilities toward wife and toward children that were involved in marriage. When Kay explored his finances, she found that he was planning to marry with enough money for a two-week honeymoon and no other resources, except an insecure job with minimal pay and uncertain prospects.

It became clear that Ken thought marriage meant getting from a wife all the love he knew from his parents, only now with sex included. The thought of his own responsibilities did not occur to him; he had always been provided for. The idea that he himself would be in the parent role as an adult, now called upon to provide financially for his own marital family, had not reached him. It was evident that, having been too strongly on the receiving end from his parents, he was deficient in appreciating the needs of a wife and children. Indeed, the closer look revealed no evidence that he was capable of supporting himself if he were alone in the world, let alone capable of all the interest, energy output and giving of self involved in meeting the emotional and financial demands of a wife and children. In his psychology he had not made the transition from child receiving to parent giving. Despite his looks, strengths and talents, he was still too much a child himself for any girl to count on him for her security and happiness.

He did not even see the problem until Kay made it an issue. At first he blamed it all on Kay, on circumstances, on his parents, on his stars. Only after some weeks was he forced to face the fact that there was a real problem within himself. And this realization opened up new hope for his maturing. Not to see this means, in some young men, mounting inferiority feelings, frustrations and impotent rage. In some cases the tension rises as the youth becomes a man in years, while the discrepancy increases between the maturity he needs for living, but cannot achieve, and the infantile orientation, which he cannot rid himself of because he cannot perceive it.

The engagement was broken, but Kay said she would see if Ken changed. This unhappy experience brought him for analytic help and may have saved him, his wife and his children from the suffering of a marital failure. Perhaps no one is more than 70 percent mature, but a certain minimum is essential for making one's way through life—at least 51 percent, let us say, and preferably over 60 percent.

The war intervened, and I am not sure of the end of the story. There was enough to work with in this young man, however, that with good analytic help and his experience in the armed services he may well have gone on to mature sufficiently to work and support a wife and children and have a reasonably good life, with the recognition that he must think not entirely of his own desires but also of the needs of others, especially his wife and children. (I did recently hear that Ken was holding a job in a small college, and the marriage was surviving.)

Whether coming into money solves many or any of the marital problems arising from the husband's limitations as the breadwinner, I do not know. Perhaps if this is his only major deficiency as a husband, if the other eight components of marriage are adequate, if this is a circumscribed area of pathology, then maybe money could keep the ship of marriage on an even keel.

In a way, the ability to earn a living has been primarily a male problem; for despite permanent argument and endless variations in our culture, breadwinning has long been the basic responsibility of the man, as running the home has been for the woman. Therefore, failure in the wife of responsibility for the home and children is equivalent to the husband's failure in providing the necessities for it. One certainly sees in an office practice numerous examples. Women's liberation may change all that, but many happily married women think they have a "good thing" and want to hold on to it.

Fred was about as adequate a husband, father, provider, friend, citizen and all-around good man as one meets in a lifetime. Frances, his wife, was his equal except in one area. This only came to light gradually, just as a husband's inhibitions in earning often emerge only after some years of marriage.

Frances was unusually intelligent, attractive and capable, but it began to be evident that she had no interest in any responsibilities having to do with the home. She could spend endless energy on community affairs but never had time to call the plumber. She was praised by all who knew her as the finest secretary the bridge club ever had, but she moaned like a martyr when she did any accounts for the home. She was indefatigable at tennis, but the mere prospect of replacing a burned-out light bulb in the home made her feel overburdened, and this item was placed on a list of things she would do when she had time (and anyway, she reasoned, it was a man's job). When someone phoned about any sort of problem, she gave sage, balanced, disinterested counsel, speaking for hours on the phone; but brief phone calls to the butcher or baker or laundry wore her out. I need not go on.

In her personal relations with the children, two daughters and a son, she was a fine mother, judicious and sound and full of humor. But her failure to provide a well-run home introduced tensions between herself and her husband that inevitably embroiled the children and damaged their emotional development. Frances in the home was the counterpart of Ed, in our earlier example, at work. In anything that was not an obligation, that meant to her *play*, she was superb. But in anything that involved domestic *responsibility* she was either entirely derelict of else did what was required so grudgingly and with such a martyred air that Fred and the children were enraged and hated to accept whatever she did do. They came to hate any dependence on her, and she treated the normal, even the minimal obligations of wife and mother as inexcusable demands and impositions.

Her parental home had been a rejecting, unhappy place; her only pleasure had been playing with other little girls, at a neighbor's. She developed in her marital home the same pattern as she had had in her parental home as we all do in some form—the same pattern or some reaction formation against it. As long as she could play and be praised, she was a happy child, throughout her life. When she had to carry responsibilities for the home, she became martyred, irritable, hateful and withdrawn.

By the time this pattern came out clearly, the first child had arrived and the second was on her way. Fred recognized this childishness in his wife and feared for her welfare if he sought a divorce. Fred was sociable, and his business required some entertaining. Frances liked being entertained but hated being the hostess herself. Fewer and fewer friends came to their home. Fred located a small cabin in an idyllic setting near enough to town for weekends. Frances raged against the idea of owning it because she feared she might somehow be expected to have some responsibility for it. They grew further and further apart as the decades slipped by. Fred made a life of his own while living in his own home with a wife who was so distant as to be almost a stranger. He would not desert her or the children. But he learned bitterly that no marriage at all is sometimes better than a bad marriage. He also learned to make the best of his wife's good qualities and to appreciate the children, for whom Frances had, in some respects, been a really good mother. He learned to enjoy what he had, and he enjoyed life as best he could without the warm affection of a wife.

In childhood he had been accustomed to much affection and closeness. Now, although he tried to accept it, the deprivation and hostility he endured from Frances—the much give and slight get—and the isolation in his own home resulted in mounting strain. Yet he was not of the makeup to seek in another woman what his wife did not provide: the normal, honest loving and being loved between a man and woman. He did not break down. He only developed common psychosomatic symptoms, the warning signs of the stress, signs that his life was being shortened. He was being killed slowly by the passivity of his wife, by her emotional pattern, which she did not will, which she did not put there, but which was her inevitable reaction as a small child to the rejections and restrictions in her 0–6 by her own parents. Her personal relations with Fred had been good enough for them to fall in love, court and marry, but these good feelings had been corrupted by the narrow pattern of her inner childish rejection of domestic responsibility. Love is easy; marriage is very difficult.

References

Saul, L. J. (1971): *Emotional Maturity*, 3rd Ed. Philadelphia: Lippincott, p. 207.

SECTION IV:
SEX OUTSIDE MARRIAGE:
EXTRAMARITAL SEXUAL
REGRESSION AND OTHER
TYPES OF INFIDELITY

To a man the disappointment of love may occasion some bitter pangs . . . but he is an active being—he may dissipate his thoughts in the whirl of varied occupation. But woman's is comparatively a fixed, a secluded, and meditative life. She is more the companion of her own thoughts and feelings. Her lot is to be wooed and won; and if unhappy in her love, her heart is like some fortress that has been captured, and sacked, and abandoned, and left desolate.

Irving

You lie and hate it and it destroys you . . . .

Hemingway

There is only one kind of love, but there are a thousand imitations. (Il n'y a que d'une sorte d'amour, mais il y en a mille différentes copies.)

La Rochefoucauld

It matters little for an old heart like mine, which has but one or two chords left whole, how soon it be broken altogether; but a young heart is one of God's precious treasures . . . and suffers many a long pang in the breaking; and woe to them who despise Christ's little ones.

Charles Kingsley,
Westward Ho!

*And eyeless Nature that makes you drink
From the cup of Love, though you know it's poisoned . . .*

Edgar Lee Masters,
Spoon River Anthology

We are now acquainted with some common varieties of marital difficulty, the emotional forces that underlie them and what we find when we follow these forces back to early childhood. The difficulties have been intramarital, between husband and wife. There are marital problems, however, that involve a third person. We will first consider one particular form of infidelity, which, because it is primarily a return to behavior characteristic of adolescence or earlier, we will call "extramarital sexual regression." We will illustrate some of its dynamics for people at different ages, and mention only briefly some of the other forms that unfaithfulness takes.

14
MONOGAMY AND INFIDELITY

If a person has achieved a reasonable degree of maturity, has a good intelligence and lives at such a time and place that he can carve a niche for himself in the existing socioeconomic cultural conditions of his society, then he can be expected to make a good life for himself and his family by contributing to society itself, giving value for value.

There are, however, a number of conflicts that seem to be *built into* the mind of every individual (Saul, 1977a, p. 275). For example, there is the tendency to continue the old familiar patterns of childhood versus those forces impelling one toward patterns of maturity and adult living: the forces of *development* and *maturity* versus the opposing forces of *fixation* and *regression.* Then there are the conflicts between *"narcissism"* and *object interest*: one's interest in oneself and one's own welfare and status, prestige, self-esteem and vanity versus one's interest in, love and consideration for others. There is a conflict between *love* and *sex*; and a conflict between tendencies toward *monogamy* and toward *promiscuity;* both of these are usually related, especially in the male, to his "oedipal conflict" with his mother.

The last-named conflicts are of central importance for relations between the sexes. It seems that all the urges that relatively normal men and women feel toward the opposite sex eventually tend to coalesce and concentrate on one particular individual. Such urges not only include the physiological sexual desire for intercourse and orgasm and trends to cooperation in all the processes of reproduction and the rearing of young, but also include the psychological tendencies to dependence, identification, companionship and other trends, infantile and mature, many of them unconscious. Even if these needs were not themselves in conflict, they would be too much to expect one other human being to gratify. So some degree of frustration in marriage is inevitable.

In addition to monogamy, occasionally seen elsewhere in the animal kingdom, human beings seem to be attracted more or less strongly to members of the opposite sex *outside* the monogamous union. The nature and strength of these *promiscuous* trends and the control of them, as of the monogamous ones, is powerfully influenced by the psychodynamics of the individual formed by his childhood emotional pattern.

Promiscuity may be antithetical to monogamy (excluding from our discussion homosexuality, fetishism and other variants), but not all nonmonogamous or antimonogamous trends are promiscuous in the sense of being indiscriminate. This attraction to healthy, hand-some members of the opposite sex varies enormously in outcome: it may remain a loose, free attraction to each healthy, attractive, heterosexual individual, or it may settle on one in particular, in addition to the spouse, or on a series of such persons. This attraction may remain just a feeling, conscious or unconscious, confessed or repressed, or it may be acted out in differing manner and degree, ranging from relatively calm erotically tinged friendship to full, passionate sexual relations.

Both the form and the strength of the monogamous and the countermonogamous drives are quantitative matters, varying in desire and in outcome as behavior, determined by one's early life relationships with those closest to one. Monogamy requires considerable maturity; faithfulness in adult life is usually the outcome of steady, faithful love relations between the child's parents and toward the child itself (Saul, 1977a, b).*

If the most intense feelings of a child were toward a member of its own sex, parent or sibling, then the sexual feelings in following this channel tend toward homosexuality. For example, from birth a girl's father was hardly ever present, and her main feelings centered on her mother. These feelings were needs for love and appreciation, intensified by her mother's neglect and depreciation; rebellion against her mother's harsh authoritarian control; and hostility and hate toward her mother because of this traumatic treatment. The whole storm of her conflicting feelings as a tiny child centered from birth on her mother. Later, she had a good, although relatively weak,

---

*It has been estimated that more than one-half of the population now indulges in affairs with a 60 percent male, 40 percent female breakdown (*Today*, February 12, 1978, p. 15).

distant relationship with her kindly father, which was a rescuing force in her life. In adolescence she had a few intense homosexual affairs, repeating the vortex of feelings around her mother, displaced to other girls. Eventually, however, the pattern toward her father emerged dominant, and she married. This only occurred after therapy, which she could accept with a male analyst chiefly because of her childhood relationship with her father.

We have pointed out that a male's attachment to his mother forms a pattern that he invariably repeats to some degree toward his wife (see Chapter 2, "Love, Sex and Psychodynamics"). Good warm feelings toward his mother lay a foundation for later good feelings toward his wife.

Trouble can arise, however, when the emotional pattern toward his mother is conflictful and unhappy, for example, when a mother is consciously or unconsciously too seductive sexually. Ted's mother would "race him to bed". He would always win and then, from the age of about four until he was eight, he would watch his mother disrobe completely at the foot of the bed before donning her night-gown. He mentioned it to her once, but she dismissed his interest with the remark, "I have a body and you have a body," as though it were of no consequence. He remembered thinking at the time, "Who are you kidding?" Ted's mother was not only seductive, but at the same time she strictly forbade him to look at her nude. He grew up sexually overstimulated by her but also inhibited by her forbidding his sexual responses. When Ted married, he repeated this pattern: he was aroused by his wife but felt that sex with her was unsatisfying. This led him to turn to other women in a ceaseless search for and flight from his mother-figure; he was attracted to his wife but inhibited sexually with her and diverted his interest and potency to other women.

Inevitably, receptive-dependent needs play an intrinsic part in these dynamics. Whether sexual feelings are stirred up or not, the child (whether boy or girl) is dependent upon the mother (or substitute) under normal conditions of upbringing. She tends to all his physical needs when he is a baby and a toddler, later getting him off to school, feeding him, settling him in at bedtime, and so on. Later, dating becomes part of the pattern: the son is permitted and even expected to date and turn his sexual interest to girls who are "exogamic," that is, nonincestuous, outside of the family. When the man marries, the whole pattern toward his mother tends in time to repeat itself toward his wife. She becomes the woman of the house and often, in the young man's unconscious, the new "mother-figure" in the home, an image that is intensified if children arrive and she becomes a mother in reality. Then the husband may become overly dependent upon his wife, lose sexual interest in her and turn his sex drive away from his marital home, just as he turned his adolescent sex drives from his parental home (upon which he was dependent emotionally, financially and in other ways) to his dates.

It is this pattern that causes a man to "live in sin" with a woman with full sexual interest, only to lose his potency immediately after marrying her. And, *mutatis mutandi*, the same pattern is seen in women. For example, a young woman was apparently oversexed and insatiably desirous of a man whom she had seduced and with whom she was living. A few weeks after their marriage, she lost all desire for him, rejected him sexually and turned her sex urges toward another. She had been overly close to her father, who brought his mistress into the home and at the same time unrestrainedly depreciated the girl's mother. This girl resisted identifying with her mother, the depreciated and helpless, masochistic wife, choosing in her mind to be the mistress preferred by her father.

For a man to transfer to his wife the pattern of dependency and inhibited sexual feelings he had toward his mother is relatively normal and healthy. But if these motivations were too strong or if there was a warping in this childhood pattern, if his mother treated him badly by omission or commission, especially prior to the age of about six, then such trauma can cause enough warping in the emotional development to produce psychopathology, i.e., serious emotional disorder of one kind or another, which is carried from childhood toward his mother into the adult relationship with his spouse. Such disturbances can contain frustrations and hostility toward his mother that will erupt as anger and hate, evidenced directly or indirectly, toward his wife.

Of course, a woman's human relations are also directly tied to the relationship she had with her mother in childhood, and like the male's are repeated in her marital relationship. And a daughter's treatment by her father can help her to mature adequately or have traumatic effects.

A man grew up from 0 to 6 with a father who treated his wife like a servant. The father came and went as he pleased, never letting his wife know if or when he was coming home for dinner, or whether he would be away on business for a week, or where; he demanded attention and service when he was at home and freely brought his mistresses home with him. To his son, he was a loving, giving Santa Claus. The man's wife, utterly rejected, debased and ignored, had little love left give her son. So the son quite naturally identified with his gift-giving, freedom-loving, self-indulgent father, and upon marrying he treated his wife and children as his father had so long treated his mother.

As we have emphasized, everything in the emotional life must be understood quantitatively. In the above example, we move out of the relatively normal sexual, dependent and submissive feelings of the small boy toward his mother, which, while containing the "oedipal" problems, form the base for a good, close relationship with a wife; and we move into the realm of psychopathology, the area of emotional disorder. A girl who marries a man who had poor relations with his mother during his 0–6 takes a great risk. Conversely, a man who had warm, close, secure feelings with his mother may remain faithful to his wife even in the face of such abuse as might drive another man to divorce.

No one can control his genes or into what family, era, socioeconomic conditions or time of war or peace he will be born. His personality, his dynamics, will determine how he reacts to his environments and behaves in them, whether or not he played any part in shaping them. But obviously, while the deepest motivations and reactions stem from the childhood emotional pattern, the external forces are also powerful. This is seen historically in women who were born into residual feudal circles of England, pressured to marry only to produce male heirs as links in inheriting landed estates and titles, and who were not treated primarily as persons in their own right. These women often responded with hostility and used their femininity and power as a weapon, becoming promiscuous and making scandals mostly as revenge for these external reasons, rather than because of trauma during 0–6, frequent as that was.

References

Saul, L. J. (1977a): *The Childhood Emotional Pattern.* New York: Van Nostrand Reinhold.

——(1977b): *The Childhood Emotional Pattern and Corey Jones.* New York: Van Nostrand Reinhold.

15
IN THE TWENTIES

Some time ago, impressed by the return to teenage behavior of a series of male patients who were past 50, I contemplated a paper on this subject with the working title "Late Life Regressions." But then I realized that this adolescent acting out was just as common in the forties, in the thirties and even earlier, as well as much later, even in the sixties and seventies. Here is a sample:

An apparently wholesome, clean-cut American couple, whom we will call Hank and Helen, court in college and marry a year after graduating. Hank is then well established on a stipend in graduate school, on his way to becoming a clinical psychologist. They are very happy and have a daughter. When she is six months old, Hank begins to have some doubts about his choice of a career. These doubts increase. After some months he decides that he should take a year off and "think about it."

This decision is typical, but usually a bad sign. Doubts about career? "Take a year to think about it." Embroiled in an extra-marital affair and don't know what to do? "Think about it." Sometimes to this is added: "Talk about it," endlessly, compulsively. As though certain basic orientations, motivations and feelings could be resolved by meditation; as though one must stop living while thinking. Why didn't Hank go ahead with his training, which would always be useful in any field, *while* he sought a more satisfying pursuit? I have often found that the person who must do nothing while he tries to find himself professionally has an inner block against doing anything. He resists any prolonged, responsible training and work, and is acting out an unconscious wish to do just what he is doing: nothing. He is thinking of what to do, but living out what he more deeply wants—the passive-dependence of the small child, who is active kinetically, always on the go, but incapable of channeling this diffuse energy into any serious sustained responsibility. For this reason such persons often take aptitude tests but do not follow through.

Hank took his year off, and on their small capital they lived inexpensively at a sort of camp. Something came out of his thinking, but it was not certainty and drive in his career; it was the extension of his doubts to encompass his marriage. Now he was not only unsure of his choice of profession; he began to doubt his choice of a wife. It is not uncommon for these regressions to occur about the time a child is born, sometimes because it strikes some specific emotional vulnerability (such as the arrival of a preferred brother or sister in the person's childhood). But most often, I think, it is because of retreat in the face of added responsibility. A child really seals a marriage, binds one so irrevocably, and imposes such lifelong weighty responsibilities.

Now Hank thought about his marriage also, and, typically, he believed that to do so he must withdraw from Helen in the meantime. He could not send his baby daughter back while he thought about her too, although doubtless he would have liked to. But he did pull away from his wife and slept in a different room—and they were in their early twenties, when the sexual drive is at its peak. This was a rather bad sign. Sex is so powerful a drive that the regression must be alarmingly powerful to stop it.

His wife came to see me. One cannot be sure of such things in a few interviews, but from all I could learn and discern she seemed as emotionally healthy a girl as one meets. This was apparent in her descriptions of her parents and her feelings for them, in her present relationships, in the course of her life, in her outlook, earliest memories and dreams—all the criteria we mentioned before. I wished I could give her a more hopeful picture of her husband's future. But here she was, married only a few years, with a baby of six months and a husband who had gone into a severe regression away from her and the child, as well as his career. His withdrawal of interest and responsibility in both areas was unprovoked by any perceptible external pressures; apparently it was a symptom of a deep inner weakness. He was one of those who regress at the very threshold of getting started in life—in career and in marriage. Some of these young men regress all the way to breakdown. Even then, however, they may with the resilience of youth and over a period of years gradually come back to some level of workable maturity and adjustment in society and marriage.

Underlying Hank's passivity was an extremely infantile passive-dependence. He had been much babied and overprotected by his mother. She hovered over him and helped him with everything. He was kept living in a symbiotic relation with her. His healthy maturational forces of growth drove him enough toward independence to work and marry. But his pattern toward his mother of passive-dependence led him to seek the same sort of envelopment by other people—by institutions such as school and church and, after marriage, by his wife. He often dreamed of his wife with a baby, and he associated the idea of a baby with himself in relation to his mother. Thus part of him—too large a part—continued to feel like a baby toward his wife, as he had been toward his mother. Then when his child was born, he had dreams of being pushed out, dreams of actual rivalry with his own child for his wife's devoted attentions.

Fortunately Hank's drives to maturity were fairly strong, and the insight and support he received from his analyst succeeded in less than a year in tilting the balance in the direction of responsible, productive activity. He began to move out of PRD (passive-receptive-dependence) toward RPI (responsible-productive-independence). He began to realize what was going on. He stopped sitting and "thinking"; he found a satisfactory job, and he reestablished the feelings of a husband and a father toward his wife and child. He was turned from the way in to the way out, at least for the present.

Hank regressed from both occupation and marriage. Sometimes only one is affected centrally, the other secondarily, as in the man who is dedicated to his job but neglects his family.

A young man in his mid-twenties has finished his training and is on the first rung up the ladder. An accountant, he has an excellent job with a large firm and is doing outstandingly well. He has a good-looking, steady wife, and three fine children. We will call him Richard and his wife Ruth. Off to so good a start in career and marriage, strong, good-looking, popular, young and healthy, he has much for others to envy and much for himself to be thankful for.

But so treacherous are the latent emotional patterns of early childhood that, rather than counting his blessings, Richard starts an affair with another woman, and before he knows it he feels himself to be half "in love" with her—he is attracted to her sexually. But if one penetrates to what is behind attractions with such destructive consequences, one almost always finds that an early childhood pattern is being acted out, a pattern in which hostility is generally the central force, truly unconscious but no less implacable hostility, usually toward the mother. Fall in love with an emotionally mature, stable and superior girl, marry her, have three healthy, happy children, and then all but murder their spirits by allowing oneself to become involved emotionally and physically with another woman. I think this only happens when the triangle fits a preexisting childhood pattern. Thus Richard continues his work while his withdrawal of love and his unexpressed unconscious hostility wreck the wife whom he has accepted and the children he has helped produce, the human beings for whom he has the greatest, most personal biological responsibility.

A married woman, a patient, once rejected something I was saying as "just typically masculine thinking." Whatever limitation this implied, men have formulated a certain wisdom among themselves. For the married man it may be terribly hard to learn to "look but not touch," but it is essential for his own selfish welfare.

A traveling man with ample opportunities to be unfaithful once told me that he sometimes took advantage of these opportunities, but only if they were sure to be transient and purely physical relationships. (Of course, sex is a component of mating and reproduction; so it cannot be *purely* physical.) He said that as soon as he saw in himself any flicker of emotional involvement, of serious personal interest, then he immediately broke the relationship—definitely, finally and completely—for, although he enjoyed his fun, his sex as play, he was most positively not going to do anything that would disturb or threaten to disturb his marriage.

A young wife, true to her husband, who has been away for two years in the Service, met a man who attracted her irresistibly. He was married and was also in the Service. She decided to yield to their mutual desires because he too would soon be gone. But that very day she received a letter from her husband overseas. He so completely trusted her that she could not betray his confidence. She broke the date. She and her husband both went through the war faithful to each other because, powerfully as they were tempted to indulge in sexual affairs, highly as they valued them, they valued far more their marriage, their home and their children. And on being reunited each wanted to greet the other, to look deep into the eyes of the other, with a sense of complete honesty and openness, which could only rest on a mutual faithfulness. I sometimes wonder if faithfulness is not more common among those species of birds and mammals who mate for life then it is among human beings, so many of whom are neurotic, that is, warped in their relationships by the way they were treated by their parents, especially from 0 to 6.

16
IN THE THIRTIES

We have stressed the basic finding that different wives—and husbands—react differently in accordance with their own individual dynamics, formed chiefly by the emotional influences upon them during early childhood. One girl of high caliber, Polly, had been married to Peter for about ten years (they were in their early thirties) when he began going out with other women. Polly, a girl of integrity and spirit, saw only one solution: Sauce for the gander was sauce for the goose. If he had affairs, then she was free to try them herself. There were three children, and she would not break up the home. So she had her affairs—very few, each long-lasting, each with a very superior, carefully chosen man, with whom there was the highest mutual regard and indeed love, and always with a man who was single or a widower or divorced, so that Polly was sure that she was in no way damaging a home. On this basis she saved her own home and kept relatively good relations with Peter. The children thereby were raised in a reasonably harmonious, stable marriage. How much heartache and psychic pain underlay her solution, I do not know. But one such woman, after telling me how well this solution worked for her, muttered as she left my office, "But it's a shitty life."

Some women are totally incapable of such a solution. In their dynamics they are strictly monogamous, one-man women. The thought of sex with a man other than their husband is not only not inviting, it is repulsive to them. Sometimes, however, if the terrible emotional strain and pain of the husband's unfaithfulness lasts long enough, even such an utterly devoted, loyal, one-man woman may turn to another man herself, turn in the way that Polly did, with no hostility to another home, seeking an unattached man who offers love, emotional as well as physical, and some healing and balm to the open wound inflicted on her heart by the husband who for so many years was her only thought.

Another girl, Rosemary, had a sound marriage and two children. Her husband, Rex, was perfectly open about extramarital sex, and could be because in their particular psychology, it was "only physical," it was always strictly within the bounds of the physical, and devoid of emotional involvement. At least this was their conscious attitude. When he visited a foreign country in the course of his business, he wrote amusing letters about sex with girls of other races, times, and customs. Rosemary freely spoke of her amusement at these transient, physical adventures of Rex's. She in turn was always touched by lonely men, and occasionally consoled them by providing the best of consolations. Rex did not mind until, in one case, there was a flicker of emotional interest on the part of Rosemary, and then in jealous anger he put his foot down.

Another outcome is quasibigamous. Shortly after I began my practice, Sheila, an attractive woman, consulted me about her husband, Sam. He had no interest in treatment for himself but came for one visit. It was possible to be of some help to his wife in the following situation:

Sam, a successful businessman, had been devoted to his wife and to their five children for over 15 years. He had always had an eye for other women and an exaggerated sexual interest in them, but had not let it affect his behavior, home life or career. Suddenly a full-blown affair erupted with a woman, Shirley, who had a husband and four children. He found Shirley irresistible, and she found Sam the same.

As is typical in these cases, rationalization played its part in self-justification. Sheila had freely admitted her part in the squabbles from which probably no marriage is free. But Sam gradually built this up to such distortion that it appeared in his mind that there never was love or good times or children or a home. With the passage of time his rationalization grew. He seemed to deceive himself with the conviction that he was a long-suffering husband driven by a merciless shrew into the companionship of another woman.

Shirley eventually divorced her husband and got an apartment for herself and her children, and Sam shared it with her. Sheila, torn to the quick, continued to keep her home together for the sake of the children and because she knew nothing else to do. So Sam lived with her and remained a good husband and father in this, his own home, but also divided his time with Shirley. In short, he now lived in two families.

Sheila survived this kind of life; and for the sake of the proper development of the children, she maintained in their minds as best she could a good image of and relationship to their father.

Perhaps all such compulsive infatuations as that between Sam and Shirley are the product of two disordered childhood patterns meshing in some way, a *folie a deux,* a joint neurosis, which causes prolonged pain to the respective spouses and to the children still in the formative stages of their development and certain to be damaged for life. (See chapter 24.)

Five years after the war there had been no change in the situation, except the growing up of the children and their departures from the two homes. Ten years later Sam and Sheila were divorced. Sam had ruined his career and also his marriage, and injured the lives of his wife and children.

"Sin" is said today to be an old-fashioned word. Many people do not like to use it, perhaps for the old-fashioned reason: it arouses uncomfortable feelings of guilt. The Bible is called old-fashioned by many moderns, but the virtues it teaches are still true today. Both Old and New Testament describe human types and their behavior, and put forth rules to live by that make survival for individuals and society possible. The seventh commandment ("Thou shalt not commit adultery") is not popular today—because adultery has become so popular. Some even see adultery as the wave of the future. But its effects upon most of the individuals I see have been devastating. It is for most people a terrible thing, a cancer eating into the soul, and no amount of pleasure seems worth it.

17
IN THE FORTIES

The turning of a man away from his own wife and children to another woman is, as we have said, seen at all ages. Sometimes, it strikes like lightning; the childhood pattern explodes like a time bomb. With others it is slow, creeping, insidious, an almost imperceptible engulfment in emotional quicksand. This analogy is apt, for many husbands resist this slow sinking; often they fight against it, and once engulfed they feel not happiness but torment, not release from the bonds of marriage and convention, but an entrapment from which they cannot escape, from which they cannot any longer *will* to free themselves.

This disintegration of will is one of the ultimate tragedies of the mind. We have used a concept of the mind with three groups of forces:

1. *The id:* the biological urges, such as for food, shelter, love, sex, mating and survival.
2. *The superego:* the results of training and identifications in forming ideals, standards, morals, ethics and conscience.
3. *The ego:* (a) the powers of perception (of outer world and our own impulses and reactions), (b) integration of these perceptions (through memory, reason, intellect) and (c) the executive powers of directing our behavior, that is, decision, direction, control and will.

These three parts of the mind of course are part mature, part childish. If a child is reared with love, security and respect and has models of harmonious, mature relations in his parents, then all available evidence shows that this child will become an adult with predominantly mature motivations toward responsible, constructive love for others in his id, superego and ego. We all have residual childish, egocentric, hostile patterns of impulses within us. These impulses appear in our dreams, even in our waking fantasies—images of selfish, grasping behavior, of the most abandoned profligacy, of every kind of sexual act, of unrestrained hostile, destructive deeds. But this does not mean that they need be acted out in real life, and they are not, except as crime. There is a diagnostic term that, although not official in the psychiatric nomenclature, should be. It is the most dire of diagnoses: "irrational, pathologically hostile acting out." It includes a person like Hitler, who, although not crazy in the sense of losing a grasp of immediate reality, is not normal either as seen through his acts of destruction that cause suffering and death, which he tries to justify by unrealistic rationalization.

Should education not make clear to the young, as forcefully and consistently and repeatedly as possible, this distinction, between what exists in our own minds and in drama and story, and, in contrast, what exists in real life? We all have these hostile impulses and therefore the fantasies they create. We live in a world of such fantasies: on television and radio, in the theater, in stories, and throughout our schooling in literature. Yet every extravagance of sex, promiscuity, perversion, licentiousness, brutality, sadism and criminal action must remain entirely internal, entirely in the fairy-land of fantasy, while we live as responsible, productive, loving family members, friends and citizens. (Those who act out any of these impulses are criminals and have no place in society or must be controlled by society.) In the mature adult these impulses, the results of lingering childhood dangers and frustrations, must be very weak, relative to the mature motivations of the id, superego and ego. They must be weak relative to the strengths of the moral, ethical standards of the superego and relative to the judgment, control and willpower of the ego. The more mature the id impulses are, the greater the drives to responsible, loving productivity and good will, the less strain there is on the conscience and willpower.

This abstract formulation is meant to remind us of the simple "structure" of the personality, which is useful in giving a model or picture of the interplay and balance of forces that make each person what he is, in impulses, wishes, thoughts, fantasies and behavior. And it is meant to emphasize the fact that we all have all sorts of urges and temptations, but we do not all act on them. Any man would like to wake up with some other beautiful blonde or brunette in his bed; but what is a fleeting or not-so-fleeting fantasy in one husband becomes rank and brutal desertion of young wife and child in another. Yet in view of the other forces in the personality, if a man has mature impulses in his id, such as love and responsibility, if he has mature standards of behavior and a conscience, if he has maturity of judgment and self-control, then his behavior will cause him sharp pangs, conflicts and torments. And in the end these may help him to become a more fully mature person, who provides much greater enjoyment and satisfaction for others and for himself.

This I had learned before Mel came to see me at the request of his distraught wife, Madeline. As she pictured it, he was having a fine time extramaritally with another woman, May. Mel came—a man of 46, stocky, broad-shouldered, attractive in looks and personality, and at first glance direct and straightforward. A second look revealed that aura of inner suffering that one sees so often in men around 45, an aura that seems to appeal to certain women. His expression reflected anything but happiness, peace or freedom. He was hollow-eyed and tragic in his seriousness, and although he could smile and had a sense of humor, the impression he gave was one of anxiety, conflict and depression. His wife, Madeline, seemed like a perfect mate for him. She was about 5'4" and had frank blue eyes and a trim, perfect figure, although she was 40 and had three children. Her suffering was undisguised.

May was 21 and just out of college. Mel had been slipping into the involvement with her slowly and inevitably, bit by bit, over the past four years.

Mel's marriage had been good but not ideal prior to May's presence on the scene. The hostilities between his parents had made him insecure personally and had split his identifications. He could not very well side with one parent without feeling disloyal to the other. His wife, Madeline, was distinctly deprived in childhood, but well enough treated by her parents to develop a strong ego and strong moral standards (part of her superego), with the ability to keep repressed her feelings of being too little loved. She was one of those small, vivacious girls, capable at anything she attempted. Mel was very dependent on her and afraid of losing her. She was not always easy to get on with, because of her readiness to feel unloved and her resentment because of this. But the marriage worked: the sexual aspect was entirely satisfactory; the children were handsome, and they were well brought up, except for the squalls between their parents, and the relations between them all were generally satisfying.

Mel was in the sales division of a large company and was away frequently on business. He met May. Mel and Madeline lived in a suburb; May had an apartment in town. She encouraged Mel. We can understand how, unhappy within himself because of his own inner patterns of feelings, he was responsive to the accepting smiles of a fresh young college girl. His need exceeded his judgment and his will. His marriage, satisfactory though it was, had its storms and tensions, and had the demands and resentments of a wife who felt insufficiently loved, felt anxious, and was drained of energy by three children. Here was May offering herself, the great diversion, the great refreshment. It took between one and two years for the affair between Mel and May to become full-blown, for all reserve to be dissipated.

With it, as is frequent, a general deterioration was evident in Mel. He began to see less of his friends and more of people who drank heavily, were more promiscuous, cut corners in their business dealings and were generally less honest and responsible toward their families and fellow men. Some were living together out of wedlock. Most were less conscientious in business and less well-off or secure financially. Briefly, they were people with less integrity, stability and responsibility. They condoned, even accepted, more readily the living out of this kind of hostility against wife and children—and also accepted what went with it: the lies and behavior that a man uses more and more in his efforts to deceive a true and faithful, if human, wife who is doing her best to preserve the home and do what is best for the children. The "other woman" often becomes an addiction. The husband may try to break off, but as with alcohol or tobacco, when they fill a neurotic need, he is not able to; he lacks the "ego strength." He cannot break off, and he cannot stop the lies and deceits that are exactly like those of a drug addict who stops at nothing to indulge a craving that he himself has come to despise. The superego (standards, ideals, conscience) and ego (judgment, control, will) have yielded partially to the pressures of the childhood pattern. Mel vowed that he did not want this involvement with May, that his wife and children were his only loves. There was a compulsive element in his seeing May—and generally behind compulsions of all sorts is hostility. This is another form of oscillation: he loves his wife and children and home, and wants to live with them in love, but is unable to give up the girl, who exerts every wile to hold him.

For brevity I will only give a few salient features of what I learned of Mel's dynamics. He had always had a problem about women, had to have their love, but felt insecure and lacked confidence in his personality and in his potency. Even though he was past 45, with a wife and three children, he was trying to prove something to himself with May—in a way using her to prove that he could have a relation, an affair, and be successful, uninhibited and sexually potent with a girl who, in his mind, fitted a certain category of women.

The disturbed elements in his childhood pattern were: contention and hostility between his parents, and considerable neglect by his mother, for whom, like Madeline's mother, children were a burden. As a result he clung too much to his mother while repressing his resentment to her, and was resentful of his father for treating his mother harshly. He could not identify wholeheartedly with either father or mother as adults upon whom to model himself.

Now in his marriage he had (as we so fatefully, inexorably and unconsciously do) recreated the outline of the childhood emotional interplay. Instead of two parents he now had two women. He craved the love of each one and clung to each like a child, but at the same time he was living out his hostility unconsciously by causing them both suffering—and of course causing his children not only present suffering but damage for life. The result was a torment of guilt, so that from the situation came not happiness but anguish.

Wife and paramour corresponded to mother and father, but not in a strict, narrow way. Mel showed the "split mother image" commonly seen in these cases. Madeline, his wife, meant to him in part the mother whose love he must have, but whom he resented because of her lack of giving. He spited her, unconsciously, by going to May. But also, Madeline and the children represented demands and responsibilities, and he fled from them to May, who was mother in the sense of escape from the burdens of family obligations, a person who consoled him like a mother. But she was also a playmate with whom he could identify, someone who meant rebellion and escape. I suppose all men would like such a dream girl, one free and loving and always available but without any expectations, demands or obligations, just sex and play and an inexhaustible fountain of love and affection. But the Mays have their needs and childhood patterns too, and sooner or later they must end the idyll. The day comes, this year or next, when she will demand the marriage she has hoped for but never suggested. Then come the tears, the rages, the threats, the gestures of suicide. And the man is guilty and weak and now afraid and confused, his capacity for decision paralyzed. But are there also girls so hostile and so masochistic, so lacking in the mating and reproductive drives that they are satisfied forever to be "the other woman," smashing a marriage while getting no marriage for themselves? There is no end to the variety of ways in which childhood patterns shape the designs of adult behavior.

Analysis was relatively new in Chicago in the 1930s. Mel had been to see an analyst of the type that believes that if he mostly listens passively to the patient, who lies on the couch for five meetings a week, and that if this goes on for enough years, all will come out well. The analyst refused to see Madeline   He said he was not concerned with the marriage or other "externals"; his patient was anxious, and his task was simply to make the unconscious conscious. We know today that this is one of those half-truths: the analyst cannot step in and direct lives or live them for his patients. On the other hand, he must have a down-to-earth, realistic, practical knowledge and grasp of what is going on. Otherwise the patient, free-associating on his back on the couch for five or even three days a week, goes off into a demi-world, a confusion of fantasy with reality, of past with present. What his conscious ego gains through some insights it more than loses through failure of enough reality-sense to use the insights effectively. As a result he regresses more and more, lives more and more in fantasy, becomes more and more childish and dependent upon the analyst. He often takes the silence of such an analyst as sanction for whatever he is doing. But the most malignant consequence is the feeling that what he does in reality is not particularly important; it is just something to free-associate about.

Mel told me that he was doing what he was doing because of this and that incident in childhood, which amounted to "his father and his mother and his brothers and his sisters and his aunts." As he talked, it was clear that analysis was for him an intellectual exercise, a play of fantasies and memories, which was of no realistic, practical use to him in clarifying and dealing with his problems and those of all concerned. In fact it had the opposite result: as he sank into this never-never land, he thought the analyst was sanctioning whatever he was doing, and that this meant they were somehow getting "deeper" analytically. This encouraged his retreat from reality into childishness and confusion. He was all but killing his wife by his behavior; he was involving the girl; he was doing irreparable damage to his children; he was lying, cheating, deceiving; he was abandoning his friends for more or less disturbed, immature personalities, slipping from his mature functioning, risking his job and career—but he was free-associating. As he sank deeper into the so-called analysis, he sank deeper into his problem, into regression and confusion.

This twilight state is a sinking back or regression into the attitudes and feelings of early childhood. These feelings develop and are transferred to the analyst (transference). Unless they are recognized and properly handled, the patient becomes more and more toward the analyst like the dependent child he once was toward his mother and father. For this to occur on a strictly limited basis is an aid to insight. The patient sees in his feelings toward the analyst the emotional forces he has been struggling with unconsciously, and through this knowledge he is helped to help himself in reducing, resolving and controlling them. But if he is not helped in this way, then the regression is useless therapeutically and does more harm than good.

Usually, following the old infantile pattern, the patient represses his hostility toward the analyst and is not aware of it; but it still produces guilt toward the analyst, as it did toward the parents. There is little chance of the patient's seeing all this, even if it is pointed out to him, if the analyst has not dealt with it properly from the beginning; and there is as little chance of extricating himself from the analysis as there would have been of separating him as a child from his mother. Typically he believes that he is just on the verge of a great insight—as though he would gain such insight if he has not done so after two or three or more years, and as though an insight alone would solve such situations. Often the hostility in the transference to the analyst is displaced to a wife or to others in life, thus compounding the problem rather than relieving it.

This is no criticism of analysis itself. It is only to point out some relevant misconceptions and misunderstandings of 30 and more years ago which, with progress in the field, are avoidable today. But of course one must be as careful in choosing his analyst as he would be in choosing his surgeon, his lawyer or his automobile mechanic, or anyone having much responsibility for his well-being and happiness.

Madeline, with her sincere, honest, fine ego, was in anguish over this situation such as no human being (or any animal, for that matter) should have to suffer. Mel's behavior struck directly at her own specific emotional vulnerability. Her pathodynamics were, in brief: lack of love and interest from her parents, making her cling excessively, but in a controlled and hidden way, and making her resentful and hostile through deprivation, while loading her with guilt for her hostility. For, if she showed her hostility, she would lose what parental interest and love she had. Besides, it was against the strict moral code of her family, which dictated that a child must have only feelings of love for his parents and siblings. In addition to these reactions, she took over her parents' attitudes toward herself, seeing herself as relatively unlovable and unwanted. In reality she was charming, cuddly and appealing, and sort of heartbreaking. Also, fortunately, she had been sufficiently loved in her 0–6 to be of the spunky breed.

"I am terrified," she said, "that Mel will leave me, but I'm afraid I may deserve it. I have demanded too much and lost my temper at him too often. And now that I'm terrified, I'm afraid he will want to get away so much more. We get on well when we are away alone together. I couldn't sleep at all last night. I couldn't change the subject in my mind. I have a feeling of doom. If he should leave me, I couldn't exist."

[This does not convey the tensing, blanching, tears, clasping of hands—the effects of inner writhing with psychic pain.]

ANALYST: Have you other close relationships to people?
PATIENT: Except for the children, no. I have good friends but all my feelings that really matter are attached to Mel. He is the only one. Do other marriages have such happenings as this and survive? I'm afraid I demand more of Mel than he can give. I am not close to people because if I were, they would get to know how I really am and would not like me. I feel awful at times when I find myself wanting to treat the children the way my mother and father treated me; I want to be just the opposite. When I found out about May, I was so furious I could have killed Mel. Of course I don't mean that. I mean that I said the most awful things. I screamed at him. It was the first time I was openly mad at him. He said he was sorry about this girl and did not want to hurt me, but that he was glad it was out in the open. Yet he insists that he loves only me and the children. He is very good with the children.

This inadequate sample is meant to give a little of the flavor of our conversations. There is no need to describe Madeline's dynamics further. Only one major point should be reemphasized; namely, the high, strict moral and ethical standards of her parental family. Largely because of these standards and her consequent guilt and self-depreciation, she searched her soul to find whether it was chiefly her own doing that had driven her husband to his infidelity. She did, I think, contribute to it, but this was because of the deprivations that they both endured in childhood, the deprivation, resentment and guilt that drew them together in the first place, the deep-seated underlying feelings that they shared and that made them understand each other. If her husband had not had his particular dynamics, including the weakness of his ego's controls and judgment and of his superego's principles, he would not have taken up with May. and his tensions would have come out in some form other than infidelity. We will mention a few brief examples of this later. In this marriage we see a one-man wife devoted to a no longer one-woman husband— actually, it appeared, to a two-woman man.

If Madeline in truth had contributed to Mel's extramarital involvement, then one would think the course of common sense would have indicated that his analyst, instead of refusing to see her, would have called her in (she would have come willingly; in fact, she requested to come), made clear to her where her behavior was pushing her husband and advised her to get some help in modifying the patterns in herself that were threatening her home; in which case Mel would have had the realistic expectation that his wife would change and become more as both she and he wanted her to be.

At any rate Madeline saw the dilemma she was in. If she reacted with hostility to Mel's behavior, then she feared that she would drive him into May's arms. But if she tried to ignore it, then why should Mel not go ahead and enjoy May, since his wife raised no objections? The same conflict existed in regard to sexual relations. If Madeline assented, and their sexual relations were always mutually gratifying, then was this not condoning May? But if, tormented by the thought of lying in arms still warm from embracing May, she refused, then would not cutting herself off as Mel's sexual outlet drive him all the more to May? If she accepted his behavior, did she not sanction it and relieve his guilt for it? But if she opposed it, did she not make him feel so guilty toward his family that he would try to excape it by leaving? Incidentally, the idea that if a marriage is good sexually, it must be good in all other ways does not hold up in my experience, as this example shows. Nor does the reverse hold true.

Madeline felt that she should divorce Mel, which she had ample grounds to do. But he was the only person she deeply loved with the constancy of the craving she had had for her parents. Then too she would be left alone with the care of three children, for whom no father was probably worse than a faithless one. At times she felt the situation to be intolerable, felt that she was not the kind of woman who could or would share a man like this and live with this kind of hostility directed toward her.

Madeline was struck on dead center. All she could do was try to stand it and wait out May—knowing, though, that this might mean waiting years or forever, or that the vagaries of her husband, now embroiled in treatment with an analyst who would not or could not tell anything to anyone, might lead to his wanting to marry May. Where his unconscious hostility and guilt would lead him was unpredictable. Standing it also meant seeing friends, who gradually had deserted Mel (for such behavior cannot long remain secret). It meant going against all her own standards by snooping in spite of herself—looking for lipstick on shirts, stains on underwear, odor of perfume on jackets; wondering about every trip; watching the mileage on the car. Because of Mel's deterioration she was always doubting, always suspicious as to whether he was deceiving her or being honest, telling truths or lies, worrying about his every absence. It meant the decay of all trust in him. And then she feared that her very dissolution of confidence in him, inevitable as it was, would itself jeopardize re-establishment of the marriage. And with her own high standards and tendency to self-depreciation, she despised herself for her behavior, or even the impulses to it, although they were only those of a wife trying to defend herself and her brood against the inroads of a woman who was a stranger, a ruthless or thoughtless neurotic or criminoid home wrecker, heartlessly stealing a husband and father. (In reality, the other woman is usually another lost and suffering soul trying to save herself.)

What this all comes down to is how the individual's personality will react in the given circumstances: stay on despite suffering, keep the home harmonious for the sake of the children in spite of everything, turn the children against their father, as revenge on him although damaging to them, expose the other woman and attack her legally or divorce; suicide and murder are often thought of if rarely committed. In the absence of any practicable solution for a given person, the triangle is apt to continue until something gives, someone breaks, or fate intervenes. Distorted childhood patterns, caused by faulty upbringing, trap a person and head him unconsciously to create his own suffering and that of those closest to him.

In this case fate took the form of an international criminal regression, against which background whether or not a mate was loyal seemed suddenly of less consequence; a regression in which groups sought their own egocentric gratification and power; a regression in which all the sadistic fantasies of tens of thousands of disordered, frustrated, hostile childhoods were wreaked in reality upon helpless victims; a regression in which powerful groups of men and women brought about death and agony for the most selfish satisfactions and goals, when cooperation could have made a more secure and happy life for all humanity. This hostile egocentric regression resulted in World War II. Although marital fidelity paled in significance against this background, it was one of the very values, one of the manifestations of emotional health and maturity for the individual and, through the children, for the race, that we fought to preserve.

Two years after the war I received a letter, of which the following sentences are excerpts.

"I have a lot to thank the Navy for. It took Mel away from May and away from his analyst, and maybe it was good for him to get away from me. Maybe it's only because I'm a woman that I never believed that the 'Army Builds Men,' but the Navy did something for Mel. Maybe it only pulled him back to reality. It did bring him back to something more like the man I married. Maybe I was unfair to Dr. ——— [his analyst]. I've heard that the real results in psychoanalysis sometimes come only in the years after it is over. Maybe Dr. ——— did a good job after all, but I can't help the feeling that he drove Mel into a mixture of utter confusion and utter egotism. However it was, Mel came back less egotistical and more realistic. He looked up Dr. ——— but found that he had moved to Los Angeles.

"He started with another analyst and this has been very different. He keeps Mel's back off the couch and his shoulders to the wheel.

The floozy [May] used every trick to hang on to Mel—offering her all, playing on his guilt, tears, threats of suicide—but in the end she married someone else. And *they* moved to Los Angeles. Mel was getting so upset before the war that I was sure he would lose his job. Now he is working well again. The company is humming and Mel is overworking, often at night. Once I might have objected, but now I'm so thankful it is not another woman that I wouldn't say a word. I don't dare uncross my fingers, but the children have a father and I have a husband again. Could he have proven to himself in the Navy whatever he was trying to prove with May? Because now he doesn't seem so—well, so restless and compulsive.''

Madeline had gotten help with her own problem, and with May gone, Madeline and Mel had had a fresh start, with something learned, we hope, of life and of themselves; they had gained a wholesome respect for the unconscious forces that motivated their lives, and were grateful for having saved their home for the children, with all it meant for their future lives.

The outcome is not always so fortunate, and one reason among many is that there is a point of no return, beyond which the marriage is only rarely reconstituted. This is the point at which one or the other partner "goes cold." The husband, even against his wishes, may lose all feeling for his wife; he may even go to the extremes of defenses against her by a sense of repugnance (like the young man who could no longer bear contact with his beautiful young wife). This coldness may develop in reaction to his wife's hostilities to him; it may develop from his inner problems, which have transferred his attachment to the other woman, leaving for his wife, to whom he was once devoted, only the rejection and hostility of his whole emotional pattern. So, too, the wife may exhaust her tolerance for her husband's disloyalty with another woman, or may go cold because of other behavior of his, or from a pattern in her own makeup of which the husband is an innocent victim. (For example, see Ben and Brenda, Chapter 11.)

18
IN THE FIFTIES

When "extramarital sexual regression" occurs in the fifties, the external situation is apt to be different from what it is in the forties, thirties or twenties, although the underlying dynamics of the individuals still give it its particular form. In the fifties the children are usually grown up, and some or all have left the nest, are away at school or out in the world, and perhaps married and settled, or beginning to be. They say there is no fool like an old fool. Certainly childishness is more striking at 50 than at 20.

Norman, of medium, rather stocky build, with serious dark eyes, was in his early fifties and was at the peak of his career. In fact he had his business run so well by an excellent manager that it was no longer so taxing and demanding. He could take it a little easier.

Although he had been faithful to his wife, Nel, except for a possible brief slip or two along the way, he had always liked to flirt with women. Most men do; his flirting was just somewhat more evident than the average—more conspicuous, less controlled. Like so many men of any age who have been too strongly dependent upon their mothers (whether from overindulgence or overprotection or deprivation or whatever), Norman always had an eye not only for women in general, but a particular woman in any given situation. On a train, boat or plane, at a party or a meeting, at the theater or any entertainment or sport, he would always select one particular woman to fix upon. In age she might be anywhere from barely past childhood to 50 or more, although the younger ones were preferred. If she had feminine charm, figure, face and manner, Norman would be "in love" with her for that brief place and time. This is probably not unusual among men. Some carry it to philandering. Some become Don Juans and may never marry. Others are well aware of this perennial series of light, sexy loves, but whatever their fantasies they do nothing to jeopardize their marriages. Very literally, they look but do not touch. The wise wife will not try to hold the reins too tightly if she and the children have the husband's basic love and know he will never let anything disturb their home. But Norman now touched as well as looked.

In his early fifties, he finds himself in love with Nancy, a sophisticated woman of the world about 12 years his junior. He tells his wife, Nel, that he is in love with Nancy, but is not ready yet to talk about it. He explains that she is no common woman but a very superior person, and then wonders why his wife is angry at this. Nel, a determined woman, will not stand for it, but will not rush into divorce after nearly 30 years of marriage and four children. She suffers as much as any wife in such circumstances, but she has a strong ego (i.e., sense of reality, judgment, standards, control and character). She watchfully waits and finds an excellent job that she likes. Norman sees that she is withdrawing from him and really will divorce him.

Strength consists in part in who is more dependent on whom. An affair can be a great culminating experience, but to have one at the expense of open hostility and rejection to and from the wife who is one's anchor gives one pause. Of course we are speaking only of a man's own egocentric feelings and not of the suffering and damage to his wife and children.

There follow months of Norman's claiming he has broken off permanently with Nancy, only to have it turn out, as is so routinely the case, that he is lying. The usual series of deceits and deceptions and the deterioration of ego and standards follows, until he is no longer to be trusted in anything. Then Nancy sees what the situation is, gives up hope of marriage and rejects Norman.

Now he has to struggle to reestablish a relationship with his wife. He has now regressed to behavior like that of a naughty, guilty child. He was "not ready to talk about it," but now he can think and talk of nothing else. He is so threatened, so preoccupied, that he cannot be trusted with the simplest responsibilities. The business continues, thanks to the efficient manager.

He struggles to get back on his feet psychologically as well as to reconstitute his marriage, for his wife finds him too much of a strain to be around. She turns out to be the stronger; he is more dependent on her than she on him. He finally sees an analyst, who finds the task of analyzing him a difficult one. There are some persons in whom the progressive and regressive forces are in about equal balance;

and some of these people react to awareness of these forces, that is, of what is causing their feelings and behavior, with a burst of insight that is almost like a religious conversion, and which signals a shift in the direction of maturing.   But Norman's ego was weak and was corrupted by lying and deceiving his wife, which also warped his judgment and his grasp of reality.   His control and will were not strong.   He had so far retreated into passive dependence on Nancy, as well as on his wife, that there was no potent force of masculine pride and independence to spring into play at the spark of insight. Instead he was one of those who react to understanding of themselves with a "so what?"

Such a man presents a special problem in analytic technique.   A completely passive procedure can do more harm than good.   With his passive-dependent-submissive wishes already so strong toward both his wife and his mistress and dominating his whole feeling and behavior, Norman could easily sink into this childish attachment to the analyst, too.   He might tend to use the analyst's sympathy as sanction for his regression and release from guilt, and the whole situation as a comfortable retreat into fantasy, letting the analyst do everything and hoping somehow, sometime, to emerge cleansed, purified and mature.   On the other hand, if the analyst accurately interprets and correctly points out reality, Norman may feel that he is not getting support for his regression, and leave treatment.   If so, he probably will have been saved much time and money, and his wife will have been spared the protraction of vain hopes.   But with a real will to solve his problem, and with an analyst who sees the psychological realities clearly enough, Norman's retreat may be halted and he may start on the long, slow road back from childishness to relative independence, effort, productivity and responsibility.   Fortunately he was prevented from sinking deeper into childishness in life and in the analysis.

Norman had the virtue of honesty.   With his full consent, all aspects of the situation were freely discussed with his wife, Nel, who was by now bitter enough, but still understanding and still loving. Despite her disillusionment and disgust with him, she would not abandon him as long as there was any chance of his getting back on his feet.

Fortunately, Norman and Nel's children were grown and away from home; it is a bad thing for children at any age to be disillusioned in one parent or in the stability of the relationship between parents, but at least when they are no longer small twigs, bending them will not cause such serious warping and damage to their personalities and lives as it does in the earliest years.

Nancy meanwhile saw that there would be little satisfaction in her future with Norman. He was too weak, too dependent on her, too unreliable, too untrustworthy with women, finances and alcohol; he was an insecure bet as a provider, even if divorced, with an ex-wife to support. The excellent manager kept the business going, thus assuring some stability of income. It sometimes seems that if there were nothing, if the wolf were at the door, the husband would be compelled to make a mature, responsible effort. Necessity is a hard master but under him we become potent, as Freud said. But by no means is this always so.

Norman continued working but his effectiveness, which should have been at its prime, dwindled. This is seen in men who relinquish important positions and become involved with another woman, or other women, and with or without alcohol sink into companionship with questionable characters. Some, like Ed, ("Passivity and Regression") have never gotten started, but here we speak of those who have worked, often successfully; then, at what should be the peak, they decline. It is a great emotional strain to be around an extremely dependent, attention-demanding, passive person, however outwardly charming he may be. It can be utterly exhausting. A man may be wealthy and shower his wife with gifts, but the underlying childish demands, the hanging on her emotionally, may drive her to divorce him to save her sanity. Or she may announce that there will never be a divorce. In this case, Nel did not divorce Norman, but she did build her own life.

Nel had the emotional and physical strength and the intellectual ability and knowledge of people to finally locate a position in industry that suited her talents. She became the breadwinner. Emotionally she achieved a workable independence of her husband. She grew to enjoy her job, her independence and her income. Norman came to terms with this. Less was required of him, but he had to accept an apartment in which his wife was not always there to greet him. As Norman accepted this, Nel came to like the arrangement and even to be grateful to Norman for her freedom, which she now cherished, and to which he, whether willingly or perforce, now acceded.

She no longer cared too much whether he saw another woman or not. She felt free now to do just as she pleased. In this case she did nothing so far as men were concerned, but she relished fully the knowledge that she was free to have affairs if she wished. Thus the marriage was saved by working out a new kind of "fit" between them. When I heard from them a few years after the war, they were healthy, rather youthful grandparents, who, in spite of spells of turbulence, had pretty much come to terms with the relationship as it now was.

Again we caution that most endings in such cases are not this most fortunate. The regression, as we have seen, it not always limited to a retreat from wife and children; it can involve the job instead of the family, or it can encompass both. And, especially when it includes both the domestic and occupational fronts, it is occasionally part of a general regression of the personality, with or without alcohol. In the extreme, the person is so childish as to be unable to make a go of life and must spend some time in a mental hospital or its equivalent.

Norman's case causes one to wonder how it is possible psychologically that a man, who for most of a lifetime has held a responsible position in his work and who has been relatively stable as a husband and a parent, can in his fifties regress so far that he cannot function in any of these capacities. If he drinks, there is a tendency to blame it on the alcohol. No doubt the dynamics differ greatly from person to person; in one such instance, they were as follows:

The man was much more dependent upon his wife than he realized. His flirtations, which rarely went far, had been on the pattern of escaping dependence upon his wife (in childhood, upon his mother) by playing the strong man to weak women.

In his fifties, however, one of these women drew him into an all-out affair. The usual deceptions and lies to his wife ensued. As is so frequent, his wife's suspicion was aroused and was readily confirmed. After initial attempts to win back and hold him from "the other woman," her hurt and dismay and subjection to lies and deceit more and more caused her to withdraw emotionally. Her reaction was in part jealousy and simple self-protection against rejection. The result for the husband was a diminution in her previous stalwart, unwavering strength and support. His dependence had lost its sustaining rock. His whole personality structure was shaken. He lost interest in the other woman, and also in his work. He began to drink. His regression became more apparent. The other woman lost interest in him. A vicious circle was generated with his wife. The less reliable and the more childish he became, the more his wife was forced, for her own security and that of their children, to stand on her own. The more she did this, the more she withdrew, the more childishly helpless and irresponsible and alcoholic her husband became.

Even if the wife understands all this and forgives and forgets and welcomes back the husband, with or without the other woman, the regression may have gone too far for the husband to reconstitute the marriage. If he can relate to his wife only by feeling like a helpless, dependent guilty child, the outlook is poor. And whether or not he can be helped by analytic psychiatry depends, as usual, primarily on the balance of forces in his makeup.

Sometimes the man has regressed so far that he becomes a hostile, masochistic person. His passive aggression, that is, his helpless irresponsibility, may have put him unalterably on the road to destroying himself and dragging down his wife and any others involved. If he is in the grip of forces that cannot be influenced, even by therapy, then his wife may have no choice but to rescue herself and the children as best she can.

19
A TEMPTED WIFE

There is no worse evil than a bad woman; and nothing has ever been produced better than a good one.

Euripedes

*No better lot has Providence assigned
Than a fair woman with a virtuous mind.*

Hesiod

Nearly every kind of problem is seen in women as well as men, for little girls are as often traumatically reared as little boys, thereby developing disordered feelings toward others as part of their childhood patterns. When one deals with the basic needs of small children, the sexual difference between the parents sometimes is secondary. If one needs food, shelter, care and affection to survive, it can be of less consequence whether this is provided by the mother or the father. This is particularly true if intense feelings do not develop toward one or the other parent, especially that parent of the same sex. Once the pattern is formed, other emotional forces and other early experiences determine how transferable this pattern is from the parent to others. Therefore, a girl who has had a certain kind of experience with her mother can transfer this pattern to her husband, just as a man transfers it to his wife. Within certain limits and modifications (for example, male aggressiveness fuses more easily with hostility, and femininity with receptivity), husband and wife are interchangeable. One might say that if each had had the childhood of the other, then in the marriage each would have had in his dynamics the makeup of the other. But, for the present at least, the husband more often bears the burden of the responsibilities for breadwinning and the wife has relative loneliness and isolation within the home and the exhausting, unremitting demands of small children for care and attention. And in wars, which are still with us, the two roles still differ.   But however great the socioeconomic differences, the same pathological patterns are seen in both men and women; and the deeper one looks, the more alike they are.

Thea had a model husband a few years her senior.   Since she had married at 20, by age 43 her three children were grown and left home to start out in the world.   Terry, her husband, at 45 was vivacious, youthful-looking, self-assured, athletic, kind, personable, popular and devoted.   He was interested in his business and extremely successful at it.   His easygoing nature and success in business gave Thea freedom for her own pursuits in the home and in the community, with ample time for golf and bridge.   She had always been a good mother.   How could she at 43 risk all this for the sake of a clandestine affair with a neurotic man (call him Brad) a few years older, who had a wife and not yet fully grown children?   It is hard to believe that this behavior does not contain a large component of masochism, that is, tendency to self-injury.   She feared it and therefore came for help in understanding it and dealing with it.

The marriage had not been ideal, but how many are?   Her husband, attractive as he was, had ample opportunities and was tempted to have an affair here and there; but he simply was not the type.   Thea with all her freedom also had been tempted, and for all I know may have yielded; but if so, it was in so quiet, brief a fashion as to arouse no attention.   If it occurred, it was not deep, and it was transient.   But this present involvement with a rather petulant, demanding man threatened the whole structure of her life: husband, children and financial security, with all the freedom and privileges that it provided.

Our point is only the obvious one that wives can be as unfaithful, surreptitiously or otherwise, as husbands.   It is worth mentioning an example of the variability of the forms masochism can take: A woman soon found that her husband was cruel and tyrannical.   She could not defy him to his face, but avenged herself secretly by starting an all-out love affair.   Some women—and men—damage themselves by being caught.   But this affair was kept hidden by her for 20 years.   (So it can be done.) However, this woman was reared with a strong conscience.   She developed enough guilt to generate severe anxiety and some psychosomatic symptoms, which brought her for analytic help.

Thea had been raised in a home with the highest standards and had been well loved.   Her childhood background was excellent except, as

nearly as I could tell, for three features: she was a little too much
adored, there was a little too much emphasis on being the best
(narcissism, "bestism"), and she was pressured and molded a little
too strongly and consistently in this direction (of vanity, egotism
and prestige) by her proud and doting parents. She must be the
best in grades, in athletics, in extracurricular activities; she must
marry a wonderful young man—and her parents were thrilled when
they first met Terry because he was the living ideal that they had
held for her. Throughout her married life he was perfect in her
parents' eyes. If she had seen him with those eyes alone, the marriage
would have been idyllic. Her parents had also imparted to Thea
good, mature standards of social behavior, and had taught her,
for example, that one to whom so much had been given owed
something to society, to her fellow man. Unfortunately there was
just enough unspoken overpushing for Thea to rebel. But the rebellion was repressed because she received so much real love that
she loved her parents in return and identified with them and consciously accepted their standards, which, moreover, her judgment
told her were mature.

Now, at 43, with her children grown and out of the home, living
with a husband who was often away, with so much freedom, Thea
felt in her own mind the old pressures and the old rebellion, and
the wish to toss them off and be free at last, to be free before the
final imprisonment of age. She wanted freedom from living up to
the standard of contributing socially; she revolted against being,
in her own eyes and those of all who knew her, such a mature,
superior person. The good and mature had been vitiated by the
internalized parental pressure toward it, pressure by the most loving,
well-meaning parents, who could not quite wait for her own maturation but had to force her growth.

As might have been expected, the neurotic Brad, who attracted
her, represented in his own dynamics a similar underlying rebellion.
But Thea's parents had been loving, and she loved them; she could
not thus throw over all their standards without feeling hostile to
them, and such hostility in the face of love could only generate
guilt. Hence her conscience, her superego, would make her choose a
form of rebellion that must somehow assure its own punishment;
her freedom, if she declared it, must be in a form that would punish
her, make her suffer. And indeed if her affair with Brad materialized

and became known, she would be ruined. This sort of rebellion is common enough in adolescence, but, as we have seen, may not emerge until the period of freedom that comes when the children are grown and have left home.

Other dynamics were also present. The give-get problem we discussed in an earlier chapter appeared, as was to be anticipated, when her love needs turned from parents (especially her mother) to her husband. As is usual, or rather inevitable, her husband could not give her all that she as a young child desired and received from her parents. Her husband was another striving contemporary like herself, with his own dependent-receptive love needs turned toward *her* for satisfaction. Frustrated by Terry's being only a husband and not meeting the residual childhood longings for the overly strong adulation of her parents, Thea generated mounting resentment against him. Handsome, wealthy, successful as he now was, he had been sufficiently deprived as a child to have relatively little warmth to give.

Also, Terry fitted her pattern of jealousy toward her three younger brothers, who were three, eight and ten years younger. Thea was pushed out of her position as the only child by her brother, Tim, who was three years younger. When her parents raved about his wonderful qualities, Thea fumed, and her resentment burned slowly but constantly against him. Now she transferred to her husband this early hostility and competitiveness generated in childhood toward her brother, Tim. She had to rise above Tim then, and above Terry now—depreciate him, emphasize his every deficiency— although her reason saw clearly his superior qualities. But the pattern dictated that she must win out over him, be the only favored child. In childhood she yearned to be favored over her brother in the hearts of her parents; now she craved this favor over her husband in the eyes of the world and in her own eyes and those of another man. She was filled with guilt and self-reproach for these hostile, selfish, ungrateful feelings, of which she was herself partly aware. She felt the hostility but did not, until treatment, recognize the internal source in her childhood pattern.

Of course many people have younger sisters and brothers without this degree of hostility to husband or wife. There are many reasons why such a pattern develops and why it is transferred to one's spouse. One reason is that the intensity of the sibling rivalry is largely determined by the parents. If they so adore the first child and then switch their adulation to the second or third, the first will react strongly. Certainly the pattern of sibling rivalry causing marital problems is extremely common.

Sometimes the hostile, depreciatory competitiveness is intensified by some special qualities of the second sibling or by unavoidable circumstances. One girl's sister suffered for some years during infancy from a chronic illness that focused much of the parents' anxiety and attention upon her, removing it from the girl who for three years had been the adored only child. Ever after, the girl strove ambitiously, had to be superior, had to win every boy, and after marriage developed these hostile competitive feelings toward her husband, whom she tried so hard to love and be a good wife to. Another girl, Vicky, had a twin brother who was preferred by her parents. She hated him for being a boy, to which she attributed his being favored over her. She must, simply *must,* share everything with him, do every little thing he did, have everything he had, be with him constantly. When she married, she followed the same pattern with her husband, and at first both she and her husband mistook this for love. But soon she could not even permit her husband to have his work to himself. She must share it. Togetherness masked old hostility to the brother, the favored male, and became pathologically exaggerated. The husband was ruggedly stable, but eventually she herself went into a severe depression.

Thus there were at least three sources in the emotional patterns of childhood for the slow buildup of Thea's hostility to her husband—irrational, unrealistic sources, not caused by his actual feelings or behavior: rebellion against pressure for too high standards, excessive expectations and resentment for displacement by a sibling.

The husband as breadwinner, being financially independent and having an occupation to hold his interest and take his mind off these marriage problems, is in quite a different position from the wife who is financially dependent upon him and psychologically has no other great area of her life to occupy her. Despite divorce laws, the husband as wage earner has a great advantage psychologically over the wife who relies on him for support. He is burdened with the breadwinning, but he has the great benefit of this whole area of interest and human relations in addition to the financial income his work provides. Perhaps the hold of a hostile wife on the husband is through the children, whom he loves and whom he knows need a good mother.

At any rate Thea's present dynamics, as just sketched, demonstrate the tendency toward potentially self-injuring regression. At 43 she was struggling with emerging conflicts of her childhood with her parents, which had been for the most part covered over all these years, surfacing when life's pressures mobilized them.

She obtained analytic help but treatment was difficult. She so greatly enjoyed the outside affair that she did not wish very strongly to be helped to forego it or no longer to desire it (which would be most unlikely); but she did see the potential damage to her husband, her children and herself. Typically her dreams were not of happiness with her lover, but were of being ill or apprehended for a crime or of some other form of suffering or retribution. In these dreams, as well as in the realities of her life, she could not fail to perceive the punishment she would inflict on herself for a neurotic freedom sought by hostile rebellion, rather than a real freedom from the inner pressure of the old conditioning. It was within herself that the conflict lay and must be resolved. Testing in life might well be important but need not be masochistic. If she enjoyed an affair, it should not cause suffering to her family and herself.

The goal of treatment was for her to achieve the freedom she wanted through necessary shifts in her own attitudes so that she could live rationally and more by her ego, her own sense of reality, her own judgment, and less by feeling that even her mature behavior meant, irrationally, compliance with parental pressure. If every good thing meant to her subservience to her parents, she would continue to rebel endlessly and to punish herself, and yet never resolve her conflict. Treatment got her on the road to this goal. It moved her toward reducing her strong masochistic trend toward punishing herself by destroying her marriage and with it all her security and position in life. It is dangerously easy for an established, respected, secure wife and mother to transform herself almost overnight into a lonely outsider looking in.

Getting on the way out, on the way to the goal, is about what we settle for in such a case as this at the present stage of analytic knowledge. If a person is well on the way out of the childhood fixation, regression or conflict, then we cannot complain too much about the *rate* of the progress. That, given the correct personality and skill of the analyst for the given patient, is a matter of the balance of emotional forces in the patient. The earliness of the injurious treatment by the parents (trauma), its consistency, the amount of balancing off by good relations and other considerations determine how deep-seated and fixed the pattern is and how amenable to analytic treatment. Thea did not manipulate herself into the status of an ostracized, impecunious divorcee.

20
FAITHFUL REGARDLESS

*The dog is promiscuous . . . . But the wolf is monogamous. He mates for life,
is intractably faithful, and if widowered will probably not re-mate but will
remain a bachelor to the end of his days.*

Ardrey

*I refused to be drawn into a divorce
By the scheme of a husband who had merely grown tired
Of his marital vow and duty.*

Edgar Lee Masters,
Spoon River Anthology

From the samples of marriages we have sketched, it must be evident
that whether a husband or a wife is faithful emotionally and sexually
is predominantly a personality characteristic. It is, as we have
stated, a matter of the main dynamics in the marriage relationship,
which are shaped by the childhood emotional patterns.

Thus, some husbands carry on outside affairs with no provocation
from their wives whatever, whereas others under extreme provocation
never stray from the marriage vows, never become involved with
another woman. This is not a matter of sexual potency or desire.
The same holds, of course, for wives who are faithful in feelings
and body to their husbands. Some, even under provocation and
temptation, do not wish an outside affair; some are even repelled
at the thought, in spite of or because of being accustomed to full
gratification with mutual orgasm in the marriage. Others feel deprived and unloved at home and strongly desire from another what
they feel the spouse does not provide, but their dynamics are such
that they do not know how to take such a step or are unable to do
in real life what they dream of in secret. And there are many other
variations. It is a matter of the personality makeup or, more narrowly,
of the individual's particular dynamics toward wife or husband.

Life is complicated—it involves finding one's way externally and also dealing with all the conflicting internal mechanisms that motivate us. Therefore, we all seek guiding principles. A man or a woman in a difficult marriage often asks, "What do other people in my situation do?" This question was asked, for example, by a wife in her late thirties whose husband was involved with another woman.

He had used the usual lies and deceptions so that his wife no longer knew if he was telling the truth or not and had lost all confidence in his integrity. She feared that she would be thought a sissy and a coward if she did not righteously divorce him. But then, she pondered: what of the children; what of their financial security; would there be remarriage or only a broken home? Such questions raised doubts. She asked what other women facing such a situation did. Of course, I had to answer that it was a purely individual matter, for there was a wide spread of reactions to such a husband. At one extreme would be the woman who, knowing of her husband's mistress, loaded him with affection and gifts in her efforts to hold him. Then there are those who struggle to save their marriages until their feelings pass all endurance and drive them to separation for self-preservation. At the other end of the scale is the wife who instantly sues for divorce.

These differences are not in the wives alone, but also in the husbands, and in the relationships in each marriage. One husband is strong, independent—and inconsiderate. He goes his way regardless and lets his wife and children take it or leave it. But in another man, initiating a serious extramarital liaison turns out to be the first step in a deterioration of his whole personality, a slide into neglect of family and job, sometimes into alcoholism and often association with less reliable, less mature companions; and sometimes the slide is all the way into a mental hospital. The range of individual differences is great. Therefore, while making full use of experience, we must study and deal with each problem specifically; for the situations (age, children, occupation, social and economic level, housing, conditions of living, relatives and similar factors) and the histories and the personalities of the wife, husband and children, as well as the interactions between them all, are unique in each case.

Economic status may also be an important factor. The poor often seek extramarital sex as inexpensive compensation for the frustrations and deprivations of poverty, the difficulties in living and their hurt pride and envy, while the wealthy have the means to take a cruise and indulge every whim of their own or of their paramour.   But many of the poor are strictly monogamous, just as many of the rich are.

One man, Vic, as wealthy as he was attractive, married and then had any girl he could persuade.   He was divorced and repeated the performance.   If it took a Cadillac or a trip around the world to seduce a girl into yielding to him, he was quite willing and able to provide these inducements.   Each of his wives was loyal and devoted and deeply in love with him.   His philandering grew out of his own dynamics—really pathodynamics, for they were pathological.   It was not the money that dictated his behavior or his moral upbringing, which was extremely strict and reinforced by the weight of his church.   The critical factor, the really determining cause, lay in extreme neglect by his mother, which exaggerated his needs for the love of women and also created a deepseated hostility to them.   As an adult he transferred to women the original hunger for his mother's love and also his hatred toward her.   This gave him an intensity that most women did not in the least understand, but which, covered over as it was by much gallantry, consideration and generosity, they found irresistible.   They did not recognize that soon they would be not the recipients but the givers—and the butts of hostility as well—until it was too late, and they began to realize that they were not beneficiaries of love, but victims of demands and hate.

Another man, Ted, also very wealthy, had a wife who was unlike Vic's in that she was not a well-balanced, mature, easygoing woman.   Vic's wives gave no cause whatever for extramarital affairs; both were nice as could be; both were one-man women.   Ted's wife was full of problems and complaints and criticisms of him.   He traveled much, he had money, and he had all possible opportunities.   Yet he remained constant.   He had other reactions to the tensions she created, but extramarital sex was not his particular channel of expressing his needs, conflicts and tensions.

Cultural standards and customs are undoubtedly important.   But in seeing husbands and wives from different parts of the globe, I am struck not by differences, but by similarities.   Whatever the custom of the country, however much freedom is socially approved,

I have yet to see the sanction outweigh the power of jealousy. Jealousy is in part biological. I see it clearly in our dogs. Just pat Angy, and Shep jumps up to push her out of the way and have the attention and affection for himself. Be demonstrative to a child your dog does not know, and his jealousy may even endanger the child. Perhaps women accept polygamy in countries where it is the custom, but I cannot conceive of a woman—or a man—at least a young one—not suffering jealousy when asked or forced to share a mate.

The tiny statistical sample an analyst sees in his office practice, however, shows that the critical, that is, the weightiest, basic determining factor is the individual's dynamics. These dynamics will of course be influenced by the culture in which the child is reared. But the basic biological needs, drives and reactions are the same in all cultures.

A few vignettes will demonstrate persons who never disregard and break their marriage vows and the unenforceable secular laws, even despite provocation by their spouses. Of course external provocations, pressures or temptations play a part in illicit sexual affairs. A good man may be tempted beyond his resistance by a seductive woman, and vice versa. But husband or wife may be impelled into an affair that never would have been entered if that person had not been in a rage at the spouse at just that time. How we behave is always a matter of external temptations, frustrations and pressures causing us to react in accordance with our specific emotional patterns. We all have our Achilles' heels, our specific emotional vulnerabilities, our price. And though we may judge others, we do not know how we ourselves will react in a powerfully emotional situation unless we have been through it.

Certainly it takes considerable maturity to ride the tempestuous horses of the sexual urges, mixed as they are with the mating instincts, the dependent love needs, etc. No wonder our sexual desires often seize the bit and run wild. But I do not think that a man or woman carries on an outside affair that pains his spouse and children, damages them, in some part destroys them, unless there is a powerful undercurrent of hostility against them, however conscious or unconscious it may be. In my experience such destructiveness to one's own chosen mate and to the children one has created is not a purely incidental result of weakness or even selfishness alone. It is not merely an unfortunate by-product; it is a direct expression of latent resentment, hate, cruelty—in a word, of hostility—whether the person is aware of it or not.

My heart sank when Bill told me about his wife Bertha. Bill was an altogether excellent, sincere young man of conscientiousness and integrity, slender in build but broad in humor and good will. When he told me about his wife, he remarked in all innocence that she hated her father. "Why?" I asked. "Because," he said, "her mother hated him, really drove him out of the house and turned Bertha against him." "How early in Bertha's life was this?" I asked, and he replied, "Always. Since her childhood, since before she can remember."

It was early in my career, but I knew by then the truth of the adage that as the twig is bent, so the tree is inclined. The danger lay in the near certainty that Bertha would unconsciously act out toward her husband her pattern toward her father. The only hope I could see was that Bertha might transfer to Bill the pattern toward her mother, feel close to him and identify with him, and turn toward someone else the hostility she had for her father. The steps to marriage proceeded against the naive Bill's own intentions.

Bill's Achilles' heel was too strong dependent-love needs toward his mother, a reaction to an excess of indulgence, overprotection and anxiety on her part toward him since his birth. One cannot but be sympathetic with this, for it was well intended and was a natural response of a mother to her late-life child after the death in infancy of her first. Bill's being an only child further fixed him in this pattern of feelings toward his adoring parents, who robbed him of initiative by doing everything for him. He could not stand anyone's being unloved, whether himself or others. He was attracted to Bertha because she had this trend in common with him—overly strong closeness to mother. His own dependent-love needs were masked by his athletic prowess, his kidding with the boys and his hearty good fellowship.

They dated. Bertha was insecure and unhappy. She was grateful to Bill for his attentions, and this led to their being "pinned." She was very pretty and was appealing because of her loneliness. Bill's parents felt for her, sympathized with her. Against his judgment, Bill yielded to her tears and wishes, and the pinning became an engagement. Still he wanted to escape, but Bertha's needs and the pity and sympathy Bill and his parents felt for her eased him into marrying her, as a shoe horn guides a foot.

It did not take long for Bertha's pattern toward her father to begin to emerge toward Bill. She became critical. This and that were not right. He was just starting his career with a small but growing business, but Bertha complained about the house, the furniture, the appliances. She wanted more and better right now. Nothing Bill did was quite right in her eyes. Nothing satisfied her— his hours of departure or return, his attention to his job, his athletic recreations. She liked social climbing. He preferred friendship, fun and the outdoors. Once in a terrible rainstorm the basement flooded. He went down at two in the morning and stayed until five moving their trunks, groceries and equipment and plugging and pumping as best he could, while Bertha slept. In the morning as he was leaving for the day's work, Bertha complained that he had done a clumsy job.

The key to Bill's personality was mother-love, mostly in the form of appreciation. He had been on the baseball and swimming teams at college, and his parents traveled long distances to see him compete. Probably Bertha could have twisted him around her little finger and had him eating out of her hand if she had given him simple *appreciation*. But she did not know this, and perhaps was as incapable of giving it as she was of giving warmth, love or affection to any man; for she was trained by her mother to hate the only man in her childhood, her father.

This hostility was reflected in coldness, which encompassed her sexuality. Bertha was frigid. Frigidity need not interfere with a marriage in any consequential way. We have noted an excellent marriage with five children in which the wife never experienced an orgasm. But that wife liked sex anyway, and her easygoing husband was satisfied. They got on excellently and were the best of parents. Bertha's frigidity, however, was not confined to failure to achieve orgasm. It was expressed in a total rejection of sexual relations. She was too tired, or had some vaginal spasm, or had or thought she had a discharge. A few times a year she gave in. She never became pregnant.

Thus she was a burden and source of hostility in every area of his life—work, home, financial, recreational, social, affectional, sexual. Bill got nothing. He gave everything, and all that he gave netted only rejection, criticism and hostility. If ever a man was justified in turning to another woman for satisfaction of his simplest, most normal masculine needs for femininity, it would be Bill. And he had charm and health and a lot more to offer. Yet under these frustrations he stayed within the bounds of the marriage vows. His own dynamics, including the close affectionate, loving harmony between his parents and their harmony with Bill precluded extra-marital sexual activity as a solution. It simply was not in his dynamics of the conjugal relationship. If it had been, it might have led to other difficulties, but it might have alleviated the inevitable vicious circle that developed between them. I have not meant to be un-sympathetic to Bertha in this vignette. She was the innocent victim of her own pathological dynamics, formed in reaction to her well-meaning mother's influence. Her life was doomed to be blighted by this mother-attachment with hatred of father, no matter whom she married. I have only meant to show that Bill, also the victim of her pathodynamics, reacted to them, but not with sexual acting out.

As time went on, the vicious circle intensified. Hatred piled up between them. In some ways Bertha was better after Bill had begun to be enraged at her. Now her own guilt was appreciably relieved. The more hostile Bill became, the more justified Bertha felt in her own hostility to him. She could feel it as a realistic, natural reaction that any wife would have to such an angry man. This couple was not in treatment—Bertha never would consider it for a minute. Her pattern of hostility to her father and hence to men must have made her fear the transference of these feelings to an analyst. I thought she might consider going to a woman analyst, following the pattern of closeness to her mother, but she would not. This was in the early part of their marriage, after only a year or so. At any rate Bertha defended herself against seeing her own makeup and its contribution to the discord by projecting everything onto her hus-band—it was all his fault, he alone must change. He did see a good analyst for a time and derived considerable help in withstanding the demands, frustrations and direct hostility of Bertha.

They came east occasionally for some 15 years after the war and always stopped to see me. It was tragic to see these young people caught in such dynamics, gradually becoming hard, bitter, hostile, frustrated and aging prematurely under the strain, and yet remaining true to each other. Such prolonged tension and stress usually causes some kind of serious physical illness. Marriage can cause illness and death as well as life.

Apart from the exceptions mentioned, few wives of the husbands with the extramarital sexual regressions themselves showed any inclination toward other men as an emotional release, and some even felt repelled by the idea. However, one husband described his fidelity in a rather poignant way. Of his wife I will only say that her insecurity, caused by the crushing dominance of a martinet of a mother, made her suffer in her own mind; it kept her chronically depressed and indecisive. Her husband bore it all quietly for years, a pillar of strength to his wife and children, and never took advantage of his opportunities for liaison with a younger, happier woman. Once when he was nearing 50, he talked to me about this. "I am grateful that I am educated and financially comfortable, that my wife and children and I have good physical health, that I live in the United States, that we are settled and rooted in Chicago, in some ways the greatest city in the country. If my wife has difficulties I only feel that, blessed as I am in all other ways, she is like a bird with a broken wing that has been entrusted to my care and protection."

His dynamics—the unquestioned faithfulness and love between his parents and toward himself—permitted him to think and feel and behave in this fashion, and this strength far overbalanced the egocentric, the infantile and the sexual. Perhaps in the future authors of plays and stories will have to tell more than hitherto of not only the underlying patterns of motivation and reaction in their characters, but their genesis, how they came to be that way, how they were formed by the emotional influences of early childhood.

Infidelity is often a neurotic and sometimes a psychotic pursuit of exactly the man or woman one imagines one needs for satisfaction in life, a satisfaction always sought but never found. So many men and women of all ages who are the most successful in seductions are also the unhappiest in their relations. They pursue an ideal that is an unrealistic fantasy and that remains forever unattainable.

SECTION V:
REPETITION OF CHILDHOOD PATTERNS IN MARRIAGE

Whether we consider the rocky layer enveloping the Earth, the arrangement of the forms of life that inhabit it, the variety of civilizations to which it has given birth, or the structure of languages spoken upon it, we are forced to the same conclusion: that everything is the sum of the past and that nothing is comprehensible except through its history.

Teilhard de Chardin

21
HAPPILY EVER AFTER

Childhood patterns live a life of their own, exerting their influence throughout a person's existence. Most of us are to some extent trapped by some amount of deleterious childhood conditioning, but in some cases it does not greatly enter the marriage directly.

Danny sat in my office giving an impression, quickly confirmed, of vitality, intelligence and maturity. What then did he wish to improve in himself?

PATIENT: I must adjust to my family's having rejected me—and I can't, and I am getting irritable with my good wife. Everything in my life is better than anyone could ask for. I have a wonderful, easy, mature, congenial wife. Our children have turned out to be decent, good, successful people with good marriages and fine children of their own. I am interested in my legal work and in reading, politics, art and music. And my wife, Dina, shares all these interests except the law, my profession.

In spite of all these blessings I cannot accept the rejection by my family. It is absurd. I am 61 years old and yet am getting more and more bitter and short-tempered, and this is threatening my marriage. I have four brothers and sisters, actually they are half brothers and sisters. My mother died when I was a year and a half old. My father remarried within a year. As the children came along, I grew up with them as their brother. But I was the outsider for my stepmother, Mum. She gave me good care, but she never let me forget what she was doing for me. If I was sick, she reminded me of her sacrifices in coming up the stairs to see me or bring a tray. Yet she would be the last person in the world to think she contributed anything to this rejection. She is a hale 80, and I'll say she is a fine woman. Today, in spite of herself, she admires me. But she still shows the definite preference for her own children, all of whom are superior and exceptional.

ANALYST: Please tell a little more about those earliest years—before age six.

P: Father's marriage to Mother had been a love match. It had been a wild romance. I was a truly loved child, and my father was completely devoted to me. Mum, my stepmother, is a great woman but she has always had this aloofness to me. I was always falling, bumping my knee or arm, but she took any attention she had to pay me as a great nuisance. If I was sick, she would say, "Look at all I do for you, running up and down the stairs," and such remarks. Gradually I saw that she did not say these things to her own children. She always talked of "my brood"—and that definitely did not include me.

Today my wife and I are left out of all my family's affairs. This is especially clear and painful at the holidays. At Thanksgiving or Christmas there is never even a phone call to say, "See you after the holidays." If we invite any of them for dinner, they cancel at the last minute. Or they may just not come, and then phone two days later and say, "Oh, we forgot."

A: What is your very first memory?

P: All my early memories are about being with Father. My true mother died when I was a year and a half old, and I was with her parents until a year later when Father remarried. My first memory was, I think, before that. It was of being with Father and his saying to some people, "This is my son." Father died when I was 25. [This memory clearly confirms his longing for love, acceptance and the pride of his parents.]

Now here I am happily married, professionally successful, with lots of friends and interests, but I have this heartache. It is ridiculous to still make an issue of one tiny thing when everything else is as nearly perfect as life affords.

A: How long have you made this an issue?

P: Always. When my wife first noticed it, she was irked and said loudly and positively, "Just stop it—forget it." Later she completely refused to hear about it.

A: But you come to see me only now in later life. Is it worse recently?

P: I suppose I feel it more now. It's always been there, but the last six months or year I have not been coping with it. No one knows this. Everyone says, "Don't worry about Danny; he's made of stern stuff; he'll always land on his feet."

A: Why are you coping less well in the past year?

P: One sister and her husband who did keep some contact moved away some years ago. The two brothers and their families I sort of wrote off. In a way I don't even care that much about Mum any more. But we were very devoted to the other sister, Letty, and her family. A year ago her husband was about to do a very foolish thing in his business from a legal standpoint. I pointed this out. They both accused me of meddling. I spoke with them, and we seemed to have it resolved. They couldn't have been nicer. But in fact we never got together again. That was the last straw. And from then on my preoccupation with this began to be unhealthy, and now it threatens my marriage. I am 61, and my wife and I don't have that much time left.

A: Did you have a dream last night?

P: No.

A: Any recent dream?

P: No. In childhood I used to dream of running, and my feet would get heavier and heavier. You know that dream. Now I only dream bits of daily life.

[Did the dreams reflect trying to be free, to escape something, to reach something—love—and being blocked? We recall that he often bumped himself.]

A: You know biology well enough to know that the course of development takes the young away from the parents and the whole parental family, in species that have families. But if a child feels that the mother is too cool, the child is apt to cling, to be excessively attached, to fight for what it lacks from the mother.

P: Yes. Mum never kissed me, never put her arms around me. I used to weep about it. But as I grew a little older I developed a facade. I cried no more; I became perfectly groomed; all that sort of thing. And everyone thought I was unusually stable, a rock to whom others turned. "Don't worry about Danny; he's strong and solid." And now I cry over a book or play, but no longer over reality; for reality I just shrug.

In this instance the childhood pattern has not developed toward the spouse. It has never been *transferred* from the parental family where it is still fixated. It affects the marriage only indirectly by generating bitterness, irritability and preoccupation with it.

It appeared that Danny did not repeat toward his wife the childhood "object relations" he had toward his stepmother, but he did repeat unconsciously some of the "identification" with Mum. Just as she flagrantly preferred her brood to Dan, now Dan became more emotionally involved in this brood than with his wife. In this way, he treated his wife as his stepmother treated him, and this frustrated the marriage. He appeared on the surface to have full insight and to have transferred none of the childhood pattern to his wife. In reality, he had no insight into the identification with Mum and its subsequent transfer to his wife.

Danny presented not only instructive dynamics but a therapeutic challenge, for as these notes indicate, he came with quite thorough insight, but needed the help of the analytic situation to outgrow his childhood pattern, which, however circumscribed, had trapped him for a lifetime. It is not unusual for a person to have the most accurate, complete and penetrating insight, and yet for the emotional core of the difficulty to be remote from the kind of conscious realization that can deal with it, resolve it and be rid of it.

As in Danny's childhood dream, he is trying to escape, but his legs are heavy and he cannot. Many people are correct when they say they need not go to an analyst for the kind of insight they have, but they may need him urgently to help them *use* this insight to solve their problem. And as this example shows, the childhood pattern can intensify and the problem worsen even in the sixties, despite the most favorable life circumstances and despite unusual maturity in all the rest of the personality. Analytic treatment can be thought of as having two parts. The first is to *understand* the dynamics behind the difficulty. The second is to *use* this understanding curatively, to free the person from the difficulty. (In the process, the transference of the disturbing pattern to the analyst is usually of central importance.) This is as in the rest of medicine: rational treatment based upon thorough, accurate diagnostic understanding at all times.

Probably Danny's strengths, his ability to develop an effective facade, derived from the year and a half with his true mother, from his devoted father and from what was good in the interrelations with Mum and the half siblings. As usual, it is a matter of the balance of forces. The good relationships of his childhood gave him the soil for healthy maturation; however, these drives toward maturity could only defend against but not adequately resolve the trauma of the discrimination and exclusion to which he was subjected strongly and consistently from the age of two and a half. Apparently a sound base was laid during the first 18 months, and the next year was also good; so the seedling was off to a good start and could withstand the injurious preference of Mum for her brood, with no greater harm to Danny's whole life than what he related.

It is interesting and encouraging that Danny did very well with analytic treatment at two visits per week, despite his having been partially fixed in his pathodynamic pattern for almost a lifetime. Some analysts will insist that meeting less than four times a week is psychoanalytically based therapy and not psychoanalysis. Many books and articles have been written about this (Freud, 1940). In my opinion the essential is to understand the emotional forces behind the problem and to do what is most effective and time-saving to help the patient deal with these forces. The process, as Freud stated clearly, is one of "after-education" to correct the parental "blunders". (Franz Alexander called it a "corrective emotional experience.")

Danny, through Mum's behavior, was conditioned by her treatment to think of himself as an outsider in the family. He grew up in that setting, and what we grow up with in attitudes and feelings during our earliest formative years continues. Danny needed help in changing this set way of thinking and feeling. I believe treatment would have succeeded with one visit a week, but his particular pace was such that it was more smooth and rapid with two visits. I did not start at four or five meetings a week because stirring up and working with one's feelings so intensively is not optimum for many people. The unfolding of the emotional forces, the development of the transference—in fact, every constructive feature of the psycho-analytic process—is present even at one meeting a week if the analyst is skilled in this. It is a matter of adjusting the procedure to what is best for the individual patient. It worked for Danny during the two and a half years before the war; and the result held, as I learned by letter and upon seeing him during his occasional business trips from Chicago.

In some cases a person vows that he will never treat his spouse and children as he was treated in childhood. He becomes a model mate and parent. But there is a risk, a chance, that these mature defenses might at some point weaken and the old childhood feelings erupt. This is one reason that some "pillars of strength" sometimes collapse. It is safer to have a good, secure, loving, easy 0 to 6 at the core of the personality. But even when this is not the case, the defenses and reactions may work well and permanently.

The childhood emotional pattern of some persons is so rigidly fixed to parents, siblings and others in the childhood constellation that it can never be detached and transferred to individuals outside the family circle. Such a fixated person remains intensely involved with the characters of his childhood as long as they live; when the object of the attachment dies, the pattern is often maintained through memory. All such attachments are quantitative: some individuals can detach themselves almost totally from their childhood emotional fixation, and there is every gradation and mixture between the two extremes.

Once after a strenuous, hectic spring we arrived at our vacation spot, unpacked, had a bit of supper and at last stretched out to relax. Just then the phone rang. It was Julie—a tall, slender, violet-eyed young wife with a son and two daughters, charming, down-to-earth and practical. She had been to see me a few times before her husband was transferred by his company to a western state in which there were no trained psychiatrists at that time. On the phone Julie was in a panic. In her considerate way she apologized for calling during my vacation. She had strong self-control, but it was obviously now agitated and threatened. "I am losing my mind," she said. "I am not just saying this. I am fighting against going crazy. You know how I feared moving here. Randy had to for his job, but we are only 50 miles from where I was born and where all my family are. Now I'm all mixed up with them. I'm going out of my mind. What shall I do?"

Since there was no analytic psychiatrist available anywhere near her, we handled the situation by phone, seven days a week. It worked. She gradually withdrew from the brink. The near-psychosis was indeed a reaction to her family, especially her parents. Her father had always been and still was the complete commander. When he entered the house, all noise stopped; everything centered around his wishes and comforts; his whim was rigid law. Julie's mother was utterly dominated by him and kept the children under strict control, mostly with extreme guilt and a sense of obligation to parents. To develop guilt and obligation in a child, to make a child guilty and ashamed, is a poor method of helping him mature and form good feelings toward himself and others.

What saved Julie in childhood apparently was her escaping from her home to friends. This pattern continued into adult life. She had a good marriage in Chicago. Her upsets there were mainly reactions to letters or phone calls from her parents.

Many people throughout their lives, even as adults, react violently to their parents. Marilyn, who at 50 was a grandmother, began to have depressions. They were traceable to her mother's coming from Denver to Chicago to live. Marilyn lived on the South Side, her mother on the North Side, but her mother was solicitous, phoned and expected to be phoned almost daily, and gave gratuitous advice, thus stirring up Marilyn's childhood pattern of the old submissiveness to her mother, which enraged her. But her rage was always repressed; it generated guilt, and she became depressed.

The point about Julie is that throughout the three years of analytic help in learning to handle her violent feelings toward her parents, she remained an excellent wife and mother in spite of her terrible anxiety about losing her mind. Her marital family was affected only indirectly by her being so upset by her parents. Gradually, she disengaged her feelings from her parents sufficiently to be free of symptoms. She was for years free of anxiety and able to enjoy her marital family, friends and interests, but she found that it was impossible to see her parents without going all to pieces and suffering intense anxiety, control of which took every ounce of her strength, and which threatened her with mental breakdown and almost entire incapacitation.

Analytically we hoped that she would resolve her childhood pattern to the point of tolerating a reasonably friendly, adult relationship with her parents. But this was not achieved. Once she said, "I know they are elderly, and I am now the young strong one. I know that bygones should be bygones. I know that to go and visit for a few hours should be nothing at all. When I see my father, or even talk with him on the phone, I tell myself all this, but I can't fight off memories of childhood—of his coldness and strictness and the ways he treated me. Then I rage inside, and I feel guilty and suddenly I'm in pieces and fear losing my mind again."

This is a cruel clash—between the parents and the husband and children; but the choice is obvious. The parents have little time left and, sadly, are only reaping what they sowed. A marriage is for more than half a lifetime, and the children have their whole lives ahead of them, including their own future marriages and those of their children, down through all the generations to come. The Bible tells the wife she must leave her parents and cleave to her husband. And it is the same for the husband. It is basic biology: The general rule in the animal kingdom is for the young after adolescence to leave the parents or to be pushed out or deserted by them; for the parents have prepared them to survive on their own and to follow their instincts to mate and form their own families (or whatever the variation is for the given species).

Julie did not hesitate. Communication with her parents upset her so badly that it jeopardized her home, the well-being of her husband and the emotional development of her children, with all its implications for *their* marriages and children. Therefore, defending her home like a tigress, she reluctantly cut off contact with her parents. Isolating herself from them returned her to her normal happy life in home and community.

After the war her father sent them a gift. She assumed that it was intended in a kindly way; but it was enough to arouse her old love needs for her parents, her old sense of obligation and her rage and guilt. Again she became almost paralyzed with anxiety. Again she recovered at the price of withdrawal from her parents and became stabilized for the next few years.

After this period of stability, Julie began to feel secure enough to visit her father and mother, who were now getting old. Analytic help had achieved much reduction of anxiety, but it had never fully resolved the feelings still stirred up by her parents. But visiting her parents seemed worth a trial. She went only for a day, but that did it. Again she fought against losing her mind and required some help to regain her stability in her own home, in her own life. Julie shows the enormous power of these childhood patterns toward parents and others, and how they may stay attached for life to the original persons who provoked these reactions. In this case, except for her hot temper, they were not transferred to spouse and children apparently. In fact Julie has had one of the best marriages I know of, despite the frequent violent storms caused by her anxiety when she heard from her parents.

Reference

Freud, S. (1940): Outline of Psychoanalysis, *S. E.* 23, p. 172.

22
JEALOUSY AND PARANOID JEALOUSY

Jealousy is cruel as the grave: the coals thereof are coals of fire, which hath a most vehement flame.

Song of Solomon 8:6

We have remarked the frequent conflict between sex and love from which springs one of the problems of marriage. Because we expect complete gratification from our spouse, we usually expect to have our sex in a setting of love. Happy indeed is the marriage in which sex and love reinforce each other!

The sex drive itself, we have said, varies enormously because of dampening or overstimulation by elements in the childhood pattern. It is common to see young wives who complain that their husbands show lack of interest and infrequency of performance—but some wives move from this complaint to the opposite and blame their husbands for wanting sex all the time, dampening the wive's ardor or obliterating her desires by insatiable sexual demands upon her.

Equally common is the complaint of the wife whose husband is so absorbed in his work and other outside interests that he no longer cares about her sexually and in fact no longer has any sexual drive toward her. "Do you know how long it has been since we made love?" a patient often asks. "About two (or three or four) months, and if I do not initiate it, more than a month always goes by between times. Sometimes I think he must have some other woman; once every month or two is just not normal." The wife's euphemistic term "love making" is a feeble expression for sexual intercourse, that exorbitant consummation which can contract to insignificance in either husband or wife but can also be exaggerated beyond all reasonable proportion. Either way, sex can cause problems in the love relationship.

One young wife is jealous of her husband's perfectly normal, male appreciation of a beautiful girl passing by. Another woman, not overtly jealous, allows her husband much freedom, but if she were ever to find out that he had been involved physically in an extramarital sexual affair, even in the past, this woman's marriage and indeed her whole life would henceforth be vitiated. In this case, the wife would not mind her husband's dancing with other women or even being attracted to them, but the idea of his having physical sex with another woman would be shattering to her. If one learns enough of the childhood patterns and consequent dynamics, one finds the reasons behind these feelings. The first girl was severely deprived by her mother, who grossly favored her siblings. She grew up in a constant painful jealousy, and this remained an emotionally vulnerable area for her. The father of the second woman did not hide his mistresses from his daughter, not disguise his cruelty to her mother. His daughter saw his infidelities demolishing her mother as a person; she could not identify with her mother's masochistic jealous suffering and vowed that she would defend the respect and integrity of her own individuality.

Occasionally one sees the opposite: we have mentioned one couple who attributed primary importance to common interests, identification with one another, love and loyalty and had no great feeling about the sex act itself. They even told each other with amusement about their outside, purely physical sex adventures, such as the affair the husband had on a trip to the Orient with a girl from Outer Mongolia. But both the husband and wife cared deeply and were furiously jealous if they detected an *emotional* interest in a third person, rather than a purely physical sex attraction.

So infidelity can be considered "benign" when a couple agree on it in some form for one or both, and when it has little hostile meaning. It can be considered "malignant" when consciously or unconsciously it is hostile and destructive, causing suffering and sometimes ruining lives.

An apparently emotionally healthy young matron with an excellent marriage, three good thriving children and a successful, happy husband with whom she enjoyed sex almost daily nevertheless responded strongly to an attractive man outside the home. She would never actually do anything to jeopardize her excellent marriage, and indeed she fully appreciated her good luck, but did recognize in herself a strong need for outside contact, mostly mental, away from her daily routine. Although her marriage was good, the domestic routine was dull and monotonous for a woman with her high intelligence and varied interests and enthusiasms. She wanted to talk about these interests, especially the ones her husband did not share. She did not gravitate toward discussions with other women, for she was never close to her mother in early childhood. She became alive only when talking about her interests with men. It was hard for her to see why she should not yield to a culmination of this community of intellectual interest in physical closeness and sex relations. Feeling completely secure in her marriage, her loyalty and commitment to it, determined never to hurt husband or children or jeopardize the relationship, she could not see why intimacy with another man whose situation was similar to hers would not simply be a profoundly gratifying experience, hurting no one. She felt that in time her husband would share her view.

Is this a rational concept? Love is not sex. Although it is a sterile existence, one can live without fornication. But few individuals can sustain a life without love. For love is perhaps the greatest human experience, and its culmination is usually physical, in sexual intercourse. Does our culture exaggerate the importance of sex when it can be enjoyed without damaging others? Is jealousy mostly a cultural and personal dynamic phenomenon, or is it biological? Or is it both, in various degrees? Certainly it is strongly influenced by the pattern formed by the small child's experiences with its parents and siblings.

I once saw a 20-year-old college student in a murderous rage at another boy with whom his girl was flirting. He actually planned to kill his rival. It turned out, however, that this was the boy's first affair, and in his inexperience he did not recognize that the girl was flirting only to torment him; he was convinced that if he lost her he would never in the visible future find another girl to have sex with him. This meant he would not be successful as a male. His jealousy, which arose from fear of losing his female, was multiplied many times by his threatened male self-esteem. In another case it was the boy's extreme childish dependence on the girl that caused his excess of jealousy, as though he were a five-year-old threatened with losing his mother or an only child suddenly threatened with the arrival of a new baby.

The jealousy of a woman who fears she will lose her husband is apt to be intensified if she is not secure in her feminine attractiveness and cannot tolerate competition with another woman. And if her husband is the breadwinner, her whole financial security is at stake, as well as her appearing to be a failure in the role of wife; her self-image and self-esteem as a woman are threatened with being shattered. She faces loss of much more than a man in her bed.

There are personal and cultural factors in jealousy, both in emotional interest and in physical sexual interest. But we must face the fact that jealousy exists in animals, e.g., in birds who permit those of another species into their territory to feed but fight off those of the same species who are rivals for sex and mating.

It appears that, as with monogamy and promiscuity, there is a base of biological tendencies in jealousy seen throughout most of the animal kingdom, and these "instinctual" tendencies are modified in various ways and degrees by the influences on the child of the personalities in his family orbit and by the culture in which he is reared and lives.

A superior man had bad luck with his wife. Although all was loving prior to their marriage, shortly after the ceremony she became paranoid toward him with constant criticism and jealousy. In her eyes he could do no right. The least thing or even a most pleasant surprise, such as his bringing home flowers to her, she interpreted as stupid, deficient or hostile to herself. In a restaurant she thought he was looking at all the other women. She went to a psychoanalyst, a good one, but he was unable to get through the paranoid defense. She felt herself to be perfect and blameless in the marriage and attributed the entire difficulty to her husband, whom she now implacably hated. She progressed to the point of acting out her rage and hate against him by having sex with other men. The husband in turn had borne her hostility with incredible patience, but her infidelities were too much, and he instituted divorce proceedings. The wife now expressed her hostility by trying to get every cent of his money. But here the cultural factor came to his aid: he had ample evidence of her adultery, and society said that although she might torture him in every other way, her sexual intercourse with other men was grounds for divorce. The husband was kindly, loving and strong; he hated to use such grounds, but his wife gave him no choice. Her unconscious hostility from her childhood pattern emerged toward her fine husband but then turned against herself, ruining her adult life.

How people try to love each other but cannot is seen by contrasting the beauty of the marriage ceremony with the unhappiness in so many marriages and the rising divorce rate. One of life's most poignant tragedies is to see a vividly remembered radiant young bride some years later when she has been gripped and beaten by the realities of life and marriage. Infidelity, conflict between love and sex in the marriage relationship and jealousy are exaggerated or diminished by the conditioning influences of early childhood.

Childhood Pattern Closely Transferred

In general, animals do a lot of growling and snarling for warning and bluffing in order to avoid serious fighting; but once they have mated, they will risk injury and death in battling to keep their families. And it has been noted that the animals defending their homes are usually much more valiant in combat than are the intruders, who have no such just cause.

Guy de Maupassant wrote a story called "Love." The following is an excerpt from its ending:

Two birds . . . glided rapidly over our heads. I fired and one of them fell almost at my feet . . . and then . . . above me I heard a voice, the voice of a bird. It was a short, repeated, heartrending lament; and the bird, the little animal that had been spared, began to turn round . . . over our heads, looking at its dead companion which I was holding in my hand . . . .
"You have killed the duck," [Karl] said, "and the drake will not fly away."
He certainly did not fly away; he circled over our heads continually, and continued his cries. Never have any groans of suffering pained me so much as that desolate appeal, as that lamentable reproach of this poor bird which was lost in space.
Occasionally he took flight under the menace of the gun which followed his movements, and seemed ready to continue his flight alone, but as he could not make up his mind to this, he returned to find his mate.
"Leave her on the ground," Karl said, . . . "he will come within shot by and by." And he did indeed come near us, careless of danger, infatuated by his animal love, by his affection

for his mate, which I had just killed. . . . Karl fired. . . . I saw something black descend . . . I put them . . . into the same game bag.

Only man's colossal egotism has kept him from recognizing what is known to every child with a pet, every animal trainer, every veterinarian, most farmers and others familiar with animals: namely, that animals have needs and feelings and personalities just as humans have. The physiology and biochemistry of living processes are basically the same in animals and man, and modern medicine is based on this fact. Animals suffer from most of the same dire diseases as man: tuberculosis, heart disease, cancer, arthritis and many, many others. We are built on the same anatomical, physiological and biochemical ground plan. We eat, eliminate, need shelter and exercise like most other animals; we play as they do; we also are dependent as they are, need social cooperation, need to love and be loved, to establish families, to reproduce and to raise our young with affection, protection and much teaching.

Intellectually we are far superior. But brains do not produce happiness. We tend to worship sheer intellect, but intellect is only an amoral tool, like big muscles. It is a tool of the emotional life, which can be used for cruelty and destruction as well as to make a secure and satisfying life. Life is primarily of the heart, of the feelings. Whether or not we annihilate each other, with thermonuclear bombs, overpopulation, or pollution will be dictated by our feelings: hate, power-seeking, love. The intellect only makes possible the application of atomic power; the ways and goals of its use are dictated by the heart, the feelings, the personality patterns—the identical kinds of motivations that make the rest of the animal kingdom feel and behave as they do. And they, although far inferior to us intellectually, are far superior to most of us morally and in mature, responsible, loving behavior to their own spouses, children, friends and all their own kind. Certainly we have much to learn about our own nature from our animal cousins. They cannot talk but they often do better than man in making their feelings known: they openly reveal their feelings by their mien and behavior. If we see jealousy in them, we can be sure that it is the same deep, primitive form of response that we ourselves experience.

Besides seeing in animals the power of jealousy for their mates and young, we can deduce it from our knowledge of psychodynamics. In all close attachments between adults there is a strong residue of the child's dependent-love needs toward its mother, those deep needs which the mother and father will, if mature, respond to by giving the child what it craves. The child's very existence depends upon his needs for food, warmth, protection and cleanliness being satisfied; and the assurance of satisfaction of these biological needs lies in the feeling of being loved by the mother and father. These needs, still present in the adult, attach normally to the mate. This is part of the interdependence. The infant's needs are lessened in intensity in adult life. The mate is a contemporary, another poor suffering mortal like ourselves in equal need of tender loving care, and cannot be such a mother or father as we had in childhood and resent relinquishing—or such as we did not have, and therefore still inordinately crave.

Jealousy signals a threat to one's mate and young and home, and to the all powerful needs for love and dependence. And in addition, it is a terrible blow to the self-esteem. For as the dependent-love needs are transferred to wife or husband, he or she comes to stand in some degree for mother and father. To be rejected by the parents, whether for oneself alone or in favor of another, is to be held unworthy, insufficiently lovable by the all powerful parents whose opinion of oneself one accepts. If they think us not worthy of their love, whether or not they openly prefer a brother or sister, then we take over in some degree this opinion of ourselves.

These few remarks about jealousy are only meant to indicate some of its roots: how deep it is biologically and psychodynamically, and hence what a terrible state to suffer from or to provoke in another human being or animal.

Jealousy, like other painful feelings, can arise as a natural reaction to sufficient external provocation; it can also be generated from within; and it can be caused by a combination of both external circumstances and internal patterns. This combination of external and internal causes seems to be portrayed in Shakespeare's *Othello* (Saul, 1967).

Even when confronted with betrayal, not all men and women react with equal intensity. It all depends, of course, on the individual's childhood emotional patterns. As we have seen in our discussion of infidelity, one mate may never think in terms of jealousy or suspect infidelity even when there is cause, while another experiences jealousy when there is no external cause whatever. Reading infidelity into a situation where it does not exist or exaggerating a simple, slight, natural interest in someone into proof of faithlessness is usually caused by projecting something in one's own emotional patterns onto the other person.   When the exaggeration is extreme, and especially when it is combined with a strong element of hostility, it is called paranoid.

In psychiatric practice it is often hard to discern just what is internal and what external.   Persons with strong paranoid streaks are usually among the master rationalizers. They can prove anything, and they can pile up such arguments as to be very convincing. Often it takes a while before one realizes that they are weaving reality into their fantasies, into their emotional needs, and that it is useless to argue with them.   One will never win a point or have any influence on their thinking, for their thinking and way of seeing reality lack almost all objectivity and are determined by childhood emotional needs and patterns.

They are tendentious.   They select the facts and reasoning to prove their emotionally preestablished conclusions.   But this can be tricky.   Years ago I saw a man who was in a mental hospital for ten days' observation because he was suffering from the delusion that his wife was putting poison in the lunches she prepared for him.   It turned out that it was no delusion—she really was.   We obtained some of the sandwiches.

Another man, who had escaped from a private mental hospital, was picked up by the police. It was in the 1930s.   In the interview in the hospital, he "proved" that Hitler had gotten control of all the private sanatoriums in the country and was railroading people into them on false commitments for political motives.   So logical and convincing was he that the policeman who was present saw no signs of delusion in this.   But this man's idea was part of a whole delusional system that was entirely a product of his fantasy, and, except for his use of a few kernels of truth, built up beyond all reality.

When one sees a husband or a wife in the office and hears one side of the picture, it is very hard to evaluate the total situation, and often it still is difficult even after hearing the spouse's side. For as we have noted, one must discern not only the dynamics of each, but also the interplay of these dynamics between the two. Sometimes it helps greatly if one can get the opinion of fairly mature children or others who are in the home. But the way they see it must also be evaluated: are they reasonably objective, or strongly identified with the husband or the wife?

One wife, Sonia, accused her husband, Steve, of being unconsciously mean to her, of little cutting remarks, of driving the car in ways that frightened her, of embarrassing her by being late when he escorted her, of coldness of manner. He, on the other hand, showed how justified all this was as reaction to his wife's underlying hostility to him. She admitted this hostility to him, but said it was an unavoidable reaction to the way he treated her. Was he hostile to her, and, if so, how much was a natural reaction to the way she acted and how much arose from inner sources? To what extent did he have a streak of coldness, sullenness and hardness?

Both he and his wife had the highest love and regard for their son, Stanley, who was in his early twenties. He came to see me. I had hesitated to see him because I did not want to risk any influence on his alignment with one parent against the other. Even sympathetic listening can encourage hostilities and help consolidate attitudes and feelings. But my fears were groundless. He was quite mature and objective and loved both his parents devotedly. This made him secure enough to speak easily and freely. There was no question, in his view, of his father's unconscious hostility to his mother. Stanley had long recognized it; he had tried to discuss it with his father, but the father was truly not aware of what he was doing. The result of it all was that I felt much more secure in my understanding, for what the son said coincided with my own impression. His view came from a lifetime of living in the family, mine from a few professional hours with each parent in the office. If our views were the same, there probably was some reality in them.

Both parents accepted some analytic help—the mother by her own wish, the father reluctantly. But his resistance against it was discussed from the beginning. He gained insight into his feelings and attitudes toward his wife and the marriage began to improve. He had certain rigidities that made help very difficult, but once he was won over to acknowledging his part in the constant contention, the atmosphere improved markedly. Both understood better the vicious circle set up by the hostilities and the need to give a little more love and affection and patience and to settle for receiving a little less of these without anger.

Now we come to a man in whom the source of the problem was easily recognized and definitely internal. He was more than willing to follow his wife's suggestion that he come for an opinion. Let us call them Charlie and Carole. The marriage, he said, was only six months old but fraught with bitter fights. He had other problems, but these, he said, were minor. What he came about was his marriage.

PATIENT: The trouble began almost as soon as we were married. This was strange, for we had lived together for nearly a year before the ceremony, and all went beautifully. We had no fights and were very happy. Then Carole had to go home to California because of an illness in her family, and we were separated for a few months. We could hardly wait to be together again and to be married. At the time of my vacation from my job—I'm an accountant—I went to California, and we were married there. Almost at once, before we left on our honeymoon, a strange thing happened. I felt that Carole was being a little too friendly with an uncle of mine who was present. I was jealous. I'm still not sure but that she may have had some feelings for him. He was about 50, but youthful and attractive. It seemed that something changed in me after the ceremony.

The honeymoon lasted three weeks, and we were pretty happy; but I was not at ease. When we got back, we had people in, and then they invited us to their house. I had old friends, married couples, who had never met Carole. One of the couples were close friends of mine, though nearly 20 years older. Carole talked to the husband alone for what seemed to me too long a time. I became so jealous that I was in a rage at her. I tried to hide it but couldn't, and we had a big fight after we got home that evening.

Carole has a part-time job as secretary in a business firm. There are men around, of course, and you know how they feel about secretaries. There are one or two I'm suspicious of. They make me so jealous that Carole is going to give up the job, although we need the income until I'm a little better established, and we start a family.

Recently we went on a vacation to the shore. We used to go before we were married. This time she eyed the good-looking men on the beach, and this enraged me. In the evening I took her out to dinner, but in the restaurant I could see her interest in other men. I got so mad I just walked out and left her there. We have our good times still, but more than half the time we fight, so that I'm afraid she will leave me. There is always a particular man that I think she is in love with in preference to me. I am getting to doubt whether she really loves me.

ANALYST: Could this jealousy be all in your mind?

P: I guess maybe it is, but I can't help feeling this way. I need your help with this. I know it is my problem, but I think she does have this interest in other men. I get so mad I call her all kinds of names, and it is hard to keep control of myself and not hit her.

A: As you tell this, it sounds rather unrealistic if I follow you correctly. You are jealous of your wife's being in love with a man, but it seems to be a different man every day. If it's someone you know, it's usually a man who shows no interest in her, or sometimes it's even a total stranger. Do you seriously believe this?

P: Well—I guess I believe it, and I don't believe it. One moment I'm sure it's true and can't stand it. And then at another time I think it's foolish. Of course, I'm here because I think it's my problem, and I know I must learn to trust her.

I have given only a small sample of the discussion of jealousy with him; the rest was of the same nature. He came for help because he sensed that it was his internal problem, but still he could not help believing his own delusion: that his wife was really rejecting him in favor of some other man with whom she was in love, but always in a quite unlikely, unrealistic way. But of course I would have to see his wife.

The interview continued:

A: Please tell me a little about the highlights, the main features of the emotional relations in your home during your childhood, as far back as you can remember.

P: So far as I know, my home was normal until my father was killed in an auto accident when I was about four years old. I do not remember him, but I seem to have only good feelings about him. After that, everything changed. My mother had to get a job. My younger brother and I hardly ever saw her. She was in and out. She went out with other men, trying to find a second husband, and she did marry one. But after my father died, the main thing was that she was distracted; she lost her interest in my brother and me, and was always leaving us to find a job, to do her job, to go out on dates, to be interested in something or someone else.

About two years later, when I was about six, she did remarry. This man had two children of his own, and then they had one together. This stepfather never talked to us. He acted as though we didn't exist. And Mother gave all her attention to him and the other children. When I was nine years old, I was sent away to boarding school. My mother hardly ever wrote and never came to see me. I had trouble with a teacher and with some other boys. I wrote her, but she never did anything but tell me to be patient. When I got older and began to get jobs outside of school hours, she became interested in me; but then I gradually began to see that it was for the money I earned. Sometimes I hate her and hope I never see her again. But I think she loves me in her own selfish way, and I still hope that she will be good to me, write me a good letter, be interested in me rather than always in something or somebody else.

A: What is your very first memory—one of those little scraps long before continuous memory?

P: I was about five. It was Mother's birthday. I went in to see her. She was not alone. A man was there talking with her. I was terribly embarrassed and did not know what to say. So I just left. I felt that this was the wrong thing, and I went to my room and cried.

[This expresses in one poignant scene the essentials or his childhood situation and his reactions to it.]

A: Any other very early memory?

P: I remember waking up at night and seeing something on a table that scared me. It turned out to be a glove of Mother's.

A: Have you a recent dream—did you have one last night?

P: No, but I dream frequently. They are mostly nightmares: somebody is killing people and is going to kill me.

[This masochistic dream seems to indicate strong hostility, probably guilt and certainly fear, as in the second memory where it is connected with his mother.]

A: Any other kind?
P: Well, lately I sometimes dream that Carole is with some other man. I had one crazy one. She was taking care of a little boy about seven years old, and I had the idea that when he grew up she would be in love with him and have an affair with him, or leave me and marry him.
A: How do you get on with people?
P: Quite well. But I'm not easy with people. I have a few fairly close friends. But I guess I'm shy. I just can't be a "hail fellow." I go to parties and meet people, but I don't have much to say. I just don't make acquaintances easily.

Now these pieces fit together very well. The central pathodynamics, as seen in the early history and earliest memories and dreams, describe a pattern that accounts for the delusion of his wife's interest in and love for another man. Charlie's delusion is not fully psychotic, for he knows, although he cannot fully believe it, that it is a product of his own mind. His grasp of reality is otherwise sound: the disturbance is circumscribed, confined to this one area in relation to his wife. Apart from this the marriage is excellent. Therefore we can consider this severely neurotic rather than psychotic.

This neurotic delusional jealousy is the simple, direct continuation of the childhood pattern toward his mother after the loss of his father. The mother was interested in other men and then fell in love with one and married him. Now he continues this pattern of feeling toward his wife. The rage at his mother for this rejection in favor of job and another man is repressed and projected. It appears in the dreams as nightmares of someone's killing others and threatening the patient. This killer is the representation of his own inner repressed rage at his mother, for whose love he still yearns, and at his innocent wife, toward whom he continues the childhood pattern.

Why did these ideas of Charlie's develop immediately after he married Carole, and not while they were going together and even living together out of wedlock? Our guess was confirmed by later material: the reason was that although he had been rejected for another and unloved since he was about five, his healthy core until then gave him the mental strength and maturity to stand this until his marriage. He was able, in other terms, to build defenses against his feelings. He withdrew somewhat from close *emotional* relations with anyone. He kept buried his love needs, his feelings of rejection and frustration, his jealousy and his rage. All was bottled up within him. He never dared give in, even in thought, to his dependent-love needs for his mother—for if he did, he would suffer the pain and anguish of neglect, rejection, jealousy, and of the rage and hate that these aroused within him. He could not believe that any woman would really love him if his own mother did not, and he did not dare to open his hopes and longings to one. Even when Carole lived with him, he could not believe it. But when the ceremony was over, when she had now ultimately given herself to him, the rejected child's deepest love needs could no longer be contained. They welled up and broke through his defenses against them. But with them came all the rest of the pattern: the feelings of neglect and rejection by his mother for another man, who gave nothing, but to whom his mother gave the love that he, the child, so needed and craved. This whole pattern erupted suddenly toward his wife, rather than emerging gradually over some months and years, as is probably more usual.

Lawyers who examine witnesses are reputed to develop over the years a sense for whether a person is lying or truthful. The analyst from his professional experience with many persons develops a similar sense for what is going on. Years of experience form a kind of baseline. This is, of course, only a guide. In this case the material seemed clear and convincing, rather than almost impenetrable, vague or only suggestive, as it is in others. But of course I talked with Carole several times to get her view of Charlie. It would be dramatic, and a good story, to report that, as she saw it, the impression Charlie gave was false and misleading, but the opposite was true. There were serious difficulties, but not in perceiving the dynamics and the interplay between this husband and wife. What she told and what she related coincided with my impression of Charlie, derived from the first interview with him, and confirmed by many more. Carole herself had had a period of analytic work, and with her permission I talked with her former analyst, who added further corroboration. Of course, I was eager to know something of her makeup and of how she may have played to Charlie's problem. From her former analyst and from herself I learned the following:

Carole had been overprotected by her mother and overly attached to her. This heightened dependent-love need for mother, with an underlying repressed resentment against her, probably formed one of the strong common elements in the dynamics of both Carole and Charlie, made them understand each other, identify with each other, love and marry. I do not mean to oversimplify. There were other features in the attraction. For example Carole, as a loved child, tried to satisfy her needs vicariously, by rescuing and mothering small animals, and now by rescuing Charlie, who in part was so appealing because of his insecurity about being loved or lovable. At any rate Charlie was completely a one-woman man, and had never gotten close enough to a woman other than Carole, nor risked a rebuff sufficiently, to have ever had any other sexual affair. And Carole was entirely a one-man woman. She had been firmly attached to her mother, and transferred this attachment to Charlie. Defiance or resentment in the form of sexual acting out was not part of her dynamics. She slept with Charlie before they were married only because she was certain in her own mind that they would marry. Or she never would have given him her virginity, which she prized and held for her true love and husband. Her analyst felt sure of this; her associations fully supported the truth of this and revealed no dynamics in behavior, fantasies or dreams to the contrary. She was another example of fidelity and infidelity being mostly characteristics of the individual personality. Sexual acting out is a favored mechanism of some persons, while others do not have it in their makeups—they have other mechanisms.

Charlie suffered from his jealousy and the rages that went with it. The rage was projected, as we saw in his dream of the killer; and the anxiety in this nightmare and in the second memory was a symptom in real life. His anxiety was increased by the guilt he felt for his hostile outburst at his good, innocent and devoted wife. He attached this anxiety to all sorts of things—fear of thunderstorms, of flying in planes, of bugs; and typical of how irrational man's intellect, of which he is so overweeningly proud, can be, he immediately felt sure that every pain or ache or common cold was cancer, but this did not prevent him from smoking two packs of cigarettes a day.

It is hard then not to think that the human mind, nature's greatest achievement in the development of intellect, at least on this planet, is a biological failure emotionally. The very need for love, intensified because unsatisfied in childhood, led Charlie to do things for which he despised himself—things like suspecting his loyal wife, spying on her, flying into accusatory rages at her. Then he reviled himself for this, consciously in the self-recriminations, unconsciously during sleep in his nightmares and while awake in his depressions and irrational fears and anxieties, which built every minor occurrence into a portent of impending tragedy. His craving for love, his dire need, isolated, alienated and estranged him from others who would have given the love; thus the need, by its own excess, defeated itself. This is one of the greatest ironies of life—that a wish, by being too strong, too importunate, can prevent its own gratification. Another irony is that the innocent child must pay throughout his entire adult existence for abuses visited upon him through no fault of his own by parents who themselves may have been well meaning.

One could hardly find a better example of a person's gaining sharp insight in the very first interview, confirmed by all later material from him and other sources, but nevertheless reacting with rigid resistance against change. The stubborn fixed pattern only softened through hard analytic work at three meetings a week over a period of three years. Insight alone can be powerfully helpful in some persons but have little effect in others. However, insight is the *sine qua non,* the essential base, for any rational treatment designed to relieve symptoms permanently by changing the underlying pathological childhood patterns that caused them and by helping the person outgrow these patterns. So the dynamics were clear, but the treatment was difficult because Charlie was so fixed for so long in these attitudes and reactions. But gradually he learned to discriminate between what was an appropriate response in childhood to his mother's treatment of him, and what was an unrealistic response in the present situation to his wife. At least he was turned from the way *in* to the way *out* of his problem.

Reference

Saul, L. J. (1967): Othello: projection in art, *J. Amer. Medical Assn.,* **200**(1): 145-146, Apr. 3.

23
THE IMPORTANCE OF BEING MARRIED

The variety of relationships between the sexes seems infinite in any time and culture. Gail Wallace and her husband bring up two interesting points: the importance for the one to be married and the need of the other to avoid it; and how jealousy, that green-eyed monster, that can motivate crimes of passion and suicide in some people, can be of negligible consequence in others.

Gail presents not the usual *internal* neurotic type of emotional problems but one that seems to be *reactive* to her external life situation. But to what extent has she unconsciously made a difficult situation like this for herself?

She was a small, dynamic, attractive woman with a strong personality, the typical still-youthful woman in her late forties with grown or half-grown children.

She said, "I sometimes think that my marriage is the best that can be expected, that it is at least average, but at other times I think of my husband who died when I was 35, leaving me with five children. It was then I met Gus, and he fell deeply in love with me, and we began living together, planning to get married as soon as his divorce came through. He was already in the process of divorce when I met him; so I had nothing to do with that. But when the divorce came through, Gus turned against the idea of marriage. Instead of being enthusiastic about getting married immediately, upon arrival of the papers he cooled off, and we have never officially been married—we have just lived together as man and wife for the past ten years. I think of it as a common-law marriage. Very few people know we are not actually married. Gus seems to be frightened at the idea of my actually being his wife. It raises all sorts of problems. We have to protect the children, although they are grown up now, the youngest being in early adolescence, and they introduce him as their stepfather. He should have told me if he did not mean to marry me and just asked me straight out if I would live with him. Now it is a burden for me. It would be different if he had said, 'It's too upsetting for me to marry you.' He is two or three years older than I, a brilliant man, successful in business."

I asked, "How do I fit in here? Of what help can I be?"

She answered, "I don't quite know. We did both go to a marriage counselor about two years ago, but it was such a negative experience for me that we went only twice."

"Why," I asked, "did you go to the marriage counselor?"

"Because we were having marital problems," she said. "Gus told the counselor the positive things but also all the things he hated about me; I was so hurt that I did not want to go back. Then Gus did go to a psychiatrist, and he has gone to see him on and off for nearly ten years, not regularly but whenever he felt the need. But he never has asked me to come along. It seems to me rather odd that the psychiatrist never wanted to see me. I wonder if Gus has a sort of conspiracy to keep me out of his life. One time I drove him to see his psychiatrist and he asked me to wait in the car like a chauffeur. I guess that is why I am seeing you—it's a dilemma, whether to try to live happily with him or just give up. He says that I live in a dream world and should accept my position. He does have a good relationship with his children and with my children. I can't really look for another husband, a real husband that is, while I live with Gus in his world as though married to him; I can't look for a husband while Gus supports me."

"Have you seen a lawyer," I said, "about the common-law idea?"

"No," she said, "but that is a very good idea; I will go and at least try to clarify my legal status. Gus does not yet know that I am seeing you. He is out of town. He feels quite satisfied, of course . . . he has me as wife and as mother to the children and to run the home; he has work he likes and his only problem is to get me to accept the 'marriage' that we have. Eight years ago, when his divorce became final, we went looking for a house as man and wife. Now he says I forced him to look together.

"Before he was divorced, Gus was proud to introduce me as his wife if we were out of town. He was always delighted to have me along, but now he says it is just my imagination. Now he does not want me to be part of his life; he wants compartments. He wants me and the children at home, and he keeps an apartment in the city because he is high up in the company, and he wants me to just accept that."

I said, "Why do you say that it is a rotten marriage? Because you are not really married?"

"No," she said, "we were happy together once, but now he just wants a wife to be at home when he comes."

I asked, "Do you think he sees other women?"

"Oh, he has a whole list," she said, "at least a dozen available girls he is in touch with constantly by telephone. He meets them through his business, and although he is not good-looking, he is attractive to women. And then, of course, he has money to spend on them. He always pursues much younger women. He says to me, 'I'm tired of you being suspicious. I *have* to see other women.' Another time when I asked him if he were seeing other women he said, 'I thought we had that all settled.' He also said, 'You have more than most women: a beautiful home, four cars in the garage, servants if you want them,'; but I replied that I have nothing in my name."

We made an appointment for a week later, and agreed that during this time Gail would get legal advice, to determine if she had any common-law marital status in relation to Gus; I said that I would speak with his psychiatrist and tell him that Gail was seeing me, and ask if he had any comments.

Her closing remark was, "If we were happy together, it really would not matter so much if we were married or not, but now I wonder if he is not just trying to get me out of his life. A month or two ago he said to me, 'I am going through a difficult period.' He never mentioned what it was. 'I would not blame you if you left me.' I asked him if that is what he wanted and he said, 'No.' Maybe he said, 'I guess not.'"

"Men have a tendency to make women into mother-figures," I said.

She answered, "I think that is exactly what he does with me. There is still a lot between us. He says everything is my fault. For example, the diminution of sexual relations, but that is just not true. At other times he complains that I want too much sex. I don't think that is true either. I have always had a strong sex drive, but I think once a week is not too much. He got very tense after we started to live together as man and wife; he seemed to feel trapped. He would be willing to talk to you . . . he loves to talk about himself. He does it all the time and alienates people socially because he talks only about himself. When he and I are alone, he dominates the conversation even more.

"After my first husband died, I was a widow with five charming children and a warm, friendly house. Gus, like many others, just loved to be at my house. He has been divorced twice, by the way. I think he would never throw me out. He would probably support me in this house with all the cars and the swimming pool for the rest of my life. After he returns from a trip, he is glad to see us all; but in a while he begins to talk only about himself again, and he goes to live in the apartment he has in the city, and will not include me. It used to be that he would phone and say, 'Get a sitter and come into town and have dinner with me.' Now he just gets someone else, but he also wants to come home to a comfortable house and have all his needs taken care of by me. This has been building up for the past two or three years and for the last year it has been quite obvious. I have no details about his chasing women."

When we met a week later, Gail had ascertained from the lawyer that she did *not* have a common-law marriage, that she had no status or rights whatever in relation to Gus under state law. And when I spoke with his psychiatrist, I learned that some of the women with whom he socialized found him attractive enough to accept him sexually. After a brief discussion of this with Gail, I asked her what were her husband's complaints against her.

She said, "He thinks I am a manipulator. He thinks I try to pry into his private life, but I think it is only just the normal interest of a wife in her husband. He resents it bitterly if I ask to go on one of his business trips. And he resents me if he phones and cannot reach me any time he wishes. He says we have three phones in the house and yet he cannot reach me. He also complains that I do not take good care of the automobiles. He wants them in perfect condition all the time. He resents it if we are invited to a party and I accept for us, assuming that he will go. He also resents it if I phone him anywhere, at any time, to ask him where he is . . . in other words, if I reach him through the office. Once when his mother came to see us, I thought she was not entirely normal; and she was so critical and difficult that I could not even cook lunch for her. This infuriated him, but it seemed much wiser to go to a nearby restaurant.

"When my own father was 52 he went to Texas, ostensibly to get a job, and we all thought he went to meet one of my older brothers there, but he never came back. In other words, my father just left us and was separated from the family for nearly 20 years and sent no money. My mother was then 45, and she got a full-time job to support us. Then another brother invented something which could be widely used, and my mother inherited some money from an aunt; so they became well-to-do, even a little bit wealthy. Maybe when my father just vanished, it was something he had wanted to do for a long time but never dared. I do not understand it. We children loved Father very much, and he loved us."

This was a good opportunity to inquire about the patient's 0 to 6, and I asked her who were the most important people for her emotionally during those early years. We needed to discover if anything in Gail's dynamics played a part in her getting into the marital situation of which she now complained.

She replied without hesitation, "Only my mother."

"Can you give me a few details?" I asked.

She said, "Well, I was happy with her. In a way, I made no real distinction between Mother and Father. Aunts, uncles, and cousins all would drop in."

"Did you have trouble with any of these people?" I asked.

"None," she said, "except with Sister when we were teenagers, when my sister became ill for about four years. I had wonderful relations with our brothers. After Sister recovered, we had a good, loving relationship with each other. We had fought some until then. My mother was beautiful and could do anything, domestic and artistic. She and I were always very close. When I was in high school, my mother developed a little business in the home. She worked hard, but it was always in the home; so she was always present. Because Father seemed to go from one job to another and was not financially dependable, Mother worked to help support the family. At one time Father tried a business of his own, but it did not go. He worked in various factories. He came from a wealthy family and was not really trained for anything. We all turned to Mother, who was the real head of the household. She had more education and was an avid reader. Father was handsome but more the playboy type without any money. Both Father and Mother came from large families. The first time I ever broke away from Mother was when I married my first husband. He finished his schooling, and we seemed to be nicely settled down. Together with our children we lived in my mother's old house and were happy. Then suddenly, within one year, my husband died of cancer. He was still in his thirties. He and my mother had been close and now my mother and I drew even closer. All my brothers and sisters were then out on their own."

I asked, "What is your first memory?" and explained that I was not referring to continuous memory, but I wanted those fragments as far back as she could remember.

Gail replied, "I guess the first was about age four. We were to take a bath in a washtub in the kitchen because there was no heat elsewhere in the house. Mother would wash me and stand me to dry by the coal stove. [Theme: closeness to Mother.] The second memory, also about age four, was of my brother being born in Mother's room upstairs, and I was crying and felt lonely. [Theme: some displacement from Mother.] Third memory: I was playing in the yard with my brothers and sisters where we had a tree house and a wagon in which we pulled each other around. I always thought that everyone else in town was rich, and we were poor. We would be happy when my uncles came to visit . . . we loved to have them visit. [Relationship with peers, siblings, some deprivation.] Memory four: we had a big vegetable garden and we all worked in it together, and I think of a lot of sunshine; we had a sunny garden and a sunny house." [Emotional warmth and acceptance of work.]

These early memories seem to indicate a close, happy family surmounting financial difficulties by cooperation and enjoyment of each other. Of course the second memory indicates some loneliness and repressed sibling rivalry.

"Have you any dreams that you remember from early childhood?" I asked.

"Yes," she said, "I had terrible nightmares of a big head coming at me, maybe coming closer and closer and getting bigger and bigger. Also another repetitive dream: things were coming and going too fast." [Did this indicate confusion in the big family meeting all its problems?]

"Do you have any recent dreams, like last night before this interview?" I asked, "or any current repetitive dreams?"

"Wait," Gail said, "I remember! I was sitting at a table and other people wanted to come and sit at the table too. I thought we were enjoying each other's company, but then they all left and I was alone. They had deserted me, they had no concern for me. Also, I had a recent dream of Gus with his second wife from whom he was divorced . . . they were back together and had excluded me. That had really happened. Also I have an occasional dream that my dead husband returned; another time I dreamed that he came back, and I was in a dilemma, not being sure whether I was married to him or Gus." [Feelings of desertion socially, and by Gus, with confusion about her present position and feelings. Probably partially wants to get rid of husband, but then would feel lonely.]

"Have you had a recent physical examination?" I asked.

"Yes," she said, "two years ago. I have always had perfect health until about six months ago when I had some distress in my chest when I took a deep breath. The doctor said it was psychological, not physical, so apparently I am in good health. The whole family has been against Gus and my relationship with him, but since Mother became ill, they have softened in their attitude. The trouble was, I was left alone suddenly when my husband died. I was only 35 and had five children; I believed everything Gus said. I still think that in the beginning he was not lying. I believe he really loved his two former wives, although later he divorced them. I think he really loved me when he promised to marry me. I think he was sincere when he said he would marry me just as soon as his divorce was final. I am still young and strong and could get a job, but I am not a career woman. I would like to be married; I think I am cut out to be a wife and mother."

I did not say anything, but in my own mind I agreed with her. This was supported by the history of closeness to her mother and identification with her, the presence of all the children and the pleasurable visits she described from members of the family.

The following week I again asked Gail the question about her 0–6 because she had given me nothing thus far that would indicate her having a masochistic trend that involved her in this frustrating situation, living as a wife and mother without the marriage she desired. Nothing clear-cut had emerged in the first inquiry about her 0–6; so I determined to pursue it further. Was there inevitable "hard luck" (in the early death of her husband), or did she unconsciously contribute something to bringing about her situation?

I said, "Let us go back to your 0–6 again and delve a little deeper. Who did you say were the main people in your life?"

She replied again, without hesitation, "My mother."

I asked, "Why do you say that?"

Gail said, "She read to us a lot. Mother would nap on the couch on Sundays, and one of us would lie down on the couch with her. We brushed her hair; we were happy; we went on picnics. We all played together mostly, more than with other kids. We hung around Mother while she was cooking; she made us candy and popcorn. We were not aware of it at the time, but life must have been hard for her with five children and a low income. She was a creative person: she made little favors when there were parties; she made all the clothes we kids wore; she made our bread and did a lot of canning. Mother spent lots of time in the kitchen. Mother and Father would go out with friends, and we never had baby-sitters because some of us were always old enough to take charge. Then Mother taught school for about a year. She put up and sold foods of various kinds too, from our home. Father was working but not making enough money. Mother would work late at night, sewing. We were busy with schoolwork and sports . . . Father was trying to earn a living, but he was no businessman; and we just went along that way.

"Then both Father and Mother got good jobs, and one day Father left, and Mother kept her job and also went back to her home businesses. It was then that my older brother made his invention and started his manufacturing company and employed Mother; then they had enough money. By now the rest of us were all out on our own, getting married and so on. I was close to Mother all those years.

"Coming back to my current problems, Gus has told me that my daughters by my husband are sexy, but he never indicated that to them and only talked to me once about it. All the girls do not fall for Gus; he must work hard to get some of them. He not only has an inferiority complex, he *is* inferior."

"How do you mean?" I asked.

"I began to see it only when we began hating each other . . . to see what other people had been pointing out to me for years. Possibly there is some lack of refinement in Gus, but the main issue is that he wants all the privileges of marriage without its commitments. He doesn't deserve to get put down, but he does. I guess Gus just lacks a cultural background. It is paradoxical, though, because he is interested in art and music; but I think he mostly gets his women through money. I think what he really wants is for me to marry a rich husband, sort of unload me, but he realizes that is unlikely. On the other hand, he does not want anyone else to have me. He likes to have separate lives, with me as his wife who is available at home. He wants to keep his wife compartmentalized, away from the rest of his life and his other women. He wants to control everything. First he looks for a 'mother,' but then he wants to control her by money and his own charm. He is ambivalent, has a mixture of love and hate toward everyone. I am not concerned about his having any possible sexual interest in my daughters because, as I told him, I trust him and they can take care of themselves. Gus says he wants to get rid of me, but I think really he would never let me go because he has such a mother-attachment to me.

"I am still not sure whether or not the best thing would be to remain with him and try to work things out, but I cannot look for another husband while I am in this position, living in his house. Perhaps he would move out and go live in the apartment without me; then I could be free to look."

Gail provides an interesting contrast to those wives who are thrown into an unbearable frenzy of jealousy at any hint of their husbands' interest in another woman. It seems that most wives who react excessively had more or less deprived childhoods, and are therefore to some extent insecure about being loved and valued. Gail, on the other hand, seemed to have had a secure, stable, close relationship to her mother, father and siblings. There was some rivalry with one sister, who was close to Gail in age, but this was not a great issue apparently. There seems no doubt that in her 0–6 pattern, Gail's mother was indeed the central figure who held the family together, always available and providing a model of stability for the children in the face of their financial problems, and their father's unreliability. Identification with her mother's steadfastness in the family is probably why Gail still continues to make a go of her marriage, in the face of Gus's refusal to make it legal and his acknowledged infidelities and direct preferences for other women.

Of course, I was most interested in meeting Gus. He agreed to come in for an interview. He seemed rather brilliant, but also defensive, habitually saying, "You are trying to tell me this or that," until I had to point out that he was putting words into my mouth. He seemed to have charm, and I could understand why women would be attracted to him. He did not seem heartless or incapable of love, but rather to be another poor suffering mortal. Gus could not settle down and enjoy his beautiful, charming, efficient wife because he felt that if he married her, she would have a club over his head, that she could sue him for adultery and take away the one thing that really meant his whole life to him, namely his business. But he did not enjoy his compulsive philandering either—it was mostly, he said, only a physical release and incomplete at that. His previous two marriages ended in divorce, each time because of his wife's suspicions that he might be interested in other women. Apparently he had never had a fully gratifying, well-stabilized relationship with a woman. It was no surprise that this situation traced back to a disturbed relationship with the first woman in his life, his mother. I thought Gus needed analytic help more than the unhappy but emotionally more secure Gail did. It seemed to me that he could not continue as he was without some kind of disturbance from the strain, whether psychological or psychosomatic. Thus the interview with Gus shifted some emphasis in the clinical picture: from a cruel person who refused the status of wife to a woman who lived as his devoted wife, he became a suffering mortal who was incapable of enjoying what is probably the greatest gratification in life for a man—closeness to a good, loving woman. And this Gail seemed to be. While it was still reasonable for Gail to want to legalize her de facto marriage, the shoe now seemed shifted to the other foot: should she commit herself in marriage to a man who was incapable of a stable, satisfying or even satisfactory relationship to a woman? And if she left him, would he break down in some way? Now Gail, not Gus, seemed to be in the stronger position. Should analytic help be advised both for Gus, who seemed headed for trouble, and for Gail because of a possible, but not evident, kind of hidden masochism that attracted her to a man who kept her in a painful position without financial, social or legal security and who could not be a loving husband?

What would be the goals of therapy for Gail? The great unanswered question in her dynamics remained: had she a masochistic trend which led her to maneuver herself unconsciously into such a position? Consciously, Gail sensed no masochism, only "rebound." No sooner was she happily settled into a loving marriage than her husband died, suddenly leaving her solitary, sexually passionate and frustrated, with children to care for. Now there appeared a man in the process of divorce, a man with charm, kindness, generosity and money, ready to marry her when his divorce was finalized. She drifted into an affair with him, getting attention and apparently love, and certainly sex and financial relief and the offer of a new marriage. Was this simply force of circumstance and nothing more? All men and especially women are prone to such rebounds and may well beware them! The old sexual codes may be seen in today's world as stuffy, square and out of date; yet the wisdom of the ages cannot be ignored with impunity or without risking a price. Gail was sure that Gus was in love with her and would marry her; she felt there was nothing she had done then that had led to her present ambiguous position.

When Gus's second wife found out about his affair with Gail, she used adultery as her complaint in the divorce action. This so weakened his legal defense that Gus was forced to give her some of his business stock and income. In his current relationship with Gail, Gus realized he could not relinquish his sexual affairs with other women, nor did he wish to; he had embraced these affairs as an essential area of his life. He reasoned: "I cannot give up these other women. If I marry Gail, some of the women will be reluctant to go to bed with me as a married man and may even refuse, making the seductions more difficult. And as Gail knows about my affairs, she can easily get evidence. Then, just like my last wife, she can sue me and take part of my business, without which I could not live."

I asked Gus if he had thought about a premarital agreement with Gail to prevent later difficulties. He had already gone into this with his lawyer, who told him a premarital agreement would be valueless if Gail, once established as his legal wife, should sue him on grounds of adultery.

I wanted to see Gus further to try to determine if his fear of marriage was based on realistic grounds, or whether it had some paranoid coloring, or both. I found it difficult to visualize Gail suddenly trying to ruin him financially on grounds of adultery, especially knowing her personality makeup as revealed through her memories and dreams, all of which indicated adjustment to a large family. And she had been content to live with him ten years as a good wife and mother to his children as well as to her own, wanting this domestic life beyond all else.

The one clue to some masochism in Gail's childhood pattern was the potential hostility her father may have felt toward her mother because of his being so poor a breadwinner, hostility perhaps that he felt to all the children for being burdens on him, culminating in his bolting without notice. Could Gail have a pattern of feeling that this is how men treat their families, and therefore harbor hostility toward father-figures, mixed with guilt so repressed that these feelings did not appear in her first memories or dreams, those infallible roads to the unconscious? Unlikely, I thought, but not impossible.

Gus had lived his early life with two females: a sister two years older and his mother. It seems that his father walked out permanently before Gus was born. Here was one similarity to Gail's history, but it occurred at the very beginning of his life. Gus's mother was destitute and helpless with two babies. One of her brothers came to the rescue, providing the essential money for survival but giving no love, warmth or human interest. These were the male models, then, for Gus's early years: total disregard by the husband for the wife and the mother of his children and total abandonment; and, from the brother, mainly money but no consideration or love. Under the strain of living a solitary life and assuming complete responsibility for home and children on insufficient funds plus indebtedness to a brother who ignored her, Gus's mother kept her sanity but was often extremely upset. She did not always bother dressing, often going about her housework almost nude. This was probably too stimulating sexually for the little boy. His mother gave him the little she had left to give emotionally, but it was not much. Constant control of her emotions was sometimes beyond her energies. In a way she was a heroic figure, carrying on at all and raising two children in her solitary, near-poverty surroundings.

Soon Gus spent most of his time out of the home to get away from it all, getting what he could from the streets. He was usually the last child to go in at night. When Gus was near adolescence, his mother was remarried—to a kindly gentle man to whom Gus soon became warmly attached. Gus was most devoted to his mother until her death, and remained close friends with the stepfather.

Gus's dynamics fitted a common pattern for philandering—early sexual seductiveness by his mother's near-nudity left the idea of a sexual object but a tabooed one, from his earliest years. He quickly reconginzed this when I pointed it out to him. "Yes," he agreed, "I always feel as though I am looking for a perfect love which I never find." Interestingly but not surprisingly, Gus was uncertain in his potency.   He would seduce Gail, a maternal woman with children, but then feel dissatisfied sexually.   Then he would yearn for a young girl, thinking her to be an ideal mate.   He had made such conquests before, and he thought he would not ruin a young girl's life if he could give her everything she might want.   He thought that "sex with a fresh young girl would be heaven on earth."   Whether his two-years-older sister played a role in his childhood pattern and influenced his current desire for young girls (beyond their representing escapes from his mother fixation) did not appear.   But Gus employed this type of thinking in order to argue against marrying Gail, superior and desirable though she might be.   In his view, he could seduce women with less difficulty if he remained unmarried— and then there was always the chance he might meet "the perfect girl" and find "the perfect love."

We discussed the fact that he was sacrificing the excellent reality he already had in good, beautiful, superior, devoted Gail for a perfect love that only existed as a fantasy in his mind, a dream of finding the original love of his mother—a love that was tabooed but lived on because of the unavoidable deprivations at her hands, although she had done her best.

These very early deprivations left Gus with a sense of loss, and seduction and rejection by his mother, herself rejected; and his father and uncle gave him a model of men who abandoned the women who were wives and mothers, leaving a residue of unconscious hostility to women.   His first two marriages, although not at all bad ones, failed, and now he feared legalizing another one.   Because of this unconscious childhood pattern, it was comprehensible for Gus to fear marrying Gail, if only for *her* sake.   Compulsive philandering was for him a symptom, an intelligible part of his childhood emotional pattern, his search for the "perfect" (mother's) love.

What attracted Gus and Gail so strongly to one another?   Perhaps there was some similarity or "mesh" in their dynamics.   Perhaps it had something to do with the common experience of having fathers who walked out on their families, although Gus was not yet born when his father left, while Gail's father left when she was grown. But one clear element in the dynamics of both was the centering of their emotional lives on their mothers.   Here Gail was more fortunate and healthier emotionally because her mother had qualities Gail could identify with and from which she drew stability and strength.

No doubt Gus's search for a mother appealed strongly to this maternal identification in Gail. Because of this, she could have so much tolerance and so little jealousy in the face of philandering by Gus, who she felt was a deprived child emotionally beneath his worldly sophistication and business success.

Although Gus was not conscious of it, his two prior marriages to women who were two or three years older than he was may have mobilized parts of his childhood emotional pattern: rejection of mother by her husband and brother, and Gus's own escape from the home into the streets. Was this a deeper reason for his unwillingness to marry Gail? But he thought his reason for avoiding marriage was realistic fear that Gail would turn and ruin him financially. Was this an unconsciously produced idea, formed very largely from guilt for promising Gail marriage and then withholding it, as well as guilt for his unconscious anger at his poor mother because of the unavoidable deprivations by her? If so, he compensated for this resentment most of his life by showing devotion to his mother while perhaps displacing the resentment from her to all other women through seduction. But the overcompensation for the resentment against his mother, plus identification with her, made Gus a sensitive and generous person. He was generous with money just as his uncle had been generous to Gus's mother.

By now I had become concerned for Gail if Gus *did* marry her. I also felt concern for Gus if Gail gave up and left him, for underneath he harbored a strong sense of deprivation and dependence on his mother. I did not think that Gus, now over 50, wanted to be "cured" of so enjoyable a symptom as philandering and turned into a stable husband; but as long as he had a well-motivated therapeutic urge, I was willing to continue with him (with the full encouragement of his former analyst, with whom all this had, of course, been discussed, and who disliked seeing Gus only sporadically), learning more of his dynamics and providing such help as analytic therapy could offer. It seemed to be achieving a noticeable relaxation of tension and a corresponding increase in inner peace.

Gus had a long series of business trips, which coincided with my own vacation; three months passed before he again came to see me. In the interim, Gail had written me a friendly note saying that all was well, and she was enjoying life. It was postmarked Florida, and contained no return address. When Gus arrived for our session, he told me that Gail had changed; she had been going off on trips with friends. She never told him who the friends were, where she went, or when she would return. He thought the friends must be wealthy because they apparently paid all Gail's bills. They must have been large bills because some of the trips were out of the country. Gus assumed the "friends" must include one particular man and that the company of a beautiful, passionate woman like Gail must have led to their sleeping together. He was not bitter about this, but told me his thoughts with a neutral and mostly friendly tone. Gail's only explanation, he said, was that she went off with friends because Gus would not take her along on his business trips. He had always excused his refusal on the basis of squabbles they had when he did take her, although it was pretty clear that Gus liked his freedom on trips to have the companionship of other women, this being apparently essential to his emotional balance. But Gail's trips ostensibly changed nothing at home; she continued to sleep with Gus, doing whatever he wanted. The children, his and hers, now nearly grown, were around, and the whole family took vacations together. They would often go away for long weekends or a week together. I wondered if Gail had begun to think that "what's good for the gander is good for the goose," felt unbound sexually and was on the look-out for an eligible husband. Gail was so beautiful and intelligent that she would never marry just for the sake of being married, but only if there was mutual love. Meanwhile, I guessed that she enjoyed travel and sociability and was keeping an eye out for a husband on a mutually loving basis. All this I could only deduce while waiting for her to come in to see me—if she cared to.

It was touching in a way to see this couple, not in a frenzy of jealousy but each permissively tolerant of what behavior answered the other's needs.

I thought that Gus, with his early deprivation, frustrated intensified love needs toward his mother and repressed hostility, might become disturbed if Gail finally left him. But he told me his story and included the possibliity of Gail's leaving with such calm that I had hopes of being wrong; maybe he was not so dependent on her as I had thought. Perhaps the other women—probably mother-substitutes to some extent—took care of his dependent-love needs adequately. Perhaps his running from home into the streets signified a rather high degree of independence. It was Gail who had said that she thought Gus might be trying to get rid of her. Gus spoke of other women, and one in particular, who were anxious to marry him, but I could not help wondering if this was fantasy, and whether these women, even if they did agree to marry Gus, would not do so more for his money than out of sincere love such as Gail had given him all these years. Yet Gail's warm love might have stirred up the love needs and their frustrations of his childhood, and he might be more comfortable without it.

Further speculation was valueless. Although Gus wanted "the agony over with," i.e., wanted Gail to decide whether to leave him or settle down with him, he was basically more placid and relaxed than he had been. Meanwhile, Gail gave no sign of her goal or of where her behavior might be leading.

Then a period of two years passed before Gus came in to see me again. His hair was now frizzy, his shirt was of a strange bright orange hue that did not quite match a brown jacket open at the neck, his pants were nondescript, and he wore black socks in shoes that were obviously too expensive originally to permit the description "down-at-the-heel." He told me that he had been working hard on his own business, which involved traveling a lot, and that he was now a multimillionaire. He had not seen Gail for nearly a year. He was living exclusively in his center-city apartment and had no occasion to go out to the suburban home where Gail still lived, although he continued to send her money for her support. Gail went on trips with her own circle of friends, and told him quite frankly that she was looking for a husband. This suited Gus all right . . . he had become a confirmed philanderer.

He had purchased a camera and showed me excellent clear color photos of some of his women. Each was more beautiful than the next—not only beautiful, but charming and interesting-looking. The first looked about 36, dark, alert, vivacious. The next seemed to be about 42 with an intelligent, serene, maternal kind of beauty. The third was a pretty little girl, no more than 25. Gus said that he had broken off with the first girl and told me that the second, whom I thought looked the most mature and beautiful, did not "turn him on"; in fact, she seemed to turn him off. The "youngster" of 25 was presently living with him in his apartment.

"It's a myth that age makes any difference," he said. "She turns me on, sometimes four times a night! I hate to hurt her, but I must get rid of her. She has hangups I never suspected. She has a form of vaginitis that isn't serious, but is hard to cure, and it makes sex painful for her. She has a phobia about contraceptives and refuses to use a diaphragm or intrauterine device, or to take the pill. So I have to use condoms or coitus interruptus, which I haven't done for years. She is going home to visit in a few weeks, and somehow before she leaves I'll tell her not to come back. She's a good artist . . . she made this shirt I'm wearing. When she goes home she will sleep with a boyfriend there, whom I know. I've told her about the other women, and she takes it all pleasantly, and isn't hurt or angry. It's hardly like living with a woman—she is such a child—like one of my daughters years ago."

I could not help but think that the basis of personality is always the psychodynamics of the interpersonal relations, and that when life is not cruel and tragic it is apt to be sad. Perhaps Gus was less unhappy that if he were married to Gail. But in essence he had millions of dollars, and those beautiful and desirable women—was really a wealthy philanderer—but was far from happy, and underneath may have wanted to be back with the warm domesticity of Gail and the children, although he had not fully faced that situation. Eventually it became clear that Gus had satyriasis, i.e., was oversexed and dependent upon sex instead of love for happiness. The 25-year-old girl came to see me once and told me: "What I want is to love and be loved and to be close to the man I love, but all he wants are orgasms."

24
INFATUATION: A COMPULSION NEUROSIS

And I scoff at my own heart—and do its will.

Johann Wolfgang von Goethe,
The Sufferings of Young Werther

She's beyond love, I remember thinking, it's some crazy obsession, there's no anchor . . .

A. Myrer,
The Last Convertible

John Ludlow was 22, tall and handsome, personable, brilliant, athletic. In college he could easily have been a big man on campus, but no athletics or political or social positions interested him strongly enough. He was universally popular, although few of his many friends were intimate friends. This was true with girls also; John dated many but never became deeply interested and involved. He had the gift of psychological understanding, and realized that he did not want the responsibility for a girl that closeness would entail. So John absorbed himself in his studies, doing brilliantly, and the months slid quietly by.

Yet all was not as calm internally as it appeared on the surface. John confessed to an indefinable, disturbing sense of dissatisfaction, tension and anxiety. His only love was painting, but he judged it impractical for financial security and decided to pursue a career in engineering. The idea of getting away from his home area occurred to him, and, after due consideration, he arranged to spend a year at M.I.T., in Massachussetts. This worked out satisfactorily; he made friends with a few other students, and he enjoyed M.I.T. hugely, with its stimulating courses and athletic facilities so readily available. John did well in his studies, and at year's end felt more relaxed than at any other time he could recall.

As the end of his last quarter of school approached, John began to grow anxious. On the long train ride home for summer vacation he became uncomfortable as he approached familiar home territory. He realized gradually that the discomfort was anxiety, and he felt it mounting in intensity into a full-blown claustrophobia. He felt trapped in the rushing train, not in control of his position, frightened. John managed to control the fear, which he realized was irrational, and he arrived safely at home without incident; but he was still having difficulty controlling his anxiety. When he consulted me, and we discussed the incident, some explanation for his anxiety emerged:

Returning home aroused John's old pattern of childish dependence and submissiveness, of not being in control of his own situation, of being in the power of others (just as on the express train he could not get off when he wished but was in the power of the crew). This plus the feeling of being a dependent child frightened and enraged him.

He was a first child, much wanted and loved from conception. Later, however, his parents began to squabble, but never with the serious intention of separating or divorcing, and always with full, unswerving love and devotion for each other and for John. Nonetheless, these arguments somewhat upset John, particularly when he would hear his mother disparage his father, and he failed to understand their noisy but superficial nature.

At this point, John met Timmy, who lived nearby, and who was only a month older than John's 18 months, but of a much bigger build. The boys became close friends. Timmy's parents were impressed by John's intelligence and energy, and they held him up as an example to Timmy, whose father treated him harshly. Timmy reacted to this treatment by turning his hostile aggressiveness onto those who were weaker; John became a target for that hostility. It was only years later that John's intelligent and intuitive mother phoned me because John was showing symptoms of severe compulsion neurosis. He would erase a whole page of homework and redo it more than once, or he would be in great doubt about whether to put on his pajamas and go to bed or to get dressed again. This culminated one night in midwinter with John rushing down the street nude. His compulsiveness and anxiety traced to Timmy, who had beaten up John since their friendship began in babyhood, and had dominated him psychologically for years thereafter. For example, Timmy had forbidden John to have other friends and to date girls. He had so ridiculed his urinating as to make John "pee-shy."

Obviously John should be separated from Timmy, but John raged against this and insisted Timmy was his friend, his best friend, his only friend. Despite his anguished protests his parents kept John away from Timmy, and his symptoms immediately began to diminish to the vanishing point. Then came proof positive:

John's symptoms would suddenly flare up, but each time without exception they could be traced to an encounter, usually accidental such as at a school athletic event, with Timmy. Gradually John was able to defy Timmy's command to have no other friends. He established many pleasant friendships with boys and girls, but nothing as intimate as he had had with Timmy during those baby years.

The attachment to Timmy had several roots: consciously, John felt that by breaking off the relationship and escaping Timmy's domination, control and beatings he would be a coward; so he must stay and face the consequences no matter what. This led to a foolhardy bravado in other areas of his life as well. Combined with repressed rage, it made John accident-prone, smashing up autos he was driving and sometimes himself. In college fraternity life he submitted to inexcusably cruel hazing rather than leave. Eventually the hazing made him so ill physically that he had to withdraw from the fraternity.

His dependence on Timmy was deep-seated and unconscious, locking John into the attachment. He must have had some identification with Timmy, but it was never clearly evident; John never openly exhibited Timmy's trait of bullying or controlling those weaker than himself, except possibly later with his mother and his wife. In his suffering, John turned to his mother and became fixated in an excessive dependence upon her with some unconscious hostility. This made him feel like a dependent angry baby and so hurt his pride and self-esteem that he tried to boost his self-respect by feeling superior to everyone else. This need to feel superior was revealed clearly in his later infatuation with Marge, the girl he met after graduating from college. When the infatuation was frustrated, John described the situation this way: "Now the baby gets its comeuppance and crawls on its belly for help from the very people it had so looked down upon."

I think it is generally agreed that behind all compulsive symptoms lie anger, rage, hostility—all intense enough to cause the symptoms. Therefore, although John denied it as a child and insisted on clinging to Timmy, his compulsive symptoms strongly suggested violent hostility to his playmate, which was repressed. John clung to this masochistic position despite the beatings and control he suffered from Timmy, and the domination by Timmy over his entire life. He did not want to feel himself a coward if he broke off the friendship, and he was also tied to Timmy by dependency plus unconscious rage and hate. The upshot was a severe compulsion neurosis with (at its height) a transient psychotic break at about age ten when he ran nude down the snow-and ice-covered street; he recovered from it as soon as his parents separated him from Timmy. So the pathogenic relationship was avoided, but its dynamics were never worked through therapeutically. As a by-product of the relationship, John was thrown back into an exaggerated dependence upon his mother as a refuge from Timmy. The origins of the dynamics were thus unusual in that the trauma was not at the hands of his immediate family, but the result of an outside relation to a neighbor, Timmy.

When John returned from his year at M.I.T., he decided to have one last try at painting as a career. He graduated from college and arranged for graduate work in art in a neighboring state—away from home, but only a day's drive by car. All went well for nearly a year. Clearly he had a talent for painting but not genius; more and more the realization was forced on him that no matter how assiduously he applied himself, he could not depend on art for a livelihood. So John decided to return to engineering for security, although he did not enjoy it. He continued to be popular with fellows and girls alike, and life flowed with reasonable smoothness—until he met Marge.

Marge was outstandingly bright, beautiful and charming. She and John became close friends and then sweethearts, with Marge in the role of pursuer. John tried to keep his distance, but Marge insisted on getting engaged. Then she insisted on his marrying her. When he refused, it led to a fight and a breakup. His natural defenses were protecting him against an intimacy with a person whose own dynamics were certain to arouse his early childhood patterns. These patterns were not entirely repressed, however, as was evident in his inability to get Marge out of his mind during their separation. But he did control himself enough so that he did not contact her. Six months passed.

Then, whether by accident or her design, John met Marge one day in the street near his apartment. He approached and gently embraced her. She invited him to her apartment and there told him that over the past six months she had been unable to feel anything for anybody. This inability to feel was clearly not normal for a physically healthy girl of 22. It was probably a defense: "If I can't have you, I will withdraw from everyone!"

John resigned himself to engineering as a career although he was bored by that type of work. He and Marge began a short and intense courtship. Marge had difficulty in deciding whether to marry John, but soon got John to give in. They were engaged just before John started graduate school, and the wedding date was set for the next summer so that John might devote himself fully to engineering school for a year.

Some weeks before John's first semester finals, Marge came to his apartment and announced she was breaking off the engagement. Acutely upset by this, John nevertheless managed to pass his exams. Then John calmed her down, and they decided not to break up. But when he talked to Marge later, he realized she was too unhappy to continue their relationship. The next evening he called Marge to tell her that he felt it would be best to end the engagement. But soon they again resumed dating, and finally in the summer went through with the wedding as originally planned.

Marge's complaints lit up without delay, complaints I had heard so many times that it sounded like a cry echoing down the ages: "He is just like a child! I am starving emotionally and physically."

Marge came to see me for an interview, and the childhood pattern she revealed was one of deprivation: her mother, she said, showed no love or even interest in her and turned her over to hired help to raise. She still suffered under this frustration, and it enraged her to think about it and about the bullying she received from her father (like Timmy's bullying of John?). The whole pattern was repeated, of course, in her marriage to John. Nothing he did felt to her like enough, whether sex or emotional interest or work around the apartment. Under her hostile criticism he began to feel more and more inadequate, and it became increasingly difficult for him to study . . . the strain of her complaints was telling. Marge felt he was destroying her, and he felt *she* was destroying *him.*

Three years later, before his graduation from engineering school, Marge told John that she was divorcing him. This seemed another hostile act on Marge's part, for it disrupted John just before his final exams. But perhaps Marge was so desperate emotionally that she could wait no longer. Her own need impaired her consideration and love. Two months later their divorce was finalized, and John was plunged from bitter unhappiness into unbearable agony. His major task was to hold onto his sanity, and then to pass his last exams, maintain his fine academic career and graduate with a good record after three long years of professional studies.

One evening soon after the divorce was final, Marge appeared at the apartment, ostensibly to pick up something she had left. They spent the night together as man and wife. She could not stay away from John; as long as she was friendly to him, he felt almost comfortable and able to study and not in danger of suicide or losing his mind. But Marge said she could not stand seeing him because when she did, she wanted sex. This she simply could not bear. So it was "off-again-on-again" at short, intense intervals, just as before the engagement and during it and the marriage, and just as destructive. Marge confessed to John that she had spent a weekend with another man. She made it clear that this was to preserve her peace of mind and did not include sex. John now found himself unable to study, eat or sleep; he lost 20 pounds and began drinking. He could find no relief—once he smashed up the apartment, and he constantly fought an urge to shoot himself. He dated another girl but felt no rapport—nothing. He could not get Marge out of his mind; he could not live without the thought that somehow, someday, they would be reunited.

When John and I talked, I said, "Give it a year . . . try to control yourself and further your career; then let us see how Marge is and how you are."

Obviously infatuation exists, and people destroy themselves and others by so-called love. We have remarked that sex is not love. Neither is infatuation. I never saw Marge again, and could learn no more of her dynamics than what she had revealed in our single interview. But I did know John's dynamics in detail from our interviews. On his part, this infatuation with Marge was almost a precise duplicate of his feelings toward his childhood playmate, Timmy. His five years with Marge both before and after their marriage were not years of love, of each bringing to the other understanding, enjoyment, support and happiness. They were years of fluctuating torment. Marge felt John was making her mentally ill, and she wanted to escape; he felt the same way toward her. At times he hated Marge for her treatment of him, but later he would be overwhelmed by guilt because she (he thought) only wanted love, and he did not give it to her. He repeated identically his old refrain about Timmy: "He is my friend, my only friend; I cannot live all alone without him." In the intimacy of engagement and marriage John's defenses against the childhood pattern toward Timmy weakened and then collapsed. The divorce shredded all his defenses, and he was again the helpless little boy, bound to Marge as he once was to Timmy by dependence, identification, submissiveness, hostility and guilt, returning daily to be "beaten up"—now psychologically by Marge, controlled and directed by her. He was losing all self-respect, all sense of identity and integrity as a person, becoming like a newborn infant, which is still part of its mother. This was all intensified by the sexual and mating elements that pervaded all the emotional forces in the childhood dynamics. John's five years with Marge showed little love, but a preponderance of the repetition of neurotic patterns toward Timmy transferred to Marge, a truly sado-maso-chistic clinging together to torment one another to the point of disintegration. After their divorce, Marge and John were each threatened with a psychotic break that fortuantely they both resisted. John was a loved child with a basically wholesome emotional pattern toward his parents from birth. But he repressed it into an infantile, hostile dependence on his mother, to whom he would pour out his troubles on the telephone, sometimes for hours on end, exhausting her.

No doubt infatuations grow out of a variety of dynamics, including ones different from John's and Marge's, dynamics shaped by other childhood patterns. But my long-held suspicions were confirmed by John: infatuation is a compulsion. It is in the true sense a "com-pulsion neurosis," a severe type of neurosis bordering on psychosis. When it is mutual, shared by two partners, it becomes a *folie à deux*—a so-called love, which is not love at all but a form of madness, of borderline psychosis, with each playing into the other.

Hope lies in therapeutically working through the still unconscious hostility existing in both individuals. John's hostility showed in his act of smashing up the apartment; in his almost consciously deciding to fail his final graduate exams out of spite; in moments of conscious hostility to Marge; in his taking to drink; in impulses to shoot himself, and in other destructive urges against Marge and against himself; and in the direct torment he caused his mother and father. It is true that a man can be destroyed and even commit suicide because of rejection by a woman and a woman can do the same if rejected; but this occurs, I think, only when the attachment or infatuation is the expression of a severe neurosis or psychosis, a serious disorder of the childhood emotional pattern that swamps the mature realistic part of the individual's personality.

John was a mature, realistic, superior young man in that part of his personality which developed from good relations with his loving, devoted parents. When that part was in control, he was entirely normal and rational, a fine and able person. Perhaps Marge's exertion of her will over John, insisting that he marry her, aroused his latent submissiveness to Timmy, the playmate who for years, from infancy, dictated his life. In any event, the childhood patterns of Marge and John were certainly mobilized by their emotional interaction, bringing not mutual harmony and satisfaction but hostility, suffering and destructiveness, even to the brink of ruin. When John was caught up in his compulsive submissive attachment to Timmy, his mother could end the relationship because they were both children; John's good relationship to his parents developed into the normal healthy part of his adult personality. Now, however, although he could see these dynamics, John struggled in agony to accomplish his separation from Marge, his current "Timmy-figure"; but he struggled in vain, for he was also bound by the power of sex and the mating instinct. He knew his separation from Timmy had led out of suffering into emotional health. If only the pattern established toward his parents could predominate over the Timmy-pattern he now felt toward Marge, then his mature, sane, realistic, excellent qualities would relieve his suffering, helping John shape a gratifying life eventually with a good marriage to a normal girl and a satisfying, rewarding, successful career, with his painting as a hobby or an avocation.

As a symptom of compulsion neurosis, infatuation can be expected to have whatever varied dynamics eventuated in this neurosis, with the fight-flight reaction and especially hostility in some form as a common element. In addition, there will probably be a pathologically intense dependent attachment to some person in very early childhood, probably before age three.

John summarized his problem as a two-fold one:

The results of the close personal relationship with Timmy were, as we have seen, disastrous. John was beaten up and controlled by Timmy in a sadistic fashion. Although John turned to his mother as a refuge from Timmy's aggressiveness, he also felt insecure and angry at being so dependent upon her.

Both these patterns—the one toward Timmy and the one toward his mother—merged in his relation to Marge with the "Timmy" pattern being the stronger of the two. In fact, John unconsciously tended to repeat the Timmy pattern toward all those with whom he came in contact, especially if the individual possessed dynamics at all similar to Timmy's. If the person did not possess a Timmy-like personality, the basically sound relationship that John had established toward his parents asserted itself. So John was able to make friends, some of whom were relatively close; but he drew back from the prospect of the intimate relationship that marriage entails. The key to establishment of real intimacy for John seemed to be in whether he could be the dominant figure in the relationship. As long as he could be in control of the situation, keeping his dependent and submissive tendencies in check, John could gradually ease into an intimate relationship with someone like Marge in spite of the fact that she possessed to some extent the Timmy-like domination and hostility. So John could feel comfortable around Marge and even intimate during the time *she* was doggedly pursuing *him*. When his dependence on her developed, then his problems began: his dependence left him open to psychological control and domination through Marge's threats of a breakup. During the intimacy of their marriage, fueled by Marge's complaints of his lack of attention and his nonexistent laziness concerning housework, John's Timmy-pattern began to assert itself. In addition, his pattern toward his mother was transferred to Marge; Marge became the dominant one by her threat to divorce him if he didn't obey her in all ways and give her all the attention and affection she felt she deserved.

When he was around Marge, John felt threatened, dominated, controlled, insecure, inferior, angry and hostile, just as he had felt toward Timmy. His hostility became directed toward his friends and later toward himself in the form of a water phobia and serious suicidal impulses. Only occasionally did he manifest his anger openly toward Marge, since to do so would be to alienate himself from the person upon whom he was so dependent. The pattern that caused John the greatest problem in his relations with other people was the Timmy-pattern. He tried to escape his difficulties in his feelings toward people by retreat into excessive dependence—upon his mother and later upon Marge. This dependence upon Marge and on her love and goodwill was an important element in the infatuation. He fought off his own temptation to be controlled and dominated by his barely repressed hostility, making life almost unbearable for his loving parents by his masochistic behavior of drinking and threatening suicide, and holding them on the phone for many hours at a time and then ignoring them.

A letter from John arrived a few months after he graduated from engineering school, finishing high in his class in spite of being divorced just before his final exams:

> I have been unable to get off for a vacation in Texas, apparently paralyzed by indecision. I can't even make myself fix up my car. The terrible hostility I felt toward Marge has greatly diminished, largely I'm afraid because I have separated myself from her, but this hostility has been replaced by a debilitating despair. I feel that I am back where I started after graduation from college, with no direction, no joy in anything and frightfully alone.
>
> I've lost five years with nothing to show for those years but some unsold paintings, a sorry marriage and divorce, an engineering degree and months of severe emotional illness. I *have* gained a number of insights into my psychological dynamics, but right now I would gladly trade them for a decent marriage and a satisfying career. My defenses are gone and most of my sustaining illusions. You are probably right: I have no genius for painting, only a talent that I need to develop. But that remains to be seen . . . it may be that I have not yet found the proper medium. My own estimation of my abilities, however, is not high.
>
> As early as I can remember, I have felt that I was destined to one defeat after another; I think that is one reason that I am not so eager to travel to Texas and visit my successful friend in Houston. I dislike the idea of going out there defeated. But then if I stay home much longer I feel that I am going to go under. So whatever I do is motivated by sickness and desperation rather than by joy or desire.
>
> I realize that, from your perspective, my problems seem relatively inconsequential. I am still in good health, have a good job, etc. But from my point of view, looking back at the ruin my life has been to date, I can project nothing but more of the same sickness and loneliness that has characterized my existence since my earliest years. My friends have gone forward with their lives. I don't think that I have advanced an inch

since high school. And work is no longer the panacea it once was—it is just no good and totally unsatisfying working for oneself. I have tried being bourgeois and that did not work. And while Marxism is the most attractive and humane social system I have encountered, in practice it appears to serve people no better than capitalism. The reason for this failure and perhaps the failure of any social system no matter how soundly constructed in theory apparently lies in the fact that mankind cannot even remotely live up to his own aspirations. The system becomes an outlet for individual aggressions rather than a means to social well-being.

Thus I see no direction—art, family life, work, politics—in which to turn. In spite of all I have been through, I feel that I have changed very little. I am afraid of being alone as I have been most of my life. Even as bad a marriage as Marge and I had is preferable to being alone. I am also tired of having to get through each day clinging by my fingernails to tenuous hopes, to drink, drugs or the company of friends. The effort seems pointless, the returns nonexistent. When I was young and sick I had time and an uninformed hope on my side. I have neither now. Fresh starts at my age (26) and in my condition are not promising. It is either in me to continue striving or not, but at the present I can't seem to break clear of this feeling of complete and total despair.

But enough of this whining. It is time to head South. I will write before I return.

John

John reacted to his situation with the desperate state of depression he dreaded. Basically, its dynamics soon emerged: an infantile regressive helplessness that hurt his self-esteem and caused frustrated dependent-love needs for Marge, which, hurting his pride, generated a paralyzing rage. Analyzing this childish dependence and the rage it produced seemed to help diminish his acute suicidal impulses and his excessive need for refuge in alcohol.

Here is another example, with dynamics that differ from those of John and Marge. In this particular instance, I knew the woman's dynamics better than those of the man:

Jenny, divorced from a passive and ineffectual husband, clung to Joe for several years even though he was a married man with nearly grown children, and even though after the first two years Jenny realized intellectually that Joe would never divorce his wife to marry her. However, she still persisted in her demands for closeness and attention. She declared her passion for Joe, and still hoped he would return it. She convinced herself that he did "love" her after all, and that she "loved" him and contributed greatly to his life. Joe came to see me a few times and complained about Jenny's attachment, her interminable telephone calls, her incessant emotional demands upon him. Yet she could not see or accept his rejection because it was so intolerable to her.

Her childhood pattern was this: there was love from her parents, which is what gave her the strength to keep going after the complete rejection by Joe, who had finally refused even to see her. It was this parental love that helped Jenny resist suicide. But despite the parental love there was also enough rejection and deprivation to keep her fight-flight reaction aroused. Her father responded to her anger in kind. He became severely punitive. Then her mother would be consoling. Jenny would respond to this treatment by becoming contrite and apologetic, which made her father come around to being sweet to her. This part of her pattern she acted out almost precisely with Joe.

A prominent element in this part of her childhood pattern was her chronic anger at both parents when she felt they did not listen to her or give her enough attention. She then was determined to get the attention as well as being very angry, and in retrospect she realized that she was bound to her parents by both the anger and the determination to get the attention. This constant rage was also present in her determination to force Joe to "love" her.

The whole pattern was intensified by the sex and mating instincts. Joe was an attractive man, and Jenny's merciless self-destructive obsession with him made a vicious circle; she was not free to form a relationship to any other man, and thus cut off from other men by her own masochism, she poured her entire libido into her longings for Joe.

Two concluding remarks: Although there is no conclusive evidence, it seems likely, as mentioned above, that in the dynamics of infatuation there is a pathologically intense dependent and also submissive attachment to some person in early childhood. When infatuation is so strong that one individual dominates another's whole emotional life, as Joe occupied all of Jenny's (although she continued to hold down a job), and the frustration of the overintense dependent and submissive love needs produces borderline psychosis and even suicide, then the pathological childhood attachment may well turn out to be before age three. It may turn out to be an almost totally frustrated attachment to a family figure, usually a parent, at this early age, or (as in John's case) to someone outside of the nuclear family.

Infatuation that is as destructive to both partners as it was between John and Marge and as it was with Jenny is only the extreme of the mixture, which we broadly call "love" and "hate," of constructiveness and destructiveness that enter in some degree into every marriage and nearly every human relationship. Freud thought that generally the least hostility (the least "ambivalence," as he put it) in a human relationship was that between a mother and her baby son. Marriage is successful if husband and wife both have sufficient love, tolerance and patience to triumph over the negative, hostile destructive elements.

Prenatal Fixation

The therapeutic struggles were considerable in keeping John realistic enough and motivated sufficiently to get through engineering school and then to hold his job against his almost irresistible hostile dependence upon Marge and his mother, and his passive desires to give up all effort, living on his parents' money as long as he could manage to get it. During these struggles I often wondered if his extreme dependence and hostility were entirely reactive to the pressures upon him in babyhood, or if there might be some genetic impairment of the drives to independence, interest and accomplishment.

I often would think of Bill and Gail, as emotionally healthy a couple as I had ever met; my wife and I saw them when they were first proud parents, a few weeks after the birth of their first child. My wife remarked as soon as she held the baby, "You are a tense little thing." He was indeed—not only with us but with Gail, his mother, and so he remained. Little Billy was never as warm, cuddly or responsive as his two brothers, who arrived later at two-year intervals. This emotional distance which was so evident from birth, continued as part of Billy's personality. He was never close to his parents or brothers even though he was overly dependent upon his parents, and he showed little warmth to anyone. Although at times he was sweet and ingratiating, he made no close friends and was relatively unpopular in school and with the neighborhood children. This was partly because he was so self-centered, so inconsiderate of others and so readily hostile to them, whether boys or girls. Billy antagonized everyone and then complained bitterly that people did not like him. His parents were truly loving and sought advice on how to help him; for they feared for his future if these patterns continued, patterns which were easily traceable all the way back to birth and certainly not reactive to any lack of true, warm, deep parental love and tender care.

And often I would think of Phyllis, a young woman of 30, who complained violently about her inability to marry or achieve any rapport with others, or to have any interest in anything, much less hold a job of any kind. In this case also the absence of rapport with others, including her parents, her dependence on them, her hostility to them and her passivity were extreme, and apparently traced back all the way to birth.

The overall impression of these individuals is that there is a fixation of a part of the personality at a *prenatal stage;* something has failed to develop adequately in the transition from the placental, unborn condition within the mother to the neonatal stage of interpersonal relations between child and mother. And it is this inability to relate emotionally to the mother that so distresses both the child and the parents as time goes by. The child grows physically but fails to socialize properly or form any close, gratifying love relations with parents, siblings and substitutes, and later with other persons.

It is a difficult and lengthy process to ascertain that this partial prenatal fixation is present in the psychodynamics. If it is, it usually carries a guarded prognosis and means that analytic therapy will be even longer and more difficult than what is required to correct interpersonal traumata that occurred in the first year after birth.

If partial prenatal fixation exists, it may well turn out to be the key to understanding borderline and psychotic characters.

SECTION VI:
SOME TYPES OF PERSONS AND CIRCUMSTANCES

25
THE OTHER WOMAN

Mary Alstop came to see me because she was nearing 30 years of age and was not married and raising children, this being her dearest wish. At the same time she was madly in love with a married man who had three small children, and Mary was hoping that he would divorce his wife to marry her. This had been going on for over six years. There was much more to Mary than her striking surface beauty. She was also highly intelligent, psychological and capable in many ways. Her manner was subdued and slightly distant. She had been married in her early twenties. Apparently she and her husband were in love with one another when he was a student, and she worked hard to send him through college. After he graduated, she expected him to take care of her; but either he was incapable of doing so adequately, or Mary's demands were too great—she felt dissatisfied and complained that her husband did not really work for two years. Therefore, she divorced him, against the advice of her own family.

Since their divorce, her former husband had gone into the world of business and made a considerable success. Mary did not tell me how or why he had become so successful after two years of passive withdrawal, but only complained that he offered none of his income to her. He was apparently settled in a new marriage that Mary believed, whether out of wish or judgment, could not last.

Before coming to see me, Mary had been so upset (although not overtly depressed) as to make a suicidal attempt or at least a gesture, but one that was alarming enough for her family doctor to send her to me for evaluation and referral.

During our first interview I asked her what she considered to be the most important features of her 0 to 6, the years from her birth to about six years of age. She replied as follows:

"I felt that I lost my mother. This was from the time I was a year and a half old and was left with relatives, and I felt my mother had abandoned me. My first memory is of my mother coming home from the hospital when I was two years old, with my sister. Then I remember a year later when she left to go to the hospital to have my younger brother. Then, about two months after that, she entered the hospital again for an operation. Each stay was for a week or two. [The main theme of these memories seems to be loss of her mother's presence, and her love and care, which were turned toward the new babies.]

"When I was about six I felt different from my brothers and sister. There was my older brother and the younger sister and brother."

"How did you feel different?" I asked.

She said, "I felt I was not loved." As she seemed reluctant to pursue this, I asked her the following specific question:

"Whom do you consider the most important person or persons in those early years from birth to about six?"

She replied, "Mother. Mother is the one I wanted most, and I did not want anyone else. [This confirms the theme of the memories—intensified but frustrated needs for Mother.] Later, when I was a little older, about seven or eight, there was my father's father (paternal grandfather), who treated me as somebody very special, who would take me with him to visit friends and go all kinds of places with me. This was a good relationship until it got perverted. I adored my grandfather like a god, but then he did some nasty things with me, sexually, but I could not tell my parents. I thought maybe because he was my grandfather he was allowed to do these things, and I should not complain. I did not tell my mother about it until I was 17 years old, after my grandfather was dead. But I found out what men want at an early age. I fear finding out things about myself."

"Like what?" I asked.

"Well, that maybe I am a nympho . . . I was once accused by a fellow of being oversexed, and then this affair with Howard, a married man, is against all my Sunday School training. Only a year or so ago I went off on a vacation. I was not looking for anything, and I met a lot of married men, and since then I have gotten all these calls from all these married men. With my ex-husband, as long as I was a mother to him the marriage went all right, but when I wanted to be a wife and settle down, and wanted to start a family and have him choose a career, then he did not want the responsibility.

THE OTHER WOMAN 301

I did all the bills, the paperwork of the household; but when I wanted him to take care of me, he could not do it." [Was she unconsciously looking for the mother she felt deprived of, with intense demands and feelings of frustration and anger?]

I asked, "Were there any other important figures in your childhood?"

She said, "My father, but I really never had a father. [This confirms the theme of her intensified attachment to Mother alone, uncompensated by a good relationship to Grandfather or Father.] He was so busy, working on two jobs because the Depression was still on, and he felt lucky to be able to have work and bring in a little extra income. But besides that, he never bothered with us. My father and mother never got along . . . Father spoke of his 'wasted years,' meaning the years of his marriage. I was always afraid of him because he always yelled and was angry. When I got married, I didn't want my father to give me away. There was no relationship with him; he was never there. When he came home, he was tired, and we must not talk because we might wake him; or if he came home for a meal, we could not talk at the dinner table because Father wanted to talk with Mother. When he drove us in a car, he would not stop so that we could to to the bathroom. He would not let us sing in the car or play any of the games children do when they take a long trip. He was mean. He never showed any feeling, but I could always see the great anger in his face. He was never able to say 'I love you,' but now, today, he takes pride in me. He thinks I am intelligent; he is proud of my job and my income. He fought with Mother all the time.

"Maybe those weeks of separation from my mother would not have been so traumatic for me if I had been secure with my parents, but I was *not* secure, especially because of their fights. [This sounds correct. She was not secure with others in the family. Moreover, if she had been secure in her mother's love she would have tolerated much better Mother's absences and the arrival of the siblings.]

"Now my sister seems to be separating from her husband. Her little daughter is only two, but already says, 'Father does not love Mother, he loves somebody else.' I did not recognize that in my own life until I was eight years old and saw Mother crying. Father never kissed Mother, nor did he come home at night. I can't remember it, but I know there must have been strong effects on me of hearing

Father and Mother fight when he finally did come home. And then, also, I knew about Father having an outside affair."

[At this point there went through my mind something supported by later material, namely that Mary was probably identifying with the other woman. In the place of her own mother she would not have been loved by Father, who was in love with another woman; she, as a child, would have Father's love if she were the other woman. The same holds true regarding her sister and her sister's husband: she seems to identify with her sister's daughter and the comment, "He loves somebody else." But I said nothing for lack of sufficient evidence.]

"My first memory," she said, "was not really of Mother coming home from the hospital with my sister but with my younger brother. Mother has admitted that she hates men because of how they hurt women, the way Father hurt her, the way my sister's husband is hurting her, the way my ex-husband hurt me. If my sister divorced, I would like very much to go live with her and her little daughter.

"My mother was only four when her father died, and Mother was in a foster home while her mother worked. I don't like this interview at all," she suddenly said.

"Why not?" I asked. "That is very important to know."

She replied, "Because my past is so painful to remember."

"What is the worst part of your past, what is the most painful?" I inquired.

She said, "Feeling not loved by Father. I felt a constant striving to be perfect or else my parents would leave me. If I were perfect in every way, they would not leave me, and they would love me. I felt Father's rejection, but I never gave up trying. But I knew that if I came to him, he would always turn away. Openly I wanted Mother. I asked her to love me, to hold me, but I wouldn't try that with Father because I was convinced that he did not love me; so I shut him out of my life emotionally for years. I felt that Mother loved me more than Father, but not as much as she loved my brothers and sister. My older brother was the first-born, and that's why she loved him. The youngest brother was the baby, and I guess that is why I felt different. I *was* different. And often they got sick, and Mother had to take care of them.

[This is all part of her present life pattern: she clings to the married man, feels his rejection, but never gives up trying; she feels that her mother loved her less than the others.]

"Let us continue with your earliest memories," I said.

She said, "Well, I corrected the one . . . when Mother came home from the hospital with my younger brother, I was about three and a half. That is, my feeling was that Mother was coming back. My second memory was of Mother being away at the hospital, and there was a woman taking care of us and Father was there. I remember a Christmas time, although nothing specific. My grandmother was there; she was an invalid. She was a bitch . . . she hated me since I was born and told my mother that I was bad, that I was no good. I felt I had to be perfect, or Mother would not love me; I felt she was the only one that loved me at all."

I said, "Then you did feel loved by your Mother?"

She replied, "Yes, but only at times and not as much as Mother loved the others, and certainly not as much as I needed and wanted. My older brother and I fought all the time. I threw things at him, but now we are very close. He is five years older than I, but has never married."

I asked, "Do you have any idea of the reasons for his not marrying?"

She said, "Only that he cannot find the right girl to marry. My sister, who is a year and a half younger than I, I wanted to be best friends with. She had a lot of outside friends. I would give her things and do things for her. We fought some, but not like with my brothers. We shared a room, but we were never as close as I wanted to be. My younger brother is not a 'loner' like my older brother, but he has rejected the family. He has all his own friends. We did not have much of a relationship, but it has been better in the last few years. He cares, but he will not admit it; he never shows open affection for anyone, but he has been open in his hatred of Father. We all felt that we were compared to our older brother, who was very intelligent and smart at school. Unless I got all A's I felt that they did not approve of me. They certainly disapproved when I made my first suicidal attempt, and when I started the affair with Howard.

"They thought it was unfair of me to divorce my husband. They forgot that he had not worked for two years. I want to be free to live my own life, without the interference by my family. My sister is just like my mother." [It seemed that the family did not actively enter Mary's life and interfere with her, but that Mary's own continuing overstrong needs for their love made her so needy of their approval that this need interfered with her independence and made her overly submissive to them.]

I asked, "Were there any really good relationships with any members of your family?"

She said, "Well, it was somewhat good with my sister, but she is just like my mother. The relation with Grandfather was good at the beginning when he treated me special, until the time he ruined it all with the sex."

"What," I asked, "Is the best relationship you have had with a member of your family?"

"My mother," she replied, "but she had to divide herself among all the children. I wanted to be independent, but I wanted them to approve of me. My father said that I had a mind of my own when I was two years old, and that I was a good baby, a good child, and gave no trouble. I still cannot stand a word of criticism. The first time I gave a party, some of the guests could not come, and I felt it as a personal rejection. Now I feel they come because there is no charge, and they are moochers."

"So either way," I said, "You feel unloved."

"Of course," she said, "I know."

[At this point we have a picture of no good relationship with a male in early childhood, which would provide a pattern for a good marriage; there is a strong, frustrated longing for her mother. This is common enough in women with marital difficulties: their basic emotional involvement is often with their mother—a woman—and therefore no mere male satisfies them. The frustrations with men and, more deeply and usually unconsciously, with women usually feed an unrelieved anger at others with guilt and anger at oneself. Guilt is a natural result of hostility toward one whose love we desire. I said nothing at this point, but confirmation came from what Mary later told me.]

I asked how her feelings of being unloved could be connected with her unsatisfactory marriage. She replied, "I don't know. I do not like myself; I think that's part of it. For a while I told myself that I liked myself, and I was happy. That is the only period in which I did not want to die, but that was a great lie."

I said, "Do you know why it is that you do not like yourself?"

She answered, "I hated myself for a long time, and I think it was because I was hurting everyone. I was hurting Father, Mother,

Sister and my ex-husband. Howard thinks I attempted suicide because of him, but he was not in my mind at all. I didn't think that he loved me at that time. I wanted to do things my way, but they all didn't approve. They didn't approve of my separation from my husband. The only one who understood at all was my older brother. He said no matter what I decided to do, he would stand by me. [Here again is her frustrated need for love from her parental family in the form of approval. This, combined with not liking herself, suggests a lack of approval and being valued in her early years. She may well have simply taken over the family's rejecting attitude toward herself, expecially the attitude of her mother.]

"How about your hostilities during childhood?" I asked.

"Well," she said, "I was taught in Sunday School from the age of two that I must love everyone and not hate anyone. But then I heard them call my mother an alcoholic just because occasionally she had one single drink; so I left the Sunday School. Even today, if I fight, I am always the one who must apologize. I guess I have a lot of guilt feelings. I met a man at work, and this summer he got a divorce. I liked him and wanted him, but then he married another woman.

"Howard and I are going to destroy each other. Even if I get him, I won't get what I want, that is, a child. [I thought to myself that what she really wanted was not a child but a mother, and, of course, a father.] I am just terribly lonely and terribly hurt. [This was certainly tragically true.] I saw another analyst for a while . . . he was quite young, and I think not very experienced, but since the work with him I feel just as lonely and just as hurt. For long periods he would say absolutely nothing, and I just hated that. [It was touching and painful to see this beautiful, intelligent and capable girl, with so much to give, in such agony and going to waste.]

"I get hostile when the family is too demanding. I want to stay away from them and do my own thing. I am hostile to my sister because I wanted her to be my best friend, but she never phones unless she wants something from me; she never calls just to say 'hello, how are you?' Then I withdraw, and probably that's not a logical thing to do."

After a brief pause: "I have often thought I would like to be like a spider. I would take up some man, and when I got him thoroughly in love with me and thoroughly involved, I would just turn on him and throw him out and try to destroy him.   But I never really could do that."

This frightening bit of dynamics motivates much human cruelty and violence all over the world: the child as an adult tends to identify with the aggressor of his early years, his 0–6, and to revenge himself by doing to others what was done to him in early childhood.

Mary's dynamics thus far have shown her unconscious dependent-love needs, unconscious fear and hate of Father and the fact that she had no good relationship with him or any male in early childhood; they indicate a basic, strong longing for her mother's love that was frustrated and led to hostility, guilt and masochism—and all of this leading her to unconsciously resisting and fearing what she consciously so desired, namely, closeness to a man in marriage, lest she be rejected and frustrated as she felt herself to be during childhood.   Such close-ness would not work on the pattern toward her mother; toward Father; or toward her younger brother, with whom she felt com-petitive and jealous, as her first memory revealed; or toward her older brother or sister—there was just no pattern of a good relation-ship to sustain a marriage.

Further material represented Mary's mother as the one her father did not love; if she wanted to be loved by her father, Mary had to be "the other woman," the one her father really preferred.   I think this gave her the identification with the other woman that seemed to play a role in the way Mary unconsciously kept herself in a position of loving a married man with children, who apparently had no intention of divorcing his wife to marry her.   Mary was frustrated in this situation but nevertheless continued it.   It was possible that, if she went further down this blind alley, she would use it as a defense against getting married and having closeness with a man, as a result of the childhood dynamics explained above and for fear a husband would eventually reject her just as her father rejected her mother—treating her just as Mary believed all men treat their wives and are mean to all women.

Mary's dynamics put her in a bind: if Howard did not divorce his wife, leave his children and marry her, then this situation would mobilize the feelings of deprivation by Mother and rejection by Father, and the frustration would be so great that she would react with rage, probably mostly turned against herself, possibly resulting in suicidal attempts.   There was little relief because if Howard *did* marry her, did leave his wife and children, her guilt, in addition to the rest of her dynamics, would be more than she could stand. Either way, she was at an impasse, caught in an intolerable situation (Saul, 1966). Her childhood emotional pattern was so disordered that suicide was her constant state of mind, and the strength of the suicidal trend merely fluctuated. When Mary said in the interview that she and Howard were destroying each other because they loved each other too much, I asked her what she meant by that. I told her it sounded impressive that love was the same as hate and one could destroy another individual by love, but what does that really mean? She replied, "Well, he is destroying me by not marrying me. Maybe I have sometimes thought I would like to destroy him. We do love each other deeply, and in the end I think he will marry me." [Which seemed like clinging to her mother or her father for the love she felt she would never get.] (Now, years later, Howard is well settled into his marriage and happy that this affair with Mary is finished.)

I could not help but think, "How long, O Lord?" Will children ever be raised properly, with love, respect and understanding, so that we will not continue to gaze on such tragedy as this, typical as it is: a perfect girl, straight and beautiful, intelligent and capable, wanting only to fulfill herself as a woman and be loving and useful, yet doomed to frustration and misery and possibly even suicide by the inexorable dictates of her inescapable childhood emotional pattern, imposed upon her through no fault of her own?

Reference

Saul, L. J. (1966): Sudden death at impasse, *Psychoanal. Forum* 1(1): 88–93.

26
FEMME FATALE, DON JUAN, BACHELOR

Sometimes the most charming, alluring, irresistible girls make the most difficult wives. This is apt to be the case when the girl's dependent-love needs have been intensified by her childhood experiences and seek gratification through her feminine sexuality, when her cravings for romantic sexual love are really childish needs for parental love. [The child's receptive-dependent needs easily fuse with the feminine, but usually conflict with the masculine ideal.]

Edith's father died, and her mother had little time for her. The child repressed the pain of rejection, and she repressed anger, and the guilt for the anger as well. As she grew up, the full force of her repressed, internally frustrated craving for parental love was channeled into her feminine desires for love from a man. Thereby she became incredibly appealing—a femme fatale, attaching to her any man she cared to attract. But when she married, the whole pattern of childhood emerged toward her husband, as is usual. Within months he became, in her mind, in large part the depriving mother of her childhood. Her mature wifely love was vitiated by the unsatiated demands and rages of her childhood, repressed but never outgrown.

Often the quality of a child, of a little girl, in a woman is itself especially appealing—for various reasons, depending upon the makeup of the man. It often stimulates normal parental protectiveness and the masculine sense of power and mastery. If the girl has much guilt and longing for punishment channeled into her femininity, then male sadism is also aroused. Thus the disturbed childhood patterns, depending on their nature, affect in different ways the sexuality, as well as all other aspects of the personality—inhibiting, warping, deflecting and intensifying.

Boy-craziness, or nymphomania, and girl-craziness, or satyriasis, may arise from reinforcement of sexual desire by exaggerated childhood dependent-love needs and also other emotions, most often hostility. (We have already remarked that most compulsions express, in

some part at least, the pressure of underlying, frequently unconscious, hostility.)

A common result, in the man, is Don Juanism. The particular
dynamics that one Don Juan showed was a simple manifestation of
the "give-get" interplay. An unattained woman meant to him
"get"—the promise of all the closeness he still craved from his mother,
now enhanced by full adult sexual desires for the girl. But when
she yielded and fell in love with him and looked to *him* for love,
sex, affection, responsibility, for the gratification of her own needs—
when he was to "give"—then she no longer was all that his childish
desires demanded. She now was no longer the giver but the getter.
Hence he lost interest and soon felt coldness, even repulsion, for her
and felt that she was only a drain upon him, trying somehow to
exploit him. And so he would turn to a new girl, seeing in her
the old promise of getting, only to go through the same process
of disillusionment.

Sometimes he would look backward to one of his earlier, discarded
flames who had withdrawn her love from him, and, in proportion to
her unattainability, he would feel increasingly that he had made a
terrible mistake in leaving her, that she was, after all, the true love
he had been seeking. If he returned to her, and, being tempted,
she yielded again, then to her sorrow the pattern would be repeated.
Some men with this "give-get" conflict do, however, mature enough
to handle the giving and responsibilities of marriage, although sometimes only after disillusionment, irritability, hostility and varying
degrees of depression.

One outcome among many of resisted overattachment to the
mother is the perennial bachelor. It is probably entirely a matter
of the quantitative balance of emotional forces whether the result
is this or something quite different. And of course permanent
bachelorhood, like everything else, can be a result of many different
backgrounds and dynamics. It is a final, common path of various
motivations. Art, the man referred to in "Double Bind," who
could not bear to be married or to be alone, who could not live with
a woman or without one, who was powerfully, irresistibly impelled
toward one woman, and then equally compelled to escape from her
to save his sanity, was a kind of bachelor, an unsuccessful bachelor
and an unsuccessful husband, caught between the Scylla and Charyb-
dis of excessive attraction and repulsion.

In contrast was a man we will call Tony. He was attracted to women, to one in particular, but weakly. Far from feeling that living alone was driving him out of his mind, that being alone in an apartment was not to be borne, that to eat dinner alone evenings was torment, Tony relished this life for its peace and freedom. His small apartment was his castle, his retreat, his haven. When I asked him about eating alone in restaurants each evening, he said, "But I am not alone. I have the best of company—the books that I most enjoy reading." Tony was the despair of the nubile beauties. One in particular began an all-out affair with him a few years back, but as mating it progressed no further. Tony felt unwilling and unable to marry her and felt guilty about continuing their relationship. But she clung, still hoping, and he never insisted on breaking off, probably could not quite do so. He feared marriage, feared being tied down, feared being committed forever; he liked the freedom and serenity of his own life. His feelings of loneliness were not strong. His urge toward women in general, toward this woman in particular, and toward living in a marriage were weak. Why?

His central dynamics were these: He was an only child. Upon him was vented the full force of his mother's maternal drives. She was a powerful personality, dominating her husband, her home and Tony, her only chick. She was controlling and anxious (a common combination). For example, she worried so about his eating that she tried to control it almost to the mouthful. The child reacted against this by losing his appetite, being almost unable to eat at all. Only when he was left alone did he come to enjoy a reasonably normal intake. Small wonder with this conditioning that he continued, though nearing 40 years of age, to prefer dinner alone, with a good book. His mother's satisfaction in his school work was not aggressive and therefore did not cause him to react against it. It "took." He enjoyed intellectual pursuits partly because they provided an escape.

When I first saw him and inquired about his conflict over marrying the girl (Tess), he said he hesitated to marry her because he was not sure of what people would think, whether they would approve of her. I tested him with "How can you care what people think or say? The only question is whether she is right for you. If so, let others think what they will. 'To thine own self be true,' and they will respect you for it." This was enough to start tracing back the "they," which, as anticipated, led to his mother. He was not sure his mother would approve of his choice. His father played almost no part. All paths back from his various current patterns, whether being alone, liking books, being overanxious about his health, taking care about food, preferring solitary restaurant dinners, needing approval for his choice of girls, all led back to Mother.

He had a dream of a man about his own age marrying a woman in her late sixties. His first thought was, "Does this mean I want to marry my mother? That is strange. I still think of her, though she has been dead ten years. I do want to please her. I fear to go against all she told me. But I always fought with her."

"Why?" I asked.

"I never really knew. But from the time I thought of coming to see you, I've thought quite a bit about my childhood. And I think it was because of her constant domination and her anxiety about me—my looks, my health, my food—everything I'm anxious about now."

This theme led to his defenses against his mother and his wishes to escape from her orbit, which he failed to realize until he finished college and started work, that is, until he was out of it enough to see it. And this led to his dynamics vis à vis Tess.

She was a girl with a similar unsuccessful masochistic rebellion against her mother. This similarity was the positive element in their attraction. Her rebellion had hurt her: the repressed anger and the guilt had kept her from a good marriage and from a job worthy of her looks, personality and ability. This corresponded to the first memory Tony had: he hurt himself on a toy his mother had given him.

The negative elements in his attraction to Tess lay in those qualities of hers that appealed to his repressed rebellion against his mother. Tess was so unlike his mother that his mother would surely disapprove. She was of different socioeconomic and religious background. But he could not marry her, for she represented defiance of his mother—a defiance of his internalization of her training, her imperatives during his childhood. The mother herself was dead, but he could not go against her, against his partial identification with her. Equally, his rebellion would not let him marry a girl who signified giving in to his mother.

Further, he did not really want to marry Tess wholeheartedly anyway, or any other girl. He liked her because she was totally apart from his mother, she was weak and needed him, and to his mind she was not at all a mother—figure; she appealed to his strength and not to his submissiveness. He was attracted in an adult, masculine, sexual way to her, because she was so novel, so different from his mother, from all his mother stood for, and from his own attitudes toward his mother.

But as was indicated by the dream of marrying the elderly woman (only a small sample of the evidence), part of him had not relinquished his childhood need for the strong older woman. Tess' appeal was in being so unlike his mother, but she could not win against the other part that felt that she was somehow imperfect and inadequate—because she was *not* the strong mother (and because she did not embody that perfection that his mother wanted for him, her only child). Such a man usually feels that the strong woman who represents his mother has no sex appeal. If he tried sex with such a woman, one stronger than himself, he would be impotent in some degree. The weak girl, dependent and submissive to him, arouses his masculinity, including some normal sadism. She is the weaker one; he can do as he will with her sexually; therefore with her he is potent. But she does not satisfy the need for the mother, which has not been outgrown.

So Tony was not torn almost asunder like Art, but was in balance on dead center. No girl could move him, for she fought an unseen adversary in his own unconscious, the living memories and the unconscious aftereffects of his deceased mother. In Tony the balance of forces was in equilibrium, so that motivation for change by analytic therapy was insufficient for resolution. He felt no real urge to marry, or for therapy.

27
DIFFERENCES IN BACKGROUND: THE "UNSUITABLE" MARRIAGE

Let me not to the marriage of true minds
Admit impediments.

Shakespeare

"I know what you are getting married for. . . . But are you friends with her? . . .
talking and so forth? . . . does she laugh at what you think is funny? . . . you will
be young and high-spirited only a little while. How will you get along unless
you are friends and like the same kind of jokes?"

Scoggins

Let us turn to a young man and his sister, three years younger, whose father was from Beacon Hill and whose mother was from Chestnut Hill. They came to Chicago because of business and lived on the North Shore. The family was more than comfortable financially and ranked high socially. The children went to the best private schools. When they were grown, they met leaders in every field and thus had wide connections and many opportunities for good careers.

The son, Lou, started off in a large industrial company and did brilliantly, but resigned. He repeated this experience in another position. He then got a job on a ranch doing manual work, where he met the daughter of a Mexican laborer. He fell in love and brought her to his home to meet his parents. They were horrified by her manners, her faulty English, her lack of money, her different religion, her background or, in their view, lack of it. A battle ensued, but Lou stood up even to the threat of disinheritance. He thought that his parents' objections to Lillian were to superficialities. To him she was a lovely and a loved child; he thought her natural, genuine and free—close to the real feelings of people and animals. Not that he could have understood it and put it just that way at the time. He became a Catholic and married her. He served in the war. When I last heard from him he was running a ranch. He and Lillian were extremely happy and had five apparently happy children.

His sister Marian never married and was isolated and lonely. She had been the favorite child, although the parents had loved both children deeply. But the mother, especially, was too protective and restricting and always expected the children to behave perfectly. The children lapped up all the love from the parents and were addicted to it, but to be assured of it they had to be perfect. The children could never express the least anger at their mother or dissatisfaction or withdrawal because she would take this as meaning they hated her. Lou, as the less favored one, was able to express some spontaneous feelings in childhood, some self-assertiveness, some hostility. But Marian, being so doted on, needed to keep her parents' adoration, and to do so had to be faultless. When grown she felt totally inadequate, for she felt that she had no personality of her own. She lived by subservience, by trying to please everyone, through suppressing her own feelings. She hated this, and therefore she hated herself and she hated everyone. Life, she said, was torment.

Few persons, I think, can survive without breakdown if they have no human relationships. In many breakdowns and suicides the precipitant is severance of the "last libidinal tie," the loss of the last close human relationship. Marian clung to a tenuous stability by working with those on the fringes of society, those on skid row. Marian's hostility came out more masochistically, more toward her own self, than did her brother's, whose rebellion was sufficiently open, effective and free from guilt for him to achieve a gratifying life. Marian was "loved" more; she felt that to keep this love she must conform more. Hence she could express herself less, and felt more guilty about the natural aggressiveness and hostilities of childhood, the normal drives to activity and the ordinary angers that any child would feel at the inevitable frustrations. (Guilt is in part a product of anger at someone whose love one craves.) Therefore, her rebellion was more subterranean; she hurt her parents only through damaging her own life.

But the main dynamics were the same in both brother and sister: to keep their mother's love they had to be flawless and excessively virtuous. This was too extreme for them to tolerate. Without realizing it, they turned against their mother and all the standards to which, with the best of intentions, she tried to mold them. Persons of the same social class and background, such as those with successful businesses, all reminded them of the parental mold, and they fled from those in fear and resentment, seeking a life of their own, on their own, seeking their own identity. Whether this can eventuate from a childhood in which the mother (or father or both) was not also in some way hostilely controlling, I do not know. But this outcome in some form or degree is frequent. In another family, for example, a daughter refused an inheritance of some millions, went off on her own, married a teacher of a different background and had a good life. Her brother stayed close to his parents and repressed his rebellion until he was in his forties, when, to the grief of his wife and children, he took to wine and women, in the company of immature companions of dubious probity.

There are several morals to be drawn from this discussion. The chief one for our present concern is that similarities in social, financial, religious, cultural, educational and other areas are not the fundamentals for a happy marriage. True, they can make a marriage—or break it—or prevent it entirely. But these factors are not rock bottom—they merely operate in accordance with each person's underlying dynamics. Compare this family with the family described in Chapter 9, "A Paradigm of Marriage."

28
HOME AND CAREER

With "the pill" and the growth of the women's liberation movement, some changes in our social ideology have become obvious. Are these changes a new development or only old conflicts, the long-range emancipation of women, coming out more openly into the national consciousness? Rather than attempting a sociological discussion let us look at some clinical facts: here are three sisters who consented to being interviewed; they seem like normal, healthy young women, from a loving home and with excellent human relations and enjoyable lives.

The oldest, Helen, has four children ages twelve, nine, seven and five. Her husband Paul is devoted and hard-working. They are middle class and able to live in a pleasant suburb, but it has been a great help financially to have Paul's income supplemented by what Helen earns working in the office of a local business. This work quickly engaged her interest, and the money provided her with amenities such as clothes and occasionally tennis or a movie or dinner out that they could not afford on Paul's income alone. Of course, the job took time out of her housework—time from cooking, cleaning, picking up, laundering clothes, plus the other endless details of maintaining a home for six people. Helen managed to get some help and kept her home and work in relatively good balance, escaping the insatiable demands of the children while at the office, and keeping from being swallowed up by the business by retreating to her housework.

As her success and involvement at the office increased, and she was asked to work full-time, her conflict intensified. "If I had known about this in college," she said, "I would have done it differently."

"How would you have done it?" I asked. "Would you have not had the children?"

"Oh, no," she replied, "I would have, for I wanted and still do want the children."

"In that case," I said, "what would you have done differently? Would you not have come to this same point, with both children *and* career?"

"Yes," she said, "I guess so, but I would have known and been prepared. Maybe I would have started the career first. Maybe I would have taken a graduate degree in business administration. I might have done it the same way, but I would have had a *choice*. And I would not have felt that if I did not marry on graduation from college I was a failure."

In sum, Helen is in conflict between her deepest concern, home, and a career that tempts her, takes much time and makes her a casual although excellent parent. Is her interest in business bad for the children's development? Thus far the children have reacted with an appreciation of her independence and, by identification, much independence of their own, which is good. Helen has a full, conscious problem in distribution of her time and energy between home and career. The quality of her mothering is so superior that the basic principle of "love them and leave them alone" seems to be working perfectly in her case.

The youngest sister, Stella, has a driving, ambitious husband, Jim, who is extraordinarily devoted to Stella, the children and the home. The oldest of their three children is five. The other two are still in diapers. Stella and Jim can afford to live in a suburb, but just barely, and cannot afford much in the way of baby-sitters. Fortunately, although Stella has more than she can handle, she is young and strong. At one point recently she came to see me because of anxiety and unintentional weeping. It was evident in a single visit that she was greatly overburdened, but felt she must live up to an impossible ideal of strength and endurance and was blaming herself for her inner, partly unconscious protest against the demands upon her, which exceeded her physical and emotional resources. Once her view of the reality (the excessive demands and her impossibly high expectations of herself plus anger for not accomplishing them) was out in the open, Stella was relieved and able to accept the fact that she must pace herself for the three to five difficult, taxing years ahead. This she has been doing successfully, but she longs for the time when the children will attend school, and she will be a little more free to indulge some interests outside of home and family.

The middle sister, Mary, shows no evidence of this conflict between home and career, overt in Helen and warded off for the next few years in Stella. From early childhood Mary was the most cuddly of the girls; she loved all cuddly things such as dolls and small animals, at first stuffed and then alive. Her husband Bill earns a bit less than either Paul or Jim; they live more simply but apparently are more satisfied. Their two children are their primary interest in life. Mary shows no signs of any yearnings for a career. She is happy and satisfied with her home and children. Mary said to me, "I have no interest in women's lib. If a woman wants a career, I think she should have equal rights, but for myself, I know when I'm well off. The career I want is making a loving home by devotion to my husband and children." Nevertheless, Mary always has some simple part-time job to supplement the family income. At one point she took a more time-consuming job, but the youngest child started to wet the bed. Mary gave up the job and the child again kept dry. Both Mary and Bill said, "We have always been happy with each other, but there was not real deep laughter in the home until the children arrived."

Thus we see three sisters, all loved children, all from the same devoted parents, yet each with dynamics just different enough that two had this conflict—overt or latent—but the other sister was content to be a homemaker. Also, their frankness in talking with me seems significant; it demonstrates how openly these problems are faced and discussed today. Just what created the differences in each girl's dynamics I was not in a position to investigate, beyond establishing that they had such a stable, loving home life as an analyst rarely hears described. I can, however, point out some dynamics concerning the conflict between home and career that are commonly seen in practice.

First, we must recognize a fundamental problem: because all forms of life reproduce, and the process (of conception, birth and rearing of young) in other mammals is identical with our own, it seems obvious that there is a maternal (and also paternal) instinct. But how this operates must be questioned. Did Mary have a stronger maternal and also stronger nesting instinct than her sisters? Or was it increased by her early experiences, or were her sisters' interest in careers increased by something in their dynamics? Basically, is there a maternal instinct in humans that, like every other drive, is intensified, inhibited or otherwise affected by the early environmental emotional influences? There are alternatives; e.g., is there only a sexual instinct among mammals, and if they all knew consciously what it would lead to in the birth and long, difficult process of rearing the young, would they all seek contraceptives? Probably only humans have this foreknowledge. Will they therefore gravitate toward enjoying sex but avoiding its results in procreation? Will wanting or not wanting children be primarily determined by early emotional influences, by the person's own dynamics, by his childhood pattern, with much less force of instinct than we had believed?

Those patients I have seen who have strong wishes for children and deep love for them, who really enjoy children, seem to be individuals who were themselves very much loved during childhood and have an identification with their parents that makes possible their own love of their children and grandchildren. But there are also those who were deprived or rejected in childhood and unconsciously strive to give their children what they themselves lacked.

I have seen many very disturbed young persons, ambulatory schizophrenics, mentally disordered, some even hallucinating, who were attracted to each other by similar dynamics and because both were so helpless in the world. Not uncommonly, such couples meet in a mental hospital. Often out of neurotic, even psychotic, reasons they insist not only on marrying but on having children. Does this threaten a situation in which, by natural selection, the more healthy mature personalities will advance their own careers and therefore society, but have few young, while many of the very sick ones reproduce the species and raise children who by heredity or by identification will themselves be disordered mentally?

29

PSYCHOLOGICAL BLINDNESS IN A RELATIVELY NORMAL COUPLE

There is a kind of marital problem which is somewhat frightening because it is not necessarily the result of psychopathology, any definite emotional disorder in husband or wife, but occurs with high frequency in otherwise normal, intelligent, well-intentioned couples who love each other and try sincerely to do what is best for each other's well-being and happiness, and who try to make a good marriage for their loved children. The following is a composite of five marriages typical of the point:

Cora was a full-blown blonde young woman of erect posture, a little above the average height. Her energy, wide interests and knowledge and her outgoing personality combined to make her most attractive. Chester, her husband, was an attractive man, for about the same reasons; they made a handsome, successful couple, welcome in any circle or group, with three active children.

One Saturday in March, Cora found herself trying to achieve a modicum of order and neatness in the children's rooms. It struck her with some distress that this was a job she had not particularly planned for and did not relish at this time. Cora supplemented the family income by doing editorial work for several prolific doctors who wrote professional articles. She was also taking graduate courses and writing a Ph.D. dissertation. She did not have to work to assure the family's security, but wanted to use her mind and benefit others. Cora had planned to clean the house from 7:30 to 9:00 in the morning, cook breakfast for the family and drive the children to their various activities. Then she would spend the day until dinner time catching up on her editorial work and getting some time to herself. But this was not to be. Chester had stayed up very late at a party the night before because he believed it was important for his connections and his future. Cora waited up till his return and then, exhausted, finally dropped into bed. But Chester was not ready to sleep and wanted lovemaking first. This particular Saturday morning he had to get up at 6:30 for a meeting. Cora had asked him not to wake her, but to let her sleep the extra hour. The temptation of her presence without her attention was too great for Chester, however; he could not stand getting up all alone and quietly leaving. So he was noisy enough to wake her and also the children, for which he apologized. Cora got up tired, cooked breakfast for the entire family and by the time each of the children was delivered to his activity and she had cleaned up the kitchen, it was two in the afternoon. Then there were phone calls to be made, and it was three o'clock, with none of her editorial work done and not a moment's break.

Pouring salt in the wound was the thought that Chester had accepted a major job for their church which would consume the next three weeks, and now he had no time to do it. He accepted this responsibility some months earlier because he thought it would be helpful to his image in the community and valuable for his career. Now, to "bail him out," Cora was unofficially doing the job for him, taking hours out of her day.

While she was in this mood of fatigue and pressure, trying to pick up the house and hoping somehow to get her editorial work done, the phone rang. It was Chester calling to say he would be free early and wanted to have dinner earlier than usual. He would be home by five. Cora controlled her rising anger, got in the car and drove around picking up the children. She hoped to get dinner on the table no later than 5:30. Handling her brood with one hand and the cooking with the other, she met her time schedule. But Chester did not arrive by five o'clock as he had said he would. By 6:30 the dinner was overcooked; so Cora decided that she and the children would eat. Chester arrived at seven feeling guilty but still with some expectation of being greeted as a minor hero for his long day's work. When he didn't get the greeting he anticipated, he became irritable, but did cooperate in getting the children to bed, helped to clean up the kitchen and then did some of his own take-home work. To relax he then decided to watch a sporting event on TV. But he felt he could not do this alone—to enjoy it, he needed Cora beside him, boring though it was for her and the kitchen not fully cleaned up.

At 9:30 Cora was exhausted and wanted to go to bed. Chester finally turned off the TV but had a lot to talk over with her and continued in conversation until 11:15. Cora, still exhausted, dropped into bed. Fifteen minutes later Chester crawled in beside her, wanting sex. Although she had always been highly sexed, Cora now felt that for her it was just another chore in the endless list of the day's demands upon her. She was healthy and normal sexually and had always readily come to climax before, but now she did not want the climax, and resented being made to have an orgasm. Cora told Chester this, but he was insistent, for this had become his routine, no matter how late the hour.

In Chester's mind, his behavior was only that of a healthy male toward his wife. He had become psychologically blind to his excessive demands upon her, demands for attention that a small child might make upon his mother. He was blind to the fact that he made Cora miserable and angry by his demands, and was actually undermining her health. She thought of an outside affair as some relief but was too loyal for that. Not, she told me, that a wife or a husband cannot have a purely sexual relation outside marriage while remaining intensely loyal and faithful in basic devotion; it is a matter of how he or she takes it emotionally, but also of how the mate feels about it. Cora had fantasies of divorce and remarriage to an older rich man. She developed a number of psychosomatic symptoms and feared that her very life was in danger. Chester saw himself as loving, devoted and potent, with no concept of himself as an incessantly demanding small child. He failed to *identify* with his wife, to see to what extent he was crushing her integrity and individuality, i.e., her development into a person in her own right, with her own interests and activities beyond serving husband and children.

It is hard for a child and virtually impossible for a young child to comprehend that his or her parents can want, let alone have, a life of their own. Cora's interest in writing led her to the editing job. Now that work had rekindled her creativity; she wrote some pieces of unmistakable interest, originality and merit. During their engagement Cora and Chester had discussed their prospective marriage in detail: they would have children, Chester would undertake half of their care, and Cora would have enough freedom to develop as a person in her own right. Chester was not only willing but enthusiastic about her having interests of her own outside the home.

Although their vows of sexual and emotional fidelity were kept, their fine premarital agreements on the human, responsible, nonsexual aspects of marriage were crumbling. Chester either burdened her, or let her burden herself, with excessive responsibilities including his, such as the church job. He rarely expressed an interest in reading anything Cora wrote, but he tried to delight her and the children with his own new-found skill at making vanilla muffins. Even healthy physical sex, that great binder of marriage, had become for Cora a demand upon her and therefore a source not of gratification but of mounting resentment and rage. This girl, whose whole body once trembled in ecstasy at his touch, was beginning to dislike the entire process.

In this marriage and other similar ones, the fault is by no means all the husband's. This case is presented only to illustrate a common form of psychological blindness in the husband, which usually is found to derive from his repressed original self-centered dependent-love needs toward his mother. Even when Cora explained all of this to Chester in clear and definite terms with ample examples, he was unable to comprehend it and see her outlook as another human being. In other marriages it is chiefly the wife who is psychologically blind and demanding. In some marriages each partner alternates with the other in periods of psychological blindness to the other's needs.

If Cora's husband could be made to see her outlook clearly, then they would both have something to discuss openly and work on together. Such a problem will not usually be solved rapidly, but if both work with understanding on the difficulties that exist between them, then often steady progress can indeed be made, though it might take five or even 15 years to reach an equable, gratifying relationship.

The following is a verbatim interview with Cora, the wife in the preceding composite description of psychological blindness:

PATIENT: I guess the point of this session is to go over what we tried to do on Monday . . . .
ANALYST: Right.
P: Which is a recitation of problems of marriage with two active, busy people.
A: Relatively *normal,* busy people.
P: I'm not so sure of that! But we'll give it a try. May I ask you this: is what we are going to discuss apropos of the childhood patterns in marriage? Because I am going to get to that in the end.

A: Yes.

P: I seem to be caught in a double bind. Chester seems to be saying, "Be there when I want you to; be the nice warm body I can crawl into bed with; make sure there is food in the house for me to have breakfast; come on outside with me when I am clipping the hedge; be the lap I can put my head on when I am sleepy; take care of the kids; get the cello; take care of religious school; baby-sit on Saturdays when I work; come to my office parties when I want you to; come to the business dinner-dances when I ask, etc. Be there when I want you to, and every now and then I'll have some time for you."

Now you mentioned once that loyalty keeps people from affairs, and I have talked to you about loyalty before, about fidelity and disloyalty. And I thought you could be loyal and still be *sexually* unfaithful. I don't consider Chester disloyal or unfaithful to me because he spends all that time with his work. I don't know how to work independence into this . . . whether it is sexual independence or intellectual independence. I don't understand what the difference is; I think you can still be very loyal to a human being . . . I am basically loyal to Chester. You may say I am wrong, that I am deluding myself. But I have this tremendous respect and affection for him. At the same time I feel his message to me is, "Go and be independent." I am working as hard as I can to get the independence that I seek, but I need some emotional support and that includes relationships with people, whether women or men . . . and that seems to be part of it.

It's a double-bind message; I don't know what to do about that. "Be there, but be independent."

I remember you said once that might be the reason I couldn't get my dissertation done. I don't think you were talking so much about the hours as the emotional quality of it.

When I told you all this last week, I remember we talked about Chester's dependence. On the one hand he was a tremendously competent person, helping others and doing his work brilliantly. On the other hand, he had this dependence. Somewhere in there he lost his ability to empathize with me, really to be in touch with another human being. I don't think it's just me; I think it's the children too. I don't think Chester can empathize with people. I remember once saying to you, 'Could that have something to do with the fact that he was a premature baby?' and had been in a preemie nursery for the first couple of weeks. . . . His people are loving, kind people but are not like my mother. With them, it is much more intellectual. His mother has great respect and devotion for people, and she is tremendously proud of her children, but I think she has encouraged a kind of independence in them, which means that they can't connect with people. Chester's mother was adopted, and that may have something to do with it . . . she had some problems with her relationships to people. In fact, she was adopted by her mother's best friend. I think it was before she was 20 months old. She's always had problems; she didn't want us to adopt any children.

Chester's father came from a very unconventional family too. I get the feeling that they were absolutely devoted, loving, wonderful people. The point is, they both loved their children and that is why Chester is so wonderful. It's just that he doesn't have this ability to connect . . . he had a nursemaid when he was small because they were rich enough, and maybe he didn't get that kind of loving. . . .

A: Are we discussing Chester's dynamics now? Because if so, I want to ask you a question. First, the two things in my mind are:

In regard to his being premature, there has been a little work in this area on imprinting, but I don't think anything conclusive enough to answer your question.

The other question is, could it be in part the behavior of a loved child who takes his mother for granted? The child grows up, Mother is always there, he is loved, everything is provided, the family has enough money to own a house that offers security, there is plenty of food, Mother's lap is available to put his head down . . . could it just be his oedipus?

P: Sure, as the older of two children . . . .

A: And so Mother is independent, and he says "Fine, Mother be independent," but he is accustomed to Mother being there whenever he needs her.

P: I think that might be partly so, but I also feel some people, some women, learn to empathize. I am very sensitive to Chester's feelings and his needs, and I get pleasure out of satisfying them. But it is definitely a *mechanics* problem.

A: Meaning the mechanics keep you exhausted all the time, more than you can handle?

P: But it is not just that. It is my childhood pattern. It's being ignored and treated as though my time is not as valuable as his.

Oh, here is something additional: I went to Urbana on Monday with a friend to this lecture, and I came back on Tuesday morning. This male friend gave me a long detailed description of a person he tried to hire from Washington, D.C., a man who was wonderfully qualified for this job; he had fought for this fellow and gotten a tenured position for him, spent a lot of time and energy, and then the man said he couldn't come because his wife didn't want to leave the part-time job she had. Now this man was teaching in Washington, and the wife was a second wife, and it was just a part-time job for her. But the man said she didn't want to leave. My friend said, "She is a typical selfish, mid-thirties woman," and he sort of looked at me and said, "I know what I am saying to you because this is a phenomenon that we see; women have to learn to accept part-time employment." And a little while ago, the chairman of my department said, "You have a husband to support you," and I said, "But I have to pay someone to take care of the house and the kids," and he said, "If my wife paid anyone to clean our house, I'd divorce her!" So there was a man who wasn't sensitive to what he was saying; not that he was especially saying it to me, but he was making a comment about how odd that was from his poverty background, to pay someone to do the housework, not realizing it was necessary for me to pay someone to do the work so I could study. And now coming back from Urbana here was my best male friend saying the same thing to me! He was saying, "What could be so important about her part-time job?"

So he was saying that, because there are part-time jobs in his department that don't have to be tenured, he fills them mostly with women. He thinks that is good for women, to have part-time jobs. Of this woman who had a part-time job, he said, "It was *only* a part-time job." Her selfishness kept her husband from taking this great opportunity. What I couldn't communicate to him was that first of all, we don't want part-time jobs . . . we want full-time jobs. Somebody gets them.

Why not women as well as men?   Secondly, if you do get a part-time job and commit yourself totally to it, it doesn't matter that it is part-time.   If it matters to you, it is just as important perhaps for you to stay with it as for your husband.   It is a terrible pity that it becomes a "win–lose" proposition: if I win, you lose, or vice versa.   It shouldn't be that way.

I have to say that every time in my marriage Chester has wanted to do something, I have gone along with him because it was a good step forward for him.   Every time he has done it, I have lost two years . . . I have lost a total of eight years out of my life with the four moves Chester has made.   No one can say I am selfish; no one can say I have been selfish.   The point is, I am going to have to be selfish now, and you even might criticize me and say, "But you have a husband who earns $20,000 a year; why do you have to go to work?"   Do you see what I mean about double binds?   I not only get it from Chester, which is bad enough, but I get it from all the other people except you. . . . I get it from my mother still.   She was very concerned about the children; she thinks they are going to suffer.   I am not sure the children will suffer in the first place, and in the second place, we suffer.   I have no evidence that the children will suffer; I *know* that I suffer if I don't do things.   As a matter of fact, there is a lot of evidence that children who have mothers working in things they love are better off.

A: You may be right: love them and leave them alone.   If the mother develops her interests and personality, by identification and although they might get less time and attention, they get a model for maturity.

P: I should remind my mother about that!

A: Referring to your friend's comment about the wife who wouldn't leave her job: "It's the typically selfish woman"—it is not that; it is the fact that marriage involves all kinds of compromises.   Some like it fat, some like it lean, and so you get together and see what you can work out that is the best for both partners.

P: But you see, in my marriage I don't feel that Chester has ever made a concession, not one.   Can you tell me, has he?   If I hadn't come to see you and spent the money on my treatment, we could have taken a couple of bang-up trips, but he hasn't had the time, frankly.   I am trying to think of

anything in my life that has taken something from him.. , . Am
I wrong?

A: I don't think so; I think maybe it is my fault, in that you got
Chester to come in to see me once or twice, but we never got this
particular issue (of who gets what from whom) out that sharply
and in that clear a focus.

P: I thought we did.

A: We got out the issue of what he wants, or what he would put
up with . . .

P: What do you mean, put up with?

A: Put up with your career. But he doesn't behave in a way that
makes it practical, I think, on two counts: the one is mechanically it takes too much time for you to do all these things,
and keeps you exhausted. And the other is, emotionally— your
being in the situation of having no support and being ignored.
And the double message: "Oh, sure that is great for you to have
a career, *but* you have to be Mama too, to me as well as the
boys, while I go my own way and contribute nothing emotionally."

P: That's beautiful!

But I do think that to let a spouse be free, he or she should
do as much as possible with his or her gifts, giving as much moral
support as you can to the other and having enough sensitivity to
respond to the needs of the other. If this could only be done
equally in a marriage, if there could only be a fluid relationship
so that the needs of each were met in terms of time and emotional support.

Maybe in some ways I treat Chester as a parent-figure. If he
were to talk to you over a period of time, he might also feel that
I have a dependency on him. That would be interesting to see,
if it were a burden to him. I don't think he is sensitive to it.
He might say, though, "Why doesn't she hurry up and finish
up her dissertation so she can go to work and supplement our
income?" He might feel that is the most important thing. "Why
does she treat me as the money-bringer?"

A: But you are trying to finish everything up.

P: Yes, as fast as I can. But I am slow about it.

A: You were describing the normal interchange in a marriage;
how each marital partner takes it, of course, has to do with
the childhood pattern.

P: But why can't I (as Chester would say) work out my childhood patterns and learn how to handle them so I don't bother him? When he would say this, my response would be: "But you married me, and you are ignoring me—your childhood pattern is to ignore someone you love; you have to alter your childhood pattern too or else we don't stay married!"

A: I may be prejudiced because of our working together and my overidentifying with you, but as you said before, women *have* emotional needs.

P: Don't men?

A: Yes, but not *only* men. If he treats you as a woman and lays his head on your lap, and you do the cooking and handle everything else, always doing what he wants, you can have emotional demands also. Not just men, but women can have them. A patient of mine not so long ago knew this when he was 21 years old, when he was still in school. He said, "I don't want to get emotionally involved with a girl because I don't have the energy to take care of her emotional needs." And that wasn't even a marriage situation; he just didn't want to be too involved with a girl. Of course, there was a lot more to it than that, but that is the way it came out. And I thought, "Smart boy!"

P: You see, Chester was exactly like that. He never slept with a woman until he went to South America when he was about 24 years old. And it wasn't that he was such a Puritan—he and I haven't talked about it too much—but I think he couldn't get close to someone. I think he was aware of his inability to have that kind of relationship and maintain it.

A: That's right . . . you sleep with a girl, and she has all kinds of emotional demands to make; it isn't just a physical thing, that's the hitch about sex, and that brings up something I guess we ought to discuss another time: sex in connection with loyalty or fidelity. If it were only the physical sex it would be simple; you know, it feels good; so you do it, and that's that. But it stirs up this intense emotional involvement.

P: It doesn't always, though.

A: No, not always . . . .

P: It can, but that is where the loyalty comes in. If you are loyal to your husband or wife, then you can have these pleasurable, intense experiences, and they are just like going to a good restaurant or seeing an absolutely marvelous play, or anything that is aesthetically satisfying.

A: Yes, but it depends on the makeup of the individual.

P: Tell me how that can be; I wonder about that because I don't feel as though I could threaten my marriage . . . maybe a lot of people could, but I don't feel as though I could. I feel that I am so aware of Chester's strengths and so appreciative of them, so unromantic about other people . . . .

A: This doesn't apply to you, but we ought to go into it, with you in particular. One way in which it works is if a man is basically strongly attached to his mother, and he can go out and have sex play with other women, but they never become mother-figures to the extent of his intense attachment to his mother.

P: Couldn't that be true of me, because we both know how strongly I identify with my mother? Maybe it isn't a cross-sexual thing, maybe it is simply the relationship to the mother.

A: Yes, of course.

P: I've been trying to find evidence of that female relationship to the mother as well as the oedipal.

A: Absolutely.

P: If I identify that strongly with my mother, and I know about loyalty . . . . That's why I said to you that Chester might feel I am too dependent on him. In fact, I feel very much the same toward him as I feel toward my mother.

A: Some work has been done on this; there is more discrimination in the early years than has been recognized. But as a general thing, for a baby to be taken care of, to be attached to somebody, to be loved and cared for, is the basic thing whether it is by mother or father. So it might be important, but it is secondary to what Freud called getting to the oedipal stage.

P: The word "guilt" is on my mind . . . I am not with Chester enough, we are not together enough, and now, suddenly, I have a group of men friends who all like to be with me. This has never happened to me in my life before. I have lost a sense of control over the way our marriage is going. Chester is working terribly hard; he frequently leaves at six in the morning and goes to meetings in the evening.

There is no question in my mind that I would prefer to have a realtionship with Chester than any of the other people I know, for every conceivable reason: I trust him, I like him, I respect him. But he is just not available, and I don't know now whether this is because he senses something in my behavior or attitude or feeling that makes him uncomfortable and insecure, and therefore he is going out and working hard—or even having an affair—I just don't know! But I feel increasingly remote from him. I've never had that feeling before and it scares me. It just may be that time of our lives. For a long time I have been able to say, when he worked so hard and was absent so much from me, that he was furthering his career. I could see in my own case, working on my Ph.D. dissertation, that I didn't have time to be around him; and when I had some free time, instead of selecting to be with him I might select gardening (which is what he often does), or something else.

I have to be sensitive to the fact that Chester is 40, and people at 40 frequently leave marriages, and this sense of remoteness that I feel may be something new to him; he may not have quite the same commitment I do to the marriage. He may have a commitment so long as it is O.K. for him; but when he starts feeling uncomfortable, he may not have the same underlying commitment that I have. I guess I am scared. One of the things that comes up is the rejection—he doesn't get into a tailspin, as I do, at rejection. He has some kind of strength, so that if I am angry at him, it doesn't stop him from doing his work. If I go away alone, he doesn't see that as a rejection. But I see his work and his removal from me as a rejection. I find that I am frightened, I am scared at the thought that he might leave; I don't feel as though I could cope. That's horrible; I hate being so weak.

At the same time, without the support from these other people who I know are fond of me and attracted to me, willing to spend an evening with me, talking, "wooing" but not engaging in any physical contact, I would be so alone. It has been a long time since Chester did that, if ever. I don't know why I insist that he is such a perfect being, in comparison with the other people I know. It may be that when people make choices—you know, I made a choice to marry him in the first place—they can't let themselves believe their choice wasn't the best. I can't let myself believe that Chester isn't better than everyone else.

I feel guilty getting from other men the companionship I don't get from Chester. Of course, I don't put out what they want, first of all, which is sex, because I would only want my sex with Chester. I don't think it is fair to the other men to use them as substitutes for Chester. It makes me feel so selfish. To have gone through psychoanalysis as much as I have, and developed skill at being more selfish is rather scary. I am so much more self-involved than before I began analysis; I couldn't then name the things I needed. Now, being able to name them makes me want to go out and get them, and that is selfish. I don't value that; I don't like it; I would prefer to be infinitely capable of giving. To say "Gee, I am not able to give so much as I would like because I am not getting enough" seems bad. I don't like that, having to be so economic.

A: That's not the first question; the first question is, is this really the emotional truth? Not whether you like it or not . . . .

P: But you and I have talked before about maybe getting rid of some of my need to get so much, because it was based on the child-hood pattern, the relative deprivation. So now I am a grown-up and grown-ups don't need as much as children because they are mature. Unfortunately that rings hollow, as I say it, because people—whether children or grown-ups—need *something.*

When I talk to women about it, it is clear that women's problems are different from men's. They get so little from their work because their work is so isolated. And children can't give to their mother what the mother gives to them . . . although I do get a lot of satisfaction out of my children.

But I have decided—and all I have to do now is figure out how to handle it—not to go on this trip that I had planned for myself and the children. If my work for the Ph.D. degree is done in October, fall will be great for a trip. But if my dissertation isn't done until March, for the spring awarding of the degrees, then I can take the kids on vacation in April. Anyway, all this planning for a trip suddenly seems unfair to me; it involves an unfair amount of planning on my part to get the children ready for it. I want to go off to work every morning like Chester and do my own thing, and I can't do it with all this planning.

It makes me so angry and sad ... if I want to do *my* work, I have to get somebody to care for the children, and Chester never has to face that situation.

It's like the airplane tickets for Denver ... we are going there on Wednesday. I got the tickets and did all the negotiations for our last vacation in Minnesota; so I said to Chester that in all fairness I thought he should handle this trip. But he didn't do it. So when my mother says, "When shall we meet you at the airport?" I can't tell her. So I have to go to Chester and say, "Will you please get the airplane tickets?" And then that sounds like nagging. And he still hasn't done it ... this is a busy weekend, and we are going to be out of luck if he doesn't do something soon about the tickets. If it is so hard for him to do those family things, those family responsibilities ... He took the children camping on Saturday night. He said it was restful; they went to a lake they couldn't drown in, it was so shallow. He let them take the canoe out by themselves in the shallow lake, and they had a wonderful time! He said, "I slept the whole time." I was glad for him, and the kids were happy. If I had been there, I would have been organizing them into games and taking them for walks. He can do different things with the children; they are complementary to what I do with them.

When he came back from camping on Sunday, we went to a reception about three o'clock and left there about six; we drove right to the airport, and he flew to Rochester for the night. He will be back tonight for supper. I didn't see him at all last week; there were three mornings when he left between five and six. There were some mutual friends who came over two evenings last week; when people he likes are around, he will be there, but when my friends are around, he leaves and goes to his meetings. I suppose this is not unusual, or is it? Are marriages supposed to be like this?

A: It might be both. The principal thing is that it is not unusual for men who are absorbed in what they do to put their work first. But *the degree* to which they do this determines whether it is unusual ... for instance, consistently leaving at six in the morning and coming home at eleven at night, and the persistence of that, might be unusual. I think it is a question of how well a man handles his two great responsibilities: his occupation and his home.

P: It upsets me that I come to you and spend money every week talking about ways to improve my marriage or make it work, and I don't know where Chester is going, or if he is going at all!

A: Right . . . however much we might change you, where is Chester going? The bare fact seems to be that, instead of drawing closer as you both approach 40, you are moving further apart. Is it all you, or is it both of you?

P: It makes me so sad.

A: It seems to me that there should be a minimum that he gives to his home. It is his home; he married you; they are also his children.

P: But if he took them camping, that is a wonderful thing to do.

A: But that is not marriage. Marriage is not one or two big events every year or every month. Marriage is a day-in, day-out thing.

P: Every morning or every night the children will say to me, "Where's Dad?", especially when I get them up in the morning or put them to bed. It is very hard for me because I know how they feel about him; I know how they love him.

A: So, just as I said, don't knock it when he does the special things.

P: What do I do about it now? I have four people who want me to go away with them to different places, to just be with them. I think they would like me to do my work with them; they could provide me an atmosphere in which I could work. It seems incredible to me that suddenly I should have so many people who can say, "Come to my space and use it," but I can't accept. I have asked the two grandparents if they would help, and they have said no. That is not quite fair.

A: When you ask for help, is that for a circumscribed period?

P: Yes, any period of time. But they can't. I may not have asked right. Maybe with this new decision of mine not to go away on the trip with the children it might be possible.

A: But is there a chance of your work for the Ph.D. degree being finished in October?

P: A slim one. What has scared me is that I haven't shown any of it to anybody. I've tried seeing one of my advisers but he wouldn't take the time to talk with me. He said, "Get it all done first."

A: I thought that was his job . . . .

P: When we talked about it, because I was worried, I asked him if it should be fairly polished before giving it to him. I said, "How would you feel if it were not too polished?" And he said, "I prefer that you would have worked on it before you waste my time." So I said, "Okay." That is pretty scary . . . I would like to give them a great thesis, all finished, and I am worried about what they will say when I give it to them and they don't like it.

A: How much work is there to polish it?

P: I haven't looked at it; I haven't reread it.

A: Well, one good reading might do it, don't you think?

P: Maybe. But I don't think I know really what a thesis is: I don't think it is meant to be polished, frankly. I think it is like a long paper and just has to be acceptable, not perfect.

A: It is read for content more than for style? Does polished means the thought has to be clear?

P: I don't know; I haven't dared to expose it yet.

A: If your work were all done and the exams passed by October, would that have any appreciable effect on the marriage?

P: I could go to work, and that is what you and I have said I need! I don't care what I do, volunteer work or anything; I would be in a position to get some approval from non–sex objects.

A: Right.

P: I haven't felt free to put myself in a position to do things that I would enjoy doing.

A: That's important. You will still have problems, and people have them all their lives, but then you would be coping with problems of adult accomplishments and not the problems of the student pleasing the professors. So I think that is important. Do you think it would affect the marriage favorably?

P: I think so, but I am not sure . . . because it is only my side of it. I don't know what is going on inside of Chester's head now. I think in the sense of his being proud of me . . . well, I am sure he has had as many doubts as I have had about my ability to get the degree. To get it will, in a sense, make all these years of tension a little more worthwhile. Both of our academic careers will be resolved in this degree of mine. So in that sense I think we will have a lot more closeness. One of the things I would like to do is be able to give to my kids and my husband more than I have in the past without feeling as though I am taking away from my working for the degree. So, yes, I believe it will be therapeutic for the marriage. It might not resolve the differences in the marriage because I might be creative and loving to Chester for a while, but I would go back to my work and would not have as much time to be creative and loving . . . and he wouldn't have learned anything! But nonetheless, yes, I think it would be therapeutic.

A: So that is one thing we can do . . . .

P: Get the degree to make him feel good?

A: Yes, get the work done for the degree. And is the other thing really feasible? That is, to find out what is in Chester's head? Is he going to see a marriage counselor or tell me or tell you?

P. I consider it all the time; I suggest it weekly. I think after the degree were completed I might feel more secure in pressuring him to do it. You are the natural person to see because you know everything about us anyway. But you are also protective of me.

In a sense, I feel I am not married right now, which is why I am having a very active social life. When we go away to Denver on Friday I am going to have a wonderful time with Chester, I think. But I am afraid it is going to be like going away with a stranger.

This man who came to see me yesterday is the person who phoned me after 11 years. He is just lovely, fascinating, interesting, a dear human being, with whom I have a fond memory of growing up and exploring things together. I didn't remember when we met or when we started to date; but he reminded me of the exact dates, and so we talked about it. I had remembered a different part of the relationship, and so we talked about that too. I asked him why we stopped seeing one another, because I did not remember, and he said what I suspected—that I had moved away and he wasn't in any position, wasn't rich enough, to travel to see me. And we hadn't had that big a thing going, we had just been friends.

A: The children are going with you and Chester to Denver, aren't they?

P: Yes.

A: Won't that make a big difference? After all, they are Chester's children.

P: We both enjoy them.

A: Yes, so won't that . . .

P: Make a difference?

A: Make it more like a marriage again. [Cora reported to me after the trip to Denver that the marriage was indeed closer again, and had remained so.]

P: It's just like being with fun people; those children are now big enough, so there is a lot of pleasure and fun just being with them, a lot of the time, and that is going to be very nice, unless my mother pulls her "heavy-expectation trip," and then I have to keep the kids quiet, and neat and clean, and that will be my responsibility.

A: Are you going to live in a house with your parents on this trip to Denver? You are not going to be in a separate resort cottage?

P: No . . . I know what you mean; it has disadvantages. But if she doesn't bother me about making the kids meet her expectations, we will be all right. But if she tells me that the children are not meeting her expectations—and she would never tell Chester— then she creates tension between Chester and me. She doesn't mean to, I don't think.

It's very tiresome, at the moment, this relationship with Chester. It's like a separation in many ways . . . I have a friend who has filed separation papers. Both her lawyer and the husband's lawyer say neither one of them should leave the house because if either one moves out, the other one can accuse him or her of desertion. So they are both living in this house, but they are not sharing a bedroom. He doesn't give her any money; she works. But he doesn't contribute any money to the household food or running of the house; she actually owns the house. She buys food and puts it in the refrigerator; he comes home and cooks it for himself, and then leaves all his dirty dishes and doesn't buy any food.

In my case, Chester's paycheck goes into our account and I am drawing on it for everything; so the money is not an issue. But I cook the dinner and then leave it on the stove because he is not there, and he comes home, eats what he wants and then leaves the food out. I come down in the morning, and there is all this spoiled food! I've cooked at some cost to myself, some time and energy and thought. Often, if I leave the messy dishes from the night before—not always, but often—he will clean it up the second night.

A: Well Cora, let's go back to the Ph.D. dissertation . . . it's written but not polished, is that it?

P: No, I have probably another 100 pages to do. I have 200 pages now.

A: If they were written by October, you could submit it? That's only four months away.

P: Five, and then depending on my vacation . . . .

A: If getting the degree might improve the marriage, how about having a concentrated drive to push that through in the next few months?

P: I'd like to try that, but I can't do that unless I have the children taken care of

A: How about when you are on vacation with your parents? Are there other children around for yours to play with?

P: No, it is an isolated house in the country. I am working on a very complicated idea at the moment, which is one of the reasons why I need time to do reading. It is complex, but I think I finally have a "handle" on it. It has to do with the relationship of play and art. So I am reading in aesthetics, and I am reading in play theory rather deeply at the moment. What I would like to do is give myself a month on aesthetics and a month on play, do the reading and the writing, a chapter for each, and then a month to pull the whole thing together. That is basically what I would like to do. It is a nice, clear view of the summer. The library at the college is only open from eight to five . . . there isn't any way I can work on vacation in Denver. There is just no physical space to escape from the children.

A: But your mother should understand.

P: No, she doesn't understand. In a way, she shouldn't . . . *nobody* understands how long and hard it is to get a degree. Least of all, did I know it! That sounds stupid. But people I've known have gotten a B.A. at age 21, and at 24 they were done with their Ph.D. It never occurred to me it would take me this long. I am still so far ahead of most of my peers, it's incredible! There is only one person who started with me who is done, and there are a lot of people ahead of us who are not done. I didn't know that when I started; I am not sure I would have done it if I knew it would take so long.

I was talking with this man the other night; he writes these radio things. He did a Shakespeare program for children, or really, for everybody. He wrote the whole program. I asked him how he knew enough. He said, "I had to do a tremendous amount of research on Shakespeare, theory and history. You don't just write these things off the top of your head; you do the research." So I said, "Then what?" And he said, "Then you sit down and it takes you two weeks of writing 20 hours a day, and you write it." And I said, "Two weeks! My God! If I only knew enough about something, I wouldn't mind if it took me a month," but I don't have the time to do it his way. And I don't feel as though I know enough.

These abbreviated notes from a session with Cora show the frustration so common in highly talented wives, and some of its consequences.

Cora improved rather rapidly after her trip to Denver, largely because during it she felt she received the closeness from her husband, Chester, that she had felt so sorely lacking. As we spoke of this later, she said that she had decided to accept the "lean" times during that year when Chester was so busy and preoccupied, and settle for the "fat times." This realization alone made her feel more patient with the ups and downs of her marriage.

She was also relieved to recognize the common human reaction of both women and men in impulses to turn to others when frustration passes a certain intensity. Many other wives have confessed to me that they followed through on their sexual impulses; they claim it did not injure their marriages because the impulses were not part of their personalities but only a transient phase during a period of great pressure, until they could control their lives, diminishing and coming to terms with their frustrations and stabilizing their marriages.

Nevertheless, it is a poor and risky matter for a husband to be unaware of how much frustration he is causing his wife, and how much frustration she can tolerate. One patient came to me for help periodically when she feared her frustrations with her husband would prompt rash behavior on her part. Another wife, who was almost pathologically monogamous, unable even to think of another man as attractive, occasionally would suddenly be sexually tempted by attractive men whom she might see when shopping or out alone, because her marital frustration tolerance had been exceeded.

Cora, like many of these basically faithful, completely loyal wives, suffered from a "give–get" imbalance. The demands upon her of husband, home and children were beyond her emotional capacities to give while still completing her own education . . . an education she felt was necessary for her whole future—for her interests, financial security, emotional development and physical and emotional health.

Cora had an in-depth awareness of her childhood patterns, previously analyzed intensively, especially that part most relevant to her marriage, namely the gross preference of her parents for her older brother. They had considered him the champion of the family and Cora's status was that of the little sister whose opinion was given no value or attention. Cora had mentioned the emotional support she got from other people, and this points up a situation I had seen several years earlier:

Two couples became close friends, although each husband and wife indulged in sex with the opposite husband and wife. It worked out because each wife gave the other husband something he did not get from his own partner; in return, each wife received from the other husband something she did not receive at home. The situation continued for years without sexual jealousy. However, some jealousy not of a sexual nature was eventually felt by one wife for the other: she thought the other woman was getting more from the two men in attention, consideration and support than she was.

SECTION VII:
SOME HAZARDS OF
MARRIAGE

Love is to the moral nature exactly what the sun is to the earth.

Balzac

Deceive not thyself by over-expecting happiness in the married state.

Fuller

30
AN INCIDENT OF PREGNANCY

This book is primarily about husbands and wives, but we cannot neglect to mention, however briefly, the great biological upshot of it all.

We distinguish *internal* disorders from ones that are chiefly *reactive* to forces of external circumstances. Some persons are or become disturbed, may even break down, under the most favorable conditions of life, no matter how kindly fate has treated them. Others remain stable in the face of outrageous fortune.

I had known Rosamond, as we will call her, since her girlhood. She was especially attractive in her healthiness, wholesomeness and good sense. She found her man—one of similar qualities—and they married and had three children in rapid succession. Roland was a good husband and father. He provided a small house and car and whatever the children needed, but never earned enough for Rosamond to have help with the house or children or any margin of surplus. Together they did everything, being skillful with maintenance of all kinds—painting, upholstering and the like. The children thrived and were healthy, bright and athletic. As they grew older, Rosamond began to have a little time for her friends. One thing she missed was vacations, just getting away from the same old show. Summertime was better because then she could get in some tennis at the neighborhood courts. So their lives passed in a routine, somewhat humdrum way.

In the midst of my dinner one evening Roland phoned and told me that Rosamond was weeping uncontrollably and was wild. I asked if she would speak to me on the phone. She did. I listened for a few minutes, told her I would be free after dinner, and asked her to come over with Roland in about three-quarters of an hour. This was deliberate on my part. I had judged that nothing dire would happen at the moment, and conveyed this reassurance by asking her to come a little later rather than immediately.

They arrived.   I asked Roland to wait while I talked privately with Rosamond. She was upset all right. She was wild. She was not totally out of control but was too near it for comfort. I knew her as a stable person and could not believe all this upset was from inner reasons; but human nature is full of surprises. By now the reader will have guessed the answer. This extreme hysterical state, which her husband thought was psychotic and was indeed so unlike her usual self that it could be called "out of her mind," was a violent reaction to the fact that her menstrual period had not occurred. The core of the reaction was unmitigated fear and rage—in general and at Roland in particular, whom she blamed for this.

Their children were now 14, 12, and 10. Rosamond had been a good mother and wife and for 16 years had discharged all her responsibilities, effectively but without relief and with very little time or legitimate indulgence for herself. It had been a simple life, a good life, but her "get–give" equilibrium had been out of balance— too much unremitting give, too little appropriate get.   She had been strong, stable, loving, uncomplaining.   But she had been incubating her plans.   With the youngest now 10, she felt she could get out of the house some at last.   She had found a position in an active small business.   Here she felt unchained from the kitchen and the nursery; she felt free; she had an outside interest. She saw new faces and was immersed in a larger interplay of relationships with varied persons.   She had found hard-earned partial freedom, variety, interest, change.   For her, life was beginning at 40.

And then the thunderclap.   Was she to lose all this and go back to the unrelieved restrictions and demands of pregnancy, home and a small baby all over again?   Her new life, for which she had worked long and hard and which was in all ways deserved and proper, suddenly at one stroke was threatened with destruction. If she lost it, she would be 50 years old before she would again have an opportunity for this sweet and precious share of partial freedom.   She felt trapped. And in truth she *was* trapped—by the crude physiology of reproduction and the prospective years of still more mothering.

She gave me permission to have a few words with Roland.   He could not believe that Rosamond could be so upset over being pregnant because he thought that "all women are delighted to have children." Of course, I suggested a laboratory test as soon as the result would be significant.   It came back negative, as is not infrequent in such cases. Thus the problem was resolved, and they returned peacefully to their fourth decade of life and are now well into their sixth.

In this instance I have not given Rosamond's "nuclear emotional pattern," her main dynamics and the "specific emotional vulnerability" that her missed menstrual period and supposed pregnancy struck. The reason is that it was not indicated to explore this in the emergency interview with her; in fact, it was strongly contraindicated. To go into it would have gained little at that point and probably would only have upset her even more, by shaking her self-confidence and distracting her from the external situation that so upset her. It was far better to treat this as a normal, intelligible reaction to a difficult situation that could be dealt with. In such cases it is a matter of looking into the externals before thinking of changing the patient to help her handle them. Can life be changed to fit the patient, or must the patient change to fit an unalterable situation? Is the problem chiefly *reactive* to external difficulties, or is it mostly *internal?* These questions are always among the first in the mind of the psychiatrist.

31
THE CHILDREN

Q: What is the best thing a father can do for his children?
A: Love their mother.

Train up a child in the way he should go: and when he is old, he will not depart from it.

Proverbs 22:6

If a child lives with criticism, He learns to condemn.
If a child lives with hostility, He learns to fight.
If a child lives with security, He learns to have faith.
If a child lives with approval, He learns to like himself.
If a child lives with acceptance and friendship,
He learns to find love in the world.

Whatever happens, it is the children who suffer. It is through the children that I often see the parents and their problems. Almost invariably, a child's symptoms are in reaction to pressures, conflicts and tensions of some kind in the home. "There are no problem children, only problem parents and situations." However there are sometimes dramatic exceptions in which pressures from outside the home affect the emotional equilibrium of the child. The principle of investigation is the same: exploration of the problem with one parent or both.

Jimmie and Janet were conscientious parents. Their oldest child, Jill, about nine, was beginning to have nightmares and anxiety; her *joie de vivre* was diminished; she was less outgoing, even a little withdrawn; and eventually her grades in school began to drop alarmingly from their usual high level. The parents called me. Rather than seeing the child, I asked them to come in first to tell me how it all looked to them.

By the time I met Jill, what she was reacting to had become pretty clear from my talks with her parents. As in most cases, it is much more important to remove, correct or at least diminish the

source and cause of the trouble—conflict between the parents—
than it is to "treat" the child. It was a fascinating experience to run
a clinic for children, in which I met and got to know each child a
little, but in which the basic treatment was only with the parents.
The results were most gratifying. Sometimes, as with Jill, it is
mostly a matter of reducing the contention between the parents.
In other cases it involves dealing with the mother's or father's feelings, attitudes and treatment of the children. Sometimes one parent
or both are merely misguided and require some education. At the
other extreme, one parent is incorrigible, and more must be done
therapeutically with the child to help him understand what he is
reacting to, and how to use his insights in order to develop properly
in spite of the traumatic situation with the parent.

For some years I was puzzled as to just why children seem to
react with such upset to conflict and hostility between their parents,
even if the parents both unquestionably love the child dearly, and
the child has good relations with both of them. Now it seems to
me that most generally this is because of the child's conflict of
identifications. As we have mentioned, we relate to other persons
as objects (of dependence, love, hate, sex and so on) and by identification (feeling with them, imitating them, taking over their attitudes,
empathizing with them, introjecting or taking them into one's own
mind). If the parents are in serious conflict, if there is much hostility between them, the child is torn. His dependent-love needs are
satisfied well enough, if the parents both love him, as Jimmie and
Janet loved Jill. But Jill could not use the usual paths of identification in her emotional maturing; she could not use them as patterns of adult maturity for her to grow into. For if she identified
with one parent, she was hostile to the other. In order to avoid
taking sides, she withdrew from identifying; thus she lost much of
this important way of relating to her parents and of following this
line of *being like them,* modeling herself on them, as a guide to
maturing.

A further deleterious effect on the child is the view of marriage
he obtains from the friction between the parents. Here again, if
this occurs early enough in his life and is sufficiently severe and
prolonged, then, as from all strong early influences, an emotionally
based concept of each parent and of marriage is formed in the
child's mind; and these early "imagoes" of the parents and of others

important to the child and the concepts of their emotional relations, once formed, are probably never fully erased. The child may thus grow up with a view that marriage is frustrating and hostile rather than loving and harmonious. And if the child does identify with one or both parents in this relationship, then the child to this extent brings feelings of frustration and hostility to his own spouse later.

In view of such considerations, I was eager to meet Jill but not to advise treatment unless the interview strongly indicated it. It is good for a child to have a psychiatrist as an understanding friend, but only provided he is the right psychiatrist for that child. At least as much as in the rest of medicine, the motto is *primum non nocere*—the first duty of treatment is to do no harm. We would much rather see problems within the family resolved within the family. We want to keep the parents as the main confidants and supports of the child. They are there all the time, through most of the child's life. And it is more natural for the child to solve his problems with his parents.

This need not deny the child any insights that psychiatry* can contribute, but the insights mostly can be imparted by the parents. The parents will achieve them by working with the psychiatrist on their own difficulties, and also by direct discussions of the child with the psychiatrist, who can suggest the insights and how to convey them to the child. This usually improves parent-child relations in an effective and natural way and helps the emotional growth of all concerned. Usually the analyst instructs the parents not to give insights as the psychiatrist would; they should mostly work them into dinner-table or bedtime conversations, and often they can do it indirectly by discussing some other person or a character on television

---

*The term psychiatry, as used throughout this book, always refers to dynamic psychiatry, that is, to psychological understanding and treatment based upon psychodynamics. Psychodynamics is the embryonic science of emotional motivation and reaction—the understanding of a person, his childish and mature impulses, in adjustment and maladjustment, in emotional health and in disorder. Freud made this great breakthrough in his discoveries, and now there are further contributions from all the sciences of the personality and behavior. Because of these further developments and contributions and because many analysts strongly prefer to use the term psychoanalysis in its narrow sense, restricted not only by theory but by the mechanics of treatment (for example, frequency of meetings, use of a couch and so on), it seems less controversial and more correct to use here the broad terms dynamic psychiatry and psychodynamics. Our purpose is insight and understanding, and treatment that is based upon knowing the dynamics of the individuals.

or in the comic strips. By such natural methods even the smallest children can be reached, with the parents always biding their time and waiting for the proper moments.

Of course, I mean all this as realistically and flexibly as possible, but shall not go into detail because our purpose is not a treatise on technique. Sometimes it is best for one psychiatrist alone to handle a marital problem, but the complications of so doing may outweigh the advantages. Sometimes occasional visits of the child to the psychiatrist are indicated—to the psychiatrist of both parents or, when they have different psychiatrists, to one or to the other. Sometimes it is best for the child to see a psychiatrist of his own. The child's visits, to whomever, are sometimes best kept few and far between; but in other instances systematic treatment is indicated. In these cases the psychiatrist should determine whether or not the parents are to some extent trying to *unload* onto him their own responsibilities for the child. The basic principle in all treatment is clear: *understand the patient.* In dealing with family problems it is a matter of understanding each of the personalities and the emotional interactions between them. [For an in-depth discussion of treatment, see Saul, L. J. (1972): *Psychodynamically Based Psychotherapy.* New York: Science House.]

The maternal function, like all drives and reactions, is subject to exaggerations, inhibitions and other distortions by the childhood emotional pattern. At one extreme was Milly. She had been the last of seven children. By the time she arrived, her mother was worn out and resented having yet another child to raise. Milly was a nuisance for her brothers and sisters, who only tolerated her and exploited her. She did everything to please them, even disagreeable tasks, just to get a few crumbs of acceptance, attention and inclusion in the family. Milly was the Cinderella of the family, and it was only some love from her father that saved her psyche. It was this sparse but loving relationship with her father that enabled her to marry at last and sustain a relation with her husband. Her feelings toward her mother and siblings were full of inner frustration and resentment, and following these patterns Milly had no good relationship in her adult life. Even that with her husband was far from harmonious, vitiated by many of the patterns to her mother and siblings. When her baby daughter arrived, she was the first human that Milly had ever been close to, and Milly had the child all to herself. The daughter was also dependent on Milly. She was the first human that did not fit one of the imagoes of her family, but was entirely removed from Milly's childhood patterns toward her parents and siblings. The result could be anticipated: Milly's total absorption in her baby and overmothering. Surprisingly, perhaps, the daughter survived the "smothering" very well it seemed, at least up to age 20, when I lost contact with both of them. There were three more children born to Milly, and all seemed to do well despite Milly's overprotective anxieties about them.   Milly had been rejected and excluded during her 0–6 and later continued to feel rejected, excluded and inferior in the community in which she lived.   She extended these feelings maternally to her four children and feared they would never "make it" as part of the elite in-group. There really was no elite "in-group," but Milly saw it this way because that is how she viewed her family, from whom she felt excluded.

Sally was the opposite of Milly: she was grossly neglected, rejected, undervalued.   Only two and one half years of a reasonably good acceptance from her father and the companionship of a younger sister and two cousins saved her stability, enabling her to marry when she reached adulthood. Unfortunately, her husband turned out to be a brute and threatened her very life. Sally survived and had three children. She was enormously attached to her son, her only truly good relationship. She was a conscientious mother who loved her children and wanted the best for them; but they all felt that something was lacking, and they did not get on well with Sally, becoming rather uncontrollable as adolescents.

Thus we see that mothering (and fathering also) can be strongly affected in many ways by childhood emotional patterns.

The devotion of the mother to the young is probably the model for loving, as we have said before, not only in human beings but biologically throughout the mammalian kingdom. Of course, it has its deviations and aberrations, and its examples of parents' mistreating and eating their offspring, but these instances seem to occur under exceptional circumstances such as starvation or when the animal is severely neurotic or even psychotic.

The father, as compared with the mother, is one remove from the child. He does not bear it or suckle it; he does not have the mother's intimacy of contact with it. (There are, however, always variations and exceptions—for example, it is the father sea horse who takes over the baby sea horses and carries them in a pouch similar to the pouch of the kangaroo.) The father's love for the young can also be powerful; he comes to it in part through providing for and protecting his mate and her offspring. Thus his activities, even in society, represent an output of energies devoted to the rearing of the young. It has been suggested that the creativity of men in the arts and sciences has been greater than that of women because this productivity represents the energies which the women put into the bearing and rearing of children.

In any event, and to whatever extent paternal love follows the model of maternal love, the mother's love for her child is probably the purest example and model of what true love is. Moreover, it is itself one of the central goals, if not the central goal, of the man's love for the woman, i.e., to make a home for the production and rearing of young. Such love is by no means confined to human beings, since other mammals and birds mate for long periods and even for life. In this, many of them have better records of stable marriages than do human beings.

The love of the mother for her child is not only a model for love but for maturity. The mother and her young, in humans and in other species, represent the essence of maturity and immaturity, respectively.

The offspring started life as a single cell. While within the womb it was completely parasitic. At birth it has to learn suddenly at least to breathe for itself, and soon thereafter has to learn to swallow and take in food for itself. Gradually it gains the use of its senses, powers of locomotion; gradually it comes to be less utterly, parasitically dependent upon the mother.

The mother represents the complement of this. The more parasitic the infant, the more giving must be the mother; the more helpless the child, the more protective must be the parent. The child sucks up energies, for its goal is its own growth and development. The mother pours out energies, for her goal is now to assure the best development of her offspring—not for any tangible return, not to fulfill her ambitions, not to support her, not for personal gain, but for the children's own sakes. To see them grow into lusty adulthood, able to be independent, to mate, to make their own way and to rear healthy wholesome offspring of their own—this is the essential of true maternal love and the pattern for true paternal love also.

This unselfish love of the mother for her child is also at the bottom of those feelings between human beings that make society possible. Human beings are not the only creatures to form societies. In fact almost all species do. One need only think of schools of fish, packs of wolves, hives of bees, flocks of birds. Only the exceptional species is not social. What holds these species in societies is not yet well known. No doubt it is a combination of many motives; but one powerful motive, as is evident from the study of human beings, lies in this capacity for love, which we see epitomized in the mother's relationship to the child.

"Love thy neighbor" is an ideal of Western culture, an ideal that is, as we all know to our sadness, only partially achieved. Many people try to love but cannot. And when we come to examine with great care why an individual is not able to love, we discover invariably that it is because he himself was not properly loved during the formative years of his childhood, that is, from conception to the age of six, seven or eight. Perhaps he was not loved at all, perhaps he was loved not wisely but too well, but always something was wrong in the attitudes and feelings of the parents toward him during his tenderest years; and the parent who is closest to him is usually the mother. Often, of course, it is not the mother but the father who is to blame, which recalls the quip: "What is the best thing a father can do for his children?" To which the answer is, "Love their mother."

If the child has not been loved with a primarily selfless interest in its own well-being and development, then, because of mistreatment, it develops reactions of resentment, rage and hostility. These appear in disorders of behavior, in depressions, in feelings of persecution, in headaches, in derangements of the stomach, heart and other organs. Indeed, the functional neuroses and psychoses represent, as Freud said years ago, failures in the development of the ability to love. The failure of this development means that there are inner irritants—inner feelings of rejection, for example, or of being dominated—feelings of being in some way mistreated.

These inner threats and irritants in turn generate hatred; and this hostility and vengefulness appear not only in the form of neurotic, psychotic and psychosomatic symptoms but also in behavior in life.

Thereby such hostility underlies frank criminality and white-collar criminality, and at bottom it is the grass-roots cause of war. A few evil individuals could not rise to power and lead a great nation into revolt or war if there were not a great deal of hostility throughout the population ready to be channeled by such leaders into open violence.

To rear children is not easy. Their animal instincts must be domesticated to civilized social living, but this must be accomplished without upsetting their emotional relationships with their parents.

The greatest single influence in their lives will be that of their mother, who during the earliest years is the one closest to them. If this love is pure, then the core of the child's personality will be sound, and it will be strong to withstand the onslaughts of life.

And this unselfish disinterested love of the mother toward her child should be emblazoned for us as a model of mature attitudes and behavior. From the picture of mother and child one can see what is mature and what is infantile; one can see the child's ego-centric, parasitic "demandingness" and the mother's mature capacity for meeting the needs of the still weak and helpless creature for its very survival.

The evils and suffering of mankind are mostly the results of improper childrearing, which foredooms the children to becoming insufficiently mature mothers and fathers. I have heard, although I have been unable to completely confirm it, that the Hopi and Mojavi Indians consider anyone who strikes a child to be psychotic, a matter of direct relevance to statistics on our "battered babies" and "battered wives."

But the voice of reason is persistent. As mankind gradually learns, becomes conscious of and appreciates the significance of emotional maturity and what goes into the development of this capacity, we may move nearer to these goals, and thereby further away from the results of impaired maturity and impaired capacity to love, namely, neurosis, psychosis, criminality, disease, violence, cruelty and war. We can move toward development and adaptation, toward strength, stability, cooperation.

The model is the mother's love for her child. Truly, the hand that rocks the cradle rules the world.

We have seen that personality and sexual development are complex, as are the early life experiences, marriage and parenthood; but the principles of childrearing—and when talking about the child we talk of the marriage, too—seem to be relatively simple, although practically hard to achieve. Theoretically they are not too difficult to formulate: in the first place the motto should be that of the surgeon—*primum non nocere*—do no harm. Parents should be acquainted with the pitfalls of childrearing: overprotection and underprotection, pushing a child into too much responsibility or not letting him take enough, not socializing him enough or socializing him too suddenly, too early, too harshly or too consistently or inconsistently—deprivation, domination, depreciation and hostility.

The child must be socialized, but this can be done by a gradual process that it can accept. What is of the utmost importance is to keep good emotional relations with the child. Parents ask, "Is it all right to spank the child, or is it better to scold him, or what should I do?" The answer depends upon the individual, and the touchstone should be whether, in the handling of the child, the child still loves the parent. Is it still a good relationship? Is it warm, friendly, easy? If you can socialize the child, handle him, even punish him if necessary (and I question whether punishing children is ever essential and not a symptom of mishandling) and at the same time *maintain a basically good human relationship.* you have prepared, you have preserved the pattern of good relationships in later life that is the core of a healthy personality.

This result assumes that the training of the child has been favorable to his development. If his training has not been favorable, it can either inhibit or exaggerate parts of the development. For example, the period of toilet training is usually the period of *general* training. If the parents are too dominating and too demanding in other ways, they may apply these attitudes to toilet training in particular. "You can't go to school and you can't do this and you can't do that unless you first succeed on the toilet and show that your bowels are all right." Of course, this kind of after-breakfast demand belongs to an era that hopefully is in the past. But the parent who is overly strict about toilet training is not apt to be in other respects open and broad and tolerant and helpful to the child's development.

It is interesting how often, if you analyze patients—or if you don't analyze them but just listen to their stories—you find people who have the problem of domination and submission. I saw a young man recently whose feeling was that he was unhappy about himself.

He was always more or less enraged because he always felt that he had to "be a good boy," and he had to "be a good boy" because that was how he got along. He was good, and he did get along. But it bothered, in fact enraged, him. Why should he be disturbed about it? Because he felt that in his own family the price of getting along was submission. For him, to be good was not to be good as an adult who enjoyed his life but to be submissive to his parents.

As a corollary to gradual socialization ("the inevitability of gradualness"), the parents should provide a setting of emotional warmth for the child, just as you provide the warmth of the sunshine and good soil for your plants or flowers to grow in. Provide all this, and let the child develop. For instance, if he looks cute, you don't rush over to him and pick him up and start to hug and kiss and cuddle him just because he's adorable. He was doing all right and was happy and cute the way he was, and you don't run in and do something about it, even though you have the impulse to. All of which involves a little understanding of, and object interest in, the child. ("Love them and leave them alone.")

Let us look at two brief examples of intensified sensuality of local zones resulting from unthinking use of the child by the parent. A young man's complaint was that he had irresistible impulses to kiss men while riding in trains. In the whole structure of the case there was one fact that emerged strongly: the amount of actual kissing on the mouth that his father had done to him when a baby had greatly exaggerated his oral sexuality. We see a similar situation in a patient who came from a different culture. In his culture, parents do not inhibit the sexual play of children the way we do. There, one way that little boys play together is by getting into a kind of chain, nude, pressed each behind the other, and this fellow had his anal sensations very much stimulated. As in the first case, although psychologically the man grew out of it pretty much, married and had a family and made a go of things, there still lurked latent in the background a high degree of anal sensation that was strong enough that he had homosexual fantasies, as well as a tendency to anal masturbation which led to orgasm and so on.

This is a rather typical result when stimulation of a particular area becomes mechanical. From parents who are stimulating to the child's genitals we get one source of nymphomania and satyriasis; and from parents who are afraid of any manifestation of sexuality, we get persons who are inhibited sexually. Everybody has within himself a residue of all sensations and reactions.

It is essential that the child develop through the unfolding of his nature and potentialities. This nature is to develop from a passive-receptive-dependent (PRD) child into a responsible-productive-independent (RPI) adult. Every grown-up remains a child to some extent. It is a case of enjoying *both* sides of every sensation and situation, the childlike and the mature, in ways that do not harm the person himself or others.

Some mention must be made, too, of the child's need for love that is at the bottom of most great rivalries among children. A child wants to be loved as much as or more than his brother or sister is. The brother or sister comes along, and the child fights because he wants to be loved exclusively. These rivalries are inevitable, but they can be handled if the parent is forewarned. If he knows, for instance, that sibling rivalry is a virulent thing, a powerful force that the little ones have to struggle with, then it can be fitted in with the course of development. You cannot stop it by a mere discussion. But you can help it tremendously, even in a child five or six years old, if you discuss the fact of envy and rivalry and wishes for love and keep it in the child's language. We must translate for the child and get across the feeling that we understand these things that all children experience. Sometimes it produces a tremendous effect to say that you have had the same experience yourself: "Oh, I know what a hard time you are having with little Willie, but let me tell you about my experiences with little Annie when I was only four years old." And then explain that a sibling may be a nuisance, but having one is better than growing up as an only child.

There is probably a natural competition with the parent of the same sex, but this, too, is only part of growing up unless bad child-rearing heightens or distorts it. There is a huge literature on this, but I think the child grows naturally in the masculine or feminine direction if he or she is simply let alone. The inevitable rivalries and problems in the human relations of the growing child can be handled by a parent who does not have great technical knowledge but does have human interest and sympathy and the capacity to communicate with the child. The essential point is for the parents to avoid the common abuses in childraising and keep good feelings.

To develop properly the child needs good models. If he has fairly mature, well-balanced parents with whom to identify, he can stand a great deal of abuse and still turn into a fairly well-balanced adult.   If, on the other hand, he has infantile, fixated, regressed, hostile, aggressive, passive-receptive-dependent parents, than he models himself on them.   I think that is the practical difficulty in preventing neurosis, psychosis, criminality and all the other emotional disorders that result from faulty childraising.   These maladjustments are mostly the effects of injurious treatment of the child during his formative years. We have made only a beginning in preventive psychiatry, but it seems possible in time to produce responsible-productive-independent people by avoiding the grossest abuses in childrearing.

We have seen that growth to responsible adulthood is directly influenced by the child's relationships with his parents and those closest to him in the earliest years. Healthy, honest questions about sex that are answered with openness by one's parents will help the development to normal, natural sexual and emotional maturity. If the parents are incapable of this, they should arrange for the child to see a physician or any other good professional who is qualified. Do not forget identification: we have seen that the boy whose father mistreats his mother tends to mistreat his own wife that way when he marries, with consequent warping of their children.

32
SOME LEGAL ASPECTS OF MARRIAGE, SEPARATION AND DIVORCE

When I was a much younger man, I remember my father telling me that the only time he ever obtained a successful result in a divorce case was when he reconciled the parties. On a number of occasions he succeeded in doing so. This is a backhanded way of saying that, while the other side of the fence might look greener, this is not always the case, or that those who suffer most in the divorce process are normally the children.

However, there are also many cases where the only solution is separation and divorce, or at least, a temporary separation, possibly followed by reconciliation, or if that cannot be accomplished, by a divorce at a later date.

In order to understand the legal aspects of separation and divorce it is necessary first to understand the legal aspects of marriage itself.

Marriage

Put in simplest legal terms, marriage is a legal contract between two persons of opposite sex. (Recently two young men tried to marry one another in a southern state, and the court held that marriage between people of the same sex was unlawful and not a marriage.) This contract must be made in accordance with the statutes of the particular state in which the marriage occurs.

The requirements for a contract of marriage vary from state to state. Many states have laws requiring physical examinations to ensure that neither party has any one of a number of diseases which would make it impossible to make a valid marriage contract. Also, in some states notice must be given for a specific length of time before the marriage takes place. This is known colloquially as the

---

*Mr. Duane is senior partner of the Philadelphia law firm of Duane, Morris & Heckscher. We are enormously indebted to him for this clear, concise chapter.

"waiting period." In other words, the parties apply for a license, a specified time must elapse before they receive it, and during that waiting period certain things must be done. If you want to be sure that you are contracting a valid marriage, it is well to consult a lawyer who knows the state laws. In all states, as far as I know, it is generally necessary to have witnesses to the marriage, the number being stated by statute.

Marriage ceremonies can be performed by certain designated persons, usually judges, mayors or other city officials, and in all states (so far as I know without exception) by clergymen and priests of recognized religions.

In some states two people need only stand up together and declare before witnesses that they are married. The Quaker ceremony consists of just that, and constitutes a marriage without a minister, mayor or other government official, but it does require a license.

In some states common law marriage is recognized. This can be marriage without benefit of license and occurs when two people live together and by their declarations to a third person indicate that they are married.

Living together under the name of "Mr. and Mrs." is not sufficient by itself in some cases to constitute a common law marriage; it must be accomplished by evidence showing that the individuals *intended* to be married. A man who goes to a motel for the weekend with a lady friend and registers as "Mr. and Mrs. Smith" does not ordinarily intend marriage. However, if without any marriage ceremony or license this same man and woman lived together for a considerable period of time, designated themselves as "Mr. and Mrs.," thereafter stated to various people that they were married and in other ways acted as married people, this would be evidence they had intended to be married and would probably constitute a valid common law marriage in some states.

Rights of Married People

Having entered into a marriage contract in one of the above ways, the parties immediately have certain rights. These can be classified into two groups—personal rights and property rights.

Personal rights include: the right formally to be known as married people; the legal right for the wife to be known as "Mrs.";

the right to have sexual relations without fear of being accused of adultery, fornication or other crimes; the right to bear legitimate children; the right of those children to be considered legitimate offspring with the accompanying personal and property rights that title ensures; and many others.

The second rights obtained by marriage are property rights. Automatically upon marriage both husband and wife acquire rights in the property of the other, principally the dower rights of the wife and the curtesy rights of the husband. These go back to earliest English law and first meant that in the event of the death of either, the surviving spouse automatically acquired legal interest in the real estate standing in the name of the deceased spouse. Today by statute these rights have been extended in most states to include sharing in property other than real estate. It is significant that generally neither husband nor wife can dispose of real estate owned by one without the signature of the other. In community property states this right ordinarily is even greater.

As the parties go on living together, their financial and property interests become more and more entwined. If either one dies, in most states, the survivor automatically is entitled to a definite share of the other's estate, whether or not it is left to him or her in the will of the deceased. For instance, if the husband dies and leaves all his money to his children, his wife in most states has the right immediately to claim against his will, and can take a fraction of his estate outright.

Another property right is the right to support. The wife is automatically entitled to be supported by her husband. In some states the law is changing in this basic concept: husbands now have certain rights to be supported by their wives under certain circumstances, such as when the wife has income and the husband does not, or when the wife is working and the husband is not. As women's liberation progresses, women are obtaining a large number of rights to new jobs and other rights for which they are fighting, while at the same time they are gaining many new responsibilities. Thus, in many states if a husband and wife are both working, the wife has just as much of a duty to support the children as the husband has. This right can be enforced by the children or by guardians of the children in the courts. Where both have independent income, it is a factor in the amount of support one owes the other.

Another very important property right for the wife is that she can buy necessaries and charge them to her husband, and he is liable for them to third parties.

Separation and Settlements

Now the husband and wife have been married for some time, and things are beginning to deteriorate. They nag and fight and fuss— the children get on their nerves—they don't have enough money— bills are too great. The husband is playing around with other women, or the wife unjustly thinks he is. She has found a boyfriend at the club or the neighborhood bowling alley or bar, and her husband becomes jealous. They gradually grow apart. Their romance is going out the window, and sympathetic people of the opposite sex are always willing to listen to their troubles and tell them in turn how awful their own spouses are. Perhaps the couple just realize they are totally incompatible. They might swear at one another or humiliate one another in public. One strikes the other, etc. Their dissatisfaction with each other may be more dignified, the wounds suffered going much deeper, so that one or the other is tremendously unhappy and uncertain as to what to do—and wishes to settle matters the best way he or she can. Finally one of them goes to a lawyer for advice and tells the other, who in turn sees his own lawyer, and the fat is in the fire. Their marriage is on the rocks, or whatever other cliché one wishes to use.

The Function of Lawyers

Let's assume that this couple have consulted good lawyers–lawyers who know the law, lawyers with experience in this area, lawyers who can advise on tax matters, lawyers with high standards of ethics, morals and fairness, who have sympathy for the problems with which they deal. Without doubt such good lawyers are to whom married persons in trouble should turn.

What will such good and experienced lawyers do? First they will collect the facts from their respective clients. They will ask each client to write out in longhand all his or her grievances and the entire history of the marriage: when it happened, where it happened, who was there, whether they got on well on their wedding night, whether they have satisfactory sex relations, if they were happy in each other's company, etc. And then the couple should write out a complete year-by-year account of what went wrong, what instances they consider to be grievances and causes for a separation or a divorce. These statements cannot be too complete. The more complete they are, the better job the lawyers can do.

Second, the lawyers will obtain information regarding the parties' children: their names, dates of birth and facts about the parents' relationships with the children.

Third, both clients must be 100 percent frank with their lawyers, giving them a complete list of what each owns and what they believe the other party owns. The lists should include real estate, securities, insurance policies, bank accounts, trust funds, automobiles, federal and state tax returns, and so forth. If property settlements are reached based on incomplete information concerning ownership of property and its extent, and other items involved, there is always the possibility that either party may set aside the settlement on the ground that it was obtained by a fraudulent statement of the property and financial worth of the other.

Each lawyer must then determine what his client wants and is willing to do, particularly regarding custody and care of the children.

Equipped with all this information, the lawyers then discuss with their clients and with each other their clients' stories. Each lawyer is faced with four problems:

1. Care and custody of the children.

2. Grounds for divorce: If either party wants a divorce, each lawyer must find out if either party has *grounds* for divorce or to defend against divorce. In many states it is still necessary to have grounds for divorce, although many states have laws that permit divorce by agreement of the parties, usually after a certain period of separation. The grounds and the methods for obtaining divorce available to an injured party can be judged and decided upon after each lawyer examines his client's statement of facts.

3. The question of support of the wife and the husband.

4. Financial settlement: whether or not there should be any financial settlement, and in what amount. Should it include payments of cash, division of real estate, division of the personal and household effects, the establishment of trust funds and things of that nature?

[In those cases where the individuals do not have substantial assets, some of the following points will not apply.]

All the above considerations take time and many meetings. Some discussions will be held by the lawyers with their respective clients, some by the lawyers with each other: sometimes four persons will be present—the two parties and each of their lawyers. If it appears that a separation is necessary, the lawyers will prepare an agreement covering the four points above. Usually the separation, custody and support agreement will contain a clause providing that the agreement is effective whether or not either of the parties sues for divorce. After all this has been accomplished, the agreement will be signed.

In those cases where the parties have substantial property, there are many problems, including tax problems, which arise. For example, are certain payments to be made by one party to the other based on a division of property? Are they payments for support, for instance of the wife, or are they payments for the support of the children? Are they gifts from one party to the other, and how and to whom will such payments be taxed? Also, should provisions be made in the agreement for the wills of the respective parties, covering the way they will leave their money in the event of death? Should life insurance be taken out to insure the carrying out of the agreement in the event of the husband or wife dying during the time the children are minors? Are certain payments taxable? Should joint income tax returns be filed, or should each party file his own tax return? What division should be made of the household effects and property, etc.?

There are ownership problems to be solved: who owns what, is it owned outright by one of the parties, jointly by both or as tenants in common, or tenants by the entireties, or is it community property in the community property states?

When substantial property is involved, there are chances of being severely taxed, on the one hand, or opportunities to save taxes otherwise due, on the other. Therefore, it is extremely important that the parties have on their team someone with a thorough knowledge of estate, income, gift, and other tax matters, both state and federal.

It must be remembered that agreements made between the father and mother are not necessarily binding on the children because the courts in the jurisdiction where the children are physically present have continuing jurisdiction over the welfare of the children of divorced persons. At any time either parent or some other interested party can go to a court to ask the court's protection of the children, both physically and in terms of their support and maintenance. In such proceedings the only test that the court applies is what is in the best interest of the children. All judges try to work out a fair solution to family problems involving the children of separated or divorced persons.

In connection with these agreements, it is important that they not be collusive, as that term may be defined by the law of the state having jurisdiction. In many states it is required, and generally it is good practice that the agreement for separation, custody, support and division of the property be shown to the Master in divorce, to the Court, and in some cases incorporated as part of the court decree.

It is usual and desirable that one paragraph in the agreement specifically state that the signing of the agreement shall not in any way affect either party's right to sue for divorce or to defend against any divorce action brought by the other.

Other clauses provide that each party gives up all rights against the other, except for rights contained in the agreement.

Many agreements provide that subsequent disputes between the parties shall be settled by arbitration.

Sometimes negotiations are long-drawn-out, tough and marked by great bitterness. A determining factor is the relative strength of the bargaining positions of the parties, and this depends on the facts of each case, such as which of the parties most wishes the divorce and what are the real grounds for divorce, and whether good grounds exist.

In the event no agreement can be reached regarding separation, care and custody of the children, support and division of property, the entire negotiation must be abandoned and go into litigation in the state court having jurisdiction of the parties and the subject matter. Then the rights of the parties will be decided by the court in accordance with the statutes and decisions applicable in that state. Generally speaking, such a solution of the problem is to be avoided if at all possible. Such contests are expensive, harassing, tedious and unsatisfactory, often leaving scars that never heal; and the children always suffer.

To repeat, the reaching of agreement covering these subjects is much to be desired.

It is fully realized that in the case of persons of modest means the agreement may be short and simple.   However, the provisions covering separation, custody and care of the children, the amount of support for the children, wife or husband and the division of whatever property the couple have are still a necessary part of the agreement unless the parties, in the absence of such an agreement, leave these questions to be decided by the court.

Jurisdiction

It is vitally important that if court action is necessary, matters pertaining to separation, custody, support and division of property, as well as the divorce, be decided by a court having jurisdiction of the parties and the subject matter.   It is also vital that if a divorce be obtained, it be recognized throughout the world, or at least in the United States.

No subject has caused more litigation than the question of what state has jurisdiction to grant the divorce.   This matter is still so complicated that each party's lawyer must be asked about it.   It is too complex and changes too fast to be covered in this short chapter.

If someone suggests that you obtain a "quickie" divorce in a few days, either in another state or in a foreign country such as Haiti, Mexico or the Dominican Republic, be sure to get the best lawyer you can to advise you.   Such divorces can cause serious problems, particularly if you wish to remarry.

All states, so far as I know, require the moving party or plaintiff in a divorce case to be a resident of the state at the time the case is begun.   Residence is usually defined in terms of physical presence within that state for a required period of time.

Generally speaking, if the husband and wife have been living together with their children for a number of years in the same state, that state has jurisdiction.   Other states or even countries may have jurisdiction under certain circumstances, but these circumstances and the laws in existence at the time of the proceedings must be studied and a legal opinion obtained before any proposed court action is begun.

Once the court has properly taken jurisdiction over a divorce action, it also usually acquires jurisdiction over property rights of the parties.

In most states, including those where the laws provide for granting a divorce without regard to the fault of the parties, there is also provision for alimony, which is a court order requiring one person to make payments for the other's support. Such orders are in addition to any orders for support of the children.

Today in many states the court having jurisdiction over the divorce action is authorized to order a division of the parties' property between them as equity and fairness require. This includes property owned separately by each spouse. For example, when the husband has been employed and the wife has stayed at home and taken care of the household and family, and when the husband has acquired securities and other property as a result of his employment, some courts have ordered the husband to transfer some of his assets to his wife at the time of the divorce on the theory that she has indirectly contributed to their acquisition.

While in "no fault" states fault is irrelevant in granting a divorce, it may nevertheless be a factor affecting either the alimony or the division of property, or both. If one spouse has been guilty of serious misconduct, his or her alimony may be reduced or even eliminated, and the share of property that the spouse is likely to receive may be similarly affected.

Grounds for Divorce

Originally, under early law, adultery was the principal legal ground for divorce. Times have changed! Grounds differ from state to state and country to country. The most generally recognized causes today are adultery; desertion for a definite period; cruelty, both physical and mental; insanity; and inability physically to consummate the marriage. In recent years some states have passed statutes establishing so-called no fault divorces, whereby it is possible for the parties to agree to be divorced after having been separated for a certain length of time. Such agreements must be properly made and recorded in court or other proceedings.

The Catholic Church does not recognize any causes for divorce. For a couple to terminate their marriage and be able to remarry in the Catholic Church, the marriage must be *annulled*, i.e., found never to have existed.

In some Protestant churches, only the innocent party in a divorce may be remarried in a church ceremony, and sometimes hearings are held by a lawyer appointed by the church to determine which spouse is the innocent party.

It is best for those to whom the views and rulings of the religious denominations to which they belong are important, to consult their priest or minister before contemplating or commencing actions for divorce.

Once a divorce action has been filed in a court having jurisdiction of the parties and subject matter, usually a Master will be appointed, testimony will be given before the Master or in court, briefs may be filed, and the court will render its decision.

If a divorce is granted, a decree is entered signed by the judge, and, after a statutory period has passed to allow for appeals, the decree becomes final, the bonds of matrimony are dissolved, and each party may legally remarry, at least so far as the civil law is concerned.

In Conclusion

During this long period of working out the legal details, enormous emotions are involved on both sides; and in all my years of legal practice I have never met a doctor who could contribute more to such situations than Leon Saul, the author of this book. Lawyers are primarily responsible for negotiating the settlement and clearing things up in court, but they cannot be blind to the medical, psychological and physiological problems that have been described in previous chapters. While the lawyer can add tremendously to a constructive solution when homes are breaking up or have already been broken, his chances of a successful conclusion for both the parties involved and also their children are greatly enhanced if he works closely with ministers, marriage counselors, psychologists, psychiatrists, family physicians and other medical doctors. Acting as counselor in domestic marital problems usually represents a financial sacrifice compared with other kinds of legal work, but there are great rewards to be obtained for those who find themselves able to contribute to the welfare of the husband and wife, their children and other members of the family. In so doing, they have engaged in a most worthwhile effort. As my father said, the only divorce cases you really win are those in which the parties become reconciled and live together happily thereafter.

Caution: The above overview of the legal situation involving marriage, separation and divorce should be useful to anyone interested in the subject. However, it must be emphasized that in every case *the laws of the state having jurisdiction will govern,* and a practicing lawyer in that state should be consulted.

33
DIVORCE

Better by far . . . forget and smile,
Than . . . remember and be sad.

Christina Rossetti,
"A Birthday"

For the race is run by one and one and never by two and two.

Rudyard Kipling

This is life's sorrow:
That one can be happy only where two are.

Edgar Lee Masters,
Spoon River Anthology

How you live your life depends upon the uncontrollable circumstances in which you find yourself as an infant, child and adult, upon the circumstances of your own making such as marriage and, of course, upon your particular personality, which is primarily composed of your childhood patterns of emotional forces, i.e., of motivations and reactions, instinctive and conditioned. These factors determine your choice of spouse, and how well or poorly you get on in life, in the marital state in general and with your specific spouse. Some men and women cannot tolerate, let alone enjoy, so close and intimate a relation with any other person; others cannot get on with a particular individual as spouse, but do make a harmonious marriage with someone else.

We once became close friends with a handsome, healthy, charming couple. The wife, Polly, had been married before, but shortly after the first wedding found she had "goofed," and rapidly and successfully terminated the marriage. Less than a year later she married her present husband, and that marriage has lasted 20 happy years.

A young man who graduated from professional school with me and found his wife becoming increasingly hostile feared that a divorce would take an important part of his income for a long period of time. But he found that his wife could tolerate him no better than he could stand her, and she was entirely fair and accepted a reasonable settlement, giving him his freedom. He, too, made a satisfactory second marriage.

Statistics seem to indicate that second marriages are generally not much more stable than first marriages.* I guess there is no way to know if the second tries are happier—perhaps some partners, because of their age or for other reasons do not want to go through another divorce and remarriage. In my experience it takes 10 or 15 years to make a marriage; those who have learned this are loath to go through all this adjustment to a new spouse. (For further statistics on divorce in the United States, see Chapter 6.) Most divorced people tend to marry other divorced people, and most remarry soon, within an average of three years. Up to age 24, divorced men and women have the same chance of remarrying. But from age 25 to 44 the number of divorced men remarrying is almost double that of divorced women. From 45 to 65 men remarry two and a half times more than do women, which seems to argue that a woman should leave a bad marriage as soon as possible. The men who remarry have a pool of potential wives with a wider age range than women, whose choice is limited to a relatively small number of available men in their own age bracket or older (Westoff, 1975).

Those who come to an analyst because of marital problems are not a representative sample, except insofar as they exemplify those individuals who are undecided upon action and hope for guidance, through insight and by seeing themselves through the eyes of a professional with long experience. Chapter 9, "A Paradigm of Marriage," sketched briefly how analytic procedure helped to resolve the unavoidable divorce of one couple and subsequently aided both parents and their children in making harmonious later marriages.

---

*The current population report of the Bureau of Census, P-20, 297, 1976, puts the lifetime risk rate for divorce in first marriages at 37 percent; the lifetime risk rate for second marriages is 40 percent. This seems to indicate that the success rate for second marriages is not significantly different from first marriages. (We are indebted to Dr. Harold Leif, director of the Philadelphia Marriage Council, for these statistics.)

The analyst sees many individuals whom he successfully helps through the crises of decision and the sometimes inevitable divorce, but whom he is not able to aid in achieving a successful remarriage. It depends on the specific individual and the circumstances. One woman of middle age with grown children, Nora, had a husband, Francis, who was chronically unhappy and dissatisfied, and who could not stand his wife's energy, drive, success and popularity because of his own childhood pattern of defeated sibling rivalry. Once when they were house guests and his wife was the center of conversation and attention, he reacted by becoming depressed. She left that house party several days before his departure to attend one of her activities; he immediately recovered his good spirits and enjoyed himself immensely when he replaced his wife in the attentions of the others. Francis sought analytic help in an effort to save the marriage, which had been intolerable to him for many years. The reasons for his unhappiness emerged clearly: Nora, through her love of attention and admiration, struck her husband's specific emotional vulnerability (Saul, 1971), his sibling rivalry.   But its intensity was too great to be influenced therapeutically in a reasonable length of time.   His family circumstances had changed too soon after his birth, through the death of his mother: and Francis was thereafter rejected and his older sister strongly and openly favored by the stepmother.   This sense of rejection, frustration and dissatisfaction and of defeat by his older preferred sister had become too intrinsic a part of his personality to be reduced rapidly enough to save his marriage.   Not only did his feeling of rejection disturb his marriage, but it permeated his whole life.   He suffered severely, feeling like a rejected unwanted child despite his outward success.

After many years of faithfulness to Nora, Francis sought relief in friendship with Anita.   Anita had sustained a chronically unhappy life because of the inconsiderateness and unconscious hostility of her husband, and its indirect effect had been unhappiness for their children.   Over the months his platonic friendship of mutual sympathy became increasingly eroticized until it climaxed in an all-out sexual affair.   At that point, Anita felt secure enough to leave her unhappy marriage and try for a divorce, which came through in less than a year.   Now Francis, more and more desperate in his married life, decided to divorce Nora, although they were both nearing 50.   He saw it as a sort of last-chance effort to escape his misery.   Through analysis, he realized that this unhappiness lay within himself, but consciously he thought that life might ameliorate without delay what analytic help could not.   Francis had tried to change himself to fit his wife's dynamics; now, selfish though it was, he would try to change his life to fit his own dynamics.

What is learned emotionally in analysis must be worked through in real life.   But Francis had not worked through the fact that, in the depths of his feelings, the act of divorcing his wife was like "killing off" his sister, and this could only increase his guilt, fixing him more firmly in this masochistic state of misery that had pervaded his entire life in spite of every success he made financially, professionally and in the love of women.   He thought that Nora would not be hurt too much—she was from a prominent Chicago family, successful in a fascinating career, widely admired and in demand socially, a beautiful and independent personality.   To Francis, she seemed invulnerable.   Divorce would not slay her; he could afford to be selfish.

Anita lacked Nora's vivid, radiant personality; thus she was less a sibling competitor as well as more dependent and therefore less a parent figure for Francis.   But this was the only improvement in his change of circumstances.   It seemed as though fate was favoring Francis when Nora soon remarried an excellent man whom they had both known for years, whose marriage had suddenly exploded.   This should have eliminated any residual guilt in Francis, for Nora had seemingly improved her lot.   But in fact Nora found the road ahead rough and painful: she had sunk her entire life into Francis; for him, she had left her own parental home and family, embraced his whole clan and become an important figure in it.   In her new marriage she developed a new identity, with a happier husband and an interesting career open to her.   What could make difficulties in such a life? Partly, the principle of inertia, and also the fact that despite her popularity and success, she was essentially a one-man woman for whom the marriage had struck deep.   Although there was no danger of her breaking down, becoming depressed or withdrawn, she was still a "scorned woman."   Her indomitable spirit helped her control her anger, but she did become irritable and crotchety as she strove to make the new adjustment while approaching the threshold of old age.

If such a woman as Nora—stable, strong, beautiful, talented, brilliant, popular, a devoted wife and mother, absorbed in an interesting career and remarried to a superior man who loves her—can nevertheless be made miserable and irritable by an unwanted divorce and rejection, what can we expect the average wife to suffer?

If the husbands like Francis were to go on to some measure of personal happiness, much improved even if not ecstatic, then some concept of abstract morality might justify it. But happiness is so much *within* (Saul, 1977) that the dynamics which made the husband unhappy in his marriage often continue to do so after the divorce.

By contrast, the lot of a man suddenly deserted by his wife is apt to be much less arduous and tragic. The pain of rejection by his mate may be no less, but "for man it is a thing apart, 'tis woman's whole existence." Colin by age 40 had built his own small business; it adequately supported him, his wife and two children. He felt nicely stabilized in life. But his wife's "time bomb," the pathology in her childhood emotional pattern, went off suddenly for no reason he could determine. She became hostile, impossible to live with, and insisted on divorce. Colin was rocked to the core, and because he thought her somewhat unstable, he managed to get custody of their son and daughter. He lost interest in his business because he "no longer had a wife to work for." As usual, a man as attractive as Colin soon had many women "in hot pursuit." Perhaps this is one reason many husbands are so ready to leave their wives: other women are so readily available. Ancient wisdom says that the natural ally of woman is woman. Isak Dinesen wrote a short story ("The Sailor's Tale") asserting this. But today it is not so. Since "the pill" has been introduced, men can easily find plenty of women ready for companionship and sex with or without marriage, especially if the man has an adequate income. But Colin was a one-woman man, and could not indulge in promiscuous sex or remarry just for the sake of being married. He devoted himself to his children and to sports.

Gradually Colin pulled himself out of his depression. His ex-wife remained hateful, trying to get every cent from him by repeated legal actions. Then, ten years later, she remarried, and Colin, nearing 50, fell in love with a married woman of 40 who had several children. She was very proper, as was Colin, and there was no possibility of an affair. But such is the power between the sexes which we call "love" that it gave Colin the lift he needed. He became close friends with the woman and her husband, and received undisguised affection from their children. This family put in him a complete trust that they never betrayed, supporting him emotionally in the face of his ex-wife's interminable onslaughts. They considered Colin's wife to be slightly crazy, a psychotic personality (Saul and Warner, 1977) or in some way emotionally sick. Thus it was that Colin, after ten difficult years, came back on his feet with his grown healthy son and daughter, working hard to rebuild his business and thinking seriously of remarriage when he met the right woman and of rebuilding a home, but this time without planning to bring new babies into the world.

The degree of maturity in both marital partners has a direct bearing on the success or failure of the relationship; in clinical practice one sees many marriages involving such dire mistakes that they should and must be corrected by annulment or divorce. Yet if divorce ensues and the partners remarry, happiness is not the inevitable outcome, for happiness, as we have said, is so much within.

Emma Failed to act early in her marriage when a basic incompatibility surfaced, and tragedy followed: She found after a few months of marriage that Ed was subject to severe depressions. Instead of getting expert advice, she decided to "stick it out," in hopes that marriage and children would cure him. (It is not fair, realistic or workable to use marriage or the birth of children for therapy.) He got worse and became abusive; eventually Ed had periodic hospital admissions for his depressions, and between these bouts was vile and often violent to Emma and their three children. Life with Ed became increasingly intolerable for her, and they agreed to divorce. But by now Ed had lost his secure white-collar position, and divorce was more than the simple matter of separating—Emma would need support for herself and the children. Ed became even more hostile and did not want to commit any future income to their care. After much ill feeling and frustration, he moved to another state where he obtained a legal statement saying he was mentally ill and could not be expected to provide support. So the entire financial and emotional burden fell on Emma. What masochism! She had recognized soon after their marriage that Ed was mentally ill, but went ahead anyway with the birth of three children. What hostility! This typifies one aspect of nature, which sees to the reproduction of children but apparently totally disregards the mental and physical health of either parents or children.

Divorce is neither virtue or evil in itself—like intelligence, it depends on *how it is used.* Is it used hostilely and destructively, for punishment, or is it a realistic, necessary step for both and for the existing or potential children?

Some men feel that they are rationally seeking the good of both partners when they announce after many years of marriage that they want to "change their life-style" and obtain their "freedom." But the hostility shows through when they insist on their own happiness at the expense of the wife and children. Usually such a husband claims to be loving and considerate; he may make noble gestures promising generous financial support. But when these promises are written down as legally binding, he refuses to be tied down. One example is Fred and Janet. They came to see me when both were 35. They were both attractive in appearance and personality. Janet had worked to finance Fred's schooling, and his rise as an architect had been meteoric. He was financially rewarded beyond his dreams. After years of frugality, Fred was not inclined to save; with his earnings so high he saw no reason not to indulge himself with the best life offered, and he equated best with expensive. Yet a glance at his heavily-lined face told the casual observer that Fred was far from happy; he constantly complained of overwork, of being caught in a quagmire. He was a getter, not a giver, both emotionally and financially. Fred's dynamics included deprivation to the point of being almost an outcast in his own family; intense rivalry with his younger brother; a father with little regard for the mother's feelings. His father would come and go as he pleased, treating Fred's mother as a servant or slave. He would not phone when he was not coming home for dinner, or would call to say he was coming and then would not appear until 10 P.M. He might not appear for days. He freely indulged his bachelor-like existence with other women, brazenly bringing one or another of them to the house with no regard for the feelings of his wife or the effects on his children.

It is not surprising that Fred identified with his self-indulgent father rather than with his masochistic, beaten-down mother. He insisted on purchasing a huge, elegant house for Janet and the children. Janet had been frugally reared, but did her part in trying to run this mansion. When expenses of renovating mounted, she did carpentry and painting, wearing herself down physically. Fred, like his father, was totally unreliable for meals, never informing Janet of his comings and goings, and let her wear herself out on house and home while being a good, devoted mother. Besides this identification with his father, Fred also transferred to Janet his pattern of rebellion against control by his father. Obviously, a man's childhood pattern toward his father as well as the pattern toward his mother can make troubles in a marriage.

Janet was under severe strain physically and emotionally. She was up to three packs of cigarettes a day and drinking liquor to relax and get to sleep at night. But she had no insight into these incipient addictions. She saw herself only as doing her part in a marriage to a brilliant, successful man who was too busy to keep her apprised of his plans or whereabouts. They gave up eating meals together as a family; he preferred eating on his own, appearing at home only occasionally and irregularly. He failed to identify with Janet or the children, for he had slipped into an all-encompassing and egocentric identification with his father, repeating toward Janet the treatment his father had accorded his mother.

One day, after nearly 15 years of marriage, Fred told Janet that he had not been completely honest with her. He really had not loved her for several years, and had enjoyed sex with other women, although only casually with no all-absorbing affair. He seemed to think that if she really loved him and wanted his happiness, she would not be jealous but would support his actions. His confession wakened Janet in a flash to the fact that she had in truth slaved for Fred—working to finance him through architectural school, in his climb up the ladder of financial success, and managing every detail of house, marriage and childrearing, saving money, to keep him free for the climb—yet Fred had given no interest, appreciation or love in return. Her love for him died rapidly then. Fred liked the idea of divorce at that point. It meant freedom to be with a girl with whom he had just started an affair, and it meant freedom to find a new wife to "correct" Janet's faults. Janet came from an old-fashioned home, and was an old-fashioned girl to the depths of her personality. She faced divorce with trepidation but could not stand marriage to a man who did not love her and who had a mistress.

Typically, Fred made a show of great generosity for a settlement, wanting "only the best" for Janet and his children—until the agreement was ready to be signed, at which time he insisted on those things *he* wanted, with lack of empathy and identification with his wife of 15 years. In part this was out of fear of being controlled, as he once was by his father, and against which control he rebelled.

So their marriage ended. She, rejected and still under his complete financial control, saw him living with another, younger woman. Janet, who had devoted her life to building Fred's career and income, now was forced to face the world alone with the children, unequipped for a career and with inadequate income. Fred showed no inclination to marry his mistress, and I guessed he would live out his pattern of rejection toward her also.

Another couple, Roger and Alice, both 52, with three children in college, were considered by all their friends to enjoy that rarity, a near-ideal marriage. But one day Alice came to see me professionally because Roger had abruptly announced that he had been thinking over their marriage. He said it did not satisfy his needs; he was past 50 and did not have so many more years left, and would be happier if he were free to make the most of them. Therefore, he had decided to leave her.

At my request, he came twice to see me. Roger was resistant and kept reminding me that he was not coming for marriage counseling, but was only there because I had asked him to come. During Roger's second visit I raised the question of whether he was fully aware of his motivations in rejecting Alice and hurting the children after a marriage of 30 years. I questioned whether his conscience could stand this. Roger reacted with anger and accused me of beating him down with interpretations. This led to his childhood pattern of rebellion against over-control and domination by his father. Roger thought that I would try to force him back to his wife, as his father would have tried. It was the emergence toward his wife of this childhood pattern toward his father that was the basic cause of his leaving the marriage—just as he had fled from his father. Roger was attractive and, I hoped, consciously well-meaning. I certainly had sympathy for him but could not professionally stand by without raising these questions. It was about their marriage and separation that his wife had come to see me, with his full knowledge and support; he was central to it all. But Roger took the questions as threats and reacted with rage—perhaps they suggested to him emotional realities that he did not want to see. Why not? Was he involved in a sexual relation with another woman, a relationship he did not want questioned? He had married Alice when they were both very young, in large part to escape from his conflict with his father, which was threatening him severely and painfully. Here again was the age-old picture of humans making themselves and others miserable during their brief moment on life's stage.

In contrast, my friend Bruce came to mind. He was only a few years older than Roger and had recently learned that he had a heart condition which would not restrict his activities too seriously but would probably give him only five more years to live. Facing this prospect of death at about 60, his thoughts turned back over his life. He felt it had been a good one, and still was. The girl of his choice had accepted him as a husband and had been a true and devoted wife. They both had deeply enjoyed their four children. Bruce felt that he could not adequately show his appreciation for the love and the fine home life she had made for him. He gave increasing thought to how he could make their remaining years together happier for her, and how best to prepare her for the years after his death. First he asked her if she wanted to stay with him when he could no longer be fully active. He did not want to be a burden to her. Then he increased his attentions to her, trying to make her even more happy and secure. Bruce, like Roger, was eminently successful in his field. But unlike Roger, he appreciated that this was as much his wife's doing as his own. She had given him the peace of mind to work freely and effectively because he could feel secure in her faithful love and confidence, and in her care of the children, to say nothing of her efficient running of the home.

Have no doubt—love conquers all. Clinical experience proves it. So does the message of religion, loud and clear and true: "A new commandment I give unto you: that ye love one another, as I have loved you . . . ."

And again, we have the Golden Rule, found in religions the world over: "All things whatsoever ye would that men should do to you, do ye even so unto them: for this is the law and the prophets."

But you do not hear this message if there is not enough love in your childhood emotional pattern.

Alice discovered that Roger had been seeing a psychiatrist for about two months, and she arranged to have a talk with him. After this appointment with Roger's psychiatrist, she gave up hope of saving the marriage, convinced that the young psychiatrist had been won over by Roger into supporting his decision no matter what.

She now felt that she had no choice but to begin to adapt to single life at age 52. For this she asked my help. She had the self-confidence of the loved child; from the loving protection of her parents she had entered into the marriage with Roger. A life alone, with the necessity for self-supporting work, was totally alien to her thinking and experience; suddenly she was "cut adrift," without knowing how to swim, row or sail. But the love she had received as a child would perhaps give her the inner sustenance (Saul, 1972, pp. 370–377) to make a new life for herself. By now I was reasonably sure that her emotional upset was "reactive" to the external blow and not "internal," from distortions in her own childhood emotional pattern. A year later she was actively preparing for a career in business.

Although the neglect and mistreatment of wives by adulterous husbands is all too common, wives also are often hostile to their husbands, reflecting traumatic treatment in their early childhood at the hands of their parents. The question remains: are small boys naturally more obstreperous and aggressive than girls, harder to handle, and thus more apt to have difficult relationships with their parents? There are many wives with disturbed childhood emotional patterns who, subtly or directly, torment their husbands, even driving them to an early grave. Ava was one such wife: when the hatred between Ava and Wilt became completely open and life together became intolerable, Wilt asked for a divorce. She was adamant, freely admitting that she refused the divorce for no other reason than hate and vengence, taking out on him the hostility generated in her 0 to 6 against her own father for his neglect and abuse of her.

There are many different outcomes to divorce. Theoretically, in some cases, the wife finds new strength and new satisfaction in her independence, and when her husband asks to come back into the marriage, she can refuse to accept him. Such poetic justice sounds good on paper, but in the author's experience seldom materializes.

More frequently we see women such as Daisy, who years before had set off in marriage as a starry-eyed bride. With Rob she had four children in rapid succession before waking up to the fact that he— although from a wealthy family—was not only penniless but was an extremely passive character devoid of ambition and despising responsibility. Faced with the support of a wife and four children, he rapidly collapsed. Rob lacked the maturity even to try to support the family; his wife's disgust with him enabled him to get a divorce, whereupon he settled for a low-level job with meager pay. Then he disappeared. Daisy had been deprived as a child, but also had enough love and strong enough parents to identify with to develop an indomitable fighting spirit. After Rob left, by holding a variety of jobs she managed to raise the children and to finish her education— but at quite a cost! Her two boys and two girls of course had emotional problems, but they were not so severe as might have been expected. Daisy herself gave out far beyond her emotional means in working and raising the family; she had to live without a love life. There was too much going out, almost nothing coming in. She did not enjoy the freedom and independence thrust upon her and was chronically suicidal, but she never acted out these urges despite many temptations to do so in the face of fate's cruel blows.

Daisy survived partly through the realization that her children needed her, and partly through confidence in herself and her ability to make a contribution to mankind. She had a brilliant mind and the determination to make her way in the world, raising her children to be good adults and refusing to be defeated by her feckless former spouse. Daisy was supported through these terrible years by a series of analysts upon whom she was dependent; yet she felt frustrated by them and responded with anger. Like Pierre in *War and Peace,* she was battered but kept standing and came through. She was not a financial success, but she weathered the worst of life, and one had to admire her unreservedly. Daisy exemplifies one of life's most poignant tragedies: the radiant bride, filled with anticipations of love and happiness, abruptly meeting harsh realities, struggling merely to survive and doing so only at terrible cost. Once "dumped" by her husband, Daisy would never be radiant again; any future happiness would be flawed by present struggles and past memories. She would have to relinquish her dreams of happiness and settle for bare survival.

Recently I chatted with a woman of 50, five years after her second divorce. Divorced women almost invariably ask me, "Don't you think I should be over it emotionally by now?" "By now" might be from a few months to several years. I asked this twice-divorced woman what she thought, and she replied freely and accurately to the point:

"In my first marriage, I had two children, who are now adolescent and live with me. They still need me. But I don't think a woman who has children in a marriage *ever* gets over the divorce. Women are different from men; men can go on with their jobs and lives, and get other women. For a wife, divorce is in some ways worse than death. In death you go through the ceremonies and bury the person, and it is over and done. But divorce never ends. Death can of course have drastic effects upon marriage in many ways, depending upon the age of the partners, which partner dies, the entire socioeconomic setting of the marriage and the basic dynamics of the partners. However, death is an external factor like sudden uncontrollable poverty or wealth or illness, and not central to our subject, the childhood emotional pattern in marriage. Terrible as the loss of a husband can be, death is apt to be less traumatic than direct, heartless rejection by divorce. As you know, I've taken up my life and have a good career. But some scarring lasts forever. How much and how painful depends on how much guilt I have. My second marriage was a mistake to start with, and lasted only a year. Yet it has taken me five years to get over it, and I am not really over the first divorce. The children live with me, and my ex-husband is still around, usually with a girlfriend, although he has never remarried. He takes a sporadic interest in the children, and they go with him on pleasure trips. My first marriage deteriorated gradually over five years' time. I only divorced him when be became physically violent and actually dangerous to me and the children."

"You have put your situation very succinctly," I said. What prolongs the wound for a divorced woman is not only guilt, often irrational, but the whole dynamics of her personality, and of course the circumstances of the divorce.

Reviewing what I had observed in practice, it seemed to me that two forces other than guilt were equally important in recovering from divorce: pride and self-respect, and independence. In most cases the hurt to the normal personal and feminine pride endured despite all efforts to forget. Rejection of a woman by a man after she has been completely involved with him, yielded him both her body and soul and borne and raised his children, is a terrible thing. Out of *hurt self-respect, guilt* and *dependence*—plus inertia after having her whole way of life as wife, mother and homemaker destroyed—the divorcee often keeps asking what she did wrong, unjustifiedly looking for where she has failed. She does this even though she sees quite clearly that the cause for divorce lies entirely in her husband, and she can find no cause for such guilt. I often pondered these dynamics until Jessica, a suddenly deserted wife, enlightened me. When I was asking some questions about her 0–6 she said, "I think that I have a problem in never having been sufficiently my own person. That's because, during my childhood before age six and afterward, I always got along by being loved for being 'a good girl.' I loved my parents, and they were so pleased and returned my love when I was 'a good girl.' When I married I tried to please my husband, Gary, in the same way . . . now that he has rejected me and left, I can't help thinking that it must be because I failed in some way to be 'a good girl.' In other words, it makes me feel somehow his leaving is due to a failure of mine. Could that be why I feel guilty even though I know for sure it really is *not* my fault, and he even fully agrees with that? He has no complaints about me and says it is all his problem. He has just told me that he no longer sees the 'other woman' and is considering getting psychoanalytic help."

Even if we acknowledge that there are uncontrollable external circumstances that affect one's life, we must recognize that "dynamics are destiny." If the dynamics, i.e., predominantly the childhood emotional patterns, of the partners mesh closely, then the marriage is harmonious. If not, the result is friction, tension, clash and conflict. Perhaps this conclusion seems mechanistic, but I think it is true, in the same way that the heart, lungs, kidneys, liver, intestinal tract and other organs each have their own mechanisms of operation. When our organs work properly, we are totally unaware of their existence. When something goes wrong, however, we may suffer excruciating pain.

If marriage has such mechanisms of interaction, then perhaps we could use computers to predict whether the patterns of two partners would mesh or clash, and at what points. But first we would have to ask each partner key questions and program the computer with the pertinent information and answers. Today, computers arrange meetings or dates, but not so selectively as to search out the individuals' deeper dynamics, so far as I know. This would be a thoroughly worthwhile experiment, much in need of exploration. A couple planning marriage, believing they are "in love," would probably pay little attention to such results from a computer, but at least they would be forewarned and might get analytic help in advance of possible difficulties, thereby maturing and adjusting sufficiently to forestall any trends from their childhood patterns that, if not seen and dealt with, might lead to divorce. Or is this a vain hope, considering the power of the unconscious childhood emotional patterns?

The science fiction of today can herald the reality of tomorrow. Think what might result if computer predictions based on childhood emotional patterns could accurately mirror the success or failure of individual marriages, could help loving couples to meet each other. What agonies might be avoided? How many couples who might never have met each other would be brought together? Think how much trauma for children could be avoided if either future misery or future happiness in marriage could be predicted! We could move a step toward proper childrearing, creating stable homes with loving parents who give their children love, respect and understanding; and through this we could move toward a world in which people treat one another with love, respect and understanding instead of hostility, violence, crime and war.

This is probably a wishful fantasy. But there is much in the ancient admonition:

If your ways would be ways of pleasantness and all your pathways peace,
Love God and keep his commandments.*

References

Saul, Leon J. (1971): *Emotional Maturity,* 3rd Ed. Philadelphia: Lippincott, p. 207.

_____(1972): *Psychodynamically Based Psychotherapy.* New York: Science House.

_____(1977): *The Childhood Emotional Pattern and Corey Jones.* New York: Van Nostrand Reinhold.

Saul, Leon J. and Warner, S. (1977): The psychotic character, *Int'l. J. of Psychoanalytic Psychotherapy* 6: 243, 252.

Westoff, L. (1975): *The Second Time Around.* New York: Viking Press. NOTE: Although this is a popular rather than scientific book, it does refer to some serious sociological studies.

*Edgar Lee Masters, *Spoon River Anthology*

34
THE SECOND TIME AROUND

Everything that dies dies by its own corruption; all that injures is within.

Menander

It is not marriage that fails, it is people that fail. All that marriage does is to show people up.

Fosdick

It is a commonplace to say that we must make one of the most important decision of our lives, the choice of a mate, when we are too inexperienced and too suffused with sex and other feelings to have good judgment. That is certainly true. But I am not at all sure that after many more years of living one would choose any better. When people remarry, their second mate often turns out to be remarkably similar to the first. However, this is by no means always so. It probably depends on the strength and fixity of the underlying childhood pattern.

One girl, Eve, tall, willowy and shy, was from a home in which the father disdained the mother, and the mother was so masochistically submissive to him, so doormatish, that the girl could not respect her. When a senior in college, Eve fell in love with a superior young man, Reed, who was starting off well with a large firm. Passionately attracted to each other, they slept together for some months before they married. But sex is as sensitive as it is powerful. Since their meeting, he had been irresistible to her. Now, the instant they were married, she lost her desire for him.

However, in time her sexual feelings returned, and the whole relationship settled down into a happier marriage than the average. They were especially happy with their two sons. Reed was killed in the last months of the war. Eve continued to live in Chicago, but once when she was nearby, she came in to see me and told the rest of her story.

"Two years after Reed's death I remarried. Clarence [as we will call the new husband] seemed stable and devoted to me and the boys. But in a matter of months marriage with him turned out to be impossible. Clarence was just a complainer. We agreed in a friendly way on a divorce. Of course I know that any friendly agreement is against the law. In Illinois it is collusion, and no ethical lawyer will touch the case. The law in this area apparently is not designed to keep the peace. It insists that divorce must be a hostile, antagonistic, punitive process—the Adversary System. But Clarence and I decided to remain friendly and just leave the law to the lawyers."

Eve was right, of course. The only criterion for legal divorce was *guilt*. The form of the guilt is called grounds. A new approach is gaining acceptance: to handle delinquent spouses much as delinquent children are handled—not by examining the guilt of the defendant, but by seeking the basic causative factors and resorting to divorce only after trying to remove them by the use of all necessary specialists from all disciplines. The criteria of the juvenile courts, set by law and philosophy, are not guilt and punishment but what protects society and is best for the child. That of the divorce court would be what protects society and is best for the family and each of its members.

"I don't think it was the lawyers," Eve continued, "but Clarence's own makeup that turned it into a contest. But the lawyers helped. I don't blame them too much; each was honestly trying to guard his own client's interest. Anyway, somehow Clarence felt I was holding out on him, insulting him or something. I wanted nothing—no money—only freedom for myself and the boys, just to correct a mistake. But he took it personally. He gradually changed his mind about our friendly agreement and decided to contest the divorce. It made me physically nauseated to line up every complaint I could think of against him, but I had to do it. Before we married my lawyer had insisted on a prenuptial agreement to protect what I had from Reed. I told him at that time I just couldn't ask that of a man I was about to marry, a man I thought loved me and the boys and whom I loved. But fortunately the lawyer insisted and Clarence signed.

"Once I said to him in the midst of all this, 'We've been married less than a year. We know it was a mistake. Why do you oppose this divorce? You prevent yourself from being free, and it a terrible situation for me and the boys. You get no advantage. Why do you contest it?'

"He said, 'Because I get the satisfaction of hurting you and preventing you from ever marrying anyone else.' I guess he was a psychological sadist. If so, there must be a lot of them."

In the end it was a dirty business because of Clarence's makeup and because of the archaic divorce laws. At last Eve was free, after much ordeal and expense. Her years of living had not enabled her to make a better choice than when she was a young protected college girl. Is this not true of almost everyone? Of course, her judgment of Clarence was no doubt influenced by her eagerness to remarry to have a husband, a father for the children, increased financial security and everything else that a man gives a home. But then is not almost everyone's judgment strongly colored by strong emotions, when it comes down to choice of mate?

Three years later Eve wrote me as follows:

"The two years after the divorce were hell. But now I'm married again—to a good guy. I've waited for a year to write you just to be sure this one was for keeps. It's not perfect, but neither was it so with Reed. It's good though, and I'm lucky and happy. It surprises me, because Eric is ten years older than I am, and I thought he was a confirmed bachelor and that something was wrong with him because he'd never married. But he is okay sexually and is not only devoted but thrilled with suddenly having a wife and two grown sons. I just hope his burst of family enthusiasm doesn't lead him to insist on a baby."

SECTION VIII: PREVENTION AND TREATMENT

. . . believing it to be the finest thing in the world to be a gentleman; by which word he had been taught to understand the careful habit of causing needless pain to no human being, poor or rich, and of taking pride in giving up his own pleasure for the sake of those who were weaker than himself.

It is virtue . . . that maketh gentlemen; that maketh the poor rich, the baseborn noble, the subject a sovereign, the deformed beautiful, the sick whole, the weak strong, the most miserable most happy.

Charles Kingsley,
Westward Ho!

35
THE CHILDHOOD PATTERN AND THE DYNAMICS OF ANALYTIC TREATMENT

Know then thyself, presume not God to scan;
The proper study of mankind is Man.

Alexander Pope,
Essay on Man, II

And ye shall know the truth, and the truth shall make you free.

John 8:32

Insight into the childhood emotional pattern does not alone effect cure. In fact, this insight can be misused, as when an unqualified therapist hammers away at the childhood responses to trauma and thus unwittingly encourages the patient to think of himself as a child rather than as an adequate adult who suffers from problems caused by unresolved residual patterns of childhood (Saul, 1972, p. 378). Insight is a powerful tool, but its misuse can cause positive harm.

In most people, however, even insight alone can be beneficial. It is usually the indispensable first step in resolving any problem. Without it, one is groping in the dark; unless you see the problem clearly, how can you begin to work on a solution? If a marital problem is relatively superficial, then a sympathetic ear and talking the problem over may suffice to ameliorate it. If its roots lie only a little deeper in the personalities, then sometimes insight alone helps the partners solve it.

Most marital problems seen by this author, however, are found to be very deeply seated in the personality, i.e., in the reactions to trauma during early childhood, especially from 0 to 6. Usually they require some degree of resolution within one or both marriage partners to achieve a harmonious relationship. The reason for this is the nature of the problem itself: a disordered relationship to parents or others that repeats itself in the marriage. Therefore, the only secure, permanent solution is the correction of the disordered childhood relationship. If not corrected, it lurks, usually unconsciously, in the personality, only to emerge sooner or later in any close relationship and almost surely in marriage, since this is the closest one comes to another individual, and moreover, in the setting of a home; it was usually within the child's parental home that the initial emotional trauma occurred, which now revives in the marital home.

Why is it so often a person's childhood emotional pattern does not emerge until middle age or later? Recently I saw a highly intelligent, attractive, 45-year-old woman who was depressed and felt dangerously withdrawn from friends, work and life. She told me of a few difficult experiences that had precipitated her depression, such as her husband's waning interest in her and his growing interest in another woman. Such life experiences are traumatic, mobilizing symptoms if they strike specific emotional vulnerabilities in the childhood emotional pattern. In this case, as I began exploring the childhood pattern, she remarked: "I can see that I have felt this depression and withdrawal since I was a child of about seven or eight. In fact, I guess I have fought it all my life, only now I am getting tired of fighting and am tempted to just give in to it." She clearly expressed the weakening of her ego defenses, resistances and controls, one factor in the emergence of this part of her childhood emotional pattern.

By "trauma" we do not mean only a single violent incident of some kind. Trauma for a child within a reasonably stable home is in continuing longstanding attitudes and feelings that impede or warp the child's normal development to maturity. It is a process of "conditioning." For example, a child grows up receiving insufficient love and attention, or is dominated and overcontrolled or brushed aside with insufficient respect for its wishes and personality, or is constantly depreciated and negatively criticized by one or both parents (the three common D's: deprivation, domination, depreciation.) Living in such an emotional climate during its earliest, most formative years *conditions* the child to *expect* such treatment, for *this is all it has known* from adults. This expectation "spreads" from the parents or others responsible for the child to persons outside of the family, especially to those individuals who become emotionally close as the parents once were. In general, the younger the child is, the stronger, more deep-seated the conditioning and its effects.

If a child is young enough and the mistreatment by omission or commission is strong enough, the result is not mere neurosis but psychosis with severe disruption of the mental and emotional processes, including sense of reality. The reverse is not necessarily true, i.e., some psychosis may be caused by physical or biochemical factors instead of early emotional trauma; but this is not established at present, and organic, physical causes do not concern us in this book.

The deprived child grows into an adult who, consciously or unconsciously, continues to *feel* like a deprived child; the dominated child continues to *feel* dominated as an adult; the depreciated child continues to *feel* depreciated. As Freud said, "the child we once were lives on in us all," which means for life. The child reared only with love, respect and understanding expects these things throughout life from others and by identification has them to give.

If a wife feels deprived by her husband because of her own *internal* continuing feelings of being the deprived, if the husband feels dominated and depreciated because of his inner childhood emotional pattern, then marital discord inevitably arises. At that point, kindly "counseling" or even insight alone will not suffice to resolve the problems. Ideally, what is needed is the correction of these *warped internal feelings*. Because they arose from treatment by parents during the formative years, a process of *de*conditioning is needed to open the way to *re*conditioning these feelings toward others, such as one's spouse. Freud (1949) used the term "after-education." Franz Alexander (1946) aptly called this reconditioning a "corrective emotional experience." This terminology accurately describes the goal of psychoanalytic therapy and indicates its process.

The total childhood emotional pattern is the result not only of early treatment of the child but of the interaction of the child's inherited potentials with the physical and emotional influences on him during his most formative years, 0 to 6.

Early trauma by omission or commission came from other persons, parents or substitutes (was "interpersonal"); therefore, correction must come from another person. In the psychoanalytic process the reactions of the analysand to the analyst is like a laboratory sample of the analysand's relations to other persons. Sooner or later the reactions of the child whom the analysand once was will emerge toward the analyst. Thus in some way, shape, manner or form, the deprived patient will feel deprived by the analyst, the dominated will feel dominated, and so on. Meanwhile, the realistically friendly feelings between analyst and analysand keep their relationship going so that the traumatic part can be "analyzed out" in a setting of mutual cooperative exploration. If an individual has experienced insufficient friendly feelings in childhood, he will probably not be able to establish a working relationship ("therapeutic alliance") with the analyst and will prove unanalyzable. The repetition of feelings of the childhood pattern toward the analyst is the *transference*. It opens a path toward cure. If a deprived child grows up to feel deprived within his marriage, a squabble or something more serious ensues. But when the feelings of deprivation, for example, emerge toward the analyst, they can be traced to their sources in the analysand's childhood.

When insight is achieved, after-education and corrective emotional experience become possible. The analysand can then learn to *discriminate* between the *real* deprivation in childhood and the *unrealistic,* irrational exaggerated *feelings* of deprivation at present toward the spouse or analyst. He can in time, by insight and *working through,* discover what are unrealistic, persisting, residual feelings of childhood, and how they are influencing his current adult interpersonal relations including those toward wife, children and other persons. How successful this process is and at what rate it proceeds depend upon the nature, extent and depth of the analysand's disordered feelings and upon the skill, ability and personality of the analyst. For example, an adult who was too extremely unwanted as a child, too rejected and deprived from birth, will probably be psychotic and inaccessible to this method. [It has been tried in modified forms, however, with various kinds of psychotics, apparently with benefit to some (Berkowitz, 1977; Brenner, 1975; Compton, 1975; Furer, 1976; Gedo, 1977; Strupp, 1976).]

On the other hand, if the deprivation has not been that severe or has been transient or well compensated for at least intermittently, by others close to the child, or if the deprivation did not occur until well after age six or seven, then with an experienced and astute, truly interested analyst the process may go rapidly and successfully within a minimum number of meetings. And there are all gradations between these two extremes.

Lying on a couch five days a week is no substitute for accurate analysis. It is still best for some analysands, but by no means for all. For some, it even slows the process by encouraging so much *regression* to the pathological childhood pattern that this intensifies the pattern to unmanageable proportions that swamp the adult part of the personality and lead into a fantasy world, away from facing and reducing unpleasant reality externally and in the childhood pattern. Cure depends on the adult part of the personality facing, handling and resolving powerful *emotional forces* that the child could not comprehend or manage. Cure involves adapting all techniques to the individual; the analyst can do this only if he understands the childhood emotional pattern as soon as possible, preferably in the first hour or two. Of course, in marriage problems the analyst must understand not only the pattern of each partner but also the interactions between them.

What role does the analyst's personality play in treatment? Supposedly, he was analyzed himself as part of his training. Yet no matter how well aware he is of every facet of his own childhood pattern, that pattern still survives within him. To be "completely analyzed," like achieving full maturity, is an ideal never entirely attained. What is as important or even more so than being "completely analyzed" is being *mature*.

No matter how thoroughly analyzed he might be, everyone has a dynamic unconscious. Therefore, some interaction of the analyst with the patient's pattern is inevitable. This is the "countertransference." A young man was referred to a brilliant and experienced analyst. After four or five months he broke off treatment, saying he recognized the analyst's superior ability, but simply could not work with him. The analysand's problems sprang from childhood deprivation; so did some of the character traits of the analyst. The patient could hear the analyst's words and appreciate his keen, accurate interpretations, but he could not maintain a constructive transference because in his object relationship he *felt* no warmth from the deprived analyst and could not identify with him. Not everyone can be analyzed by every analyst. Just because of this interaction of deeper dynamics, the analyst's childhood pattern may facilitate therapy or hinder it or block it entirely. In all of medicine, the patient's *transference* to the physician (especially the confidence in his integrity, conscientiousness and devotion) plays a role in the patient's cooperation and the success of the treatment. But in no other medical specialty and in few other professions is the physician's true personality so intrinsic a part of the treatment itself as in psychoanalytic therapy.

The final process of cure is learning by *practice in living.* For example, knowing how dependent one is or was upon the childhood home and parents and how angry one is about this is not enough. Nor is it enough to have insight into how one's anger operates toward the analyst in the "transference," or how dependent one becomes upon him and what rage this engenders, and what anxiety this causes; or what further anger arises when one is cut off from the dependence. Insight and working through in this transference to the analyst do not complete the cure. The final freedom and growth come from practice in living with those feelings that cause the emotional problems, as one learns by experience how to alter, reduce and come to terms with them. (We have used dependence and anger for examples because in general these are the two main poles of the emotional life. We are all born helpless with dependence upon our mothers for our very existence; rage arises when the infant's demands are not met, and later the adult feels similar rage when his dependent demands go unanswered, and when the dependence causes feelings of inferiority and anxiety.)

Ideally, working through the transference results in "analyzing out" those feelings of the childhood pattern that make problems and difficulties toward the analyst, such as excessive dependence, competitiveness, submissiveness, envy, hostility and the like—and leaving only a good adult-to-adult relationship. One does not have to kill off one's parents to escape an excessive dependence, submissiveness, competitiveness or hostility toward them. To mature, the child needs to outgrow these neurotic exaggerations and achieve a good adult-to-adult relationship with his parents, insofar as they are capable of it. The transference can be of great help in attaining this maturity by providing a sample relationship in which to work it out initially.

To summarize, we have remarked that improvement depends, as in the rest of medicine, upon the balance of forces:

1. The severity of the disorder, involving how early in life the disturbed patterns—the pathodynamics—were formed, and how powerful, deep-seated and widespread they are in the personality.
2. The health and strength of the counterforces toward maturity, resolution of the disorders, adaptation and health.
3. The uncontrollable circumstances and happenstances of life.
4. The skill and personality of the physician.

The curative process involves four overlapping elements: (1) insight, (2) development of the transference (of the childhood pattern toward the analyst), (3) working through in the transference and (4) working through in life.

One might see the overlapping elements in the transference that occur before insight. Sometimes long before a person consults an analyst, the working through may have proceeded quite far in life. Yet for a thorough corrective experience, the working through must be seen and accomplished in the transference as well as in life, and this working through may occur over a period of years simultaneously in transference and in life. The last step in the curative process— working through in life—is part of learning about oneself from experience, and reopening maturation by overcoming, reducing, outgrowing the traumatic childhood pattern. This goes on for the rest of one's life, sometimes facilitated by occasional visits to the analyst, which often prove of appreciable help for many years, even interminably (Saul, 1972). Meetings with the analyst, perhaps every few months or more or less frequently, often catalyze the individual's insights and save much time in achieving a calmer, more satisfying life, even if such visits (by telephone, if more convenient) continue for many years.

A highly perceptive patient wrote me: "I can see why I had to work through what I did recently with you . . . I have remained 'task-oriented,' my emotions have not been heavy . . . I have been losing weight, terribly slowly, but consistently. I have been exercising, trudging through the snow or swimming as far as I am able daily. I feel less dependent on everyone. I feel remarkably good about myself and life, and remarkably serene and sure of myself. I have been so hardworking and efficient lately—my! 'Neurosis' takes up so much energy. If I stay this normal I will eventually be able to accomplish an awful lot more with my life. The time and money I spent on you was well worth it."

If every child were properly reared, we would not need psychiatrists except possibly for some forms of nonpsychogenic, toxic disorders of the brain. Physically healthy children raised from birth with love, respect and understanding would probably be free of neurosis, psychosis, criminality, violence proneness, irrationally hostile acting out, revolution and war—and intrafamilial hostilities. Such individuals would then be free to love and work and play, and raise properly the next generation of children.

Not every person seen by an analyst, especially for marital problems, is psychoanalyzed. If a man or woman is aware of severe anxieties or homosexual trends or any other deep-seated personality disorder that he or she wants to work out before getting married, or even to become able to marry with improved chances of success, then psychoanalysis may be indicated, along the lines described early in this chapter. No other procedure may hold as good hope of success. With other problems, not only may psychoanalysis be unnecessary, but a different approach to understanding the individual's dynamics may hold more promise of therapeutic effectiveness.

For example, if a husband announces one day that he is leaving his marriage, the general mode of proceeding in such a situation would be somewhat as follows:

The wife, reeling from the blow, is at first in need of emotional support, if only in the form of having the analyst to talk to and to vent her feelings on. Then the principle becomes the basic guideline of psychotherapy—Truth. If the truth does not make us free, nothing will. This involves a dynamic diagnosis of the wife, an understanding of her dynamics with details of her childhood pattern, to learn her strengths and her emotional vulnerabilities, just where this rejection by her husband threatens and hurts her the most. Something of the husband's dynamics can be learned from the wife, who usually knows his childhood pattern well enough to relate its major features. Next, the husband is asked to come in so that the analyst may hear directly from him about his wife's dynamics and his own. If the husband seems to be acting in a neurotic, psychotic or pathological way, he should know it, whether he goes ahead with his behavior or not. Even if he wants no interference or insight, he owes it to his rejected wife to reach some understanding of what is going on psychodynamically within them both and between them. This will give the wife insight to help her in handling the difficult, painful rejection to the best of her emotional ability. And it may save the husband from a threatening internal neurosis or even psychosis. Of course, there are wide variations in this general procedure. For example, Enid, the wife in "A Paradigm of Marriage," wanted a divorce, and it was important for Edwin to have what insight he could into her reasons, namely, his own unconscious hostilities. The dynamics must be thoroughly understood, but in using them therapeutically, "circumstances alter cases."

In this chapter we have given a condensed description of the dynamics of psychoanalytic treatment. Such treatment in full scale is resorted to only when it seems well worth the investment of time, money and emotional energy for the individual. Marital problems are usually handled by seeing both partners and proceeding in a down-to-earth, common-sense, realistic manner. This means trying to understand the cause of the husband's or wife's unhappiness, determining if it can be resolved in some direct, simple fashion. The analyst learns whether practical, external measures will help, or whether the antagonisms are deeper within one or both personalities and must be dealt with more analytically. At the extreme is a spouse who announces that he or she does not want to save the marriage, that the decision is final and not open to discussion, but meanwhile develops neurotic or psychotic symptoms requiring treatment for an emotional disorder so deep as to be a serious personal problem only incidently related to the marriage. In such cases the individual needs therapy for the neurosis or borderline psychosis, and the marital chips must fall where they may.

There are, of course, all gradations of intermediate situations in which analytic work is indicated. Compare, for example, the following two couples:

Larry could not have been more typical of the young man who eagerly marries early but then rapidly finds the reality quite different from his anticipation. One day, without warning but with characteristic egocentricity and with what he considered admirable honesty, he informed his wife that he no longer loved her and had another woman. Under the impact of this blow, his wife, Glenda, came to see me. The immediate task, she felt, was to keep from "coming unglued and falling apart." This was not difficult; she seemed basically stable. Glenda was also highly intelligent, beautiful, sexy, realistic, spirited. Here was plenty to work with. There was no evident reason why she should not learn from this painful experience and make a new and excellent marriage. But one never knows what dynamics lurk beneath the surface awareness. I try to discern the childhood patterns in the first or second meeting with a patient, whatever the crisis. When Glenda arrived for her second visit, I explained that it was always good to understand these things beyond the surface appearance, and that we should continue to meet to explore further. She reacted against this suggestion, and I questioned what she feared. She never came back, but left assuring me that I had helped her enough so that she could handle her own life. I told Glenda that I would feel easier if we knew her dynamics. But I could only respect her independence.

Eight years passed, and then one evening Glenda phoned me in considerable distress:

After that second visit, although she was reassured that she would not "come unglued," the emotional pressure and suffering continued, and she sought relief in an affair with a sympathetic man who happened to be married, with two children. To Glenda's surprise, she then found that she was pregnant, by her own husband she hoped, but they nevertheless were divorced as soon as possible. Larry gave her no support; so she had to struggle to support herself and her son. Her lover moved with his family to a distant city after their affair, which lasted two years, leaving Glenda plugging along alone. Larry became alcoholic; she felt he was something of a psychopath because he had begun phoning her, threatening to tell her lover's wife of the former affair with Glenda. This was the reason why she had called me in such distress, asking for advice.

"I do not feel it is my role to run the lives of others," I told her, "nor do I think anyone can assume that role. I can only ask your own opinion of a few suggestions: how about starting with the truth? Phone the wife, say you are no homewrecker, that you admit the affair, but it was under extreme pressure of Larry's rejection. The affair has been long since over and forgotten, a mere incident of the past when you and your lover were both young and immature, and you hope she will see that, not letting it injure her marriage because you certainly do not want her to suffer as you have."

In retrospect, it is obvious that Glenda had a strong streak of masochism that should have been analyzed; while consciously wanting marriage, she would unconsciously manipulate herself into a position of loneliness, financial insecurity and struggle that would torment her and damage her young son for life.

Compare the situation of Larry and Glenda with that of Gary and Vicki, a couple just entering their thirties. This time it was the husband, Gary, who came to see me. He and his wife were drifting apart, he said, and she was losing interest in sex. This increased his interest in other women, and he was having an affair with a most attractive girl, who was divorced and wanted to marry him. But he and his wife had three small children and needed help with their marriage, although neither one knew if it could be saved. Vicki was already seeing another analyst. So Gary started seeing me therapeutically. His father had been away most of the time, and Gary had been brought up almost entirely by his mother and aunt. His mother was physically seductive, often walking around the house partially clad. She was quite strict about being looked at and over-controlling in general, provoking a rebelliousness in Gary that mostly took the form of sexual activity. This gave him a tendency to philander, and now meant rebelling against his wife, which con-stituted his part in their marital problem.

Vicki's childhood pattern centered on hostility to a brother nearly her age, whom the parents shamelessly preferred. The clash of her unconscious childhood emotional pattern with Gary's was contributing to the destruction of their marriage. But there was enough maturity to work with, and three years later it was clear the marriage would survive. Open fighting had disappeared, and their children had a reasonably harmonious stable home. Gary and Vicki were not idyllically happy, but were infinitely more so than Larry and Glenda.

This does not mean that good psychodynamic therapy always works, but does show that it is worth trying in preference to dis-carding a relationship—rendering asunder what has once been joined together—especially if the union has produced children.

References

Alexander, F. and French, T. (1946): *Psychoanalytic Therapy*. New York: Ronald Press.

Berkowitz, D. (1977): The vulnerability of the grandiose self and the psycho-therapy of actingout patients, *Intl. Review Psychoanal.*, 4(1):13–22.

Brenner, C. (1975): Alterations in defenses during psychoanalysis, *Kris Study Group Monograph VI*, Bernard Fine and Herbert Waldhorn, eds., pp. 1–22.

Compton, A. (1975): Aspects of psychoanalytic intervention, *Kris Study Group Monograph VI*, ibid, pp. 23–97.

Freud, S. (1949): *An Outline of Psychoanalysis*. New York: W. W. Norton, p. 67.

Furer, M. (1976): Construction and reconstruction in the tripartite treatment of a psychotic girl: paper presented to the Margaret S. Mahler Symposium no. 1, *J. Philadelphia Association Psychoanal.* 3(4):121–128.

Gedo, J. (1977): On the mode of action of psychoanalytic therapy, presented to the Chicago Psychoanalytic Society, Mar. 11, 21 pp.
Saul, L. J. (1972): *Psychodynamically Based Psychotherapy.* New York: Science House.
Strupp, H. (1976): Themes in psychotherapy research, *Successful Psychotherapy*, J. Claghorn, ed., pp. 3–23.

SOME ADDITIONAL REFERENCES:

Chance, E. (1959): *Families in Treatment.* New York: Basic Books.
Mudd, E., Mitchell, H., Taubin, S. (1965): *Success in Family Living.* New York: Associated Press. (An interesting and illuminating systematic study of 100 "successful" families in the various aspects of their relationships and functioning. Each chapter has an extensive bibliography.)

36

SOME RAPID RESOLUTIONS
In Adolescence
In Midstream
In The Decline

Fascinating as are the processes and problems of treatment and results, they concern us only insofar as they illuminate the dynamics of marriage. Three examples at different ages show that when the emotional forces are in favorable balance, they can tilt quickly toward improvement in a person or in a marriage.

In Adolescence

A young college man, Ray, had felt so fatigued for two weeks that he could hardly move. Although he was an athlete, he could now hardly walk for more than a few minutes. College had begun but he felt unable to leave home to attend. Nothing in the routine of the interview provided any clue to the trouble. Asked about present relationships, he said these were fine. Girls? Fine, too. But I noticed a slight hesitation. He tried to pass it off, but I insisted. I had to force his response, saying, "There is something with a girl that you are not telling me." Finally he blurted out, "I had my first sexual affair with a girl this summer. She ended it a few weeks ago. She slept with another man she had told me about."

Apparently his need for a woman, including all-out sexual relations, was intense. But he doubted seriously that any other girl would have an affair with him. Losing the first girl made him think he would have no girl for sex. He was not ready or financially able to marry, nor would he have married this girl anyway. "Where does the girl live" I asked. "Just a few blocks from me," he said, and then he started—almost jumped. "What!" he exclaimed, "You aren't saying that all this is because I want to be near *her*?" That was sufficient. His pride was strong. To think that he was still dependent on a girl who met his devotion by tossing him over for another! It was unbearable, unthinkable. Shocked at himself, he was jolted back to his usual self. He left my office, told his parents he was straightened out, and shot back to college without delay.

Of course, what had happened was that he had been in the midst of an adolescent rebellion against his own submissive dependence upon his parents, especially his mother. Intensely conscious only of the powerful sexual attraction to the girl, he had, all unconsciously, developed the same dependence on her. When the interview made him aware of it, it hurt his pride painfully and mobilized precipitously the full force of his rebellion and the assertion of independence. It was a successful "blitz-analysis." The result held, but after graduation he returned to go into the whole conflict more thoroughly and did well in outgrowing the tendencies to become submissive and dependent on others. He no longer needed to show his independence only by fighting his tendency to be dependent. As he genuinely grew to be more independent, his hostilities diminished, and he could relax and enjoy life more and more. He exemplifies a typical, frequently seen adolescent problem and how, if the balance of forces is auspicious, it can tilt toward cure through a single burst of insight.

In Midstream

It has been remarked that the deeper working of the human mind only becomes comprehensible through its struggles with suffering. Certainly if one but listens openly, with relative freedom from preconceptions and clichés, to patients who come for relief from psychic pain, one hears many fundamentals clearly and directly stated with but little disguise, and often sees clearly the meaning of feelings and thoughts that are unconscious, or more or less unconscious.

Sylvia was an attractive woman of 40, married with two sons, ages 10 and 12. When she came to see me with the common complaints of anxiety and depression, I wanted to hear her story as she would spontaneously present it; and I had in mind supplementing what she told me with the usual data used for dynamic understanding: a picture of her present life, recent dreams, early childhood (0–6) emotional pattern in her family, earliest memories and the course her life had taken. But the main point was quickly reached:

PATIENT: I have been tense for some time—really some years I guess, but worse in the last six months. I've come to see you because now I've been snapping at the children, and I can't stand the thought of hurting them. I know the most sensitive time is before the age of six, but I can't believe it won't hurt them at later ages also to have a grouchy, ill-tempered mother. I notice my feelings in the rest of my life also, but do my best not to show them. We have many friends, including a few good close ones. I do a lot of things in our church and community. We play tennis regularly. We are in perfect health and have a good life. It seems silly to feel this way.

ANALYST: Will you tell a little more about your relationship with your husband?

P: He is a fine person, devoted to me and the children. There is some tension there though. I feel I can never entirely please him. He is always somewhat dissatisfied, no matter what. He comes home in a reasonable mood but pretty soon he acts cranky and critical. He may even flare up some and then apologize. His apology is sincere enough, but this goes on and on. [She seems angrier and angrier as she talks.] He is a lawyer, and makes occasional out-of-town trips . . .

A: Why do you stop?

P: [Hesitatingly] I can hardly believe what I'm saying—that I'm really glad when he goes; it's a relief. But I miss him when he's gone. I want him back, but when he comes, I get tense and wrought up again . . .

A: Again you are silent. Is this hard to tell?

P: Yes. It is awful. I feel so disloyal. And I feel I'm invading his privacy and mine.

A: We might pay a little attention to why you feel this way about what really amounts to simply being honest about your feelings. But I can easily understand your hesitation about this in a new situation, and will try to make it as easy as I can for you.

P: I guess you're interested in dreams.

A: Very much so. [Not infrequently in approaching feelings which are difficult to face, a person goes to a dream. And this dream usually reveals in disguised form what is being held back. Therefore, I am glad to study the dream.]

P: In a dream I had about two weeks ago the boys and I were at the tennis court, chatting and happy. Then we noticed a log there. But it turned out to be a big dog. It seemed to be friendly, but then I thought it was dangerous and might attack us.

A: What does the dog make you think of?

P: About a year ago we had a dog. He was quite a problem in the house—house-breaking, worms, ticks, everything. It was more than Myron, my husband, could take. He tried so hard to be patient, but he lost his temper and I lost mine. I shouldn't blame him, but he makes me so tense. We really have a very good marriage but . . .

A: Again you are silent. The associations to the dog lead again right to anger at your husband. Could it be that you have not quite wanted to face the truth about this? Is it possible that his making you tense really means that he makes you angry, and that your anxiety and depression are the result of bottled up anger at him, which you have not fully acknowledged and which just simmers?

P: [Here is one of those significant expressions and pauses that are difficult to depict, but which show that a psychic reality has been touched, often show it more clearly than the words that follow.] Maybe . . . it could be. Maybe I've sort of sensed something like this for some time.

A: If it is so, then we should discuss it further in another visit. And also, should I not meet your husband? Would he come?

P: I think so. He is really a fine person. He is away on a trip now. As soon as he returns I'll ask him to phone you.

[It is always interesting to see this more or less conscious awareness. In this case it is semi-awareness of the anger at the husband. One might see it the other way round, as more or less unconscious. Technically, it would be called preconscious. In ordinary language, Sylvia dimly sensed but did not fully recognize her anger at Myron, and she had no realization of its intensity, which must have been strong in order to produce her symptoms of tension, anxiety and depression.]

When he came to see me, Myron, of middle height, stocky and pleasant, began the interview with no reluctance:

P: I am really very anxious to talk with you. I wanted to do so anyway because I've had an experience that has scared me. I haven't told my wife because I haven't wanted to upset her, but I thought I had a heart attack. A week ago I suddenly felt my heart pound and was short of breath. I took my pulse and it was about

120. I went to see my doctor. He examined me and said there was nothing wrong with my heart and that he thought there was nothing wrong physically at all, but that this was from nervous tension. I haven't had it since then.

A: What was going on when it occurred?

P: Nothing. I was dressing for dinner after a board meeting.

A: What was that?

P: You know I'm a lawyer. I do mostly corporation law. I have to do with mergers, reorganizations and the like. As a result, I'm on the boards of some companies.

A: And?

P: This was an important meeting. I had an important part in it. There was a lot of hostility and aggressive talk. I got quite a lot of it and was pretty strongly attacked, but not all openly and directly. I tried to relax and forget it when I returned to the hotel to get ready for dinner. That's when this attack came.

A: Were you aware of being irritated or angry yourself?

P: I was aware of being tense. Actually I'vs been tense ever since my mother died six months ago. I've always been rather tense, but it's been much worse for these six months.

A: What kind of feeling do you think is causing this tenseness?

P: I don't know, but it may be irritability. I must admit I've been awfully irritable, mostly with my family. I try to control it, but find myself snapping at my wife and even at the children. I feel very bad about it, but I find myself being critical and irritable, and sometimes I flare up without meaning to. When I come home after work, I'm so tired I can hardly move. When I feel nervous, I'm a little short of breath. But I had a complete physical, with X-rays, electrocardiogram and blood tests, and everything is normal.

A: Have you any more ideas about the tension? How do you get on in all aspects of your life?

P: I get on fine. Basically we have an excellent marriage. We have good friends. And I get along fine in my law firm. We enjoy the theater and tennis and have a good life. I work hard but not too much, and I thoroughly enjoy it. I have a front row seat in American business. As to tension, I only know I've been more tense since my mother died.

A: Please tell about that relationship, including earliest childhood.

P: My father was killed in a car accident when I was 12. My sister was 20 at that time, and she married a year later. I lived with my mother. Mother did some work in the home, and for the rest we got by on my father's insurance. Mother was extremely dependent on me, especially when I got a little older. She did nothing without me. She was very strict. I always tried to please her, but it was a struggle. She acted as though her life depended on me. I got engaged to a girl but I was so irritable because of living with Mother that I broke it off. Finally I did marry Sylvia. Mother did not approve. She never got along with Sylvia or even with the children. But Mother felt that *they* did not like *her*, and felt very unhappy about this. I tried my best. I did everything I could to make Mother happy and comfortable, but it was never enough. She would only have been happy if I had left my wife and children and come back to live with her, but this she did not really want.

A: Go on.

P: I always have some fear of not being competent enough, although I know that in actuality I am. And I am really very happily married and have fine youngsters. But I am tense.

A: Tell a little of the emotional relations in your earliest years, before six.

P: My sister was eight years older than I. Father was with a very large company and worked almost all the time. So I was close to Mother—very close. Father was swell, so warm, so friendly and understanding; but Mother was the power in the house. She made all the decisions. She worked hard. She was bossy and very strict and directing. But she was very kind, and I was very fond of her. She wanted me to be proper, to be a fine man, to look right, speak right, do right, and I wanted to also, and did. I would have paid quite a price if I hadn't. Father was fine and easy, never a cross word to me. We got on perfectly, really loved each other. But Mother was never happy. She was helpful to others, but strict and critical. As I tell you this, I can see that one of the strains in my marriage is because I tend to be like Mother in being too strict with my children. The children's real warmth goes to my wife much more than to me. It's the same with our friends. They are loyal to me and respect me, but their warmth goes to Sylvia.

A: What are your very first memories?

P: The earliest is of being carried or taken along by the hand, by Mother. Then I have one of doing something for Father and being very happy.

[Here the two themes are clearly portrayed—with Mother, but directed by her; with Father, but doing something for him and happy in the relationship.]

A: Did you dream last night?

P: I do remember a dream of a few nights ago. In it I was living with my mother. It was a beautiful place. I was wandering in the garden and had to be careful of the flowers. Meanwhile, Mother was cooking dinner for us.

A: Does this make you think of anything?

P: No. Well, it's not my home. That's all.

A: What do you mean?

P: I think of being irritable in my home. That's all.

A: About what do you think you are irritable there?

P: It just occurred to—maybe—hm! I'll be damned—maybe—maybe because people are not treating me the way Mother used to.

[With this tears flow. He must use his handkerchief. A sensitive area has certainly been touched.]

If the house is not picked up, neat and in order, or if someone is thoughtless, or if they don't look after me as Mother did—yes— then I get tense and irritable. And in the office too. There's always a little tension. If all is smooth, I don't notice it; but if anything goes wrong, then I feel it. I try to build a tolerance of others.

A: Because you cannot expect others to behave toward you as your mother did?

P: True. I was the only son and felt the pressure as though I were an only child. I used to pray for a little brother or sister. I was critical of Mother, but she did so very much for me. Even as I tell you about her, I feel I should not be critical because she did so much for me.

A: I guess you see the identification with your mother—tending to be like her and her model of how you and others should be. You said you are like her at home and in the office. And also your feeling of guilt toward her because of your hostility to her, a resentment that, however, has mostly been repressed. And your anger when people do not mother you as she did.

P: Yes, I see. But I don't want to be like Mother. She was respected, but she was not happy, and she did not make her family happy. She did so much for us but would not leave my father or my sister or me alone to live our own lives [tears]. My wife is so different; she will have no part of mothering me. She sends out my clothes to be cleaned and mended. She refuses to mother me.

A: You must become fully aware of your anger and what makes it. Like your wife's refusal to mother you, which may be the very best thing in the world for you.

P: Yes, I see your point. I'm sure it's true. If she let me slip into the same feelings toward her that I had toward my mother—I just don't want to contemplate it.

A: That is one of the central secrets of maturing and of psychotherapy—to avoid entrapment by your childhood patterns so that you feel as a mature adult would toward others, in a realistic way, and not as you did as a child toward your mother, or toward whomever the disturbed pattern developed. I think you will solve this well because through it all there was also real love between your mother and yourself and because your relationship with your father was so easy, warm and secure. I feel pretty sure your episode of a fast heartbeat was nothing more than repressed anger because the others in the board meeting did not treat you as your mother did, and because they did not behave as your mother, and now you, expected. And your tension is anger because you miss your mother and all the solicitude she represented. With your wife's personality as it is, I think you can outgrow the expectations toward her that you had to your mother. As you do that, she will be more responsive, warm and giving to you, and you will be less and less irritable. The vicious circle will stop; there will be less undercurrent of anger, and more giving, tolerance and warmth.

In this fortunate instance improvement did indeed start after this single interview, in which it was possible to uncover the essential dynamics. Of course, such insight alone is only effective where the balance of forces in both husband and wife is thus favorable. Sometimes one can see clearly in an hour a pattern that takes years to resolve. But here the wholesome and mature impulses preponderated; the exacerbation of demands and resentment caused by the mother's death were alleviated. And Myron was on the way out—out of that part of his feelings toward his mother which caused tension and irritability when transferred to his family and business associates.

Usually it is unwise for husbands and wives to discuss their unconsciouses with each other. But there are no rigid rules, only guiding principles. Myron did tell Sylvia of his tendency to want her to mother him and his anger when she didn't; and of his recognition of his being like his mother in strictness and criticalness although he did not want to be this way. This helped, for it only made explicit what Sylvia sensed anyway; it might not have helped if Myron himself (his "ego") had not been eager to reduce this component in his marriage. With all the love from and toward his mother, and so unambivalently toward his father, and toward his sister as well (although she was not a prominent figure in his life), he had the base for good relationships. He was not psychoanalyzed in the sense that he did not go through a "transference neurosis," that is, the living through toward the analyst of the disturbed pattern toward his mother.

This transference was apparently not necessary; the good feelings predominated. Although older than I at the time, he related to me warmly, openly and with confidence, following the pattern toward his father. We met weekly at first, then fortnightly, then monthly. The anxiety attack did not recur. His relations to his wife and children had their ups and downs but improved steadily; his tension in his profession diminished.

He could use the insight to spot his tendency to want others to behave like his mother toward him or in line with the standards of behavior she set for him and for everyone. However, the unconscious is treacherous, and I thought the time might come when he would find it advisable to return for more intensive work. But he continued to improve. Perhaps the friendly relationship with me helped, at least over the first few years. We continued to correspond for eight years after the war and to meet occasionally when he came east. Then he moved to southern California, and we lost touch. The quick collapse of the neurotic structure was most gratifying, in contrast to instances of equally clear and simple dynamics in which the balance of healthy mature forces and disturbed infantile ones is such as to be very stubborn and resistant therapeutically.

In the Decline

Let us cherish and love old age, for it is full of pleasure, if one knows how to use it.

Seneca

Age is not the obstacle to help with emotional problems it was once thought to be—the essential is still the balance of emotional forces. But there is no cure for waning charms and powers except graceful acceptance of nature, of the life cycle we are all born to, and making the most of our pleasure in the mature pursuits.

A successful business executive of 63, Owen, came for consultation because of anxiety. The suspicion, created by his story, that there was an undercurrent of rage at his wife was quickly confirmed by his report of a dream of riding into a slum area where a man attacked a woman. The slum area turned out to be his unconscious, the attacker, his own hostility to his wife. He had been fairly close to his mother, he told me, but not really close, not the way he wished, and he had repressed resentment against her. His father had died when Owen was five years old. It was soon evident that he was overly dependent on his wife, following the pattern toward his mother.

His wife was threatening to leave him, or at the very least, to have a sexual affair with some as yet unchosen man. She was enraged at Owen because he did not function well sexually. He no longer had the interest, she complained, nor gave the performance. First she thought he had a mistress. Then she thought something was wrong physically; he saw a urologist, then an endocrinologist, and tried hormones. All to no avail. Now he had developed anxiety about his sexual ability and thought that the problem was psychological, that he had developed some sexual inhibition. He had never had this problem before, except once or twice in youth when he did not function well sexually—but then it was only a transient problem under unusual circumstances.

Of course, he had thought of the fact that he was 63 and his wife 60. They were grandparents. In my opinion, this matter required graceful acceptance of the inevitable, after a lifetime of happiness, for which they could be grateful. Battling against the course of the life-cycle could only add struggle and frustration. It was, as usual, a matter of making the most of what existed, not raging against the reality while pining for a fantasy. He saw this and talked it over with his wife. She was well preserved but long past the menopause. He would arouse her without being able to follow through adequately. On her side, her own desires would arouse those in her husband. He would try or not try, and either way would more often than not leave her urges unsatisfied.

After some recognition of the facts of life, she adjusted reasonably well by having a bedroom to herself, thus being separated from the frustrating temptations of the conjugal bed. With her anger and her threats of infidelity removed, and with insight into his own reactive rage at her, Owen's anxiety diminished and his potency increased. But then he too had to face the years of adjustment to the realities of waning desire and potency. They reached a good *modus vivendi*, with mutual understanding of these tribulations of decline.

There was one untoward but revealing incident about two years afterward. Owen was reading in bed in his room. The weather was hot. He was seminude. His hand wandered idly to his genitals. His wife suddenly entered. She went into a rage because she said he showed more evidence of potency there alone than he had the last few times that they succeeded in having relations.

Such a case is typical. Certainly the gradual decline of desire has its problems no less than the sudden onslaught of the sexual urge in adolescence. Of course, a few men remain fully active sexually well into their seventies, and some probably longer. But most go through the decline in their late fifties, and for many it begins in the forties. Wet dreams and masturbation show the physiology to be intact still, but lust and potency no longer power effective performance. Even at best, the "zip" is not what it once was.

It must be strongly emphasized that therapeutic results are not easily and rapidly achieved. We have only meant to demonstrate that rapid resolution is sometimes possible when the balance of forces in the individual is auspicious for resolving or rising above the childhood emotional pattern.

We noted earlier that an understanding of an individual's dynamics can alter the childhood emotional pattern which is causing trouble within marriage or in other areas of the person's life. This leads naturally to questions concerning the results of such therapy. Clear-cut statistics would be illuminating, but none exist, perhaps because the vast variety of individual emotional problems, their kind and degree, with the use of dynamics for treatment varying accordingly.

A fine young woman comes to see me in near panic for fear of losing her mind; her husband of 15 years announces he is leaving her and then proceeds to move out of the house, giving no reasons. She cannot so precipitously face life alone when her entire existence and occupation have been her husband and children. She has no interest or training, and suddenly will be short of income, as well as having to endure the loneliness, being deprived of her husband's companionship and emotional support, to say nothing of being deprived of her accustomed sex life. The immediate therapeutic problem is to keep her stable in the face of this worst of rejections and the prospect of starting a life on her own. She manages to endure for some months, and then it appears that her husband has behaved this way because he is partly psychotic. He begins to veer back to her. Should she accept him back if he is a borderline psychotic? Should she make an attempt to get him evaluated and possibly treated?

Another wife in similar circumstances finds it more than she can bear; she becomes paranoid toward her husband, unable to think of anything except how awfully he as treated her. She is unable to have an interest in anything else or to carry responsibility. Her husband relents and wants to reestablish his home, but cannot tolerate being in the presence of his wife because of her paranoid condition.

Another woman, unable in youth to relate to other people closely, had some analytic treatment which went so successfully that she was able to marry and have children. But later she complained that her orgastic response was not as free and full as it should be, and this upset her husband. Later he was upset that she had been in treatment for nearly seven years and all was not "perfect." Of course, this was not quite accurate on his part: she had not really been in continuous treatment for ten years. Only occasionally, when she felt unhappy enough, she came in for an hour or two or possibly more at weekly intervals, with beneficial results. Such a person may have a very good marriage and life in general, even though she feels the occasional need for an analyst who knows her and can help her, who is "on tap," as it were, for decades—for example, the young woman who phoned me during my vacation (Chapter 21, "Happily Ever After"): nearly 20 years later I still hear from her, and she insists that our rare telephone conversations have saved her marriage, her sanity and her life. Enid, the wife in Chapter 9, "A Paradigm of Marriage," was helped in the same manner to get through a divorce; we describe in Chapter 39, "Mature Love," the man who was helped to avoid divorce and to save his marriage. A borderline psychotic girl met a borderline psychotic boy in a mental hospital; their parents could afford continuing treatment, and the two made a relatively happy marriage, with children, in spite of rare periods of depression and withdrawal states.

These examples illustrate that there are just no "end points"— unlike pneumonia, for instance, in which a certain percent of patients die, while another percent pass the crisis, the consolidation is resolved, and they recover.

As I review by memory and notes the patients I have seen over the years, I find that, even with sound statistics lacking, a firm impression emerges:

All the individuals got something well worth the time and money they invested in the analytic experience, whether they came for a single hour or kept in touch for 25 years. This is not surprising. To "know thyself" is only the *beginning* of wisdom, and analytic understanding enlightens all that comes after it, continuing to increase in depth and value for the rest of one's life.

37
THE PREMARITAL PERIOD

Adolescent seeking, pregnancy, children and divorce, while not central to our topic of marriage, are so germane to it as to require illustration of a few relevant points.

Humans are forever caught in a biological instinctual dilemma, being on the one hand promiscuous in their sexual urges but on the other driven to fuse these urges with permanent mating to one spouse. Before having to make a commitment to mate and family, can the adolescent not freely enjoy and indulge in sex, or is sex so involved with mature mating that it cannot be indulged for pleasure alone, even in adolescence? If an adolescent is relatively mature, sex will involve urges to find a mate and will not be free; but if there is a lack of maturity, a predominance of disturbed childhood patterns, then these will make trouble in the personal relationship with the partner and thus interfere with the sexual freedom and enjoyment. Although we may want to enjoy sex for itself, it seems that this is impossible because sex is too involved with other instincts and forces in the personality, is too interpersonal psychologically.

Adolescence can be a difficult time. The human organism at about 12 to 14 years of age suddenly feels the full force of the sexual urge. Yet the adolescent has not reached full growth or strength and is not yet mature, physically, mentally or emotionally. If this period from the burgeoning of the sex and mating drives until maturity and establishment in career and marriage lasted two or three or four years, it would be difficult enough. In a pioneering or agricultural community a boy of 18 or 19, if mature enough emotionally, could work his own land and provide for a wife and young. But the increasing duration of education means that a boy is 21 before graduating from college, with another three to six more years added if he studies for a profession. This makes him 25 or more before he has even begun his experience in life, before he has even been tested by the responsibilities of the world and of supporting himself and others. Many, as we know, collapse under the first real responsibilities and regress in different ways and degrees, some even so far as to require hospitalization. Girls, of course, encounter the same problems. What then should adolescents do in the meantime? Some guide to the answers must lie in what they *do* do and in the consequences.

First, as to the boys. We have had a double standard. A young man is thought to lack masculinity if he does not have sexual experience, say by about age 21. Some start at 14. But with whom? Experience with a prostitute does not seem a proper initiation into what will be his most valued relationship—that with his wife. But if it is a girl of as high a caliber as he wants his wife to be, will they not become emotionally involved? And, if there is mutual orgasm, will not the full force of the girl's love-needs, mating instincts and maternal urges be aroused? Will she not want marriage? And then will the young man either marry her although not in love with her, or, knowing that from the beginning he wanted sex with her but not marriage, will he reject her? And will this rejection not only hurt her, frustrate her deepest instincts, but permanently injure her self-respect and self-esteem? And if the young man is mature, will he not feel this, feel that he has "used" a fine girl, and generate a guilt that may lead him to punish himself, subtly but surely, for a long time? This is in fact a common story.

But between the prostitute and a girl of this sort is there not another type of girl, who will gladly have sexual affairs but with no strings attached? Yes, there is, but the ones I have seen are neurotic, for their sex is split off from their love, mating, reproductive and maternal instincts. A friend of mine once jokingly said he would like to meet a nice masochistic girl, that is, one who would give and suffer. So here we are again. The girl who is available is neurotic; she suffers from a disturbance in development that is not promising for her to achieve a happy marriage.

But cannot sex somehow be freely enjoyed in a setting of friendly companionship without the involvement of the mating instinct, until the right time and the right person come for this involvement as marriage? A few words are in order in connection with May, whom we met in Chapter 17 as Mel's inamorata.

May was a young woman of average good looks and with all the attractiveness of youth. What made her embroil herself emotionally with a man, who, however interesting, was twice her age and had a wife, five children and a home that had been established and apparently stable for nearly 25 years? Why would she forego young love and the freshness of starting life with her own man, a man who, like herself, came to marriage unused?   This pattern is not, however, unusual.   I have seen it in college girls and have followed the later lives of some of them.

One sophomore had a rather half-hearted interest in finding out why, when she wanted so much to marry and have a family as soon as possible after graduation, she should be having heavy affairs now with a series of boys and be sleeping with them.   A healthy young junior thought life quite simple: a girl should have her fun while young.   Maybe she was right.   My own view may be grossly slanted because it is only the people with problems who come to my attention.   This girl, so frank, direct, honest and outgoing at that time, phoned me from St. Louis some eight years later.   She was in a panic—pregnant by a married man and shaken by the realization that, now 28, she was having a continuous series of dead-end affairs, with no marriage in sight.   She sensed that somehow her sexuality had broken loose from her mating instincts, and she wanted help.

Another college girl went through a period as a freshman when she was so attracted in every way to much older men, between the ages of 40 and 60, that she turned away from them as a defense, as an opposite reaction, when they were friendly to her.   Her dynamics showed (among other interplays of motivation) suppressed rebellion against her parents, chiefly her mother.

Then there was an apparently quite normal, controlled girl, Andrea, who also had a penchant for older men.   She later moved to another city, but when she was 28, she came back to see me.   She had just broken off a clandestine affair with a man of about 45 who had a wife and three children, and now was attracted to a man less than ten years her senior, about whom she had grave doubts.   We will call him Al.   I referred her to an excellent analyst in Milwaukee, where she lived.   Her doubts were justified: Al was a sadist.   His ex-wife had not been able to get away; she had felt that her life was in some danger, and would be more acutely so if she made any move.   So she took advantage of a visit to the pediatrician as an excuse and left her husband and abandoned her child.   Of course, Al raised a furor, but in the end she was free legally.   He pursued her and threatened her until she moved to Canada.   The analyst suspected this ex-wife of being paranoid and Andrea also, but it turned out that their fears were realistic.

The girl's material showed a strong masochistic, self-punishing tendency. In childhood her hostility was much repressed. All was love; yet she had dreams of all sorts of disasters happening to herself. These dreams involved her younger brother. As nearly as could be discerned, the issue reflected an overindulgence, overprotection and overcontrol by her parents, especially her mother, during the first year or two, generating an overstrong dependence on her mother. The arrival of a brother when Andrea was two and the turning of the parental attention toward him therefore caused an intensified hostility in Andrea. But the family's standard of never expressing hostility, only love, caused Andrea's hostility to be repressed. She was able to repress it, but at the cost of turning it against herself down underneath.

The psychiatrist did his best to analyze this masochism, but Andrea persisted in acting it out. She married Al despite all she knew about him. The psychiatrist told me that her parents had taken the opportunity to phone him to blast him for trying to prevent their daughter's marriage to the man of her choice, although she had told them her fears soon after the one time they had met the fiancé. (If parents can understand and advise and be sure the fiancé is entirely mature, loving and flawless after one or two meetings, I admire and applaud their insight and sagacity.) Six months after the marriage, Andrea called her psychiatrist again: her husband's pattern toward his first wife was repeating itself with her. It included physical sadism. She told her psychiatrist this, thanked him for his past efforts to forewarn her, but said she could not come to see him because of fear of her husband. After the war when I saw the psychiatrist, I asked about them, but he had heard nothing further. Then, less than a year later, he wrote me that Andrea was dead, of what I never found out, but the psychiatrist was suspicious of Al's sadism, especially since he was a chemist and could easily make himself expert in toxicology.

In different personalities, hostility and guilt take different forms and involve sex in varied ways. Since those people with problems are the only ones who contact me, perhaps other girls whom I do not see find happiness in a series of sexual relations before marriage, or outside it, or in these affairs with older married men. Statistics on this matter would be interesting. The only generalization I could make, very broadly, from the situations like Andrea's that I have seen or have known about, is that a strong sado-masochistic component is the common element, a strong tendency for the love and sex and mating to be deflected into a path that causes suffering, sometimes extreme suffering—to the man, his wife and his children— and punishment to the girl herself. To her, at the time, it is "true love," an infatuation from which nothing can dissuade her. But the truth is that one must use one's head in guiding one's heart because often one's heart is largely directed by darker forces, infantile patterns full of hate and sadism and destructiveness directed to others and to oneself. The head, the ego, the highest powers of reason and judgment must be aware of these forces, or one will as Wilde wrote, "kill the thing he loves," and himself also.

How sexual freedom before marriage is working out since the introduction of "the pill" is a complicated matter, and it is just because it is so complex that the outcomes are so individual. This complexity arises from the involvement of sex with other major forces in the total personality.

In the first place sex is a physiological reaction of body to body, but neither body exists without a personality. Sexual intercourse is not, as is often said, a simple bodily function like urination or defecation or eating a meal (anyway, who enjoys eating alone?). It always involves the two personalities. When one's most secret, most utterly egocentric sexual fantasies come to reality, they are always altered by the interplay of the personalities. At least this is true except probably for criminals or schizophrenics, who are incapable of identifying with, feeling with, another person. Putting it most conservatively, it is very difficult to keep personality out of the purely physical act. Sex involves another person; it is part of an interpersonal relation.

This is not surprising, because sex is part of reproduction; further, it is part of the mating instinct. In humans and some other species, this is a cooperative undertaking between male and female—building the nest and rearing the young. Whatever the exact underlying instincts for mating may be in human beings, there is no doubt that human children do not mature normally to emotional health unless reared in a secure home by both a father and a mother. I do not mean to say that some excellent adults have not come out of broken homes or orphanages. (In these cases, good fortune has provided adequate substitutes for the parents.) I am speaking of the base—the complete, loving secure home—and not the exceptional situations. Sexual intercourse is part of the mating instinct, of an interpersonal relationship, and hence cannot be dealt with as though it were an isolated act. It is sometimes split off, as we have seen, but perhaps this situation is usually or always pathological in some degree.

In our examples, the problems that arise from trying to satisfy sexual desire as though it were an isolated, independent function emphasize how involved it is with the mating instincts and the total personality. The adult personality is the result of a long development, which follows the emotional attachments and reactions of earliest childhood. Thus sexual indulgence is intimately involved not only with mating but with all the other forces in the personality, both the infantile and the mature.

One of the chief of these forces is of course the young child's consuming need for love and care from its mother. And in adults these dependent-love needs usually seek satisfaction from the person who is desired sexually. As we have just noted, sexual desire usually follows the original path of the childhood attachment (imprinting, Chapter 2). This is clearly seen in adolescents who normally leave home, but then feel lonely and crave love. This craving is combined with sexual desire, so that their needs for love now include both forces and draw in other motivations as well. If enough of these desires and motivations are drawn in, then they experience the feeling of "being in love." If the infantile forces predominate over the mature ones, then the feeling can be infatuation, with some warping of their sense of reality and responsibility and a disregard for the welfare of the "loved" one for the person's own sake.

Some relatively mature personalities do not handle their sexual relations or even their feeling and behavior toward the opposite sex in a mature fashion. This is most clearly seen when sex is used for neurotic "acting out," that is, for following childhood patterns of behavior toward others, rather than sex and mating being expressions of the mature motivations of the healthy adult. Hence sex can express hate (as in lust-murder) or infantile dependence ("clinging vines" or passive, dependent men), grasping ("gold-diggers") or any other feeling, as well as or rather than mature love and responsibility. Sex has "content"; it serves as an outlet, pathway, channel or drain for every kind of feeling and tension, mature and immature. It is also the great consolation and diversion. Between couples who deeply attract each other it is one of life's culminations. But because of the intrusion of powerful, often disordered, infantile desires into the mature motivations and mating instincts, parents, educators, churchmen and others concerned have justified fears that the adolescent who rides these wild horses may unconsciously and unintentionally cause serious harm to himself and to others.

We have mentioned a college girl who said, "Isn't it strange that I have all these affairs when what I really want is a good marriage and children." A woman may be promiscuous although she wants more than anything else to be a faithful wife and mother. How this can occur is illustrated by a young woman of considerable beauty whom we will name Beryl. The key was expressed in a poignant dream: "In the distance I see my mother; I get near her, feeling so happy, she looks at me and says disdainfully, 'Oh, it's *you*.' Then I realize that she had thought that I was my brother."

Beryl longed for marriage, for a husband to love and be loved by, for children and a stable home. Yet, in her mid-twenties, she could say with only slight hyperbole, "I must have gone through a thousand men." She would meet a man and long to be close; soon she would be dating him, sleeping with him and perhaps living with him. But she would want to be *so* close to him that he would feel uneasy and begin to withdraw. This would threaten and enrage her; she would storm at him in a temper tantrum. He would feel threatened and defensive. Soon she would pick a fight, and in a matter of weeks the affair would break up in anger. She was beginning to see this pattern in her own behavior and to see the instability and neuroticism of her various men. Her own pattern was readily traced back through the wreckage of her passionate, turbulent, explosive affairs to the emotional suffering of her childhood. She had a brother, Bart, two years older, who was openly adored by her mother in shameless preference to Beryl. In preadolescence Beryl mentioned this to her mother, who confessed that she had always felt something special for Bart. He could do no wrong, Beryl no right. Her father was only a peripheral figure, absorbed in his work. But he had feelings of love for Beryl as a child, and this saved her from psychosis.

As is so often the case, the partially rejected child becomes overclinging and fights desperately for what is deficient, like an animal half-starved for the succulent food that is so close yet denied. And the constant, unsatisfied, emotional hunger sustains a ceaseless underlying resentment, ever ready for bursts of rage. Longing for her mother's love, combined with resentment, produced guilt and the feeling that she deserved punishment. If you must have someone's love and are dependent on him or her, how can you burst out in rage at that intimate person? Hence Beryl's anger stayed subterranean and was mostly vented on herself (like stumbling and hurting oneself when in a rage at another person).

Toward her brother Beryl felt the adoration of the younger sister, and her longings for his love and affection were increased by her mother's rejection. But she also felt hatred toward him out of envy and jealousy of his being preferred by her mother. All these feelings were eroticized. From an early age Beryl took every opportunity to go nude in front of her brother. Only once, however, was there any physical contact: when she was about 13, she entered his room nude when he was undressing. They got on the bed but at the first touch panicked. That was the end of any overt eroticism between them, and the incident was never mentioned thereafter. But her patterns toward both her mother and her brother underlay Beryl's relations with boys, and they came into the open when she was in her early twenties and went all the way sexually. Then appeared the too-intense love needs, the feelings of rejection and frustration, the rage, the picking of fights exactly as with her brother, the final breakup, the intolerable loneliness, the longings for marriage, the new man and the old cycle. Through it all, however, she was able to work steadily and support herself. If the balance of forces and the choice of analyst are propitious, even problems such as Beryl's can be helped eventually and the girl, despite her wild oats, may find the right man for herself and make a go of the marriage she so deeply wants.

Whether or not there are girls who just have their fun and then, when ready and when they meet the right man, settle down, I know that there are such boys. Their sexual adventures satisfy a curiosity prior to marriage, and then they are better able to settle down with the wife of their choice. Men are always ready sexually, and, willy-nilly, with a woman or not, by wet dreams or masturbation, will have their emissions with orgastic overflow about three or four times a week, whether they wish it or fight it. Some who have been embroiled with girls have concluded that it is best to rely on this safety valve and marry as early as possible.

In a way it seems a great loss that youth, as yet uncommitted to the weightier responsibilities of career and family, cannot freely enjoy something that exceeds all other immediate pleasures and culminations as does sex. But humans have many built-in conflicts. Why indeed should sex come in full force before a child is yet an adult? Why should the emotional development be so readily warped by parental influences? Why the hair-trigger readiness to become hostile? Why is sex so detachable from the other instincts that go into mating, reproduction, family life and rearing of young? On the other hand, children raised with good relationships to their parents achieve adequate emotional maturity and become stable, healthy spouses, parents and citizens. Adolescents who play with sex are apt to find that sex and the other potent instincts are playing with them. They are apt to get caught in the grip of their instincts as these forces are handled by their particular individual dynamics.

These dynamics (it seems to me from such observations as have been presented here) are the strongest factor in the long run, assuming a reasonably stable environment. A still young and charming mother feared for her two daughters who were nearing puberty. She feared for their sexual behavior when the biological urge hit them. In anticipation she was imposing strict moral training in the religious setting of their church. This was fine—if it was done in a way the girls could accept and did not produce the opposite effect by antagonizing them and inciting them to revolt.

Actually the most effective and reliable control over adolescents lies in mutual love, in good feelings between parents and between parents and child. This is the great, central fact. Given this, there is little cause to worry about girls or boys injuring themselves or others by their sexual behavior. A teen-age girl (let us call her Nina) who always had excellent relations with her parents talked to me easily and freely, in a friendly, social (not professional) relationship. She told me of a girl at her school who had a reputation for sexual looseness and another who was leaving because she was illegitimately pregnant. I said, "Something must be very wrong in those families, in the feelings between those girls and their parents." She replied, "Of course. My friends and I have known that and expected something like this. The girl who is pregnant has a brute for a father. Now he will blame her, but he is the one who should be blamed; he made her like this."

There was no need to worry about Nina. She knew the physiological facts of life; far more important, she knew the emotional facts, as seen in her remark. And the essential, the real base, was her good relationship with her parents. "Sex education," in the form of explaining to the adolescent where babies come from, is of course almost pointless. Their questions should be answered as soon as they are old enough to ask them; but the parents' tone and attitude are as important as the content. And this tone and attitude will reflect the only real essential: the mutual love and trust that make mutual frankness natural and easy. So long as the girl or boy loves his parents and is sure of their love and can communicate freely with them, talking over any subject with no holds barred, being direct and open about all relations, including those with the opposite sex, because of mutual trust—so long as this kind of child-parent feeling exists, there need not be any worry about the child. That child has no hostility of any consequence toward his parents to deflect toward others to hurt them or toward himself to cause self-injurious masochistic behavior.

Contrariwise, if this mutual love and trust, this free communication between parent and child (and this is a two-way channel), is lacking, then there is no possible way that the parents can control a teenager. A teenager cannot be chaperoned permanently. If he is driven into a feeling of hostility and guilt, he can always surreptitiously find opportunities for acting out sexually, and other ways, to harm his parents, himself and others he involves.

Nina, the girl just mentioned, controlled her sexuality without difficulty until she graduated from college and married at the age of 21, with all the components of marriage unified and fused, giving herself to the man of her choice with a clear conscience and no apologies, and entering with him into a rich and satisfying love life, resulting, when they were settled, in wanted, loved children. Perhaps other girls freely have many all-out sexual affairs and afterwards re-integrate their sexuality with the other components of matrimony and settle down equally well into a stable home life. I do not know what the statistics would show. But I am sure that in the long run the major "destiny which shapes our ends" consists, barring unusual circumstances, in the essential dynamics of the individual personality, the continuation of the earliest emotional reactions to the parents.

38
PREMARITAL INTERVIEWS

The good can be won; all that we dread can be conquered.

Epicurus

The author has found most premarital interviews with young men and women to be helpful, particularly in making clear certain points. Many, if not most, young couples, although they may have definitely made up their minds to marry and would let nothing stop them, nevertheless also have certain anxieties and insecurities about taking this step. Sometimes they are not quite clear in their own minds as to what the sources of these doubts are. A few interviews should help them define them and discover something about their sources.

Many couples do not realize the difficulties of marital adjustment. I would point out the discrepancy between the Hollywood version of marriage—the glamorous girl and man who live happily ever after—and the actual statistics. Obviously brutal destruction of illusions would serve no good purpose; gentle leading to a realistic view is the only safe ground for making the difficult adjustment necessary for marriage. Certainly the differences between fantasy and reality should be clarified and emphasized. The distinction is of vital practical importance. Only a portion of one's fantasies can ever be realized. But if that is known and accepted, then one can pine less for the fantasied potentialities and enjoy more fully the actual realities.

One of the difficulties in making a marriage lies in the inability to see, during the courtship, what the relationship might be later when it is consummated. If there are ulterior motives for marriage, then the difference may be huge: one partner might fawn on the other, pouring on the flattery during the courtship with the real motive of marriage for security or money. Even with complete sincerity and no ulterior purpose, few individuals are well enough aware of their sex and mating drives, how these drives motivate them, or—even more important—aware of their childhood emotional patterns and the longings which will cause dire difficulties, such as excessive dependent love needs or urges to control and dominate, or to lean on another submissively.

It is difficult for youth to have an appreciation of the demands that marriage makes upon one's capacity for giving love, interest and attention and for taking responsibilities within the home. The *New Yorker* cartoon of the young couple standing at the altar, each one thinking of the other one bringing breakfast in bed, is all too typical.

It might be a good idea for the couple to understand the limitation of anyone else's capacity for judging who is a good mate for another person. Harmony is, of course, very largely a matter of how two personalities fit each other. Often it is a matter of how two neuroses fit each other. How the dynamics mesh may be seen frequently in those who seek premarital psychiatric evaluation, exactly as they do a physical examination, even before their engagement. This is, of course, a much better time than after the couple have been engaged for a long period and are on the very brink of marriage.

There are certain possibilities for predicting the success of a marriage. It is well established (Saul, 1977) that the basis of the emotional relationships of adult life is laid in childhood. As we have reiterated, each person follows in his marriage, usually with uncanny precision, the patterns of emotional reactions that he had in early childhood toward members of his own family. Therefore, a boy or girl who has had basically good, close relationships with both his parents and with his brothers and sisters can generally be counted upon to have the capacity for a good relationship with his spouse and children. Conversely, a young person who has had disturbed relationships with his parents during his earliest days, weeks, months or years is usually not a good risk. It may be that the balance of forces is such that this person may still turn out to be a good spouse and parent, but there is definite risk involved.

One great difficulty here lies in the fact that a person may have relationships with his parents that appear superficially to be good, but there may be important tensions underneath the surface. One must take into account the fact that every person operates on two levels, and one must try to discover the true deeper feelings and motivations. The years from conception to five or six are the most crucial and, of course, usually the hardest to find out about. It is then that the core of the personality is laid down. The child who has had excellent relationships within his own family until that age has a healthy base to his personality which is apt to make him good marriage material even though things may have gone wrong after that age.

There is a difficulty in the premarital interview itself. Here there is not the same motivation to reveal oneself as there is in treatment. Here there is not the urge to relieve suffering. Instead one or both of the pair may have reason to hide the truth in order to make a good impression.

Perhaps all couples should know the usual course of emotional development in marriage. Most couples are brought together because of identification. This is generally taken to mean similarity of interests, but in reality it usually goes much deeper than that. The similarity usually is in certain, often neurotic emotional needs and drives. Two people may be brought together because they were both deprived, or because they are both hostile to their fathers, or because both of them have an older brother or sister with whom they had problems of competition. Often the more intense the emotion toward the members of their own family (for example, the greater the deprivation each has suffered), the more the couple are brought together, the more they understand each other. So far so good. After marriage, however, the underlying patterns to the parents begin to assert themselves. Now the feelings of deprivation (or other troublesome feelings) begin to be directed toward each other. Each one feels that the other is not doing his part, not giving enough; and keeping to this particular example, the very sense of deprivation in both, which led to their falling in love, now leads to marital disorder.

Couples should be aware of the masochistic tendency, often more transparent in girls than in men, to get into a position that brings suffering. This is seen clearly in the many girls who get themselves involved, sexually or otherwise, with men who never marry them or give them happiness. Often they damage their reputations because of the relationship. If marriage is achieved, it is very often with a man who is in some way sadistic, usually unconsciously so. One hears again and again of cases in which the husband treats his wife shabbily and drives her into a nervous breakdown or to the verge of it, or else makes her life miserable. Not infrequently, however, this is the responsibility of the wife in that she unconsciously picked this particular kind of a man to marry because of a masochistic trend within herself. In addition to that she sometimes, by her own behavior, brings the man's sadism out by subtly provoking him. Of course men have this tendency also. The important point here is that neither one of the couple should make a neurotic, especially a masochistic, choice of a partner.

Another point, often closely related to this, is the matter of ulterior motives. Sometimes there is more of an element of winning prestige or money through a marriage than the young person may be conscious of. Sometimes, particularly in girls, there is an element of escaping from an unhappy home. If these motives can be frankly expressed and discussed, the marriage starts off on a much better basis, and a great deal of the undercurrent of guilt is obviated. This is of first importance because the tendency to make oneself unhappy stems largely from feelings of guilt—deep-lying guilt toward one's parents and also currently generated guilt within a marriage.

It usually seems to be healthy if each individual of the couple is able to discuss in a private interview something of his whole philosophy of sexual relations and his past experiences. This is borne out by the Kinsey report (1948, 1953), which shows that without treatment sexual patterns seem to change not at all in the course of people's lives.

The "helpability" of emotional problems should be pointed out. The analyst sees many couples who come to him after years of strife and who are on the verge of divorce, or after divorce has already occurred to the detriment of themselves and the futures of their children. Yet the basic emotional difficulties are frequently found to be solvable problems, and much of their suffering could have been prevented if they had sought help earlier. They should know that if things do not go well, it does not mean that the marriage has been basically a mistake and a failure. Sometimes the difficulty is rather deep-seated, and considerable treatment is necessary. But in many others the main point can be reached in a relatively short time, and sometimes simply a few interviews with a good person or treatment over a few weeks or a few months can be of appreciable help. Many young people are astounded to learn that the personality and motivations of an individual are not utterly fixed and unalterable, and that with help significant steps can often be achieved toward adjustment and maturity. It is, as we have stressed, a matter of the balance of forces, within each individual and between the two persons.

References

Kinsey, A., Pomeroy, W. and Martin, C. (1948): *Sexual Behavior in the Human Male.* Philadelphia: W. B. Saunders.

___ and Gebhard, P. (1953): *Sexual Behavior in the Human Female.* Philadelphia: W. B. Saunders.

Saul, L. J. (1977): *The Childhood Emotional Pattern.* New York: Van Nostrand Reinhold.

39
MATURE LOVE

When someone asks me what kinds of people and problems I see professionally, I usually say, "I have an office practice, not a hospital practice. I see the everyday problems of everyday people—like you and me." Those I am privileged to see and help are by and large quite superior persons. Whatever is causing trouble beneath the surface, in their egos (conscious characters) they have maturity, compassion, courage, emotional honesty and other fine attributes. I do not like the term "patient," although we are in a patient–doctor relationship. We deal with human beings, whose problems have mostly arisen from childhood patterns generated by their parents, as the growing child interacts with the circumstances that fate and they (consciously or unconsciously) have gotten themselves into.

These people are helped by insight, which is largely an educational procedure that exposes the more or less hidden roots of their problems and enables them to help themselves. Most problems are *basically in human relations,* in *feelings toward others.* The relation to the analyst is a sample human relation. (The term "analysand" is in many ways a more suitable appellation than the term "patient"). Insofar as the disturbing elements can be "analyzed out" of the relation with the analyst, so that only good, free, easy, friendly and mature feelings remain toward him, then the analysand has a workable model and experience for use in his relations with other people in his life. Basically analysis is simply emotional honesty and often requires a certain nobility, but always at least elements of a good character.

A man with some feelings of insecurity, inferiority and anxiety, despite his outward success, was telling me in the office about his home life. "I recognize," he said, "my wife's fine qualities, but something in her makeup makes her charming to everyone except me. People all praise her. Besides charm, they tell me of her maturity of judgment and her realism, how efficient and practical she is, and how kind, considerate and thoughtful she is. But toward me she shows none of these feelings. We used to have a loving relationship. But in the past few years she has shown, more and more, only criticism and anger toward me. It's gotten to where nothing I do is right. She sarcastically twists my kindest words around. If I am quiet with the children, she tells me I am neglecting them; if I play with them, she scoffs, 'Just another child.'

"For years I've tried to overcome her hostility to me by giving her so much attention, consideration and affection that she would be forced to soften. This worked for a little while only. Recently she has wanted a divorce. I myself have now come to feel, 'Get it and good riddance.' But I can't go through with it. For I know that she is a child underneath. She acts so independent, but she has no career skill and no other close friend or emotional support, and I do not believe she could survive without me. What you said is so true: people usually hate a person they are dependent on. And I think she is a masochist. I think a divorce would destroy her and all she has in life in her present position.

"As I visualize such a future, I could not let her do that to herself. I live in a constant stream of hostility from her; but as I see it, I have no choice but to be strong and stand it, for if I reacted as she wants me to, she would ruin her life. It is not easy for me, for I need much love. I had a lot in childhood, as I told you, and also a lot since. But I could not cause her the pain of jealousy or deal her such a blow, nor can I let her isolate and destroy herself. You once mentioned a Norse god who was a god because he could live without love. I can understand that now, unfortunately."

Perhaps this man was wrong in his judgment. Perhaps his wife would have thrived and prospered after a divorce. I think, though, from other information, that he was right. But even if he misread his wife's behavior, can we not take heart about human beings from this kind of mature love for another? Of course, when faced with such a marriage, the analyst also thinks about the man's own possible masochism, thinks that perhaps he kept himself unconsciously in a deprived position, the butt of hostility, out of inner needs for punishment, some unknown guilt perhaps. But masochism had never been evident in his previous life with his wife or with others, or in his dreams. From all that could be learned, he did what he did out of mature love.

I heard from this man some 15 years later; the marriage had held and been relatively happy—his judgment had been mature and correct, the best for his wife, himself and their children, and now for his grandchildren who were a great joy. For although his wife's childhood pattern had partially emerged and made trouble in the marriage, both husband and wife had enough maturity and strength in their egos to remain with the marriage, tolerating the discomfort while they worked through their difficulties and slowly recovered their initial loving relationship.

40
THOUGHTS FOR A YOUNG COUPLE

... Married life ... bumps, bruises, and adjustments. It is mind, not body, that makes marriage last ... keep thine eyes wide open before marriage and half shut afterward ...

A. Myrer
The Last Convertible

In the practice of psychotherapy, analysts generally do not give *advice*. There are many reasons for abstaining, but one alone suffices: even though the analyst may see the childhood emotional pattern and therefore know part of the patient's personality better than the patient knows himself, no human being knows another well enough, or all the externals, to make decisions for him. I have never liked the term "counseling" in spite of its advantages, because it implies giving advice. A good analyst does not, however, shirk responsibility or shrink from giving emotional support. But the method for doing so must be purely analytic, that is, talking over with the patient the psychological realities as they appear to the analyst, and the likely consequences of possible decisions. The analyst only knows the possible pros and cons of what he observes at that particular moment; it might be just a fragment of the reality, and even that might be distorted. In Chapter 9 ("A Paradigm of Marriage") a patient mentioned years after treatment that she could never have lived through her divorce and remarriage without the analyst. But at no time during her treatment did the analyst give direct advice or imply that he favored one alternative or the other. He did discuss the realities openly, but only when he had accumulated ample evidence to make evaluations.

The following thoughts are not advice, then, but insight gained from the experiences of others.

We previously listed nine important elements in the making of a satisfying marriage and home for rearing children. These elements can be roughly subdivided into two or three categories: mechanical, emotional and sexual. With these elements in mind, we might suggest to a young man or woman contemplating marriage something like the following:

Dear John and Mary,

You are entering upon an extremely difficult venture when you commit yourselves to the intimacy of life together for as long as you both shall live. The satisfactions will be well worth it if you preserve and succeed in achieving a reasonable degree of harmony, identification and love. Some of the problems you should know in advance; discuss them and try to reach an agreement upon them. Some problems will be relatively mechanical such as deciding who will be responsible for what tasks. Since earliest history when man provided the food by hunting, it has been the husband's time-honored mission to furnish his wife and children with food, clothing and shelter. Will you two continue this pattern? Will you have children? If so, will you, John, undertake the full responsibility of earning sufficient income to support both of you and the children adequately? Or will you, Mary, carry part of this responsibility? If you help, Mary, will John then take on part of the care of the children, a very demanding task? If not, will you have someone to help with the children, Mary, and if you care for them alone, will you be able to tolerate their interminable demands and the loneliness of the housewife's life, the foregoing of pursuing your own interests and your freedom to live independently in the big world?

It is important to define in advance those areas for which each of you as husband and wife will accept responsibility and authority. No doubt there are as many ways to distribute this responsibility as there are marriages. But in the most successful ones, no matter how important the husband might be in business or profession or what interest, enjoyment and income it provides him, when he crosses the threshold of his home the husband acknowledges that it is his wife's domain, the area in which *she* is unquestioned authority and ruler. And she in turn needs the intelligence, judgment and overall sense of reality to take this responsibility. Both husband and wife must share the responsibility and authority for (1) adequate financial security, and (2) proper rearing of their children and the emotional satisfaction of the children and each other.

Besides these relatively "mechanical" elements of marriage there are the more exclusive emotional ones.

Few couples, I think, discuss the extent and intensity of their dependent-love needs until one or both becomes so frustrated that mutual anger is already threatening their marriage. While taking her history, I once asked a young woman the routine question: "What about your dependence and love needs?" She replied instantly and emphatically, "Oh, I need lots of love and support." The give–get cases in this book illustrate just what troubles marriages can encounter because of these needs. One sees many of them in practice: the husband who is so absorbed in his own work and interests that he has meager time, energy or interest in his wife and children although he is not actually "overworked"; the man "in the gray flannel suit" who is so busy climbing the ladder of success that he has insufficient time or energy available for his family; the wife who always has some favorite television program to watch when her conscientious husband has an evening off or wants to go to bed; and so on. There are extremely few human beings who are able to live in close proximity let alone intimacy with others without developing some frustration and irritation that engender anger. Unfortunately, this problem is intrinsic to nearly all marriages. How do you handle this annoyance and anger? Is it best to ignore this friction within a particular marriage; or to give in and blast away; or to control the anger and count to 10; or to forget it for some days, and "let not the sun set on your wrath," and then having waited, judge whether to forget it entirely or talk it over when both partners are calm? Decisions such as these are essential in making a marriage, and learning to make them sometimes takes 10 or 20 years, so difficult is the marital adjustment. But in achieving it you will grow and mature, reaping the deepest satisfactions that life affords—a loving close relation with spouse and children.

Another basic area of adjustment in marriage is sexual relations. I would like to assume that between the two of you there is a full, strong, wholesome desire for sexual intercourse. I think most couples feel this force whether or not they indulge it before marriage. If either of you is in doubt about gratification in sex, it is not for me to say, in this permissive age, "try it." Sex is important for your whole personality, and "trying it" may offend your conscience and entire past training. Some boys as well as girls still hold virginity as the most precious wedding gift to their mate. I can only say that, if other problems that stand in the way of loving and being loved are solved in reasonable degree, then usually the sexual performance and satisfaction follow freely and naturally. Of course, if one or both of you have some inner disorder in the sexual response, then this probably will require treatment, whether by physical or psychological procedures or both.

To marry young can be a fine thing, but sometimes the couple is not mature enough to handle the relationship, especially if a child arrives soon. Usually the time when one marries is not a matter of thoughtful and deliberate choice, but an emotional decision. If the fit or mesh is right, the marriage will probably do well whether the couple is very young or not. Without the correct mesh of personalities there will be difficulties.

The great basic determinants of marital happiness or failure lie in the motivations and reactions of the childhood emotional pattern. But a few agreements between husband and wife can smooth the marriage path. Most couples work out dozens or hundreds of these little agreements to keep their relationship pleasant. For example, "Let not the sun set on your wrath." That is, try to conquer your anger before the day ends, before you go to sleep. This is sometimes more than one can do, but if so, the following aphorism applies: "Sufficient unto the day is the evil thereof." Every morning wipe the slate clean; make a fresh start with good feelings unrelated to the troubles of yesterday. To conquer one's anger may take some years of practice.

A pleasant custom and preventer of friction is the daily "cocktail hour." It may involve sipping only fruit or vegetable juice rather than liquor, but should be a special time to sit down together or with the children, exchanging problems and experiences of the day. Another potential harmonizer is listening to or watching a daily news program together. A couple learns what subjects are pleasant for discussion and which topics to avoid.

Every time you meet or part, express affection by a kiss and embrace. Everyone needs appreciation. Mary, when your husband puts in an especially hard day or week at work, show him you recognize his efforts and appreciate them. John, your wife has the daily drudgery of cooking. Show her you enjoy every meal; keep up the compliments. Everyone has inferiority feelings and a sense of failure in reaching full maturity. Bolster your mate's self-esteem. Try not to criticize each other except with the greatest tact and gentleness. Do not attempt to control each other, make demands on each other or interfere with the other's freedom. All this, of course, should be within the bounds of fidelity and loyalty.

In agreeing to the assignment of responsibilities within your marriage, you must settle the crucial question of handling the checkbook and banking. It is a time-consuming task. In my experience, those marriages seem to work best in which the wife handles the accounts, for she knows every detail of operating a home and how much can be spent. She relieves the husband of such details as might take too much time and effort from his schedule, and leaves his energies free for his work. The wife is usually more satisfied not only to stay within the budget but to maintain a savings plan if she handles it herself, and the husband has more time free to earn.

One word more, especially for John: if you ever forsee divorce, discuss it carefully and tactfully long in advance. Give Mary time to adjust and prepare her for this blow from which she will never fully recover. And see the best professional in your area before deciding. Of course the same advice holds true for wives who contemplate walking out on their husbands.

Although the above points are true and apt and a correct guide, you are probably so irresistibly in the grip of the mating instinct that you cannot at present hear or comprehend these thoughts or calmly consider them. But as time goes on and the everyday painful differences and frictions arise, as you struggle with them you may recall this guidance and return to these words, finding that with time and experience they have meaning for you and possibly some help.

41

THOUGHTS FOR A TEENAGER

Dear _____,

You are just entering puberty, a stage in your development that different children grow into at different ages. I am a grandfather, a physician and a psychiatrist. It would seem likely that, out of all this experience, I would have a great deal to tell you on the subject of sex that might be of help to you. I will address this to you, a boy, although I think that most of what I say will be of use to your sister and other girls also. What comes to my mind is not one big, dramatic piece of information which I do not have, but rather a series of points.

First, be perfectly open about sex with your parents, both mother and father. Of course, they know that sex is normal and that boys have erections from the time they are small babies. Therefore, there should be no shame or guilt in discussing this subject with either of your parents. Sometimes there is shame though, and if you feel it, the thing to do is discuss this feeling directly with one or both parents. I think the reason this feeling of guilt or shame comes, if it is not part of the training and atmosphere of the family, is because those differences in sex you may have noticed are connected with your mother or sisters—that is, a member of your family—and, of course, sexual feelings toward members of the family are generally forbidden in our society. Also, the atmosphere of the home may encourage you to be superior to certain things—to be above meanness, above dirtiness, above sex—but your parents' own attitudes toward sex can and should be discussed openly. For sex is a natural, realistic, inevitable function of the body. However, it is connected for various reasons with all sorts of feelings and inhibitions. Reasons for the latter are obvious: all sorts of troubles would result if everyone indulged in sex with everyone else. But your parents should not try to punish you for sexual feelings without explaining it all clearly and answering your questions about it, or taking you to talk with a doctor or minister or other person qualified to explain it physically and, above all, psychologically.

A second point involved in knowledge about sex is that, at a certain age, the juices are generated in the sexual organs, and if given no outlet while you are awake, they usually come forth during sleep as "wet dreams." Since these orgasms, as they are called, will occur two to four times a week or more, the question arises: "Why not enjoy them?" The answer, I think, is that within limits there is no reason not to. Some people think that it is a good thing not to masturbate, not to touch one's genitals, but to control the sexual urges as thoroughly as possible because such control strengthens one's will. That may be true, but I think the point here is *not* to feel guilt or shame about having such urges because they are natural, normal and unavoidable.

Point 3: A tremendous complication is introduced into sex because the urge is toward a person of the opposite sex, in other words, between you and a partner. The emphasis is on another *person*; for a boy, the urge is toward a girl. Therefore, a relationship to another human being is involved, and it becomes important not to hurt that person or to be hurt by her. The hurt can be emotional or physical. Physically, the two main risks are venereal disease and pregnancy. There are antibiotic drugs which kill the germs (gonococcus) that cause gonorrhea and the ones (treponema pallidum) that cause syphilis. But the rate of venereal disease is rising alarmingly, and one must be extremely careful not to contract it. Gonorrhea damages the genital organs themselves, but syphilis affects the entire body, and can rot any organ including the brain over a period of years. Pregnancy hurts the girl particularly. Even though in recent years people have taken a much broader view of it, it is still considered a disgrace for an unmarried girl to have a child because one is neglecting a child if it is brought into a home that is not secure, stable and loving with *both* a father and mother. The way a child is treated during its earliest years determines what kind of person it will be for the rest of its life. So it should not be brought into the world unless it can be received into a stable home made by a father and mother who love one another and can give their child love, respect and understanding, all of which are needed to raise it properly during its childhood until it becomes an adult. Pregnancy can hurt the girl, her child and also, indirectly, the boy. It is a terrible crime against the child if he is not wanted by both father and mother because an unwanted child cannot grow up to be normal emotionally.

Point 4: The sexual urges of a boy toward a girl are connected with basic emotions, including strong attachments. Once a boy is interested in a girl, he is apt to be not only interested in sexual relations but in having her time, energy, interest and attention. Perhaps even more so the girl wants *his* time, energy, emotion and interest. In other words, you become interested in a girl primarily because of a sexual urge, but you begin to make great demands upon each other. She is apt to have needs for attention and time, and also financial demands.

Naturally these demands absorb a large part of your life and also make a setting for intense jealousy. You may feel jealous and angry if she pays attention to another boy; your life will be restricted, too, if the girl becomes intensely jealous and angry with you for paying attention to another girl. This raises the question of age: is it good or bad for your present and future and the girl's present and future to have all this time- and energy-consuming emotional involvement and experience while you are very young? Usually the disadvantages outweigh the advantages, although I cannot be positive. I wonder if it gets in the way of learning? As I recall the statistics of Dr. Kinsey, college graduates began having sexual relations relatively late in life, when they were already in college and over 20 years of age. Those who had sexual relations much earlier did not go beyond grade school. It is not clear how to interpret such statistics. Possibly keeping sex repressed stimulates the fantasy and aids development of the intellect, but I do not think this has been proved. But a certain age and maturity are required before one is "ready" for a continuing sexual relationship.

Point 5: The other effect one must consider is the effect of sex upon marriage. Biologically, marriage is mating, and other animals besides man mate, for long periods or for life. Sea elephants stay together after mating for only a few weeks; this would seem to be because the young sea elephants are dependent upon their parents for the first three weeks after their birth. After they are three weeks old, they take to the ocean and are apparently well able to care for themselves. Storks nest together after flying north until the young are able to fly safely by themselves; then they fly back to Africa. Here again the parents stay together until the young are sufficiently grown to be safe. Human young require nearly 25 years to mature. So if mating is in part an instinct, causing the parents to stay together for the sake of their young, human mating as in marriage would last for a whole lifetime. The effects of your sex life on your marriage are not only important for your own happiness and the happiness of the girl you eventually marry, but also are important for your children. The old adage "As the twig is bent, the tree is inclined" expresses the essential truth. Young children are readily conditioned, and this conditioning lasts for life. This is one reason there is so much neurotic and mental illness in the world. Sex and what goes with it—the attraction to the opposite sex—can make all sorts of dangers and difficulties; but if properly handled, sex is the source of life's greatest pleasure and most lasting satisfaction: the one-to-one closeness in love of mate, sexually mutual orgasms and emotionally feeling for one another, as well as mutual feelings toward one's children. Such feelings are important for you and for your spouse, and for your children during their formative years, and also for the children's whole future lives, especially in their own mating, and for their children.

As I said at the outset, all of this applies to girls too. The sexual desires of girls are just as strong, and perhaps even stronger, than boys'. But girls do not have certain secretions that must be discharged; their secretions are only lubricants. Psychologically, since throughout the animal kingdom it is women who bear the children, females seem to be especially oriented to children and to understanding them. Women look to the husband to have the strength to give them and the children emotional support and physical security. Mother, Father and children all complement each other in the basic family unit.

References

There are literally thousands of books dealing with teenage sexuality. To mention only a few:

Johnson, E. (1977): *Love and Sex in Plain Language,* 3rd Ed. Philadelphia: Lippincott.
Pomeroy, W. (1971): *Boys & Sex.* New York: Dell.
____ (1973): *Girls & Sex.* New York: Dell.
____ (1974): *Your Child & Sex.* New York: Delacorte.

SECTION IX:
CONCLUSION AND
PERSPECTIVE

42
MARRIAGE, CHILDREN AND
HISTORY INDEX

Give me other mothers [and fathers] and I will give you another world.

St. Augustine

Over the newborn our power is that of God and our responsibility like His toward us. As we acquit outselves toward them, so let Him deal with us.

Bellamy

It takes human beings so many years to mature that one might think we would do a thorough job of it. Perhaps we do, on the average, physically and intellectually; but emotionally it seems to work in the opposite way—we are children for so long that we never get over it.

The emotional patterns with which children react to the way they are treated by parents and others responsible for and close to them continue for life. Of course, in adult life these patterns come out toward other persons, are *transferred* to them—not only to spouse and children but also to friends, acquaintances, associates, various groups in society, country and humanity. One's feelings toward his parents repeat themselves toward the world. Hence, *each person behaves in society about as he did or wished to behave in his childhood home. The home shapes the citizen. Thereby the home shapes history.*

If the child was given love and security and respect for his personality from conception through the early hours, days, weeks, months and years (from 0 to 6), then he continues to feel loved and respected and secure with people in adult life and in his own mind with himself. With this basic condition met for adequately maturing emotionally, he or she becomes a good, responsible spouse, parent, friend and citizen. However, if the child's needs for love, security and respect are not met, then (1) he feels unloved, insecure, not respected by others and by himself, and is enraged; and (2) he does not adequately mature emotionally.

The reason for the latter is that the child naturally tends to grow from his initial parasitic helplessness at birth into his relatively independent adult responsibility for himself and others. If he is unloved, insecure, unrespected, he cannot grow satisfactorily into this relative independence and responsibility for others that is the basis for being a loving, respecting husband or wife, parent, friend and citizen. Instead, since frustration of fundamental needs threatens the child, he reacts with a tendency to fight and to escape—fight and flight. Little and helpless, he can do neither. Frustrations accumulate beneath the surface, shaping an adult who is hostile or withdrawn or both, and the young animal fails to be properly domesticated to cooperation in human society.

As we have stressed, the path to maturity is apparent if one observes a good mother or father with a loved child. This relationship is strong and clear throughout the animal kingdom; we use the expression accurately when we speak of a parent fighting like a "tigress" to protect its cubs.

Just visualize the baby or small child, utterly helpless, entirely dependent for his very life on the parents. Weak and helpless as he is, if he is left without parents or substitutes of course he panics. He feels weak and inadequate and inferior to the big adults; he is competitive, fighting for his position, because being loved is his only guarantee of survival. Being helpless the child is insecure and anxious, readily threatened and frustrated, and therefore angry. His hostilities are constantly restrained by his parents (or substitutes), and so usually are his sexual desires, which physiologically can only be used for play and not for mating or reproduction. As he reaches his full size and strength, the child becomes able to mate and reproduce, and this reverses the attitudes; the child now as an adult must be responsible for himself, for his spouse and children and for his society.

Hence, *responsibility* is such a big word in the dictionary of the emotional life. We grow *out* of intense needs to *get* love and dependence, which cause insecurity, anxiety, frustration, competitiveness, and the resulting reactions of hostility and withdrawal, which lead to guilt and shame. We grow *toward* increasing capacity to be independent, giving, loving, and responsible for others, and for living and letting live in a friendly, cooperative way.

Harmony and satisfaction in marriage are difficult to achieve even at best, since marriage is so complex an interaction of feelings.

In simplest terms, the husband is part mature, part still the child he once was. So is the wife. The mature part drives the husband to find a wife, enjoy sex (which is easy), rear the young (which is a strenuous lifetime job) and support the family. But he may not relish all this to the full because the childhood part resents the demands and responsibilities, keeps him angry and impels him to escape in various ways into his own self-indulgence. The conflict between the mature and the childish parts of his makeup tends to frustrate both. The same is true for the wife: she may maturely want marriage but childishly reject the independence and responsibilities it requires. Both husband and wife may want to give less and get more. If both husband and wife had childhoods with good, loving relationships, they work out their conflicts between their childishness and maturity to a reasonably satisfying, happy solution. But if their childhood patterns of feelings toward others are full of frustration and anger, then the latter tend to repeat in the marriage, increasing its emotional difficulties. And the primitive, animal fight-flight reaction is kept aroused. Sooner or later it breaks through the mature trends and the restraints of society in some form of primitive, animalistic, sexual, regressive and hostile behavior.

In addition to the mature and childish patterns of feelings toward others, there are the sexual urges, tastes, inhibitions and activities; the physical health; and the habits and rhythms of living, such as amounts of sleep, and hours of retiring and rising. All these in each partner must jibe reasonably well with those in the other. No wonder marriage takes a lot of maturity and adjustment, and no wonder the reality is usually so different from the dream. A lot of mature capacity for taking responsibility, giving love and tolerating hostility and frustration is required. It is difficult to give up *having* a parent in order to *be* a parent. We all look for some—often too much—of the parent in our spouse. And with the fight-flight reaction kept aroused, the hostile regressive animal in humans is always apt to break out.

Improper childrearing, by not meeting the child's basic psychobiological needs, prevents its maturing to these capacities for love and responsibility—hence all the neurosis, psychosis, addiction, hostility, irrationally hostile acting out, crime and war; hence all the marital misery and the transmission of all this psychopathology, all this emotional disorder, from generation to generation. Hence marriage and history are what they are. You get love by giving it—not by demanding it.

The more we see and learn of how children are treated from conception on, the less surprised we must be at the state of marriage and of the world with all the pathologically hostile acting out and suffering. In fact, considering what children are subjected to, perhaps the surprise lies in the world's holding together at all. There is even a possibility that self-preservation will nose out pathological hostility and the need to suffer, so that we do not destroy others and outselves, by overpopulation, pollution of the environment, exhaustion of resources or some form of nuclear disaster.

Of course, I am aware of the risk of being judged too optimistic for concluding that wanted children, reared from conception with love, respect and understanding and with reasonably mature parents as examples develop into adults of good will; and that if all, or most, adults were of good will, we could solve most of the world's problems by reason, in an attitude of social cooperation. We still need to merge the psychological clinical findings in individuals with the findings of the other psychological and behavioral sciences, including ethology. For the effect of man's long childhood, especially the early period, of imprinting, conditioning and other learning, is to mold to a large degree and more or less permanently the many powerful animal instincts. Checks are formed against hostile aggression by love, identification with kind parents and training; and such forces strengthen the social cooperation seen in all animals (Allee, 1951). These early experiences thus shape the overall pattern of thought, feeling and behavior, that is, the personality, in each human for life; hence the vast range from the psychotic lust-murderer through every variation to the man or woman of genuine, responsible good will.

It is glaringly obvious that the disease that wreaks such havoc upon humanity, imposing enormous burdens when latent, and killing and maiming by the millions when active, is not heart disease or cancer or any other nonhuman agent—it is *man's irrational, pathological* hostility to man (Saul, 1976). The only danger to man is man. The extent and intensity of the hostility and violence of humans to their own species is unique in the animal kingdom. This exaggerated, destructive hostility goes beyond the normal, useful fight-flight response of other species in nature. It is a symptom of emotional disorder, of failure to mature emotionally. It is the essential step in all psychopathology. In broad perspective, it is the breaking through of the disordered animal in man because of a chronically aroused fight-flight reaction kept stimulated by improper socialization and abuse in the earliest years. It is true that divorce and discord in marriage usually bring out the worst in people: the naive, automatic egocentricity and selfishness of the frustrated, threatened small child, and the reflex attack response of the animal, transparent through the veneer of civilization with its legal procedures. It includes such mistreatment of the child as underprotection or overprotection, deprivation or spoiling, domination or premature responsibility, dotingness or depreciation, hostility, violence to the child, and over-discipline or absence of socialization. These kinds of disorders in interpersonal relations from 0 to 6 stunt and warp development, making hostile emotional cripples instead of mature, loving, responsible husbands and wives, parents, friends and citizens. The contrast between mature adults of good will and those of egocentricity, cruelty and violence is dramatic despite all the intermediate mixtures. There is still hope that by making every child a wanted child, by assuring every child the love, security, respect and understanding that it needs as much as it needs food and shelter, we can prevent tormented marriages, mental illness, crime and war. "If we had one generation of properly reared children we might have Utopia itself."

References

Alee, Warder (1951): *Cooperation Among Animals.* New York: Abelard.
Saul, L. J. (1976): *Psychodynamics of Hostility.* New York: Jason Aronson.

> Ah, love, let us be true
> To one another! for the world, which seems
> To lie before us like a land of dreams,
> So various, so beautiful, so new,
> Hath really neither joy, nor love, nor light,
> Nor certitude, nor peace, nor help for pain;
> And we are here as on a darkling plain
> Swept with confused alarms of struggle and flight,
> Where ignorant armies clash by night.

Matthew Arnold, *Dover Beach*

INDEX

INDEX